School of American Research
Advanced Seminar Series

DOUGLAS W. SCHWARTZ, GENERAL EDITOR

SCHOOL OF AMERICAN RESEARCH
ADVANCED SEMINAR SERIES

Reconstructing Prehistoric Pueblo Societies
New Perspectives on the Pueblos
Structure and Process in Latin America
The Classic Maya Collapse
Methods and Theories of Anthropological Genetics
Sixteenth-Century Mexico
Ancient Civilization and Trade
Photography in Archaeological Research
Meaning in Anthropology
The Valley of Mexico
Demographic Anthropology
The Origins of Maya Civilization
Explanation of Prehistoric Change
Explorations in Ethnoarchaeology
Entrepreneurs in Cultural Context
Southwestern Indian Ritual Drama

# Southwestern Indian Ritual Drama

Advanced Seminars are made possible
by a gift in recognition of
PHILIP L. SHULTZ
for his efforts on behalf of
the School of American Research

# SOUTHWESTERN INDIAN RITUAL DRAMA

EDITED BY
CHARLOTTE J. FRISBIE

A SCHOOL OF AMERICAN RESEARCH BOOK

UNIVERSITY OF NEW MEXICO PRESS • Albuquerque

**ELMHURST COLLEGE LIBRARY**

Library of Congress Cataloging in Publication Data

Main entry under title:

Southwestern Indian ritual drama.

(School of American Research advanced seminar series)
 "A School of American Research book."
 Based on an advanced seminar sponsored by the
School of American Research, April 3-8, 1978.
   Bibliography: p. 345
   Includes index.
   1. Indians of North America—Southwest, New—Rites
and ceremonies—Addresses, essays, lectures. 2. Indians
of North America—Southwest, New—Dances—Addresses,
essays, lectures. 3. Indians of North America—Southwest, New Drama—Addresses, essays, lectures.
4. Indians of North America—Southwest, New—
Music—Addresses, essays, lectures. I. Frisbie,
Charlotte Johnson. II. Series: Santa Fe, N.M.
School of American Research. Advanced seminar series.
E78.S7S585            299'.74           79-2308
ISBN 0-8263-0521-0

© 1980 by the School of American Research. All rights reserved.
Manufactured in the United States of America.
Library of Congress Catalog Card Number 79-2308.
International Standard Book Number 0-8263-0521-0.
*First edition*

# Foreword

This exceptional volume on the ritual drama of Southwestern Indian groups provides a rare insight into the sources and processes of this most human activity. Through case examples and general discussion, emerges a genuine understanding of why ritual has always been so near the core of human culture. The prologue establishes an important context with an extended operational definition of ritual drama that is used productively throughout the volume. Then, with a range of disciplinary perspectives and using the methodologies of music, dance, ethnology, and linguistics, the authors present Southwestern Indian rituals and their components in engrossing detail, not only describing performances but also considering such rarely addressed topics as composition, creativity, rehearsals, the role of the audience, meaning, and dynamics. To examine just the diversity of obvious functions manifest in these rituals, socialization, reaffirmation of core values, fertility, curing, and the promotion of group solidarity is to provide an awareness of the importance of these ceremonies in the larger cultural system.

The groups covered and the ritual aspects considered are Zuni Kachina Society Songs, Hopi Ogres Drama, Picuris Deer Dance, Mescalero Apache Girls' Puberty Ceremony, Navajo House Blessing Ceremony, Navajo Shootingway, Papago Skipping Dance, and Havasupai Song. However, beyond individual cases, the broader contributions of this volume include critical evaluations of earlier work, new approaches to the generation and analysis of data, insights into change and process, and theories of composition and the origin and function of vocables.

## FOREWORD

The final chapter presents an important assessment of the state of research on ritual drama in the Southwest and makes significant regional characterizations. The results of the seminar discussion include techniques of dramatic presentation, dance, backstage activities, the role of singer, the role of women, and the cultural transmission of ritual. All of these elements make this an extraordinary volume: for professionals, it is an invaluable source of detail and theoretical stimulation, and for generalists, who have been fascinated with the ritual drama of the Indians of the Southwest for centuries, it is a unique and sensitive exploration into the nature, complexity, and poetry of ritual drama as well as the delicate sophistication of the craft of anthropology.

School of American Research                      Douglas W. Schwartz

# Preface

Southwestern Indian ritual drama was the topic of an Advanced Seminar supported and sponsored by the School of American Research from April 3 to 8, 1978. When the seminar was officially proposed in August 1976, both the complexity of the topic and the necessarily preliminary nature of the endeavor were realized. For these reasons, the focus was narrowed to allow concentration on the music and dance components within ritual dramas. Participants were chosen according to guidelines established by the School and an ongoing commitment to studying ritual drama in the Southwest. They included those with methodological specializations in ethnomusicology, dance ethnology, linguistics, and ethnology. Eleven scholars were invited to participate; the nine who actually attended the seminar were Donald N. Brown (Oklahoma State University), Claire R. Farrer (University of Illinois at Urbana-Champaign), Charlotte J. Frisbie (Southern Illinois University at Edwardsville), J. Richard Haefer (Arizona State University), Leanne Hinton (University of California, Berkeley), Joann Kealiinohomoku (Northern Arizona University), Don Roberts (Northwestern University), David McAllester (Wesleyan University), and Barbara Tedlock (Tufts University). Gertrude Kurath (Ann Arbor, Michigan) actively participated from afar and prepared a paper for the volume; we regret that this was not also possible for Robert A. Black.

The success of any Advanced Seminar depends not only on the scholars, but also on a number of others whom we would like to

# PREFACE

identify. Foremost among these is Douglas W. Schwartz, president of the School of American Research. From the time of the original discussions about the feasibility of such a seminar through to the completion of this volume, Dr. Schwartz has been a source of encouragement. He unselfishly gave of his time and energy, and while we were in Santa Fe, proved to be a most generous host. Both to him and the School of American Research, all of us owe a debt of gratitude for providing the setting, housing, and transportation which made possible our week of intensive discussions. In addition, we would also like to thank Ella Schroeder, who efficiently and graciously managed the Seminar House during our week there, and cheerfully ran a number of errands for us all. Likewise, much credit is deserved by the kitchen staff (Jennifer McLaughlin, Sarah Wimett, and Paul Kisly) for their preparation of consistently delicious meals.

The editor is also grateful to the Research and Projects Office, Southern Illinois University at Edwardsville, for its assistance with photocopying, postage, and some of the telephone expenses incurred between February 1 and October 1, 1978, in relation to the seminar. The preparation of the final manuscript would not have been possible without the skills and dedication of Ann Van Horn, secretary of the Anthropology Department at the same university. The late Wanda Driskell (former director of publications, School of American Research) also deserves thanks for her moral support and editorial suggestions, as does Elizabeth Hadas (managing editor, University of New Mexico Press), for working diligently with expertise and sensitivity to make this volume a reality.

Finally, to all of my colleagues who shared in this endeavor, the editor would like to say thank you for participating both as a group and as individuals. Without your cooperation, enthusiasm, and willingness to work, critically evaluate, and discuss issues far into the night, and yet bounce back with a smile to another day, the seminar would have been impossible.

# Contents

| | | |
|---|---|---|
| Foreword | | vii |
| DOUGLAS W. SCHWARTZ, GENERAL EDITOR | | |
| Preface | | ix |
| 1. | Prologue | 1 |
| | CHARLOTTE J. FRISBIE | |
| 2. | Songs of the Zuni Kachina Society: Composition, Rehearsal, and Performance | 7 |
| | BARBARA TEDLOCK | |
| 3. | The Drama of the Hopi Ogres | 37 |
| | JOANN W. KEALIINOHOMOKU | |
| 4. | Dance as Experience: The Deer Dance of Picuris Pueblo | 71 |
| | DONALD N. BROWN | |
| 5. | Motion Pictures of Tewa Ritual Dance | 93 |
| | GERTRUDE PROKOSCH KURATH | |
| 6. | A Calendar of Eastern Pueblo Indian Ritual Dramas | 103 |
| | DON L. ROBERTS | |
| 7. | Singing for Life: The Mescalero Apache Girls' Puberty Ceremony | 125 |
| | CLAIRE R. FARRER | |

CONTENTS

| | | |
|---|---|---|
| 8. | Ritual Drama in the Navajo House Blessing Ceremony<br>CHARLOTTE J. FRISBIE | 161 |
| 9. | Shootingway, An Epic Drama of the Navajos<br>DAVID P. MCALLESTER | 199 |
| 10. | *O'odham Celkona:* The Papago Skipping Dance<br>J. RICHARD HAEFER | 239 |
| 11. | Vocables in Havasupai Song<br>LEANNE HINTON | 275 |
| 12. | Epilogue<br>CHARLOTTE J. FRISBIE | 307 |
| References | | 345 |
| Index | | 361 |

# 1
# Prologue

**CHARLOTTE J. FRISBIE**
*Department of Anthropology*
*Southern Illinois University at Edwardsville*

The Southwestern United States has attracted and fascinated anthropologists since the earliest days of the discipline. The region, populated by a large number of America's first inhabitants, is characterized by cultural pluralism. Despite a long and well-known history of contact with a variety of cultures, Southwestern Indians continue to be distinctive in a number of ways from others around them. They maintain autonomous languages, dress, cognition, beliefs, and ritual dramas. The continuing encroachment of outsiders, with their religions as well as technological, political, and economic interests, and their desires to control, seems to do no more than slightly perturb the existing systems.

To understand the reasons for both continuity and change, anthropologists as well as scholars from other disciplines have been studying Southwestern Indians for well over a century. Thus contemporary anthropologists have access to an enormous body of literature based on data gathered over a long period of time utilizing a wide variety of methodological approaches and theoretical perspectives. Yet despite all the data and the attempts to synthesize them through explanatory models and interactional perspectives, no one can claim that ultimate truths have emerged or that we now "understand."

Anthropologists interested in ethnomusicology and dance ethnology have been as attracted to the Southwest as have their colleagues in other specialties. Before the turn of the century, ethnographers such as Jesse Walter Fewkes, Washington Matthews, and Matilda Coxe Stevenson were recording songs and discussing musical instruments, dance costumes, ritual calendars, ground plans, body movements, archaic language in song texts, change, and a variety of other topics. The work by ethnographers and popular writers continued through the decades, gradually being augmented by the more specialized studies of Frances Densmore, George Herzog, and Helen Roberts. Occasionally scholars tried to synthesize what was being learned (for example, Jeançon 1927; H. H. Roberts 1927, 1936; Chesky 1941; Kurath 1953; Nettl 1954; *American Anthropologist* 1954). The decade of the 1950s saw the establishment of the Society for Ethnomusicology in 1955 and the initial studies of Southwestern Indian dance by Gertrude Kurath, a dancer-ethnomusicologist-anthropologist; with these events, specialized work by ethnomusicologists and dance ethnologists began. The number of specialists and activities expanded rapidly in the 1960s, and continues to do so at present. Since the last attempt at synthesis (Frisbie 1977), further work has become available.[1]

While the pace of research activities continues to accelerate, one of the problems faced by researchers is that of finding time to analyze data and develop meaningful statements which can then be shared with colleagues interested in similar matters. One goal of the Advanced Seminar on Southwestern Indian ritual drama was to alleviate this problem while simultaneously expanding the data base for Southwestern Indian studies. The seminar was designed to encourage, facilitate, and motivate participants to return to tapes, notes, and other field data already collected but not as yet processed for publication.

Another goal of the seminar was to assess the current state of work on ritual drama among Southwestern Indians. In this portion of the endeavor, we were not reacting to any one particular statement on the topic, but rather trying to forge one by pooling our knowledge, field experiences, methodological approaches, and theoretical perspectives. We arrived in Santa Fe with diverse academic and geographic interests, and with varying degrees of commitment to one or more theoretical perspectives ranging from structural-functionalism to ethnosemantics, symbolic structuralism, and dialectical process.[2]

*Prologue*

Part of what happened during the week can be most aptly described as a "sorting out process," an articulation of our own ideas in reference to those of others, and a search for a common meeting ground from which, once again, to depart. By the end of the week, we had refined our thinking to the extent that a mutually acceptable working definition became possible. On the basis of the studies in this volume and our critical discussions of them, the following definition emerged:

> Ritual drama, in dealing with life itself, is a process which serves to unite humans with other humans, as well as humans with other-than-humans, the revealed with the unrevealed worlds, the visible with the invisible. The process is accomplished through a variety of multisensory, multilayered experiences entailing "cultural performances" (Singer 1958) by actors for reactors. Specific elements of ritual drama, as reflected in the chapters in this volume, include story line, characterization, multiforms, layers of meaning and aesthetic events, and a degree of stylization or formalization that allows recognition and identification of the forms, but does not make impossible the expression of individual or group creativity.

As with any operational definition, we expect our own work as well as that of others to modify the concept.

The Advanced Seminars are designed to stimulate an exchange of ideas among scholars; they are followed by a period of reflection and an opportunity for revision before the ensuing volume emerges. This volume, like others in the series, was designed to allow individual authors to develop their own thinking about the topic. In our case, the ideas about ritual drama are presented through studies of selected Native American, traditional, ritual dramas, all of which occur in the Southwest. The focus is limited by a necessary concentration on public and accessible ritual dramas, and by an emphasis on traditional ritual dramas rather than on those involving the Native American Church, Christian churches, or currently emerging dramas.

The first chapter in the volume, by Tedlock, represents a new frontier in the understanding of Zuni music. A variety of approaches lead her into Zuni ideas about music, classification of songs, musical aesthetics, and an in-depth comprehension of the process of composition. Rejecting the earlier, yet still pervasive idea that native theories of composition are rare, if extant at all, she presents evidence for a unified body of theory about the compositional process and explicates that process.

Kealiinohomoku's chapter considers the drama of the Hopi ogres. Unlike the other ritual dramas discussed in this volume, this one has children as its central focus. Taking particular perspectives which derive from training in theater and dance, she provides comparative and updated information about the Ogres drama, relates this to broader insights into Hopi ritual drama, and correlates the drama with Hopi child-rearing philosophy. By inference she suggests a set of guidelines for analyzing drama, and develops models for ongoing fieldwork and the analysis of ritual drama.

The chapter by Brown on the Picuris Deer Dance augments the limited literature on Picuris ritual activities and provides a summary of published sources on northern Tiwa dance. Of particular importance is his attempt to add another dimension of analysis to his earlier work on the classification of Taos Dance by using extended statements from participants to uncover participants' perspectives and individual understandings of the Deer Dance. An examination of these understandings enriches the anthropologist's own analysis of the ritual drama.

Kurath's chapter adds another methodological dimension to the volume by its consideration of filming as a technique for studying ritual drama. Using the Santa Clara Game Animal Dance as a focus, she discusses the pros and cons of filming, technical problems, and the potential value of film both for analytical study and eliciting further information from participants. Her work also includes a filmography of visual resource materials for the Tewa.

The chapter by Roberts illustrates the calendrical nature of Eastern Pueblo ritual drama. After discussing Pueblo ceremonies as ritual drama and classifying them by dance type, he presents a calendar which concentrates on the years 1963–68 and the Tanoan and Northern Keresan villages. His work provides a base for studies of change in Pueblo ceremonial activity.

The chapter by Farrer examines the Mescalero Apache Girls' Puberty Ceremony from the perspective of an exegesis by a native practitioner. She suggests that such an explanation provides the data needed to consider contemporary theories of ritual. The results of such examination cause her to suggest that "rites of passage" may be profitably termed "rites of confirmation" or "rites of intensification"

## Prologue

to correspond more closely with the native view. Her notation that the elicitation resulted from a nonstandard interview technique raises the question of the contexting of anthropologist/consultant dialogues as well as another about the extent to which our queries form a portion of the data.

Frisbie's chapter on the Navajo House Blessing Ceremony exemplifies ritual drama as process and the methodological need for contextual analysis, especially that which documents backstage activities which affect dramatic structure and content. Historically documenting the development of this preventive ceremony's public version in response to the changing twentieth-century world with the attendant incorporation of Western ideas about dramatic performance, she compares the dramatic components in both versions as these are practiced today. The difficulties facing outsiders attempting to understand ritual dramas with implicit or encapsulated story lines become clear, as do the roles of Navajo singers and audiences. The nature, expression, and overall roles of creativity and individualism are explicated by examining "free" or "individualistic" prayers, so often ignored in studies of Navajo ceremonialism, and by identifying the decision-making processes, human forces, and cultural expectations which serve to limit and define these elements.

McAllester's chapter augments anthropological and Navajo studies literature by presenting a detailed, comprehensive description of Shootingway, a curing ceremonial. His analysis relates Shootingway ritual drama to Navajo philosophy and world view, expands the list of components usually cited for the latter, and questions Reichard's (1944) notion of "the compulsive word." His work supports a view of Navajo ritual drama as a direct reflection of the origin myths.

The chapter by Haefer examines Papago ritual drama inherent in the Skipping Dance. His emphasis is on the importance of historical data for analyzing the development of particular ritual dramas in their present form. Patterns from the expression of this drama, both historically and at present, are extrapolated and combined with elicited and implied thought concepts to suggest a theory of ritual drama.

Hinton's chapter focuses on particular linguistic features in Havasupai song, and provides the first comprehensive model for vocable structure and vocable formation among Southwestern Indians. Analyzing several genres of song, she discusses what a song consisting of vocables accomplishes as an act of communication and expression, and examines the internal structure of vocables and their aesthetic function. The latter discussion, in particular, reveals the creativity and nonrandomness involved in their formation and usage, and the potential contribution specific linguistic features can make to the total effect of ritual drama. The chapter concludes with a series of testable hypotheses about vocable structure and function. These deserve the attention of scholars interested in vocables as well as broader issues, such as the relationship between sung and spoken language, and the dramatic effects possible through the controlled use of linguistic elements in ritual drama.

The individual chapters in this volume cover a wide range of issues from a number of different perspectives. Some of these issues, such as composition, change, aesthetics, creativity, and the role of women are discussed in the final chapter, where we also address ourselves to questions about the kind of work that needs to be done and the varying feasibility of doing it.

We trust this volume will give readers some sense of the enormous variety of traditional, public ritual drama in the Southwest, and stimulate continuing discussions of ritual drama within a number of disciplines.

## NOTES

1. See the following: Bahr (1977); Bahr and Haefer (1978); Beck and Walters (1977); Farrer (1978); Frisbie and McAllester (1978); Gill (1978); Griffith (1978); Haefer (1977); Hinton (1977); Kealiinohomoku (1978a, 1978b); Laird (1977); Lamphere (1977); Luckert (1977); McAllester (1978); Pandey (1978); R. Rhodes (1977); Royce (1977); Sweet (1978); and Witherspoon (1977).

2. In the area of ritual drama, all of us had different ideas, derived from such sources as Bateson (1958), Chapple and Coon (1942), Geertz (1973), Grossinger (1968), Kurath (1950), Ortiz (1972), Titiev (1960), Turner (1967, 1969), Van Gennep (1960), and Wallace (1966).

# 2
# Songs of the Zuni Kachina Society: Composition, Rehearsal, and Performance

### BARBARA TEDLOCK
*Department of Sociology and Anthropology*
*Tufts University*

### ETHNOMUSICOLOGY AT ZUNI

The first person to make sound recordings of American Indian songs was Jesse Walter Fewkes, who during the summer of 1890 took his phonograph to Zuni, New Mexico. Shortly thereafter he published two articles (1890a, 1890b) which were the first methodological statements about the field use of sound recording equipment and native reaction to it. Benjamin Ives Gilman (1891) published transcriptions of nine of these Zuni songs, which he described as lacking a fixed scale; his transcriptions were the first ever made from sound recordings of American Indian songs. Two years later, John Comfort Fillmore discussed these songs and the problems with the proper notation of pitch which arose from the uneven driving power of the recording machine (1893–94). Several years later, Charles Wead (1900:78) made similar observations, concluding that "Gilman's thorough examination of these songs and his published transcriptions are unsatisfactory." Gilman himself felt that the work of Troyer, who used Frank Hamilton

Cushing as his "Zuni" informant, was more successful: "Carlos Troyer showed Dr. Cushing how he thought the songs of the cliff-dwellers could be written and preserved. . . . Mr. Cushing sang them repeatedly, until by Mr. Troyer's careful pen, they were transcribed to the satisfaction of both. Mr. Troyer has a valuable collection of about forty of these" (1898:19). Between 1904 and 1913 the Theodore Presser Company published 13 of Troyer's Zuni scores, 6 of which have what purport to be Zuni texts with interlinear translations.[1] On close inspection, however, the texts consist mostly of vocables which Troyer "translated" into meaningful English words; the transcription of the meaningful parts of the texts sung by Cushing is so approximate as to be largely undecipherable.

Troyer based several of his own compositions on Zuni themes,[2] and he also published two small, fanciful books on Zuni music: *Traditional Songs of the Zuni Indians* (1904a), and *Indian Music Lecture: The Zuni Indians and Their Music* (1913). In these and in his introductions to his Zuni scores, he reported that, for the Zunis, sounds have colors, and that these colors are related to one another in a "fixed scale," with red indicating "fa," orange "la," yellow "do," green "re," and blue "mi" (1913:35–36). These sound-colors are taught to young Zunis by "the Sunpriest and song master," who press "perforated shells of various sizes and colors" to their ears, between stanzas, in order to help them "in the perception of the sound-waves from the Sun" (1909a:2).

During this same period of romantic fancy, Reid Stacey, largely following Troyer's work, praised the Zunis for their musical achievements, specifically calling attention to their melodies, fractional intervals, fixed tones, and vast melodic ranges, which he found superior to those of the Hopis (1907:55). Nellie Barnes, in her book *American Indian Love Lyrics*, reproduced five of Troyer's rhymed verses in English (1925:23–24, 78, 79–81, 82, 83), without the Zuni texts or music. She used one of these songs, entitled "Lover's Wooing, or Blanket Song," to illustrate her theory of "crest words," which "shift the metrical emphasis, [forcing] the rhythm to bend to them" (1925:170–71). She apparently took Troyer's interlinear translation (1904b) to be an accurate guide to the Zuni text, but in fact it seldom coincides even with such recognizable Zuni words as do occur in that text.

The most prolific collectors of American Indian music, Natalie Curtis and Frances Densmore, gave little attention to Zuni. Curtis

## Songs of the Zuni Kachina Society

(1907:429-44, 556-57) published the texts, translations, and music for three Corn-Grinding Songs, one Corn Dance Song, and one Rabbit Skin Blanket Song; she did not collect any Kachina Songs. During the 1930s Densmore collected 15 Zuni songs representing three genres—Good Kachina, Comanche, and Corn-Grinding—but she collected them without texts (1957:97-111).

Turning to the general ethnographic works on Zuni, we find that Matilda Coxe Stevenson (1904:68-71) collected 12 songs of the Koyemshi (clowns, Mudheads), with full Zuni texts and both interlinear and free translations. Of all the published work on Zuni songs, the most extensive is that of Ruth Bunzel (1932a:494-98, 516-25, 534-40; 1932b:886-903), even though she depended upon George Herzog to carry out the major study of this area of Zuni culture.[3] His only published work on Zuni music, "A Comparison of Pueblo and Pima Musical Styles" (1936), included five Zuni songs; he made some generalizations about supposed contrasts between Western Pueblo and Eastern Pueblo songs, but he was really contrasting Kachina (or "Maskless Kachina") Songs and non-Kachina Songs. Bunzel (1932b:886-97) published three Good Kachina Song texts from Herzog's 1927 recordings, but Herzog himself neither published the music nor discussed this genre of Kachina Songs.

It was fortunate that Bunzel did discuss song types, structure, composition, and cueing (1932a:494-98), since Herzog had no interest whatever in exploring these native concepts and practices. She found that "each song is divided into a number of named sections, each with its own characteristic melodic features, with a system of repeats so complicated that I have not yet been able to fathom it, although it seems clear enough to the singers" (1932b:898). A few years earlier Helen Roberts, in her comparative study of Zuni and Laguna Chakwena Songs, discussed the importance of asking the singers themselves to talk about musical form: "The only way in which these points of [metrical] structure and interpretation may be definitely determined is by putting the questions to the singers themselves and discovering what are their ideas of form. That they possess such we are coming to realize more and more" (1923:184). This was quite a forward-looking statement, since most musicologists, including Densmore, firmly believed that American Indian singers could not possibly talk about their own music. Densmore, in her public lectures, repeatedly stressed that "Indians have no musical system, no rules of composition, few musical composers, no teachers and no concerts" (Hofmann 1968:97).

A recent student of Zuni song, J. R. Cavallo-Bosso, was likewise quite closed to the possibility of a native theory of song structure or composition. Although he knew of David McAllester's unpublished finding that there are Zuni names for the sections of songs of the Comanche genre, he wrote, "When I was at Zuni, I was able to find no one who knew the Zuni names for the song parts!" (1956:49). He also believed that there are no individual composers at Zuni, for "in Zuni culture as in most of the primitive cultures *all* [his emphasis] men are artists, all men take part in the work of making up songs" (1956:39).

It was against this background that I began, in 1969, the study of Zuni Kachina Songs, with attention to composition, rehearsal, performance, cueing, aesthetics, and criticism. My extended reporting and analysis of this work (Tedlock 1973) is based on 48 hours of taped interviews concerning 116 taped Kachina Songs. The song tapes in question were all made by Zunis between 1966 and 1972; the making, replaying, and discussion of such tapes is now common practice at Zuni.

## THE YEARLY DANCE CALENDAR

At Zuni the yearly ceremonial calendar begins with the winter solstice and returns in a sunwise circuit through the summer solstice to the winter solstice. This annual round of public dances, which includes Kachina Society, Bow Priesthood, and Medicine Society[4] masked and unmasked dances, consists of four main series: Winter Dances, Summer Dances, Harvest Dances, and Shalako Dances. During the first or Winter Series, each of the six kiva groups which together comprise the men's religious organization known as the Kachina Society must present a Night Kachina Dance. Eight days after the winter solstice the kiva group which will start off a given year receives a cigarette from the Sun Priest with a request to begin the Winter Dance Series. This leading position, which also holds for the Summer Dances to follow, annually rotates among the kivas in the following order: Wall, Back Wall, Corn Kernel, Dung, Brain, Small Group, back to Wall again, and so on. This sequence forms a

## Songs of the Zuni Kachina Society

counterclockwise circuit of the kivas as they have stood in relation to one another since the 1880s (Mindeleff 1891:96–99; Kroeber 1917:19).

The Summer Dances begin eight days after the summer solstice, on the evening the pilgrims return from their journey to the Zuni land of the dead located to the west of the village. Every fourth year, four days after the summer solstice, a group of about 80 Zuni men walks 50 miles to a dry lake called Whispering Waters, under which lies Kachina Village where all dead Zunis who danced as kachinas during their lifetime continue their existence as dancing kachinas. Other years this party only goes as far west as Ojo Caliente. Each year, when the party returns from the west, it is met outside Zuni by a group of kachinas from the kiva that is to present the first Summer Rain Dance. The kiva leaders then lead the pilgrims and dancers into Zuni, where they perform the opening Rain Dance.

The first Summer Dance, as well as the first Winter Dance, must be Good Kachina, considered by Zunis to be one of their oldest kachina dances. In fact, Good Kachina was once the only dance which could be offered for any of the remaining five Winter or Summer Dances as well (Stevenson 1904:654). However, by the 1920s Bunzel found that one of the variants of Good Kachina, or other traditional dances such as Child Coming Out or Mixed Animals, could be substituted, "although this is not considered to be orthodox" (1932b:887). Today, even though these series are still begun with the Good Kachina, the next five dances are almost always substitutes for it.

However, there are limitations within both the Winter and Summer Dances. Since ideally each kiva group should offer the same kachina dance for both the Winter and Summer Series, and loud drumming is taboo during the summer at Zuni, no dance which uses a two-headed log drum should be offered. Even so, as far back as 1917 the Wall People offered *hilili*[5] as their Winter Series Dance. However, someone had a bad dream and they had to dance again, this time with the proper Good Kachina Dance (Parsons 1922:199n).

The third dance series begins just after the last Summer Rain Dance in mid-September. This series, unlike the Winter and Summer Dances, consists of both masked (or kachina) dances and unmasked dances. Also, unlike the other dance series, there are no Kachina Dances which must be performed each year during this

11

season. Most of the Kachina Dances volunteered by the six kiva groups for this series are simply repeat performances of well-liked Winter or Summer Kachina Dances. There are four dances which are done only during this harvest season: Scalp Dance, Harvest Dance, *kanʔa·kʷe*, and *ya·ya*. The Scalp and Harvest Dances are unmasked Bow Priesthood Circle Dances, while *kanʔa·kʷe* is a masked dance put on once each four years by a cult group within the Corn Kernel Kiva. The *ya·ya*, which is the Dragonfly Medicine Society Initiation Dance, is a Circle Dance in which both masked and unmasked dancers perform simultaneously.

The fourth and final dance series of the year begins just after the Shalako ceremony.[6] This famous ceremony takes place after the Harvest Series is over and two to three weeks before the winter solstice. The performance of the Council of the Gods lasts only one night and morning and does not include any Kachina Songs, but the series of regular Kachina Dances begins on the evening after the major Shalako performers have left the village and continues for five days. There are six dances in this Shalako Series, one "traditional" dance from each of the six kivas. In Bunzel's time the dances were: Old Child Coming Out (Wall Kiva); Sitting at Stool (Back Wall); Slender Toad (Corn Kernel); Jemez People (Dung); Mixed Animals (Brain); and Child Coming Out (Small Group) (Bunzel 1932b:887). Today, the six traditional dances are Hopi Mixed Animals (Wall); Hopi Mixed Animals (Back Wall); Slender Toad (Corn Kernel); Wide Sleeves (Dung); Old Mixed Animals (Brain); and Child Coming Out (Small Group). One or more of these dances are done each evening in the Shalako houses; then on the last afternoon all six groups dance together in Torn Place Plaza. Each kiva group dances four times during the afternoon, whenever it wishes, and there are times when several groups are singing simultaneously. This simultaneity is called *ʔi·potikʔe·ʔa*, 'mixing it up', in Zuni because one cannot follow any single group's songs.

Each kiva group must offer at least one dance in the Shalako, Winter, and Summer Dance Series, but the Harvest Series is optional. There are volunteered Kachina Dances during the winter months at Zuni which are outside the six obligatory dances offered for the Winter Series. They are considered part of a larger class of dances which includes the Shalako Dances as well as the Winter Dances. This group of dances is referred to by Zunis in English as

## Songs of the Zuni Kachina Society

Night Dances because they are danced first during the night and then can be repeated the next day outdoors in the four plazas. When they are performed in the houses at night the kachinas do not have to be masked, but if anyone asks for a repeat the next afternoon, masks must be worn for this outdoor dancing. Any Kachina Dance performed by the Kachina Society, a medicine society, or even just a voluntary group of Zunis may be performed as a Night Dance. New songs, new dances, and even new kachinas are introduced during the Night Dances, some of which may eventually become part of the more traditional Winter and Summer Series.

When a Night Dance is repeated outdoors, it is then subject to further encores on successive afternoons. In 1919 during the Winter Series a *hilili* was repeated 9 days straight, January 15–23, which was the "longest stretch of dancing on record" (Parsons 1933:92). But in 1967 Corn Kernel Kiva danced Comanche 15 days in a row during the Harvest Series. Margaret Lewis, in her calendar of 1919, lists kachina dancing on 85 days of the year (1933:85–90). Today there are even more days than that because of the increased number of encores.

### ZUNI SONGS

Although there are a great many different kinds of songs, at Zuni, most of them fall into four main categories according to the corporate groups which own them. There are, in addition to Kachina Society Songs, Bow Priesthood Songs, Medicine Societies' Songs, and Rain Priesthood Songs. In each case, the songs are grouped into many different song strings, which in turn can be divided into two main types: Sacred Songs and Dance Songs. The Sacred Songs are used privately or semiprivately for religious rituals such as hair washing, setting up and removing altars, mixing medicine water, and making masks and prayersticks. Zuni Dance Songs are very different in character from Sacred Songs. As one Zuni put it, "Those Dance Songs, you can borrow them, you can tape them, you can just do anything to them; those Sacred Songs, they won't allow you to go near them." I only know of one string of Sacred Songs that is borrowed: the Deer Hunting Songs of the Coyote Society, which individual Zuni hunters "pick up" or learn unofficially late at night during the winter solstice celebration, just after the dancing is over. These are sometimes even passed on from one deer hunter to another without reference to the Coyote Society. The borrowing of Dance Songs, on the other hand, is common. Medicine Society Dance Songs are borrowed by kiva groups and altered to fit the structure of Kachina Songs. More commonly, individuals and informal groups borrow Kachina Society Dance Songs. In fact, all Love Songs, most lullabies, and many Powwow Songs are borrowed from Kachina Songs.

There are three genres of Kachina Dance Songs: *sawuʔʔa·we*, *teseʔʔa·we*, and *tomto·we* (see fig. 2.1).[7] The *sawuʔʔa·we* genre, which is named for the high-pitched screeches called *sawu* made in the ceremonial impersonation of female kachinas, and the *teseʔʔa·we*, which is named for the soft *tese* sound made by striking the bundle drum, are performed in all four dance series: Winter, Summer, Harvest, and Shalako. The third genre, *tomto·we*, named for the loud *tomo* sound of the log drum, can only be performed during the Harvest, Shalako, and the nonrequired part of the Winter Series.

## KACHINA SONG STRUCTURE

According to Zuni composers and dancers, the structure of all Kachina Dance Songs, regardless of genre, consists of five main parts, each with several subsections. There are two *kʷayinanne*, 'to come out with' [A], which are usually identical to each other. These are followed by two *šiɬnanne*, 'to name it with' [B], which are also usually identical to each other, except that the second one often begins somewhat higher than the first. Finally there is another *kʷayinanne* or 'coming out' section [A], which is the same as the first "coming out" section textually, but begins higher than any previous section. The large overall structure is: A A B B A.[8] These terms, *kʷayinanne* and *šiɬnanne*, are common knowledge; they occur in discussions during rehearsals and are used as cues during the performance itself. The text of the *kʷayinanne* "mentions the subject of the song," and it is from this part of the song that the title comes. The text of the *šiɬnanne* "talks about the subject of the song and tells what happened to it."

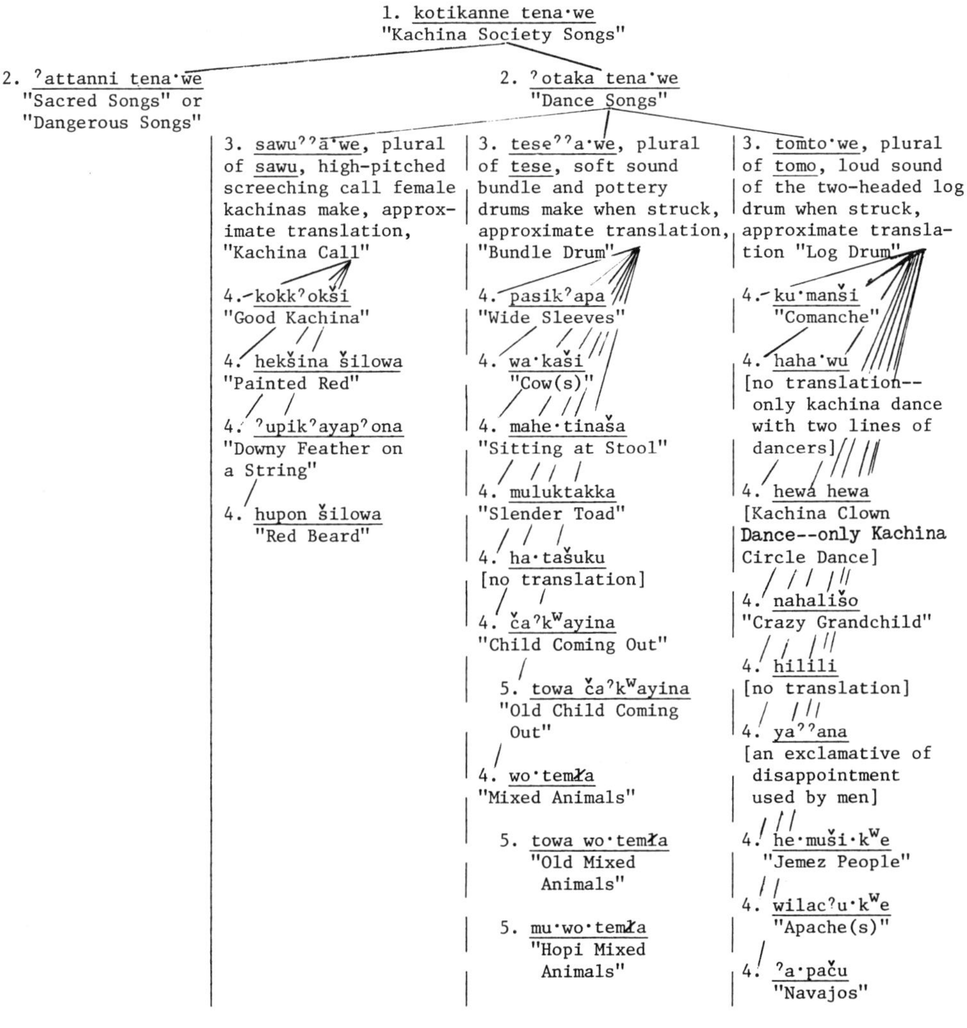

1. kotikanne tena·we
"Kachina Society Songs"

2. ʔattanni tena·we
"Sacred Songs" or
"Dangerous Songs"

2. ʔotaka tena·we
"Dance Songs"

3. sawuʔʔā·we, plural of sawu, high-pitched screeching call female kachinas make, approximate translation, "Kachina Call"

3. teseʔʔa·we, plural of tese, soft sound bundle and pottery drums make when struck, approximate translation, "Bundle Drum"

3. tomto·we, plural of tomo, loud sound of the two-headed log drum when struck, approximate translation "Log Drum"

4. kokkʔokši
"Good Kachina"

4. pasikʔapa
"Wide Sleeves"

4. ku·manši
"Comanche"

4. hekšina šilowa
"Painted Red"

4. wa·kaši
"Cow(s)"

4. haha·wu
[no translation—only kachina dance with two lines of dancers]

4. ʔupikʔayapʔona
"Downy Feather on a String"

4. mahe·tinaša
"Sitting at Stool"

4. hewa hewa
[Kachina Clown Dance—only Kachina Circle Dance]

4. hupon šilowa
"Red Beard"

4. muluktakka
"Slender Toad"

4. ha·tašuku
[no translation]

4. nahališo
"Crazy Grandchild"

4. čaʔkʷayina
"Child Coming Out"

4. hilili
[no translation]

5. towa čaʔkʷayina
"Old Child Coming Out"

4. yaʔʔana
[an exclamative of disappointment used by men]

4. wo·temɬa
"Mixed Animals"

4. he·muši·kʷe
"Jemez People"

5. towa wo·temɬa
"Old Mixed Animals"

4. wilacʔu·kʷe
"Apache(s)"

5. mu·wo·temɬa
"Hopi Mixed Animals"

4. ʔa·paču
"Navajos"

FIGURE 2.1. Zuni folk taxonomy: Kachina Society song hierarchy.

Not only the text but the melody differs for the two main song parts, as has been described by Herzog (1936:291-92). The fit of text and melody is one of the major problems that Zuni composers face. When they are dissatisfied, they say, in Zuni, *kʷaʔhi·ninaʔma*, 'it doesn't match', or in English, "It's bumpy not straight," by which it is meant that the words are not properly adjusted to the melody. H. H. Roberts (1923:179) noted this problem in her sample of three Child Coming Out Kachina Songs, in which the text "may cause a slight accent to fall where normally none would appear in the tune."

In the Kachina Call genre, the song structure, both textually and melodically, reaches the highest level of complexity within all Kachina Dance Songs. Here, each of the five main parts of the song is divided into four, paired, smaller parts. Other Kachina Dance Songs, as well, are divided into smaller subsections within the five-part overall structure, but the Kachina Call genre is by far the most complex and will therefore serve as the main example in the case of these finer distinctions.

Within each "coming out" section in all Kachina Dance Songs, there is a fixed-phrase introduction [x] sung twice, either identically [xx] or with a slight variation [xx']. It is called *penan kʷayinanne*, 'talk coming out'. In the Kachina Call genre both the Downy Feather on a String and the Red Beard Songs begin with *ho-ho-ho he-he-he*, while the Good Kachina and Painted Red begin with *ʔa-ha ʔe-he ʔa-ha ʔe-he*. This introduction immediately identifies a song for Zunis and tells them both "how far down it'll go" (the tonic) and "what beat it's got." This is a necessary part of all Kachina Songs, and Zunis can readily sing it, out of context, for each genre.

The next two parts of each "coming out" section within the Kachina Call genre each consist of a four-line song text, also called a "coming out" [a], which is repeated either identically [a] or with a one or two-word alteration [a']. The word or words altered are the names of religious persons, places, or things. They are replaced with other persons, places, or things which are contiguous with them in directional associations. For instance, in one Downy Feather on a String Song, the [a] subsection mentions thunder and lightning on Salt Lake Mountain, which the Yellow Corn Girls see and hear. In the [a'] subsection, the thunder and lightning is on Deer Village Mountain and the Blue Corn Girls see and hear it. Salt Lake Mountain, located near the Zuni Salt Lake, is the sacred mountain of the south, which the Yellow Corn Girls, who live in the north, face. Deer Village Mountain is the sacred mountain of the east, located near Grants, which the Blue Corn Girls of the west face. The Yellow Corn Girls are mentioned first, then the Blue Corn Girls, and these are contiguous directions, north then west, on a counterclockwise circuit of the four directions. Likewise the first mountain was Salt Lake Mountain of the south, followed by Deer Village Mountain of the east.

The [a] and [a'] subsections of the first "coming out" section also provide song titles. Titling is especially difficult in the Kachina Call genre, which has by far the largest song corpus (it is the most frequently performed dance genre). The Downy Feather on a String Song discussed above could be titled either Salt Lake Mountain or Deer Village Mountain but not Yellow or Blue Corn Girls. The reason for this is that the thunder and lightning located on these two mountains develop, in the "talking about" section, into rain and then a flood, whereas the Yellow and Blue Corn Girls are merely the audience, so to speak, of the events of the song.

The subsections [a] or [a'] always end with *li·ɬamm*, a word which is composed of *li·ɬa*, 'here', plus *mm*, a nonmeaningful continuant. This is also the last word of the analogous part of the "talking about" segment [b] (see below). Since song texts in this genre tell of distant events—for instance, thunder, lightning, and rain—which are coming to Zuni, it seems appropriate to end each verse with *li·ɬamm*, 'here-mm'.

The fifth and sixth parts within each "coming out" section are the *ʔiʔcʔumme*, 'to make it strong', parts of the song, [c] and [c']. They both occur five times within a given song, always in the fifth and sixth subsection of both the "coming out" and the "talking about" sections. They can consist of a new melody of one or more lines (in which one word may change in [c'], plus a line or two of vocables and emotional or affective interjections, such as, *ʔelu*, 'joy!', 'happiness!', and *hiya* and *naya*, which indicate surprise. These interjections often occur together, *hiya ʔelu* or *naya ʔelu*, and could be translated in English as 'Oh joy!' or 'Oh happiness!'. The "strong part" is the segment of the song which Zunis find the most beautiful, because "this is the part where they're really singing." This part is higher and louder and has a more complex melodic contour than anything else in a given section. The Zuni term for 'beautiful', *co?ya*, literally means 'multicolored' or 'variegated'; applied to the "strong" segment, it refers both to the greater melodic range of this part of the song, which adds variety to the song as a whole, and to what Herzog (1936:291) noted as "tonal saturation" in Kachina Songs, which here adds variety *within* the "strong part."

The final subsection is a fixed phrase coda [z], usually doubled [zz'], called *waya*, 'cover', or *ya·?ana*, 'finish'; it is repeated at the end of each of the five main sections of a song. It consists primarily of vocables like *?a-ha-ha-ha*, *?-i-hi-hi*, ending with *hiya hiya*, 'Oh! Oh!'. In some genres it is identical with the fixed-phrase introduction [x]. So, in the Kachina Call genre of Kachina Dance Songs, we have the following segments or subsections within each of the three "coming out" sections:

A [xx'aa'cc'zz']⁹
[x] & [x'] *penan kʷayinan*, 'talk coming out'
[a] & [a'] *kʷayinanne*, 'the coming out'
[c] & [c'] *?i?c?umme*, 'the strong part'
[z] & [z'] *waya* or *ya·?ana*, 'cover' or 'finish'

Turning to the subsections of the "talking about" section [B], the other main part of these dance songs, we find the following overall structure: B [yybb'cc'zz'].¹⁰ Here, [yy] is a near monotone introduction on the tonic, consisting of *hapi·me hapi·me*. The next two parts of each "talking about" section [B], also called "talking about" [bb'], replace the text [aa'] of the "coming out" section [A]. Then come two sections [cc'] which are the "strong parts." These are identical with the previously discussed "strong part" of the "coming out" section or [A]. Finally comes the coda [zz'], which is also the same as in the "coming out" section [A].

The completed structure of a song of the Kachina Call type is as follows:

A [xx'aa'cc'zz']
A [xx'aa'cc'zz']
B [yy bb'cc'zz']
B [yy bb'cc'zz']
A [xx'aa'cc'zz']

The last "coming out" section of the entire song [A] is also called *paɬtonne*, 'to cover it over with' or 'to finish with'. In the Kachina

*Songs of the Zuni Kachina Society*

Call genre, this is the section where the song reaches the highest pitches, the tonic having been raised in the second [A] (optional) and raised still higher in the final [A] (mandatory). See figure 2.3 for a Zuni drawing of a melody of this genre, which shows the last "coming out" section, also called "finishing" section, the highest part, by far, of the song. The subsection which is considered the most beautiful is the last "strong part" [c'] of the "finishing" section.

The Log Drum genre, which includes nine masked dances, has the most complex rhythmic structure of all Zuni songs, but is melodically and textually rather simple compared with the Kachina Call genre. There is no separate *ʔiʔcʔumme*, 'strong', section [cc']; thus the term *kʷayinanne* need not be applied on two different levels, as in the case of the Kachina Call genre. Instead, in Log Drum Songs [A] consists simply of [aa'] (plus the usual introduction and coda) and in [B], a new melody is simply added onto the front of the "coming out" section resulting in [bb'aa']. The term *šiłnanne*, 'coming out', can be applied to [B] as a whole or to [bb'], but this genre lacks a "true coming out" section. In Comanche Songs, what would be the *hapi·me* [y] (see the Kachina Call discussion) used to introduce the "talking about" section [bb'] is, instead, imbedded in the first line of both [b] and [b'] as follows: *wi ya hapi·me yay he lo wi ya he ne ya*.

The Bundle Drum genre, including 10 Kachina Dances which use either the *teseʔʔananne*, 'bundle drum', or the *teʔpehanne*, 'pottery drum', shows a third way to construct [B]. Some Bundle Drum Songs use the full Kachina Call pattern with a "true talking about" section, but others omit this section [bb'] altogether so that in sections three and four there remains only a "strong part" [cc']. See figure 2.2 for comparisons of the Kachina Call, Bundle Drum, and Log Drum structures (with introductions and codas left out for the sake of simplicity).

Given that all Kachina Dance Songs must have five parts with the overall structure A A B B A, in which [B] *must* be different from [A], the patterns of the three genres exhaust all the possibilities of variation for [B]. In the Kachina Call genre, the "coming out" part [aa'] is replaced with completely new textual and melodic material [bb']. Bundle Drum genre song construction, however, involves the removal of the "coming out" section [aa'] without adding anything. The Log Drum genre, like the Kachina Call genre, involves the ad-

19

| sawuʔʔaˑwe | teseʔʔaˑwe | tomtoˑwe |
|---|---|---|
| 'Kachina Call' | 'Bundle Drum' | 'Log Drum' |
| A [aa'cc'] | A [aa'cc'] | A [aa'] |
| A [aa'cc'] | A [aa'cc'] | A [aa'] |
| B [bb'cc'] | B [cc'] | B [bb'aa'] |
| B [bb'cc'] | B [cc'] | B [bb'aa'] |
| A [aa'cc'] | A [aa'cc'] | A [aa'] |

A = k̵ʷayinanne, 'coming out' section
B = šiɬnanne, 'talking about' section
aa' = k̵ʷayinanne, 'coming out' subsection
bb' = šiɬnanne, 'talking about' subsection
cc' = ʔiʔcʔumme, 'strong part' subsection

FIGURE 2.2. Zuni theory of the textual and melodic structure of the three Kachina song genres.[11]

dition of new melodic material [bb'], but it is added on to the "coming out" section [aa'] instead of replacing it.

In songs with a "true talking about" section in which [bb'] replaces [aa'], the text of [bb'] tells the outcome of a situation mentioned in [aa']. It is this situation or subject which provides most of the titles for these songs. It is as if the "coming out" part [aa'] and the title posed a question and the "talking about" part [bb'] gave the answer. In songs which do not have a "true talking about" section (for example, songs in the Log Drum genre), the "coming out" part is not regarded as providing a proper title. Instead, the titles of such songs usually refer to gestures or rhythmic figures. For example, some *hilili* song titles are: *ɬupitena ʔitelɬupnaša*, 'one with a lot of skip beats', *tomoʔʔanʔona*, 'slow beat half-timing the rhythm', and *paniˑleʔona*, 'one that goes down'—all the dancers squat at one point.

## KACHINA SONG COMPOSITION

The most common sources for new Kachina Dance Song texts are prayers, tales, ceremonies, and recent events. For example, a song

## Songs of the Zuni Kachina Society

might be about a person whom the composer saw doing something, drinking in a bar or walking along with his prayersticks. Song narrative can also originate in news items from the *Gallup Independent* (newspaper) or from television.

Song composers, called in Zuni *tena· waśeyen?ona*, are usually men, although some Zuni women are known to have composed songs which their husbands then took to their kiva group. Zunis do not, however, believe that just everyone can compose new songs. They say that there are only some people born with "song talent," consisting in part of *ce?mak ?anikʷa*, 'a smart mind' or a 'good memory'; as one composer put it, "If you make up a song and then just forget it, that won't mean anything to the people. If you make up a song you'll have to think about it all the time, keep repeating it over and over."

Each kiva group in the Kachina Society usually has two or three song composers in its membership. However, the Small Group and Corn Kernel kivas, both of which have large, active memberships, are particularly known for having many good composers. The Small Group kiva has a long-standing reputation for making new Kachina Call Songs, especially Good Kachina and Downy Feather on a String, while Corn Kernel kiva is known for its Log Drum Songs, especially *hilili*, Crazy Grandchild, and Comanche.

Zuni composers feel that good text composition within the Kachina Call genre consists of what sounds at first like the usual lyrics about rain and other blessings, which are often lines from prayers, but is "really about something today, right now." Bunzel (1932b:891) reported a clever topical Good Kachina Song text which seems to fit this ideal:

> "Say, younger brother,
> Where are you going?
> Here you go about greeting us with fair words."
>
> "Hither at the north edge of the world
> Smoke Youth
> Delights in the songs of the masked gods.
> So he says,
> Therefore he goes about
> Greeting all the rain makers with fair words."
> Thus the Dogwood clan man said to all his children.

"As dusk comes on
Who sings fairly their beautiful songs?"
Because of their words
My inner room is filled with all kinds of riches,

Uhu ehe
Uhu ehe
Aha ehe
Aha ehe

Bunzel explained that this text, although it sounded like a traditional Good Kachina Rain Song, was actually a complex allegory concerning George Herzog's musicological activities at Zuni in 1927. Here "Smoke Youth," who was "filling his inner room with all kinds of riches," was understood to be not only a Zuni filling his heart with the song blessings of the kachinas, but also Herzog filling his purse with cash from the sale of the songs of the masked gods.

The Small Group composers are considered the most creative innovators of song texts of this sort. Several years ago, there was one particular composer in that group whom many people still mention: "He really knew how to make a song out of what was happening." One of this man's best loved songs, dating from the attack on Pearl Harbor during World War II, was called "Small Eyes." Several people tried to recall the whole song for me, but they only succeeded in remembering part of the "coming out" section which said:

Early this morning
the serpents were talking.
Talking about
the floating houses
that turned over.

The composer of this song has passed away now, but there is another composer in this same kiva who is just as creative. During the summer of 1972 he composed a topical song of the Downy Feather on a String genre which will be remembered for quite some time. It is called "They Went to the Moon Mother":

["coming out" section]
ho-ho-ho he-he-he ho-o-o he-e-e
"Rejoice! Holy bundles, sacred bundles

## Songs of the Zuni Kachina Society

because of your wise thoughts
there in the east your Moon Mother spoke, gave her word
when we went up there with the dragonfly, entered upon her road.
Rejoice! You will be granted many blessings, flowing silt."
The two stars are saying [in a]       } this to all the sacred
The lying star says [in a′]              } bundles here mm.

["strong" section]
Maskers, rainmakers
soaking the earth with rain
making lightning, coming
stretching, stretching, stretching
heyo-o heye neya, hey-o heye neya
awiyo heyena, awiyo heyeney
awiyo-o heye, awiyo-o
hahaha iihi hiya hiya
hahaha iihihi hiya hiya

["talking about" section]
hapi·me, hapi·me
"By the Moon Mother's word
from the Middle Place all the way to Dawn Lake
   your paths will be complete." [in b]   }
   you will reach old age." [in b′]          }
I the masker say this to you here mmm.

A Zuni performer explained to me that this song is a complex allegory about two stars (astronauts) who went to the Moon Mother on a dragonfly (rocketship). They report to the people via the sacred bundle (Houston Control) that the moon will bless them with silt (alluvial deposits believed to be on the moon, and present in the Southwest after every heavy rain). In the "strong" part the "stretching, stretching, stretching" refers to the corn plants reaching out for the rain, the people reaching old age, and the rocket reaching the moon.

The Small Group also excels in juxtaposing the most divergent melodies in the "coming out" and the "talking about" sections. Although this divergence is characteristic of all songs which have a "true talking about" section, the Small Group composers are the most daring innovators. Not only do they juxtapose unlikely melodies, but they even quote melodic phrases from previous songs. This imbedding of extra melodies, usually done in the "strong" part [cc′] of the "talking about" section [B], is quite pleasing aesthetically to Zuni audiences and they call for repeats of such complex songs on the spot.

The Corn Kernel composers are also introducers of new melodies. In looking for new melodies, Zunis have for generations borrowed tunes from other Pueblos. On trips to Hopi, Zuni men are always trying to "catch the tune" and bring it back to Zuni. Several of the younger men in the Corn Kernel group borrow tunes from non-Pueblo sources as well. For instance, in 1971, one of the Comanche Coming Songs was borrowed from the Ute Bear Dance performed the previous year at the Gallup Ceremonial. Some melodic borrowings come from Western music, for example the "Limbo Rock" and "Swing Low, Sweet Chariot." However, if and when the audience realizes the sources of these melodies, they are quite disappointed. As one Zuni put it, "People like it until they figure out about it later, after listening to their tapes. Then they know it's just a rock tune. They disapprove of this, but it's too late, they already danced with it." To date, borrowed Western melodies have only been used in a very limited way in the Log Drum genre of Dance Songs. This genre is the most recent one at Zuni, and the two types of dances within this genre known to have used Western melodies are avowedly Plains borrowings. These borrowed tunes appear only within the Coming and Going Songs of the Comanche and Apache Dances. These ʔi·naka tena·we, 'Coming Songs', and ʔa·naka tena·we, 'Going Songs', are simple, two-part songs consisting of a "coming out" section sung over and over again while the group walks from one plaza or house to another, and a "talking about" section, sung just before they enter or leave the dance house or plaza.

The borrowed melodies in the main Dance Songs in the Log Drum genre, however, are not from outside sources. Instead, they come from Zuni Medicine Society Songs which are quite different, structurally and melodically, from Kachina Society Songs. In discussing the differences in Kachina Society and Medicine Society Songs with Zunis, one finds that the overall structure of Medicine Society Songs is: AB AB AB AB A or else AB AB AB AB AB AB A, in which [A] is called the kʷayinanne or "coming out" section and [B], the šiłnanne or "talking about" section. When a Medicine Society Song is borrowed for a Kachina Society production, the structure must be changed to conform to the Log Drum form: [A] becomes the [aa'] of all five Log Drum parts and [B] becomes the [bb'] added to [aa'] in the third and fourth parts. Zunis call these hybrid

## Songs of the Zuni Kachina Society

songs, consisting of the melody and often the words of Medicine Society Songs, but with the structure of Kachina Society Songs, *yaɬto·we*, 'Topped Songs'. Medicine Society members within each kiva group, quite naturally, are the main composers and leaders of the singing, drumming, and dancing of these songs. They add short pauses and entire half-time sections, called *tomoʔʔanʔona*, to the songs which they had to memorize when they entered the society and which they cannot, within the context of the Medicine Society, change in any way. The popularity of these "Topped Songs" is partly attributable to their paradoxical status: the composer "plays" with what would normally be rigid.

Within the Log Drum genre, the *hilili* and its variant *yaʔʔana* are the favorites. They are the simplest melodically and textually and the most complex rhythmically. For a visual comparison of the general pitch contours of a hypothetical Kachina Call, Bundle Drum, and Log Drum Song, see figure 2.3. These drawings were made by a Zuni man who is a kachina dancer, song composer, and Medicine Society member. He made the three songs equally long, though Kachina Call Songs in actual performance average 20 minutes in length, while Bundle Drum Songs average 10 minutes, and Log Drum Songs last only about 3 minutes. When I asked him why, he explained that when you learn a Log Drum Song it is just as "long" as a Kachina Call Song, but that "when you sing it and dance real fast you just clip off parts of it." He seemed to be saying that all Kachina Dance Songs have the same amount of content but are performed at different speeds and therefore, last different amounts of time. Another startling thing about the Log Drum Song contour, in comparison with that of the Kachina Call Song, is the extreme contrast in their respective heights. He explained that Kachina Call Songs sound like "the Zuni Mountains," or else "like going up stairs," whereas the Log Drum pattern is "a lot flatter, more like a mesa." He indicated two sharp pauses in the Log Drum contour, one after the first "talking about" section and the other at the end of the song. These sharp pauses occur only in *hilili* and *yaʔʔana*, the fastest (M.M.♩ = 208–220) of all Zuni dances. This wildly fast rhythm, combined with fancy dance steps, suddenly stops dead at the sharp pause and there must be an absolute simultaneity of drum, dance, and song silences or else, in Zuni opinion, the dance is ruined. This complex rhythmic development in the Log Drum genre is possible because the singing is done by a separate choir instead of by the dancers themselves, who can then keep their full attention on the skip beats and sharp pauses.

sawu ??a·we 'Kachina Call' genre

čuʔnanne 'sharp pause'

tomto·we 'Log Drum' genre

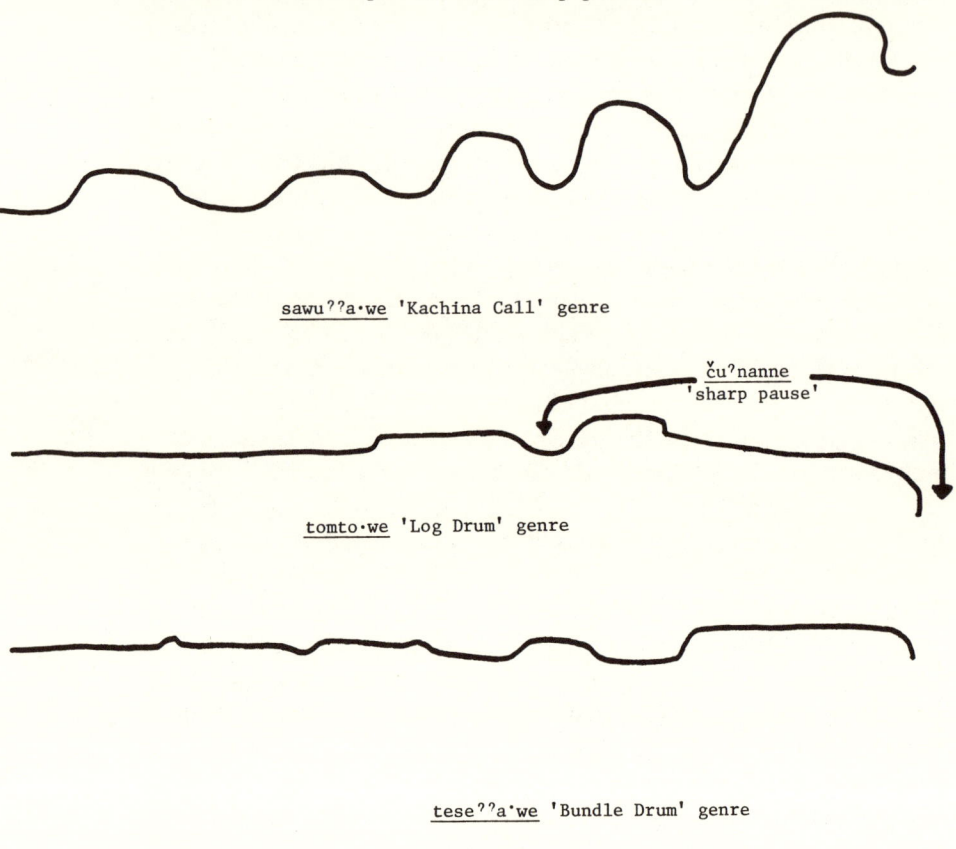

teseʔʔa·we 'Bundle Drum' genre

FIGURE 2.3. A Zuni composer's drawing of the typical pitch contours for the three genres of Kachina song.

## REHEARSAL

All Zuni Kachina Society Songs are well rehearsed before they are publicly performed, and a man who has not attended these rehearsals will not dance. A rehearsal, or ʔitečča, is usually held in the kiva from 10:00 P.M. until 1:00 or 2:00 A.M. on each night for at least four nights before a dance performance. When a group decides to pre-

## Songs of the Zuni Kachina Society

sent many new songs or a *hilili* (with its complicated rhythms and dance steps), they might rehearse almost every single night for as long as three or four weeks.

The Dance Chief and his Spokesman always arrive at the kiva before anyone else. They exchange a series of formal greetings with the other men as they enter the kiva, delivering their lines with a strong final stress called ʔ*ana kʔeyatoʔu peyena·we*, 'raised up speech.' When most of the men have arrived, the Dance Chief will ask one of the song composers, kʷ*ap toʔ łeyaye?*, 'What are you holding?' or 'What do you have in your hand?' If the composer has a song, he will sing a shortened version of it, consisting of a "coming out" section and one "talking about" section. Then he will say, ʔ*unapa*, 'Look at it,' and he may add, *šiʔnašna·we*, 'Cut some of the meat off it,' or else tell them to break the *sappokałanne*, 'backbone.' By this he means that the group is free to edit his song by removing some of the words, "taking the meat off it," or else by changing the melody, "breaking the backbone."

Sometimes, a song is accepted just the way the composer sang it. More often a song is *penappone*, 'full of words', and the group will indeed "cut some of the meat off." Another common problem is that the "talking about" section kʷ*aʔhi·ninaʔma*, 'doesn't match up' properly with the "coming out" section. If this is the case the Dance Chief and his Spokesman will remove the "talking about" section altogether and then make up an entirely new one using both a new melody and new words.

Anyone can offer a song during a dance rehearsal and the group will try it out a couple of times: "If they don't like it, they'll move right on to the next song. They won't say anything to you about it. But the next night, if you're not there, they'll say, 'Let's put it aside, maybe we can fix it in some way'." Sometimes songs are created during the rehearsal. As one Zuni put it, "A guy could be in the corner just *šowowokʔe·ʔa* ['whispering' or 'whistling'] to himself and he'll get a song which he'll then sing to the group."

Once the dance leaders have accepted a song, the composer is put in the center of the group and he begins to teach everyone his song. In songs that have long texts, the composer speaks (rather than sings) the "coming out" section once; then he repeats it a second time and the group joins in as best it can. Next, the composer speaks the "talking about" section and the group says both the "coming out" and the "talking about" sections in unison. The leaders will notice who does not seem to have it and will go sit next to him to explain the words. This is necessary with some of the younger men, who do not yet know much of the *kokka·wan penanne*, 'kachina language'. This language consists in part of the sacred words which replace ordinary words, as when *ʔamalaši*, 'horse', replaces the ordinary word *tu·ši*. In such cases, the ordinary word cannot be used in any religious setting, including Kachina Songs. More frequently, kachina language consists of synonyms for terms which are themselves acceptable in religious contexts. For example, *kululunanne* is considered synonymous with *wilolonanne*, the latter being the more ordinary term for lightning; in Kachina Songs, both words are often used together in parallel constructions. Kachina language also involves the "cutting off the tips" or the "middle part" of a word. For example, in one song in my collection the phrase, *leʔan ʔantikʷeppa*, 'that's what he said', is rendered *le-e-e ʔa tii kʷa-a-a-ha*, which Zunis who know about kachina language have no trouble at all interpreting.

After everyone seems to understand the words and knows how they go, the composer sings the "coming out" section three or four times until everyone joins in. Then he sings the "talking about" section three or four times until everyone has it. Next, they all start over again and sing each part a couple of times. Finally, just before they leave the kiva, they sing through the full five-part structure. The rehearsal ends with a prayer in which they ask the ancestors to help them get this song and not to forget it; then they all stand and stretch, saying, "May my corn grow ripe" and "May I kill a deer even if I don't go anywhere."

After several nights of rehearsal the men will start to dance to the songs. At this time they may embellish the rhythm by adding pauses or skip beats. There are two distinct types of skip beats, *ʔitelluṗnašanna*, 'short pause,' and *čuʔnanne*, 'sharp pause.' Short pauses, which are used in all dance genres, are described by Zuni composers and dancers as "punctuation." These short pauses—which occur simultaneously in the singing, dancing, and (in dances with drums) the drumming—never occur in the middle of a word, only between words. In songs that are without linguistically meaningful texts, these short pauses are inserted around "made-up-words." For example, in one *hilili* song is found *hu·niwa*, which "doesn't mean any-

## Songs of the Zuni Kachina Society

thing," and in another there is *tululina tululina*, which "imitates the sound of the drum; it's not a word but it's sort of like a *tomomoʔʔana* ['drum tremelo']." The number of short pauses in a given song varies slightly from dance to dance, so that in Downy Feather on a String, of the Kachina Call genre, there would never be more than four or five pauses, while in *hilili* and other dances of the Log Drum genre there are as many as ten or more. Sharp pauses occur in only two dance song types, both of the Log Drum genre: *hilili* and *yaʔʔa·na* (see the previous section for other details).

The final rehearsal, on the night before the dance, takes place in the house of the leader of the clown group which the kiva group selected to "play for them" during the dance. At this time all the songs that will be used are sung straight through in the same order as that which the leaders have decided upon for the actual performance. This rehearsal serves to let the clowns hear the songs once before the actual performance. This is necessary because they have an active role during the performance, consisting of both explicating the texts to the audience through gesture and helping the dancers perform well by constantly yelling out cues and instructions to them.

### PERFORMANCE

Immediately after this last rehearsal, ending at about 3:00 A.M., the dancers come out of the clown house and dance once in each of the four plazas. They are unmasked and wear ordinary clothing. At this time no one dares to watch them, lest he or she die. After this they retire to their homes where they sleep until the late morning and then have their wives wash their hair and assemble their costumes (Bunzel 1932b:895).

All costumes are alike in most dances, with the exception of the two or three *samayašeʔʔa*, 'individualists', usually friends, who decided in advance "to be different." There are, however, only certain acceptable ways to be different. For instance, in a Downy Feather on a String Dance they might decide not to be a Downy Feather Kachina, with his flat face mask, but instead a Cotton Head, with his helmet mask, big black ears, three cotton strings hanging down from the top of the head, and turquoise moccasins (see Bunzel 1932b:Plate 37d). Whenever there are individualists in the line they separate them, "with one fifth in line and the other twelfth or so, just so it'll look good."

After assembling their costumes, all the dancers gather at their kiva; if the dance is to be performed outdoors, the time of this gathering is early afternoon. They give their gourd rattles and turtle shell rattles to the Dance Chief. He prays to these, calling them *nana*, 'grandfather', and asks them for *tekʔohannanne*, 'daylight'. He does not pray to the sleigh bells or wooden rattles which are used in some of the more recent dances because "they're man-made, but turtles and gourds are *ʔa·hoʔʔi*, 'beings'." After these prayers are over, the men tie their turtle shell rattles to their legs, put their masks on, and leave the kiva in single file. As they pass by the Dance Chief he spits Payatamu medicine on them to help them attract a large audience.

If they are to perform outdoors, as in the Summer Series, they should now make four clockwise circuits of the four plazas, dancing in each of them. However, they often make only one circuit, in which they may walk through the first two plazas, Back Wall and Rat's Place, until they arrive at Torn Place, the main plaza in front of the head kiva, where they dance a few songs and then leave through Big Plaza, near the church. At this time there are often only 10 or 15 dancers and an audience of only a dozen small children, and a handful of adults. Consequently, the Dance Chief usually saves the best songs for later in the day when there will be a larger audience.

After this circuit they retire to their kiva, where their wives bring their meals to them. Then, in late afternoon or early evening, they come out again and pass through the first two plazas, saving their dancing for Torn Place Plaza. Now there are many more dancers, perhaps as many as 25 or 30. During this late afternoon dance the clowns appear for the first time that day, beating a log drum with butterflies imprisoned inside to bring out the people. However, the Summer Dances rarely have very large audiences. As in Stevenson's time, there are often more dancers than audience members (see Stevenson 1904:Plate LXIX). As Li (1937:66) noted during his fieldwork at Zuni: "Apart from those who are performing, the people in general do not attend as bystanders all the time on such occa-

## Songs of the Zuni Kachina Society

sions. As a rule they are attending their farming or other business in spite of the dances taking place in the community." In my experience, the size of audience depends upon the excellence of the songs. If a group has new, exciting songs, then they will be asked to dance again the next day. As soon as the people who did not attend the first performance hear that two or three days of repeats have been called for, they often take an interest in hearing what promise to be good songs. During the summer of 1972, when the Small Group was performing the Moon Shot Song along with several other good, new songs, they danced eight days in a row, slowly building an audience of more than 200 people.

Another large part of the audience consists of *k?apin ?a·ho??i*, 'raw beings', including dead Zunis and nonhumans. The most important members of this raw audience are the *?uwanammi*, 'rain makers', dead Zunis returning to Zuni from Kachina Village; they inhabit the masks of the dancers (rather than possessing the dancers themselves) and become visible as clouds and rain. This presence of the dead explains what is for the outsider a startling audience response to the beautiful Kachina Songs: weeping. This occurs most frequently during the first dance each summer, marking the return of the pilgrims, for "the people feel that their loved ones come back, though they can't see them." Because of this same presence, uncostumed Zunis (unlike Lagunas and Acomas) never get up and dance with the kachinas: that could be fatal.

One part of the audience, however, is allowed to dance with the kachinas: the clowns, who are considered the grandfathers of the kachinas. During the Summer Series, the Koyemshi serve simultaneously as directors and audience for the kachinas, cueing, gesturing, appreciating, and criticizing. The most common cue is *?ana k?eyato?u*, 'raise it right up', which means to sing both louder and higher. They yell this out to the dancers during the "strong part" of the last "talking about" section where the song should hit its peak. They may also have to remind the dancers to *tikʷahn ?iɫuwakka*, 'stand right', or to *tikʷahn ?otti·we*, 'dance well'. The clowns also mime the words of the songs for the audience. For example, the gesture for rain consists of wiggling all ten fingers very rapidly at chin level and slowly lowering the hands and arms to waist level.

Just as the clowns mime the text of the song, so the dancers may be said to mime the music. In *hilili*, the direction of the melody, with a sudden dip ending in a "sharp pause," is illustrated by the simultaneous dip of the dancers' yucca whips from their waists to the ground. Rhythm is most commonly marked by the stomping of the right foot on the main accents, causing the leg rattle to sound. When a singer performs such a song out of context, without dancing and without leg rattle, he finds it necessary to indicate the rhythm with foot-tapping.

If the dancers make a bad mistake in a song—for instance, if they miss an entire section—then the clowns suddenly all begin yelling at once, ʔucʔoyana·we halowaka, 'wake up you made a mistake', or yam penan ʔayyuʔhatiyahkʔena, 'listen to your words', or 'speak correctly,' or 'slow down, grandsons'. Finally, if the song is really ruined, they tell them to stop and begin again at the beginning. The audience members never call out any criticisms to the dancers; they merely start leaving the dance and do not call for any repeats. Later, when they are talking together or listening to their tapes, they will criticize both the songs themselves and their performance. However, very few songs or performances are given either extreme praise or severe criticism. From my sample of 116 recorded songs, only 4 were considered coʔya, 'beautiful' by the Zunis I talked with, 30 more were kʔokši, 'good', and most of the rest were alliye, 'all right'. Four songs were kʷaʔkʔokšamme, 'not good'. In one the words and melody were kʷaʔhi·ninaʔma, 'not matched'; two were hiš ʔemma penappa, 'very wordy' (the meaningful text in [aa'] and [bb'] was too long relative to the vocables in [cc']); and the fourth was počakkʔakka, 'ruined' because the dancers skipped the entire second "coming out" section and then had to begin the whole song over again.

During the performance, however, both audience members and clowns do express their appreciation of songs. If the clowns like a song they yell out ʔele·te!, 'that's right!' or nana·kʷe ton ʔeleʔa·wan, 'grandsons, you're doing well'. Sometimes the last "strong" part in the last "coming out" section "really gets to the Mudheads. They either start dancing with them or ʔikʔokʷeyen [giving a deer cry] or something like that. They get excited in the last part." The clowns are usually the first ones to recognize a good song and will call for an encore right on the spot.

If the audience likes a song someone will call out, immediately after it is over, ʔuhsite, 'this one again', seya, 'again', or ʔałnate,

## Songs of the Zuni Kachina Society

'once more', a request usually granted. If there are several good songs, then an audience member will come down into the plaza and sprinkle each clown and each kachina dancer with cornmeal while asking them to return the next day. If they decide to honor this request, which they must if it is properly done, then at the end of the dance, one of the clowns will announce to the audience, "People, we're telling you that in two days we will quit dancing. So friends, we're telling you to be expecting us tomorrow and the next day."

## CONCLUSIONS

Previous writers on the subject of Zuni songs—with the exception of Carlos Troyer, Helen Roberts, and Ruth Bunzel—have ignored or even denied the possibility of native musical theory and technical terminology. Troyer's discussion of Zuni "sound-colors" distorted Zuni aesthetics with a rigid notion of synesthesia or intersense modality, but the Zuni concept of *coʔya*, 'beautiful' or 'multicolored', as applied to music, does point to a synesthetic consciousness at Zuni. Roberts' call for a discussion with singers of their ideas of musical form and her assertion "that they possess such" (1923:184), along with Bunzel's report of "named sections, each with its own characteristic melodic features" (1932b:898), were hints of what a study of Zuni compositional theory and practice could reveal.

My work has, I hope, shown that Zunis have a native song classificatory system which involves a full, conscious command of the grammar of song composition and a clear understanding of pitch contour. Secondly, I hope that the idealized notion of totally egalitarian tribal behavior, which pictures everyone as an artist and generates the "group composition" theory of music, can be seriously questioned in the clear light of Zuni practice. There is a group *editing* process at Zuni, which may result in the modification of a composer's works by the membership of his own performance group, but that process has obvious analogues in everyday Western practice.

What is still lacking at this point is the kind of work that would place Zuni Kachina Society Songs in the broader context of Zuni music as a whole, including closer attention to Medicine Society Songs, and in turn place that whole more securely within a larger regional context. An obvious place to begin the latter task would be a comparison of Zuni and Hopi Kachina Song theory and practice, with an eye to such matters as the differences in kiva organization, in the role of the Kachina Cult in the ritual calendar, and in the details of aesthetic preference. Some of the differences in the music will doubtless be traceable to the influences of the Medicine Societies at Zuni. The further pursuit of that question, and the study of the Medicine Society music itself, will lead the investigation in the opposite direction, to the Eastern Pueblos. But the situating of Zuni music in the larger world does not end there; for as I have shown above, even a focus on Kachina Songs discloses such sources of musical ideas as the Ute Bear Dance, the "Limbo Rock," and Stephen Foster, and there are other songs at Zuni with Navajo, Apache, and Plains sources. The Zunis are no mere preservers of static traditions, living in tribal insularity, and a Kachina Song with an adapted melody or with lyrics about the moon shot is a solution to the problem of how to be Zuni and at the same time be of the world.

## NOTES

1. The six which have "Zuni" texts are: "Zuni Lover's Wooing, or Blanket Song" (Troyer 1904b), "Invocation to the Sun God" (Troyer 1904c), "The Sunrise Call, or Echo Song" (Troyer 1904d), "Incantation Upon a Sleeping Infant" (Troyer 1904e), "Sunset Song" (Troyer 1909b), and "Indian Fire Drill Song" (Troyer 1909c).

2. Two examples are "Rise ye, Hunters Brave" (Troyer n.d.a) and "Now Rest Thee in Peace" (Troyer n.d.b). Scores for these compositions are located in the Yale University Musical Score Archive, New Haven, Connecticut. Two other composers, Homer Grunn (n.d.) and John Comfort Fillmore (n.d.) also used Zuni "themes" in their own compositions, titled respectively, "Zuni Impressions: An Indian Suite," and "Indian Fantasia."

3. Although Herzog, with Bunzel's help, recorded approximately 180 Pueblo songs during his 1927 field trip, the collection is not accessible to researchers (D. L. Roberts 1972:248). There is, however, one tape of Zuni Social, Kachina, and Corn-Grinding songs (Herzog 1927:Pre-54-144-F) on deposit in the Archives of Traditional Music, Indiana University.

4. Here I am considering all the medicine societies at Zuni as members of a single corporate group. Strictly speaking, however, although each Medicine Society does classify individually as a "corporate group," the aggregate of all medicine societies would be technically designed as a "corporate category," since there is no overall regulation of their common affairs (Smith 1975:176–77).

5. The orthography used for this and other Zuni words and phrases follows the

# Songs of the Zuni Kachina Society

technical orthography which Stanley Newman used in his *Zuni Grammar* (1965).

6. The best description of the Shalako ceremony is still that by Edmund Wilson (1956:3-42).

7. The hierarchy of Zuni Kachina Society Songs, like the Zuni hierarchy of beings, creatures, and plants which Walker described (1966), consists of generic terms which are, without exception, inflected and nongeneric terms which are uninflected. Although *he·muši·kʷe*, 'Jemez people', and *wilacʔu·kʷe*, 'Apache(s)' appear to be inflected, the -·*kʷe* ending is, according to Newman (1965:64), an agentive which forms a collective term referring to the members of a tribal group rather than a plural form. Consequently, the one exception to this rule of uninflected form for the lower level terms [4,5] is *ʔa·paču*, 'Navajos', where *paču* refers to a single Navajo person and *ʔa·paču*, to members of the Navajo tribe.

8. I have resorted to an algebraic reduction of Zuni terms here in order to make this section easier for non-Zunis to follow. Capital letter [A] and [B] refer to large subdivisions in songs which are similar to, but not identical with, our notion of verse and chorus. The small letters [a] and [b] indicate smaller subdivisions within [A] and [B] which share the same Zuni name and function similarly on this lower level. In other words, capital [A] and small [a] are both called *kʷayinanne*, 'coming out', in Zuni, but no Zuni composer, singer, or dancer I know ever referred to song parts with an alphabetical, algebraic code.

9. See note 8.
10. See note 8.
11. See note 8.

# 3
# The Drama of the Hopi Ogres[1]

## JOANN W. KEALIINOHOMOKU
*Department of Anthropology*
*Northern Arizona University*

## INTRODUCTION

Western drama can be delineated as a phenomenal "work," characterized by a progression of events with affective content, presented in a special time and place, with a recognizable beginning, middle, and end. It is performed by human beings (or representations such as puppets) who as actors assume roles that are different from their everyday ones and engage in make-believe behavior, or experience temporary transformations. The purpose of the presentation of such a "work" is to relate a story to an audience which collectively undergoes an emotional or intellectual transformation, no matter how temporary it may be (cf. Dietrich 1953:3,6,37,38; and Albright, Halstead, and Mitchell 1955:3–5).

The two basic modes of drama are *presentational* and *representational*. Actors in presentational drama are audience-centered, and those in representational drama are stage-centered. In presentational theatre, the actors perform *about* the characters and events; in representational theatre, the actors *become* the characters and seem to live the events.

These parameters of representational drama apply to the ritual drama of the ogres as enacted on First Mesa by the Hopi and

Hopi-Tewa of Northern Arizona. The following discussion of the drama is divided into two parts. Part 1 is an exposition, and Part 2 is an exegesis.

## PART 1

### HOPI DRAMA

Hopi Indians perform dramas as outlined above, although usually the concluding episode is the only public performance. It is as if, in analogy, one could attend only the third act of a Euro-American play written in three acts. At Hopi, for example, the public sees only the "Bean Dance," the final act of the great drama of the Hopi Powamua, or the "Snake Dance," which concludes the long mythic drama that has taken 16 days for its presentation in the kiva.

Hopi ritual dramas are always representational in mode; the performers, temporarily, become the characters they portray. The concluding public performance often seems to be a colorful, nonprogrammatic, almost pageantlike display of animated Hopi symbols, rather than comprising "real" characters who are completing a complicated dramatic cycle.

### "THE VISITATION OF THE OGRES"

The major exception to the restriction of public display to Act III is the drama I call "The Visitation of the Ogres." The entire presentation is done in public, except for certain "backstage" activities. The principal audience for the drama comprises the uninitiated children of the community. "The Visitation of the Ogres" is a children's play, a very serious children's play that arouses powerful emotions in its audience.

In addition to the public presentation of the complete play, another feature sets "The Visitation of the Ogres" apart from other Hopi dramas: its dramatis personae include members of the audience—the children and some of their adult relatives. The play is in the representational mode in that the ogre characters actually become ogres. The ogres interact with members of the audience by incorporating them into highly structured improvised scenes. The younger children are not playing make-believe roles. They are play-

## The Drama of the Hopi Ogres

ing themselves in a time-out-of-joint as compared with their everyday lives.

"The Visitation of the Ogres" is performed in arena style, as are all Hopi dramas, but it is not confined to either plaza or kiva. The performers move throughout the village in which the drama appears, and at times visit other villages as well.

Non-Hopi viewers find it difficult to comprehend the meaning of "The Visitation of the Ogres." In the light of ethnocentric western understanding, the play seems to be a morality play. Some objective viewers presume that the ogres are a device for teaching children how to behave, either by punishing those who have misbehaved, or by displaying reverse models to demonstrate to children how they should not behave. Some horror-struck viewers apply their own value judgments, and interpret the drama as an unpalatable disciplinary method that will develop neurotic fears with detrimental psychological aftereffects when the children in the audience become adults. This chapter suggests that all of these explanations obscure the real purpose of the children's play.

Accounts of this play are given by Stephen (Parsons 1936a), Crow-Wing (Parsons 1925), Steward (1931), Fergusson (1931), Beaglehole (1937), Talayeswa (Simmons 1942), Titiev (1944, 1972), and field notes by Kealiinohomoku (1965-1978).

*Scenario: "The Visitation of The Ogres" or "The Pulling of the Children by 'Those Things' at First Mesa"*[2]

*Episodic Resumé.* At least one ogre woman and one ogre man plus several guards and clown-messengers have come to get children to eat. The children are ransomed with promises of good behavior and payment of food. At the end of the visit, the ogres lose all the loot in a wager with the chief of the host kiva.

*Episode One:* First announcement at kiva
*Episode Two:* First visit of ogres
*Intermission of several days*
*Episode Three:* Second announcement at kiva
*Episode Four:* So'owuhti dances around the fire
*Episode Five:* Several children are "pulled"
*Intermission for rest and lunch*
*Episode Six:* Ogres conclude visitations and go to kiva for loot

*Episode Seven:* Wager between Kiva Chief and *So'owuhti*
*Episode Eight:* Humiliation and expulsion of the ogres

*Dramatis Personae.* The Susuyukte of First Mesa, in approximate order of appearance:[3]

So'owuhti or Suyuku: The grandmother (not included in Tewa Village)

Hahaiwuhti: The mother (sometimes called So'oyok by members of Tewa Village)

Na'amu, Nataska Father: "Their Father," consort of Hahaiwuhti

Soyokmana: Natas, daughter of Hahaiwuhti, sister of the "Silly Boys"

Nataska Uncles: "Big Mouths," brothers of Hahaiwuhti. They are warrior/guards.

Heheya: The "Silly Boys" (called MukwadI by members of Tewa Village), sons of Hahaiwuhti, grandsons of So'owuhti, brothers of Soyokmana. Glossed as "Silly Boys" to mean foolish, inappropriate

Koyemsi: Mudheads. Helpers and clowns

Other ogres: Members of So'o family

Other guards

Kiva Chief (played by himself)

Kiva members who wear "civilian" clothes

Children of the community where drama is held

The families of the children, especially mothers and grandmothers

Kiva members who dress as females for the concluding public episode

*Scenario.* In the land of the Hopi live several fearsome ogre families. At First Mesa the belief is that these ogres live east of the mesas, in the area of the Navajo Nation called "Piñon," in special caves that have long passages connecting them with the Hopi world. Although they are part of the Hopi and Hopi-Tewa world, these ogres exist on the extremities of that world, and they come to the center for nefarious reasons. Their family structure follows the Hopi model, but they are otherwise morally and ethically reprehensible because they do not follow important Hopi precepts. Their primary sins are those of laziness, greed, gluttony, and sexual excess; thus they are totally out of harmony with the Hopi world.

## The Drama of the Hopi Ogres

The ogres hibernate in their cave homes during the months of planting and harvesting, and awaken when the cold winter rouses them from their stupor. They are ravenously hungry, but because they neither farm, hunt, nor store food, they must scheme to survive. They peer through the eyes of the living mesa at the Hopis who are well fed and happy because of their diligence during the warm months. They hunger especially for young, fat, salty, human flesh. They are ogres indeed, but not cannibals as many have called them, for cannibals eat only their own kind. These nonhuman ogres do not eat other ogres.

The ogres know that Hopi adults protect their children, and scold them only to prevent them from being *kahopi* (non-Hopi) adults. Nevertheless, children sometimes find it hard to follow Hopi rules, and many of them are naughty. The ogres hope that they can convince adult Hopis to sacrifice intractable children.

At First Mesa, when older children are being initiated into the Kachina Society in February and the elders are especially busy with kiva matters for the upcoming Powamua, the ogres make their bid. Winter is a good time to strike, because ritual activities might distract Hopis from the encroachment of the ogres.

The ogres process into Hopi led by the grandmother, So'owuhti (fig. 3.1). The ogres use a clever ruse to prevent the abortion of their plans for getting fat young children. They distribute to the children a tray of corn kernels and several little traps, just large enough to catch mice. They tell the children they can bargain for their lives by grinding corn, if they are girls, or by catching game, if they are boys. The ogres reason that even if they don't succeed in getting the children, they will have some victuals. These reprehensible ogres plan to live, figuratively and literally, off the Hopis.

The thoroughly frightened children have been warned by their elders that this is the time when ogres watch and salivate for children's flesh. The first visitation by the ogres justifies the threats and warnings. The children try, by being very well behaved, to convince their families that they are worth saving, and to encourage them to gather enough resources to "buy" them from the ogres. These children know they are too young, inexperienced, and weak to grind enough corn and hunt enough meat to "buy" their own lives.

For four days the children do their best to get cornmeal and meat

FIGURE 3.1. Ogre grandmother, as drawn by A. M. Stephen in Walpi, 1893 (Parsons 1936a:225). Mask and rattle of So´yok woman, drawn in Horn kiva. Hair black, sprinkled with raw cotton, a red stained tuft over forehead; face black, yellow annulet eyes, mouth red streak; white zigzag; hawk prayer-feather from mouth; black horsehair beard. Crook whitened, many olivella shells.

(the day after the first visitation is counted as "day one") because the ogres have said they will return in four days. The fourth day ends, but the ogres do not reappear. Apprehensively the children conclude that the ogres may not return, and they begin to relax. However, the children learn that the ogres always return; they should not be disarmed by the fact that they did not come back in four days.

On the morning of the Powamua, the children are terrified to see, in the gray dawn, a small fire on the southeast side of the mesa. Dancing around the fire, softly singing a scary song, is the ogre grandmother, So'owuhti. She soon makes her way up the side of the mesa and down into a kiva, where, the children are told, the rest of the ogres are meeting.

They forget this threatening situation briefly because the good kachinas come out early in the morning, to distribute freshly grown bean sprouts, green miracles that could not have grown in the barren semidesert during these cold months. Miraculously, also, their mothers and grandmothers have somehow been able to get fresh

## The Drama of the Hopi Ogres

corn, which is cooked with the bean sprouts as a springtime feast.[4] Even more exciting is the fact that these friendly kachinas make several trips throughout the villages carrying gifts: figurines for the girls, and arrows, bows, dance rattles, moccasins, and lightning sticks for the boys. These gifts remind them of their future roles, which will include caring for children as adult women, and hunting, dancing, and performing rituals as adult men.

By mid morning, however, the ogres are seen again. So'owuhti and family, called collectively the Susuyukte, emerge from the kiva that has reluctantly agreed to host them. Some non-Indians call them beggars, but this hardly seems accurate. Beggars are often pitiful and obsequious, but the Susuyukte are implacable and aggressive. They go to the households where there are children, and to the kivas, to demand food. The children cry, hide, clasp the legs of all adults in turn, and beg for protection. "Will you hold me when 'those things' come to pull me so they can't pull me away?" they plead.

Mothers ensure that for each girl there is at least a bowl of sweet cornmeal and four loaves of bread. For the boys there must be plenty of meat and a bag of tobacco to give to "those things." Some children try to run away, but those who remember previous visitations assure them that there is no place to hide from the ogres.

The Susuyukte move slowly, but inexorably, from household to household. They interrogate each child and threaten terrible penalties. At the last moment the female head of the household intercedes on the child's behalf, the purchase or trade is made, and the child is mercifully released. For children who are not visited until later in the day, the waiting is almost unbearable. At midday, the Susuyukte delay even longer by resting and eating, for an hour or longer, in someone's home.

At last, every house is visited, and the dreadful day ends. Foodstuffs given to the ogres for the children's lives have been stored for them in the host kiva. The ogres have collected enough to feed themselves for the rest of the year, but since no children are tucked away the ogres are not happy.

The ogres go to the kiva to get their loot. There they encounter the Kiva Chief, who blesses them with cornmeal and puffs of smoke. He then beguiles them cleverly and tempts them to a wager. He invites the Silly Boys to dance with a group of "girls" who are practicing in the kiva, and suggests to the So'owuhti that they will not be able to behave themselves. If they do not behave themselves properly, then the kiva members will get to keep the food that has been stored in the kiva. The Kiva Chief knows that the So'owuhti is a stubborn "old thing," and the Silly Boys are both stupid and uncontrollable.

The Silly Boys (fig. 3.2), on hearing that there are beautiful girls in the kiva, forget how hungry they are for food. They jump up and down gleefully. They promise they will behave themselves properly. The So'o, feeling more than a little miffed by the Kiva Chief's insinuations, tries to quiet her boys and accepts the wager.

FIGURE 3.2. "Silly boys," as drawn by A. M. Stephen in 1893 (Parsons 1936a:226).

Soon the "beautiful girls" emerge from the kiva. The Silly Boys are so overwhelmed with lust they do not perceive that the "girls" are either young boys dressed as girls, or old men dressed as old, usually Navajo, hags. The Silly Boys pretend to be well behaved when their grandmother is watching them, but whenever she turns her back, they try to see what sexual mischief they can do. At last, overcome with sexual cravings, they try to copulate with the "girls" in front of everyone, despite the "girls" apparent disregard of their advances. The grandmother is disgraced.

The Kiva Chief signals his men to return the loot to the kiva. The Susuyukte are told they have lost everything. So completely have they lost the bet that they are herded into the kiva to be stripped of even their clothing. In a state of shame and humiliation, the still

## The Drama of the Hopi Ogres

ravenous ogres are sent away. They return to their caves at the edge of the Hopi universe, where they will scheme for revenge next year.

### Covariations at First Mesa

The ogre visitation teams from different villages have varying numbers of alternative personnel. At First Mesa, Tewa Village regularly has three Nataska, Shipalovi has three or four, and Walpi, eight.

Sometimes, as at Walpi, the Grandmother with long, flowing hair, the Mother with tightly coiled hair, and the Sister with a butterfly whorl hairdo travel together, or the Mother and Sister form a female pair, as at Tewa.

Although the Koyemsi or Mudheads are optional at First Mesa, the Heheya (Hopi) or Mukwadl (Tewa) are crucial. They combine the roles of ogre son, step-and-fetch-it, and sexually driven clown. These Silly Boys, or foolish ones, harass the children at First Mesa by "pulling" their arms and legs—usually one Silly Boy for the arms and another for the legs. Sometimes they carry/drag the children toward a kiva before they release them. The Silly Boys also articulate the denouement of the drama because of their "tragic flaw," i.e., their inability to control their erotic behavior. The Silly Boys are jocular, fearsome, disorganized, naively stupid, and totally sensory. They are not, apparently, separate characters with individual names (unlike the Nataska, who do have individual names [Stephen 1936:183]). Whether there are two or several of them, they are "all the same."

Sometimes people laugh at the Silly Boys, though usually not before the final wager at the kiva. Until that time, onlookers avoid these creatures who often dart in unpredictable directions. If caught, onlookers are roped or humped by the Heheya (Silly Boys).

Other characters of "The Visitation of the Ogres" as performed at First Mesa are serious, formal, and purposeful. They are fearsome, but they function as teachers of stated precepts. They force the children to demonstrate publicly their ability to do chores and behave properly.

For this annual drama, the roles stay the same; the Suyuku and the Nataska will be the same next year; the Heheya and all the other characters will be the same. These roles are filled by different, unknown individuals, but that fact is not part of the drama. On the other hand, the children's roles change from one year to the next along with the improvisations in which they participate. There is no all-encompassing role of "Child." The children's roles are filled by individuals. The drama is not directed to Everychild, but to specific children, who are learning that they must change from child to adult. The preinitiation drama gives children their first experience in limbo, the "betwixt and between" as discussed by Victor Turner (1969). To the extent that the children are together in this limbo there may be the symptoms of *communitas*, again as discussed by Turner. But each child is dealt with separately, for each has problems. Each has a collection of food with which to "buy" his or her life, as well as a family comprised of different individuals who respond on his or her behalf to "Those Things." Up to this point in life, a child may have thought he or she was "something." Now children learn that they are nothing by themselves, but everything as part of a family; nothing as children, but everything as potential adults; nothing as individuals who seek to "do their own thing," but everything as responsible parts of the community. In this drama, children learn that they are expendable. They must become socially acceptable to the community or they will not be part of it.

### CLOWNS AND COMEDY

The persons who are laughed at throughout the entire drama, until the final episode, are the children. Until the wager episode at the kiva, the children are the major focus of attention; they are the unwitting clowns. Members of the community laugh at their fear and discomfort, hysterically it seems, because the anguish of the children cuts close to the viewers' hearts and interferes with unmitigated pleasure.

If the child is the clown figure for this drama, he or she is not a clown model who serves only as an example of what not to do, as suggested by many theorists about clowns (Beck and Walters 1977). A clown can provide comic relief, but such an ascription does not fit the child clowns of "The Visitation of the Ogres." Comic relief is provided by the Heheya (Silly Boys) in the denouement. Laughter during the body of the drama is directed at the children and their discomfort; this laughter is not joyful. The only relief before the final episode is that which comes after the visitation is finished at a given home.

Unpredictable comic relief does come from the often clever improv-

## The Drama of the Hopi Ogres

isations between children, civilians, and ogres. For example, women may tattle on their husbands to the ogres; children try devious ways of running away; onlookers, while trying to avoid blocking the path of the ogres, may walk headlong into one of the aimlessly wandering Silly Boys; and there is the incongruity of sexual confrontations, such as a Silly Boy humping an old woman or a young man. Humor also comes from the reversals of male/female roles. For example, when the Sister, Soyokmana, ran out of traps (that are given to boys) in 1978 to give to the Tewa Court Kiva "Boys," she gave them corn kernels instead. They retaliated by taking this as a signal to behave as females. On the day of the final visitation they emerged from the kiva behaving in exaggerated feminine ways, and "bought" their lives with bread and sweet cornmeal, much to the temporary disorientation of the ogres and to the everlasting delight of the onlookers.

### THE DRAMA AT FIRST MESA COMPARED WITH SECOND AND THIRD MESAS

The most complete family of ogres, referred to by the family name of Susuyukte, but popularly called "Those Things," is found in the Hopi villages of Walpi and Sichomovi (fig. 3.3). The next most complete ogre family visits the First Mesa village of the Tewas, called Tewa Village by its inhabitants, but referred to as Hano in the literature and by the Hopis (Dozier 1966, explains why the Tewa came to First Mesa, Hopi). The Hopi-Tewa ogre family excludes the grandmother figure, uses fewer Nataska Uncles, and refers to some of the characters by names that differ from those used in the other two First Mesa villages.[5] Informants claim they once had this figure, and that the mask is extant. No one seems to be willing to say why she is not activated for the ritual drama except that it is "traditional."

Contemporary informants claim that at one time there was but one ogre family on First Mesa that visited all households in the three First Mesa villages "on top." They claim, as they do for the omission of the grandmother figure at Tewa, that no one remembers why or when the current tradition of three families began. Informants also remember that for many years, in this century, the ogre family from Tewa Village visited homes in the village of Polacca, which is scattered on the east side of First Mesa. The practice stopped in recent years because it was considered to be "too much trouble" and took too long for the personators to make the

FIGURE 3.3. The drama of the ogres at Walpi, 1893. The Susuyukte family, left to right: Mother, Father, Daughter, Grandmother, and three Uncles.

## The Drama of the Hopi Ogres

detour. It was decided that Tewa children should come up "on top" to their traditional clan homes for the visitations.

Second and Third Mesas have regular covariations for their versions of "The Visitations of the Ogres." At Second Mesa, separate ogre families make regular visitations to Mishongnovi, Shipaulovi, and Shungopavi, as they do on First Mesa, but with notable differences. First, they never appear on the same day at the Bean Dance as they do at First Mesa, and as they used to do at Oraibi. Informants claim that everyone is too busy in the kivas to have the ogres around at that time. Second, there is but one female figure called So'o in each visiting family. She is the same figure as the Mana or Sister of First Mesa, except that she is portrayed as being very old. Third, the ogre family as it appears on Second Mesa is not as complete as the three on First Mesa. Second Mesa village presentations vary in both the cast of characters and their costumes. In 1966, for example, the Shungopavi Father was wearing the Nataska mask, but was otherwise accoutred as a Mudhead.

A fourth distinction, especially important to persons from Second Mesa, is that the ogres there are never permitted to touch the children, although the So'o figure may "catch" the children with the crook of her staff, or the Silly Boys may lasso the children with a rope.

A fifth contrast, according to an informant from Second Mesa, is that on Second Mesa the father of the household "tells on" the children, while the "grandmother is always there and always protective." The informant claims that at Second Mesa when the ogres accuse the children of misbehavior, the grandmothers say, "It's true they do such-and-such, but please don't take them." At First Mesa, the women of the household "tell on" the children in front of the gathering crowd before they defend the children.

Finally, the masks of the figures at Second Mesa are worn directly over the faces of the ogres, which makes them considerably shorter than the figures at First Mesa. At First Mesa, the entire face fits into the bill of the Nataska mask and the personator sees through the mask's mouth rather than through its eyes. The Nataska thus appear larger than life and more frightening.

Memories of the family visitations at the village of Oraibi, on Third Mesa, indicate that the major female figure was the Grandmother, and her escort was the same as the First Mesa Nataska

Father. There seem also to have been the accompanying Uncle-guards and Silly Boys, the couple's "sons," who functioned as combination clowns and helpers. When they made regularly scheduled visitations, they came on the same day as the Bean Dance, as they do at First Mesa (Titiev 1944:118). According to the account by Titiev (1944:219–20), the last visitation was in 1911. Various characters still appear separately in the kivas and in the village along with other kachinas. Sun Chief's references to "Giants" (Simmons 1942:80–84) seem to be variants of the male Nataska.

When Oraibi split in 1906 the people of Hotevilla decided that children had been too badly frightened by the Oraibi ogre family. The visitations were somehow implicated as one cause for the split.[6] Although the characters are still part of the kachina repertoire, they do not stop at separate homes, and they seem to be totally divorced from any interaction with members of the community. The Susuyukte at Hotevilla show up in kachina parades during the times of Powamua and the "Night Dances." The family walks in single file for 10 or 12 paces facing forward, then turns around and advances backward in the same line of direction for 10 or 12 paces. Hotevilla informants agree that, in theory at least, the Susuyukte could be called upon to make a special visitation to some specific child who was so delinquent that no other course seemed possible, but no one remembers this having ever been done.

Present-day residents of Hotevilla are especially critical of the fact that the ogres at First Mesa are permitted to touch the children, and they avoid watching the drama at First Mesa. At Oraibi the ogres were once permitted to touch the children. Sun Chief claims that one child who was touched soon died, and from that time on, actual touching was not permitted (Simmons 1942:85). When Sun Chief himself played the role of the Giant Kachina, he was told this explicitly (1942:181,295).

In conclusion, First Mesa seems to be the most conservative in its presentation of the ogre drama, with variations only among the supernumeraries as to numbers and types. Early in the 1970s three Nataska Uncle masks were stolen. The FBI recovered two of them in 1976, and the third in 1978. The people in Walpi were relieved to welcome back their "old friends," and rededicated them for use. Thus for a few years three Uncles were absent from the Walpi group.

## The Drama of the Hopi Ogres

Creative developments at First Mesa are reserved for the improvisations with the children, and for the concluding public episode of the wager at the kiva. The latter can include games, races, or dances, with either old men or young boys dressed as females. Sometimes these "females" are supposed to be Hopis, but often they are dressed as Navajos. On one occasion they were costumed to represent "Negroes."

### DRAMATIC TECHNIQUES

Dramatic uses of sight and sound, space and time, combine to make "The Visitation of the Ogres" a highly charged experience.[7] The Mother talks incessantly in a high falsetto, the Grandmother hoots, the Sister whistles, the Father growls and sometimes howls like a wolf, the Uncles crash their saws on the stone walls of the houses, and the Silly Boys, who are vocally mute, wear jinglers around their waists, bunches of hoofs from their belts, and bells around their garters. Something is always in motion during the public performance, so there is hardly a moment of silence during all of Episodes 5, 6, and 7. The sounds of the drama also include the voices of the children's mothers and grandmothers, who—in loud and stentorian tones—"tell on" the children, and then plead for their lives. This melange of sounds is overlaid by the children's continuous weeping, punctuated by occasional screams.

The use of space includes the entire mesa top. The Tewa group enters from the east end of the First Mesa. Both the middle village's Susuyukte, which commence and end their journey from the middle of the mesa, and the Walpi Susuyukte, which commence and end their journey from the west end of the mesa, are traveling at the same time. Their paths cross and crisscross several times during the day.

The Susuyukte move in rhythmic patterns from house to house. When the ogre family stops and lingers at a house, much action occurs "in place" between the ogres and the members of the family being visited. Then the ogre family moves on, with steady deliberation. At each stop on First Mesa the action "in place" is as follows. The Mother, Grandmother, Sister, and Father ogres all stand still with quiet feet. The Grandmother pounds her crook on the ground or gestures menacingly with it as if to grab a child around the neck. The Father sometimes lifts his bow and arrow in a threatening gesture. Meantime, the Nataska Uncles perpetually "march"—in place for a few steps, then advance to the side of the house being visited, crash their saws against the stonework and make a grating sound. They then march backward in the opposite direction for a few steps to the place where they first began the pattern. The Silly Boys bounce up and down incessantly. They vary the tempo by darting from place to place, peering in doorways and windows, jiggling up and down, randomly wandering off, then dashing back to the main figures to pick up food received from the children and delivering it to the host kiva.

The gestures of the Mother, Grandmother, and Father are spatially subdued and close to the body. The Nataska Uncles have larger gestures and extend their arms away from their trunks. The Silly Boys use many small gestures complicated by the rolling of their lassos, and the holding of their sheepskin kilts while they jiggle up and down; their gestures are enlarged when they grab the limbs of the children. Gestures can be characterized as lift-and-put-down by the female figure who walks with a staff, putting it down with each step; thrusting gestures by the Father; slashing by the marching Uncles' hands and arms; and push-pull, punch, and encircle by the Silly Boys.

The Sister has no gestures at all; her walk and stance are flaccid. The Mother, Grandmother, and Father gesticulate while the Sister endures. The Uncles are always ready repositories of power, strong but contained. They use the bow held in their left hands to push open the top part of their great mouths.[8] During the long hours of the drama the Uncles sometimes relax their intensity and gaze around.

Spatial levels are clear if the drama is viewed holistically. The lower spatial levels are filled by the children being visited, the upper ones by ogres who are larger than life. None of the dramatis personae change their own levels, except the Silly Boys, who stoop occasionally to catch a child, or the Mother or Grandmother, who climbs two or three steps whenever she reaches a kiva. An extreme change of level results when, during the concluding wager, the Silly Boys may sit or crawl on the ground to peer under the skirts of the kiva "girls," and pretend to copulate with them on the ground.

Time, as used in this drama, is both cosmic and puebloan (see Ortiz 1972). The most interesting fact is that, from a Hopi point of view, these ogres misuse time. First, they rest in the summer during

## The Drama of the Hopi Ogres

the farming days, directly opposite to Hopi practices. In Episodes 1 and 3 the Suyuku comes for the children late at night, and the Kiva Chief has to tell her that the children are in bed. Between Episodes 2 and 4 there is "supposed" to be a period of four days—reflecting the Hopi sacred number—but the ogre family does not return at the promised time. The intervening days vary from six to eight; the delay adds to the dramatic tension. The final temporal incongruity is the promise made by the defeated ogres that they will return in a year, an unbelievably long period for already hungry monsters to wait for another chance to eat.

## PART 2

### ACADEMIC THEORIES

The drama in question illustrates the "recurrent themes" of Pueblo existence as discussed by Ortiz (1972). He cites (1972:154) the special use of time (ahistorical) and space (emergence from the "middle," and the danger of boundaries), and lists (1972:139) the themes of "burlesque and caricature, mock violence, formality, masquerade, age, status, and sex role reversals, gluttony, and licensed obscenity."

Ortiz notes that deviant behavior calls attention to itself. The symbolic expression of deviant behavior is "well structured and regulated," and the deviance acts as a catharsis as well as reinforcing "commitment to normative behavior" (1972:145). Ortiz states that we learn about the Pueblo world view when we perceive the opposite of the norm. Ortiz, however, finds that these arguments do not sufficiently explain some ritual drama.

This cannot account satisfactorily for the fact that the deviant ogre family, which exists outside of the center of the world, is permitted to come into the lives of those who find them defiling. It is important to note that Ortiz (1972:139) suggests these dramas are instrumental as well as expressive. This prompts him to deduce that this instrumentality provides "boundary-maintaining mechanisms . . . as a means of insuring control and conformity" (1972:157).

The idea of instrumentality is useful for unraveling the meaning and purpose of "The Visitation of the Ogres," but while it gives us guidance, it does not provide the key. We must search further, since even the most willing Pueblo collaborators have apparently not felt the need to articulate such information.

Harvey's (1972:214) words do not lead to optimism for understanding the drama. He writes that "the native cultures obviously hold that early lifelong participation is necessary for valid understanding." Pessimism is compounded by his dictum that, "If the sympathetic person or a good theoretician can find the key so much the better for him, but it cannot ethically be revealed" (1972:211-12).

Nevertheless I believe the key to this drama is discoverable, and that its revelation will not be unethical if it reshapes ethnocentric value judgments held by many non-Hopis. Non-Hopis have viewed traditional Hopi child-rearing practices as permissive, but harsh in crisis situations. Since the Hopis are in constant contact with the non-Hopi world, mutual understanding of child-rearing practices can be beneficial.

Two features of the ogre drama's clowns do not fit Hieb's model (1972). As shown, the clowns in the first several episodes of the drama are children, and they are not deliberate clowns as are the formal, ritual clowns of Hieb's investigation. Second, the drama is not designed to make people laugh. Hieb's model is relevant to the final episode of the wager between the Silly Boys and the kiva members impersonating girls, but the final public act of the drama is not the major point here.

I agree with Hieb that neither the comic-relief nor the regression-without-guilt/socially-approved-gratification theories are adequate for explaining Hopi ritual clowns in general, and the clown figures in "The Visitation of the Ogres" in particular. "Laughter," Hieb (1972:193) tells us, "is not only a judgment on the validity of the humorous patterns, it tends to confirm the validity of the normally accepted ones . . . ." The problem with applying this idea to "The Visitation of the Ogres" is that for the first seven episodes, the laughter is uneasy.

For human beings generally, laughter helps to maintain and/or reestablish homeostasis as it resolves cognitive dissonance. In Hopi psychology, laughter shows that people are happy; happy people think good thoughts; good thoughts are necessary for ritual to be effective. This is justification enough, perhaps, for the presence of Hopi clowns, and for the inclusion of the wager episode at the kiva in "The Visitation of the Ogres," but it does not provide the key for holistic understanding of the ogre drama.

# The Drama of the Hopi Ogres

## THEORIES FROM THE MYTH

Clues might come from the tales of the origin of "The Visitation of the Ogres." In 1893 Stephen investigated the Nataska.

> I tried to get . . . to give me the theory of the Nata'shka, but he would only say that they were monsters formerly who lived in caves . . . and prowled round preying on children and people generally. Pu'ukon destroyed them. . . . They are now exhibited, he says, for the purpose of maintaining discipline among the children. If a child does wrong, or is perverse, it is threatened with the dreaded Nata'shka (Parsons 1936a:183).

Sun Chief, from old Oraibi, gives an account of the origin of the visits:

> . . . my grandfather told me the story of the giants. . . . He said, "A long time ago in Oraibi, the children paid no attention to the old people, made fun of them, tied dirty rags behind their backs, and threw stones at them. They also took food from the smaller children and fought them. The parents tried to stop this mischief but could not" (Simmons 1942:45).

Sun Chief tells an involved story about a kiva that was reputed to have members who were witches (Two-Hearts). These members were tired of the children. They performed magic with some piñon gum to create the ogres, and they charged them with catching a few children every morning at dawn (Simmons 1942:46).

The ogres emerge as more than symbols of evil because they are associated with teaching precepts of acceptable behavior. Parents are able to convince the "giants" to let the children go only after there is a promise of future correct behavior. The giants claim they will have to return if the children are not good, which contradicts the idea that the ogres are eager to come back because of their gluttony.

## THEORIES OF OBSERVERS

Fergusson viewed the ogre family as "beggars" who punished naughty children. "They all wear terrifying masks: great snouts, bulging eyes, and horns. Each carries a bow and arrows in his left hand, leaving the right hand free to receive gifts, for this is a begging expedition" (1931:127). Fergusson evaluated the experience as:

> not so pleasant for the children and very upsetting for white visitors, filled with the notions of the lasting effects of terror on

the child mind. . . . Protests to our host were met with his quiet, gentle Hopi voice: "But that is our way. He has been naughty. His mother asked them to come." Altogether it was too much for the white visitors, and they left the mesa (1931:134).

Dennis, who called the ogres "bugaboo kachinas," perceived them as either bringing punishment for bad behavior or threats to prevent bad behavior. He also called them "a very clever psychological device" to make children love their parents out of gratitude for their protection (1965:44–45).

Beaglehole perceived the experience from a pragmatic and pedagogical viewpoint:

> When the child is recalcitrant, a useful pattern of discipline is provided . . . ogres always on the lookout to snatch up the lazy or ill-tempered. The total effect of this precept and example is realistically to support the authority of the elders in the economic and general education of the young (1937:20).

Elsewhere, Beaglehole stated that "Hopi ritual has three main purposes, the production of rain, fertilization and promotion of growth in human beings and crops, and the curing of sickness and disease." He added that Hopi ritual "is heavily weighted in terms of the first two purposes" (1937:45). If Beaglehole had applied these three purposes to the ogre rituals, we might have had the key for understanding, although the first two purposes seem not to apply.

Simmons similarly noted that "the Hopi ceremonies are extremely complicated, predominantly religious, and usually performed for the express purpose of insuring rain, promoting the growth of crops, and safeguarding health and long life" (1942:18). Simmons, like Beaglehole, did not appear to try to measure these three purposes against the ritual of the ogres.

Titiev's interpretation introduces a pragmatic purpose not previously suggested.

> On all the Hopi mesas there are a number of bogey Katcinas who have the dual function of disciplining children and ridding the fields of mice and helping prepare them for the spring planting. The best known of these Katcinas are the So'yoko and Natacka (1944:216).

Titiev notes further that:

the defending kinsman is busy relating the boy's good points, arguing that he is a good hunter, that he is quick to learn the duties of a sheepherder, and that he does not deserve to be carried off. . . . [if the child is a girl,] she is relieved to have a kinswoman speak up in her behalf, saying that she is a diligent housekeeper and not lazy when it is necessary to grind corn (1944:218–19).

He includes an interesting footnote: "In spite of the fact that the So'yoko ceremony is supposed to bring beneficial results, the natives say that cold and windy weather always follows a So'yoko appearance" (1944:219).

Three new clues may be considered for discovering the key to "The Visitation of the Ogres." First is that of pragmatism, i.e., ridding the fields of mice. Second is the reinforcement of good behavior that a child receives from hearing his or her virtues enumerated. Third is that cold, windy weather follows the ogre ceremony, strengthening the idea that the ceremony is not devoted to creating moisture or enhancing fertility. There is still no suggestion of a correlation with health.

Titiev argues, "As performed on Second Mesa, the element of sex license and the routing of the Katcinas for their misdeeds serve to link the So'oyoko performance very closely to similar exhibitions on the part of clown groups" (1944:221). He considers several issues that seem to him to be related, and perceives some connection among war, warriors, clowns, humor, death, sexual excess, transvestitism, transsexual behavior, ogres, and witches. Specifically, he concludes that the sexual excess of the Heheya (Silly Boys) is associated with clowns, that clowns are connected with warriors and warriors with death. Titiev attempted to find a connection between "Clown" and "Warrior," but it became clear to him that clown and warrior (and ogre) oppose what is highly valued in Hopi society. These three, clown, warrior, and ogre, share the characteristics of promoting non-peace, non-order, non-growth, and non-life.

### HOPI HOMEOPATHY

The key is not the equation of war and warriors, humor and clowns, death and ogres. Instead it is that warriors, clowns, and ogres serve a comparable function: all three are antidotes, in that an antidote is a remedy and "includes anything that counteracts an injurious effect," according to *The American Heritage Dictionary*.

Clowns, for example, are antidotes, in the case of naughty children, for non-peace and non-order.

Clown, warrior, and ogre rituals are healing ceremonies based on the principle that like cures like. When thought of as medicine, warrior, clown, and ogre are the "same," as a class, to correct the ills of being *kahopi*. In this sense, likewise, they can be equated with death. Death is the opposite of life, and life is the quintessence of being Hopi, that is, life is moisture, fertility, growth, health, and Hopi. These qualities of life, because they are found together, are also the "same."

Clowns, warriors—and ogres—do not function solely or even primarily as inducements to conformity by presenting a model of mismeaning. In the past I have misguidedly focused on clowns and ogres as pedagogical devices that teach by reverse example. This function is probably operant, but it may obscure the real meaning.

The drama of the ogres fits the Hopi idea of medicine; like cures like, and this is sympathetic or homeopathic magic/medicine. One way to describe Hopi medicine and its theory is to invoke the "doctrine of signatures."[9]

The doctrine of signatures explains the philosophy of Hopi medicine.[10] When everything is balanced in the Hopi world there is ease and not "dis-ease." No illness is "natural," and no death is "natural." Each results from imbalance.

This contrasts with Western medicine, where some things are considered to be ipso facto "bad," such as certain bacteria that must be destroyed. In Hopi theory of health, nothing is bad by nature. Something becomes so if it is too much or too little. Balance can be restored by the judicious application of something of the same class, or associated in some way.

For example, snakebites cause swelling. If one is pregnant, anything associated with snakes is dangerous, because being pregnant is itself a "swelling." Too much swelling causes a dangerous illness (edema). If one inadvertently gets "too much snake" or has too many snakelike contacts, one must take snake medicine.

Many Hopi examples can be found in the writings of Stephen, Titiev, Simmons, Beaglehole, Steward, Parsons, and others, and more examples are revealed every day to the participant-observer. All of these examples make sense in terms of the doctrine of signatures, i.e., like causes like, and like cures like.

## The Drama of the Hopi Ogres

The three main "dis-eases" that can affect an entire Hopi community are the opposites of moisture (drought), fertility (sterility), and health (illness). Observers note that Hopi rituals give positive application of the doctrine of signatures. They are good medicine, but they are preventive rather than prescriptive medicine.

When things are out of balance, prescriptive medicine must be used. The community, a model of balance, is maintained by the preventive medicine of the ritual calendar. Prescriptive medicine, on the other hand, is usually private medicine, administered when needed by a priest or medicine man. The exception is the "dis-ease" of childishness. There are many children within a community, and they must be medicined on a community basis, as well as individually. "The Visitation of the Ogres" does both, for private improvisational scenes occur within the larger drama.

Most ceremonies in the ritual calendar promote moisture and fertility. Another reason for rituals—health and the restoration of order—explains "The Visitation of the Ogres." Hopi and Hopi-Tewa friends agree that the ogre drama is medicine. One said, "Yes, that is why it is necessary for the children to be pulled. It hurts me to see this, . . . but I know it is good for the children, and that is why I go along with it."[11]

As medicine, ogres may not be pleasant to "take," but they are necessary for people who are ill, either because they have not behaved properly or because they are juvenile and uninitiated. Initiation is the most powerful medicine of all, but until children are old enough to take formal rites of initiation, the visitation of the ogres is the best medicine for the illness of childishness. In this sense, children are *kahopi* by definition. The ogres are "like" children in that they are characterized by *kahopi* behavior, except that they are even more excessive.

### Hopi Child-Rearing Philosophy

The doctrine of signatures also helps explain the philosophy of Hopi child rearing: the child must be cured of the problems that accompany immaturity.[12] One must avoid the inference, however, that Hopis think that childhood is pathological. Hopi pathology refers only to too much or too little. Hopis are farmers and know that all living, growing creatures must start out in an incomplete form. The young corn plant is welcome for what it will become, and all efforts are extended in helping the young plant develop, ripen, and become useful. Similarly, the young child is welcome, and every effort is concentrated on helping him or her develop as a mature, ripe, and useful adult. Just as the corn is not corn until it has a ripened ear, neither is the child a human being until it is mature.[13]

All things that characterize immaturity, such as greed, laziness, and excesses of all sorts must be "cured." To be immature is a form of being *kahopi*; to be mature is to be Hopi. *Kahopi* adults are probably witches and thus pathological. Undeveloped humans must mature properly and not remain *kahopi*. Childhood ka-hopi-ness is curable; witchhood is not.

Contrast two varying Euro-American philosophies of childrearing. The Biblical approach assumes that children result from sin and they must be "saved" from their own defilement and be rid of their sinful ways. This approach does perceive of childhood as pathological. Terminology for rearing claims to "train" the child, to "break" the child. He or she is "broken" of bad habits. The child learns right from wrong for fear of punishment. The adult continues to behave in the "right" way for fear of a heavenly father, who has the power to give final and total punishment in the hereafter. The "good" person is promised rewards in the hereafter that make bearable the trials and tribulations in this life.

Another approach to child rearing, especially in America, perceives children as "real" people, lacking only in development, who must be treated with respect and given accurate answers to every question. Theories of developmental stages, such as those articulated by Freud and Piaget, suggest that development happens to a child without his or her volition. However, a family is proud if a child goes through these stages at an early age, or more quickly than the norm. It is desirable to have a child who is both precocious and "well adjusted," and to these ends the well-educated, "enlightened" parent exerts every effort. The family tends to be child-oriented, constantly involved in self-evaluation. If anything less than perfection results, specialists are consulted. The child often rehearses so carefully the role of being a child that it is difficult for him or her to develop into an adult.

Hopi philosophy does not perceive children as pathological beings who need to be "broken," or as real humans to be "respected," but as harbingers of what is to come, like young bean sprouts. With

## The Drama of the Hopi Ogres

good care children will become human and earn the right to be respected. They will not be urged to develop too quickly because that would be poor husbandry. Children are gently urged through their development by continual additions of adult responsibilities. As a younger sibling enters the household, Hopi children care for the new one. They are not expected to provide models of perfection for the infant. They are not responsible for the care of the younger one to relieve the adults in the household of extra chores, but because the care of something helps older children rehearse adulthood.

Hopi children (ages 8–10) are initiated into the Kachina Cult before they are intellectually or spiritually capable of understanding the metaphysics of the kachina. Their admission into the cult is "good medicine" for rehearsing adult (human) roles. From that time on, the doctrine of signatures is a strong influence. The choice of the first mask a boy wears dramatically expresses this, for it is believed that his first "friend" (kachina) will determine his path after death. His family carefully selects a good kachina for him to wear, so that it can enter his being and become his signature. His path is determined by the first mask he dons, even if he wears it only a few minutes. Then, he can put on a different "friend" for his first personification. His first personification may be that of a Koyemsi, but no one will want that to be his everlasting fate.

Hopi child rearing, as discussed above, elucidates features that are often misunderstood by non-Hopis. If Hopi child rearing is permissive, it is because one does not expect a corn sprout to behave as a mature plant. Bothering a child about keeping its nose clean or soiling its pants seems stupid and picayune. Adult Hopis do not have such problems, and when children are no longer children, they will not have them either. Children do not need to be taught this because they will "outgrow" non-adult behavior.

The male child is harassed, however, by his mother's brother, and the classificatory grandfathers in his paternal line, for three positive reasons. First, he learns through experience what adult Hopis will tolerate. He learns, next, that the treatment given him by his mother's brother is indicative of responsibility that he will have someday, because of obligations to the maintenance of clan knowledge and medicine. Finally, because of the harassment he experiences, he learns what he can bear—how strong he is and can be.

The Hopi girl, in contrast, does not insure her future-beyond-life by a kachina "friend." Instead she must choose a good husband.

Her first husband will be with her in the hereafter, no matter how many consorts or husbands she may have in this life, and regardless of which one she likes best. The girl prepares for a life of service with heavy responsibilities. She will be the most powerful figure of all. She will be the Mother. The path she follows on this earth will be the one she follows forever. This knowledge makes her independent, in contrast with the boy who tends to be dependent on his clan, mother, godparents, kiva mates, and his "friend." The most important article that must be buried with her is her set of wedding boots, to take her on her path. If she is happy now she will be happy then. She must have a house in this life in order to have a house in the next one. She cannot expect heaven to reward her with riches and joys she did not have in this life.

The assessment by outsiders, that punishment of Hopi children comes from the supernatural, must now be amended. By understanding the doctrine of signatures we can see that "punishment" is not a Hopi concept.[14] Instead, supernatural agencies are activated to cure a child of *kahopi* behavior. Punishment is a penalty for wrongdoing. In contrast, medicine is a treatment for illness. Punishment is a negative response; medicine, a positive one. Philosophically, child-rearing practices differ significantly between a society that punishes its children and one that medicines its children; one that inflicts pain to show children the error of their ways and one that expects children to endure something unpleasant to help them mature.

### Hopi Pragmatism

Hopis and Hopi-Tewas are religionists and idealists, to be sure, but they are also pragmatists. They know seed must be planted for corn to grow. After the corn is planted, they know there will be good results only if they work hard.

In the rearing of children they are likewise pragmatic. Small children are not wise and cannot be expected to make good choices. There is no compulsion to give "real" explanations to answer children's questions. Questions are answered with reasons that reflect a Hopi world view, but pragmatics underlie all. Children are told the reason they must not go to the well is because of the horned snakes that live there. This explanation promotes a Hopi feeling and inspires awe for sources of water, but the pragmatic reason is not told to the children. Pragmatically, if children

## The Drama of the Hopi Ogres

linger near wells they will get the water dirty, and they might even drown. One cannot afford to take chances that "real" reasons will be accepted. Children must be kept away from water sources, and they will not argue with supernatural reasons.

There is something of this pragmatism in Titiev's statement that one reason for "The Visitation of the Ogres" is to rid the fields of mice. Little boys did catch and string up mice to give to the ogres. They catch fewer mice today, but try to catch some kind of small game for the ogres. If they are unsuccessful, as they often are, there is meat available from the supermarket. Stephen reports that the ogres would accept wild game only. Today, mutton is regularly used to give to the Susuyukte. Pragmatically, Hopis realize that game is difficult to get today, so a new kind of meat is offered.

The giving of foodstuffs to the ogres may have a pragmatic reason. While it may seem to the outsider that the ogres are beggars who receive the food as *alms*, and the story line suggests that the food is given as a *ransom*, in actuality, the children's family must give payment to the ogres for their healing services! They must thank the sponsoring kiva group for providing the healing ritual, since of course it is the kiva members who get the food, and the dramatic characters are personified by members of the host kiva. It is enlightening to realize that many hidden motives are not as esoteric as they are pragmatic. It would hardly do for a mother to say, "I'm giving the food to thank the ogres."

The pragmatics of the ogres' drama is that the medicine will not work unless little children really believe there are ogres who are hungry for human flesh. Not until Hopis are adults can they be expected either to (a) enact a dramatic role, or (b) animate a "friend." Only a mature boy could, for example, be the Soyok maid who, dressed as a girl and wearing a bothersome mask, carries a burden basket and goes along with the ogres' family for many hours. Likewise, only when one has been initiated can it be understood that the person wearing a mask is not "faking it" (as one is when wearing a Santa Claus mask), but has actually become transformed into the "friend." Thus, for the drama of the ogres, the main characters are played by adults who are able both to perform and to reflect the seriousness of the occasion. The other characters of the drama, the children, behave in the appropriate way because they are naive. They are serious and receptive to the medicine.

JOANN W. KEALIINOHOMOKU

Medicinal Value of Hopi Drama

Another Hopi drama that may be a healing ritual, specifically, is the drama(s) of the clowns. Similar to "The Visitation of the Ogres," the dramas of the clowns reveal the entire drama to the audience, but the episodes can be seen and enjoyed out of context. Possibly the dramas of the clowns are primarily of medicinal value, and only incidentally, as an intellectual exercise, are they pedagogical tools. Clowns make people happy and make them think good thoughts; the thinking of good thoughts makes the deities happy and desirous of doing good things for the Hopis. In this sense, then, laughter is literally good medicine. Second, the activities of clowns that are "vulgar" or "gross" have medicinal value, to cure like desires in people by providing the antidote to excesses instead of suggesting repressions.

Obviously some of the figures in "The Visitation of the Ogres" are clowns. Yet, unlike the dramas of the clowns, the grim ogre drama is not produced to make people feel happy. It is dangerous medicine until it has a chance to "work."

The ogre drama is unique because it is the only Hopi drama that is designed to work its medicine on the uninitiated. Other Hopi dramas share publicly the concluding episodes for the major purposes of enforcing group solidarity, for entertainment, for reminding persons of the contributions of each society and clan (which "own" the societies and their rituals), and also for the magic that occurs from village-wide activation of the medicine of each ritual. In one sense it can be said that all Hopi dramas are of medicinal value, and that all of them can be understood by the application of the doctrine of signatures. In terms of the specific use of the ogre drama, however, it is the only Hopi play that seems to be devoted to prescriptive medicine and performed especially for persons who do not understand that they are being medicined.

The cast of characters differs from village to village. The origin story (a tacit prologue) and the fate of the ogres (a tacit epilogue) likewise differ in details from one village to another. Nevertheless, the essential features are consistent. For one thing, the costumed characters are never human. To be truly human is to be Hopi, and ogres are *kahopi*. When human beings come to visit, they are treated as guests. The ogres, in contrast, are not guests. They are

## The Drama of the Hopi Ogres

dealt with, but not invited in. In fact, ogres enter a home only when chasing a fleeing child, or, at First Mesa, when the Father Nataska gives special medicine.[15] The intruding ogres enter the host kiva for the pragmatic reason of storing their loot.

The numerous "children" who are part of the ogre family, such as the Silly Boys, are always in the liminal state of being neither youngsters nor adults. They are, likewise, sexually ambiguous. The Mudheads wear women's dresses for their kilts. The Silly Boys are sexually aroused by males as well as females, and in fact always lose their wager with boys who are dressed as girls.

The adult members of the ogre family are *kahopi*. They do not plant, farm, or store things for times of famine. They are lazy and try to live off the efforts of others. They procreate, but their offspring are sterile. Yet, they provide powerful medicine. When infantile or *kahopi* behavior shows up in an older person who should know better, such as a teenage daughter or a husband, that person is publicly medicined by these same ogres. Thus both initiated and uninitiated can be medicined by the ogres, but the initiated must behave as naively as the uninitiated.

A young woman from Second Mesa recalls vividly that the Suyuku was used for "warnings" and "threats" all year around, because the Suyuku could "see" the children from "holes in the stove." Suyuku was invoked especially in the weeks before the annual visitation, during which time she was included in stories. The stories her paternal grandmother told every January were "mostly about the Susuyuktu, but especially the Suyuku Grandmother." They included vivid descriptions of what the Suyuku's house looked like and what she did to children there. She claims that her grandmother told "many dramatic tales," most of them "quite short," and some of them "quite funny," but all of them graphic enough to be understood by a child.

She notes that "everyone" has to buy his or her life, however, because no one is perfect. Her father goes to the kiva when the ogres visit, and he takes food to "buy his life," because "buying one's life is a kind of purification." The ogre families visit all the kivas, where the kiva members are inside waiting to bring out their food ransoms as if they were miscreant children. Adults of the community are the "children" of the *kikmongwi*, or Village Chief. They must continually strive to be mature. Kiva Chiefs, also, are considered to be very adult. Indeed, they assume the role of "grandmother of the kiva family" and defend the kiva members from the ogres.

For children reared as Hopis or Hopi-Tewas, the drama of the ogres is medicine. For my daughter, who had been reared differently, the experience was not medicine. At age four, she was so frightened she had to be medicined by the Father Nataska. I had told her that the figures were really persons she knew who were dressed in costumes, and I swore her to secrecy. She kept the secret, but her fear was as gripping as if she had no revelation, and she actually became sick. Other children in the community, who appeared to be as frightened as she prior to the drama, seemed to recover quickly. My daughter had no appropriate frames of reference. She had no subliminal knowledge that, in the long run, no one disappeared because he or she had been eaten. Although my daughter knew people were punished for actual transgressions, she did not understand threats for "projected" misdemeanors, or being punished on principle only. Since she had not been lazy, mean, disrespectful, or dishonest she could not understand why she was being subjected to frightening threats. Hopi and Hopi-Tewa children, on the other hand, are accustomed to warnings and to curative medicine to make them more responsible. Indeed the fact the drama is played yearly, rather than happening just once in a child's lifetime, promotes cumulative values and understanding for the members of the community. For Hopi children, taught to have a world view that includes the doctrine of signatures, the medicine of the ogres is understood implicitly even if not explained explicitly.

## CONCLUSIONS

In order to understand Hopi dramas that seem otherwise inexplicable, a new postulate may be introduced. The first postulate is that persons learn by example what not to do. The second is that like cures like. The new third postulate is that healing occurs only when the illness is worked out of the system and replaced by something else.

Analogous to modern Western medicine, some medication attacks symptoms, but the disease is gone only when other medication destroys the bacteria or whatever, to permit good health to replace

## The Drama of the Hopi Ogres

poor health. Thus we have two kinds of prescriptive medicine. For example, aspirins lower the fever, and antibiotics destroy the microorganisms. Similarly, the painful medicine of the ogres treats symptoms, but another medicine is necessary to replace disharmony with harmony.

The drama of the ogres provides both kinds of medicine. The communal part of the drama cures symptoms; the improvised scenes within the drama fill the created vacuum. During improvisations children are approached as misbehaving individuals. In order for them to become acceptable members of society, to develop into Hopis, they must no longer wish to misbehave.

To accomplish this, two appropriate procedures are included in the drama: (1) Children confront their individual problems. In extreme cases, a child is "smoked" under a blanket, where fright and suffering become almost unbearable and the child feels close to death.[16] The child wants to live and no longer wishes to be naughty. The child then (2) rehearses correct behavior.

Rehearsing correct behavior follows purification even for those persons who are initiated. For example, such a person might be required to wash dishes publicly to demonstrate that she is a useful member of the household, or chop wood publicly, under the supervision of the ogres, to show that he is able to take responsibilities. Siblings may rehearse loving behavior by hugging and speaking kindly to other siblings in public. The successful rehearsal of behavior provides a guide to future behavior. Children do not lose face by suddenly becoming kind, unselfish, and industrious. They have been transformed publicly, and their transformations are sanctioned. They are more mature than they had been and everyone will expect appropriate evidence of this.

### NOTES

1. This chapter is dedicated to my daughter, Halla, who was pulled, not once, but twice at Tewa Village, First Mesa, Hopi. So far as I know, I am the first, and perhaps the only woman anthropologist who has been a participating parent in "The Visitation of the Ogres." My daughter's experiences as a child in the drama provided insights to me that I could not have anticipated. To those dear people at First Mesa who made this participation possible by accepting my daughter and me as members of their family, I acknowledge my debt, and give them my thanks with love.

## JOANN W. KEALIINOHOMOKU

Thanks are due also to the American Philosophical Society who supported my research at Hopi for parts of 1965, 1966, and 1967; and to the Wenner-Gren Society for Anthropological Research, which continued with support for parts of 1968, and in 1970–71.

2. A point of emphasis made by all persons from Second and Third Mesas is that the ogres are not permitted to touch the children, whereas at First Mesa the children are literally pulled by the Heheya (Silly Boys). This practice is called "pulling" and the drama is often referred to as "The Pulling of the Children."

3. The First Mesa ogre families from both the villages of Walpi and Sichomovi include the grandmother, variously referred to as So, So'o, Soyoko, Suyuku, and So'owuhti, sometimes spelled So'owuqti; and the mother, variously referred to as Hahai, Hahaiwuhti, Hahaiwuqti, Hahai woman, or even Ha'haiyi. The father is Namasu, or Na'amu, consort of Hahaiwuhti, variously called Natask, Natack, and most often, "Their Father." The mother's daughter is Natas, called Soyokmana, Soyok Maid, or "Their Sister." Mother's brothers, the uncles, are referred to collectively as Nataska, or Natashka, Natacka, "Those Things," "Big Mouths," giants; each has an individual name. The sons of Hahaiwuhti are the Silly Boys, called Heheya, Hehe'a; they are often called "Her Boys," although sometimes the referent of "her" is the grandmother rather than the mother. Supernumeraries include the Mudheads, more correctly referred to as Koyemsi, sometimes spelled Coyemsi, or Koyemshi.

4. Whole ears of corn that have been dried in the fall, and soaked until soft before being cooked, are called "fresh corn."

5. They often refer to the mother, Hahaiwuhti, as "So'o," or Siuwuhti, but also Soyoko, and Soyokwoman, since they have no grandmother figure. They call the father "Their Father" almost exclusively. They regularly refer to the maid as "Sister," or Siwa. They almost always call the Heheya or Silly Boys by the Tewa name of "MukwadI;" and they pronounce Koyemsi as "Guiyemshi."

6. On September 8, 1906, severe factionalism in the village of Oraibi caused one faction to leave that village and found the village of Hotevilla. Despite the claims of villagers to the contrary, Dennis (1965:44–45) reports that the ogre family did occasionally visit children in Hotevilla until 1930.

7. The mood of the affair changes from one year to the next, according to the weather. In 1966, for example, the weather was extremely cold, the day of the ogres' visitation was dark and overcast, and there were several inches of snow on the ground. The drama was more menacing than it was, say, in 1971 when the drama took place during a balmy, sunny day.

8. Men who personate the uncles and father at First Mesa have stated that the masks are very heavy and awkward because of the imbalance created by the weight of the bills at the front of the masks. Their own necks become tired from trying to throw their heads back to make the hinged mouths open and close. It is more comfortable to open the mouths manually by lifting them with the tips of the bows.

9. The following explanations are quoted from Grossinger:

> A Signature is a mark, a diagnostic occurrence in the fabric of the world. A signature indicates more than itself, than its mere denote. It is a signature *of* something, or is *left* by something. The symptom of a disease, the seal of a king, and the moraine of a glacier are all signatures. From its cognates we can learn some of the aspects and uses of the word "signature:" sign, signal, signification, signet, sigil.
>
> . . . opposition is not in fact between outer and inner worlds but between the revealed world . . . and the unrevealed world: the signature is a bridge, a circuit,

## The Drama of the Hopi Ogres

a visible mark left by invisible process—or processes which by their very nature are occluded from men (1968:6).

The Doctrine of Signatures is a single specific text derived from the initial discourse. . . . By this doctrine, we learn that the inner imperceptible qualitites (and essential uses) of objects are revealed in their outer forms. Objects with the same signature are assumed to have the same or related origins. . . . a *like* cures *like* . . . a more formal compendium of these cures is found in the body of homeopathic medicine (1968:8).

There are several traditions, some now disregarded.

There is, however, another tradition in which the Doctrine of Signatures is maintained on its own merits. . . . The simplest of these systems is a form of medical metonymy and metaphor found in Medieval herbals. For instance, we know that the walnut is a cure for cerebral diseases because it is the perfect signature of the brain.

We learn . . . Hopi men run certain races so that the speed of the running men will promote rapid growth of the planted seed. By the opposite signature a boy is told to dawdle home, picking flowers on his way, to prolong the summer and the growing season (1968:9).

10. The present discussion reexamines the concept of the Doctrine of Signatures and suggests new theoretical significance. It is not just a rehash of Frazer (1964).

11. Goldfrank (1978:49, 169–76) discusses a similar ogre family that appears at Zuni. She calls them "bogeys," describes them as being "punitive," and refutes Benedict's view that they are exorcistic.

12. This discussion presents an approach to Hopi child-rearing that differs from Dennis (1965) who takes an operational rather than a philosophical approach.

13. Goldfrank (1978:169) notes that to the Zuni priesthoods "the children are still 'unfinished' "; she does not connect growth rituals for children at initiation to similar functions for "bogey" rituals.

14. Dennis (1965) discusses Hopi child-rearing in terms of rewards and punishment and seems not to question whether his concept of punishment is appropriate in the Hopi context. Further, he does not discuss health, illness, or healing. Clearly his analysis is not parallel to the one presented in this chapter.

15. At First Mesa "Their Father" chews medicine, described as "a kind of plant that is hard to get because it grows only in the mountains. It is a root that tastes something like celery, and it is an all-purpose medicine." When a child is made sick with fright by the visitation of the ogres, the presiding woman of the household tells this to the Father Ogre, who rushes into the house, quickly puts the child down on a flat surface such as a bed or table, and removes the clothing from the child's stomach. He then rubs the child's stomach with this medicine, replaces the child's clothing, and rushes out the entrance of the house. From that time on, the child can digest the experience without becoming ill. I can find no reference in the literature to this. Perhaps it is limited to First Mesa. I personally know of two times that the medicine was administered: in 1966 for my daughter, and again in 1978, for a Hopi-Tewa child. I am told that the Ogre Father always has the medicine in his mouth during the personation in case it might be needed.

16. "Smoking" a child by holding a child forcibly under a blanket with a burning green cedar smudge is also used by the Zunis, Mescalero Apaches, and Havasupais according to other authors in this volume (personal communications: Tedlock, Farrer, and Hinton). For a description of "smoking" see Dennis (1965:46).

# 4
# Dance as Experience: the Deer Dance of Picuris Pueblo

DONALD N. BROWN
*Department of Sociology*
*Oklahoma State University*

## INTRODUCTION

The pueblos of Taos and Picuris are located on the western slopes of the Sangre de Cristo Mountains in Taos County, New Mexico. By trail Taos Pueblo is about twenty miles north of Picuris Pueblo; however, by highway the distance is over thirty miles. These two communities are the northernmost Rio Grande pueblos and together they form the Northern Tiwa branch of the Tanoan language family. The Tiwa dialects spoken in these two communities are mutually intelligible.

The mountainous environment of northern New Mexico and the access to the high plains influenced the cultural adaptations of both communities. Hunting the deer of the mountains and the buffalo of the plains was an important economic activity. The possibility of crop loss due to the short growing season at this elevation reduced the importance of agriculture. Contact with Plains tribes, especially the Kiowa and Comanche, while hunting the buffalo on the plains, or at the pueblo when the Plains tribes visited for trading or raiding, broadened the Taos and Picuris cultural inventories. Apache bands also visited these pueblos and frequently camped in the nearby mountains. The distance from European settlements limited the impact of Spanish-Catholic political domination. Compared with the other Rio Grande pueblos, this mountainous "frontier" location resulted in greater emphasis on hunting, more recognizable Plains traits, and reduced Spanish-Catholic influence.

In spite of these similarities of traditional culture, the pueblos of Taos and Picuris differ significantly today. The resident population of Taos Pueblo is now more than ten times that of Picuris. In 1970 the population of Taos Pueblo was 1,030 (U.S. Bureau of the Census 1973:11) and that of Picuris Pueblo was less than 100 (Brown 1973:270). The area surrounding Taos Pueblo has become a center of tourism with a sizable Anglo-American as well as Spanish-American population. Picuris Pueblo remains isolated from most outside traffic, although the children now attend the public schools in the neighboring Spanish-American community of Peñasco. For the anthropological fieldworker, research at Taos Pueblo remains a hazardous task, while the residents of Picuris Pueblo have worked closely since the mid 1950s with both archaeologists and ethnographers. The traditional ceremonial activities continue at Taos Pueblo, while only a dim reflection of these is found at Picuris Pueblo. It should be mentioned, however, that since about 1970 a renewed interest in traditional Picuris activities has been generated and has resulted in the revitalization of the Clown Society.

The published material on Taos dance reflects both the interest of tourists in Taos Pueblo and the negative attitude toward anthropological research. Several popular books on the Southwest describe dances at Taos Pueblo. The Eickemeyers (1895) mention a Taos Animal Dance. Fergusson (1931) provides an interesting description of the Deer Dance, while Grant (1934) mentions the Sundown Dance, Matachina Dance, and Buffalo Dance. The best popular descriptions are those by Waters (1950) of the Deer Dance, night dancing on January 6, Corn Dance, Turtle Dance, and Buffalo Dance.

In addition to these books, a number of articles have been written about Taos dance. Among them are those by LeRoy (1903), Bailey (1924), Vorse (1930), H. Jones (1931), Estergreen (1950), and Sloane (1962).

The only historical reference to Tiwa dance is found in the 1776 report of Domínguez (Adams and Chavez 1956). He describes a Scalp Dance, but it is ambiguous whether the dance is at Taos or Picuris Pueblo.

## Dance as Experience

Anthropological descriptions of Taos dance are rare. Several brief listings of dances have been published. In 1878 Morgan collected a list of 19 dances with both Taos and English names (White 1942). E. S. Curtis (1926) mentions four dances. Herzog (1936) includes a list of 16 dances and transcriptions of six songs. These are the only available transcriptions of Taos ritual dance music. Two articles of special interest are by Spinden (1915), which briefly describes an "introduced women's dance," and by M. K. Opler (1939), which discusses the transmission of the Southern Ute Dog Dance to Taos.

The most comprehensive ethnographic description of Taos Pueblo (Parsons 1936b) contains the following statement: "I am less certain of the accuracy of the following data than of any information I have recorded about the Pueblos during the past twenty years" (1936b:6). Accounts of dances by Taos informants are included as well as descriptions of specific performances of Taos dances (Children's Dance, 1932; Saint's Day Dance and Deer Dance, 1931; Turtle Dance, 1932; Buffalo Dance and night dancing, 1926). Slightly edited versions of these descriptions of the Deer Dance, Buffalo Dance, and Turtle Dance are included in Parsons' study of *Pueblo Indian Religion* (1939b).

My own research on Taos dance began in 1958 and has resulted in three publications (Brown 1960, 1961, 1976). As an anthropologist, my interest is less in dance movement than in the relationship between dance and other aspects of Taos culture. The greatest strength of this original research is probably the classification of Taos dances based on several behavioral criteria.

Although the available material on Taos dance is sparse, material on Picuris dance is even more rare. Ladd (1891) mentions a Picuris Elk Dance performed in Santa Fe in the 1880s and what appears to be a photograph of this performance was taken by Barthelmess (Frink and Barthelmess 1965). An article by Pancoast (1918) entitled "Last Dance of the Picuris" concerns the Race Dance on San Lorenzo Day, the feast day of the patron saint of Picuris Pueblo. In spite of this title, the Race Dance continues to be performed annually on San Lorenzo Day. Parsons' (1939a) brief notes on Picuris Pueblo include mention of the Matachina, Eagle Dance, Deer Dance, Buffalo Dance, Elk Dance, Shield Dance, Basket Dance, War Dance, and *Halowa* (Dog Dance). My own research at Picuris Pueblo has focused on the structural change within the Picuris cultural system rather than on dance (Brown 1973). However, the study does include a number of statements about dance and descriptions of Picuris dances by elderly Picuris residents.

With the exception of the work by Parsons, Herzog, and Brown, all of the publications on northern Tiwa dance are based on descriptions by outside, non-Tiwa, observers. Such descriptions, while interesting and useful for comparative purposes, reveal little about Tiwa perspectives toward dance, especially dance in a ritual context. A remark attributed to a resident of Taos Pueblo reveals the importance of ritual dance:

> "If the Indians of this place, Taos, give up and break the rules of their religion, according to their traditions, they (especially the old people) fear the end of the world will come." And he concludes with the touching appeal—"Now I hope you will have a better idea about why the Indians insist to dance those dances" (Bailey 1924:95).

Parsons (1936b:113) includes a similar thought in her ethnography of Taos Pueblo: "The last day will come as a result of neglecting the ceremonies, i.e., of irreligion."

The view of dance from the participant's perspective provides a dimension of understanding not otherwise available to the outside observer. It includes both culturally defined symbols and personal feelings, aspects which can be found only through participation in the specific cultural system and revealed only by statements and actions of such participants. I recently asked a Taos Pueblo dancer the question, "What is a good dancer?" I expected a reply concerning skill in dance movement and ability to keep time with the song. However, the reply was, "A good dancer is one who has a good heart, who understands what the dance is all about."

In my earlier work on Taos dance I used such categories as form, meaning, and function to analyze the dance (Brown 1976). Only in the discussion on meaning and the related classification of Taos dances did I attempt to say anything about the participant's perspective. In this chapter I would like to suggest an additional approach to the study of dance, an approach which can give further insights into the participant's perspective. This approach is based on descriptions of dance performances provided by individuals who are well experienced in the particular cultural system. Rather than viewing dance as a cultural product, or as an artistic process, dance is

*Dance as Experience*

viewed as a cultural experience. Basically, this adds a fourth dimension to the three used in my earlier study of Taos dance, the dimension of "understanding."[1]

## DANCE AS EXPERIENCE: THE PICURIS DEER DANCE

The Picuris Deer Dance generally is performed either on January 6 (Kings' Day) or August 10 (San Lorenzo Day, the feast day of the patron saint of Picuris Pueblo). It can, however, be performed on other dates as well.[2] In recent years the dance has been performed primarily on the summer date as part of the feast-day activities. These activities include mass in the church followed by a relay foot race in the morning, a dance in the early afternoon, and the pole climb by the clowns in the late afternoon. When the Deer Dance is presented as the afternoon dance, the performance begins and concludes with the Corn Dance. The specific focus of this analysis is limited to the Deer Dance.

Residents of Picuris Pueblo consider the Deer Dance to be one of the "special Picuris Indian dances."

> Them dances about Deer Dance, and Basket Dance, and Buffalo Dance, them are really special Picuris Indian dances. And Corn Dance. Anytime we dance Deer Dance, they have to dance because we are entitled to do those dances before we die. That's our dances that we never forget for the Picuris. They're like Basket, Deer Dance, Buffalo Dance, Elk Dance. All them Animal Dances are real special for the Picuris Indians. Corn Dance, we got one, too. But them other dances, like Feather Dance, Belt Dance, and them other war dances where they wear feathers, them dances are not for the Picuris. Picuris got their own dances. Them others they brought from someplace else (Tape No. 64Me8.18).[3]

The only published description of the Picuris Deer Dance is found in Parsons' (1939a:217-18) brief notes on Picuris Pueblo.

> Danced on Kings' day, but not every year. The dancers, twenty-five to thirty, come in from the arroyo east of the graveyard, past corrals on the east side and into the plaza.
> The dancers wear a buckskin mantle drawn over the head with the antlers attached and downy turkey feathers at the

points. Each side of the head, spruce twigs to hide the face. Hopi dance kilt. Skunk tail heel bands. In each hand a spruce-trimmed stick to lean over on; the dancers bend down to simulate the posture of deer. The largest "deer" is in the lead and the others follow, single file, according to size. In the rear are two little boys called . . . little wildcat, who wear a wildcat skin drawn over the forehead, the boy bending over the stick in each hand. Face, forearms, and legs spotted white, black, and yellow. Moccasins. There are two "deer shepherds" . . . , with bow and arrows, and on the back a quiver.

Two women wearing their black manta dress stand to one side of the dancers. . . .

Long ago the clowns, the Black Eyes, used to come out. There are no clowns today (1925).

### THE STRUCTURE OF THE PICURIS DEER DANCE

The Deer Dance is composed of a sequence of eight segments. Each segment consists of a distinct dance pattern (see fig. 4.1). The titles for these segments were provided by Ramos Durán and Pat Martínez, both lifelong residents of Picuris Pueblo. The brief descriptions of each segment are based on comments by these two men.[4]

1. "Deer Ladies dancing." The two Deer Ladies, facing east, side-step back and forth in front of the singers, shaking rattles in time with the drum.

2. "Going after the deer." The Deer Ladies leave the singers and, dancing with a side-step, move to the northeast corner of the dance area where they meet the entering deer dancers (see fig. 4.2).

3. "Bringing in the deer." As soon as they meet the deer dancers, the Deer Ladies return to the center of the dance area followed by the two lines of deer dancers.

4. "Going around in a circle." Upon reaching the center of the dance area, the Deer Ladies lead the deer dancers in a circular crossing pattern, the north line moving in a counterclockwise direction and the south line moving in a clockwise direction so that the deer dancers cross through the opposite line of dancers twice, and then return to two parallel lines.

5. "Crossing the deer." The Deer Lady on the north side rattles toward the south line of deer dancers. The lead dancer on the south line then moves to the lead position of the north line. When the south line dancer has reached the halfway point between the two lines, the Deer Lady on the south side rattles

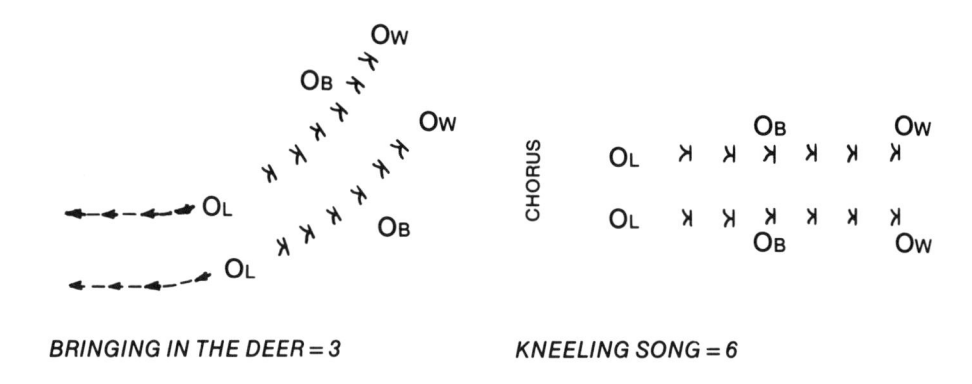

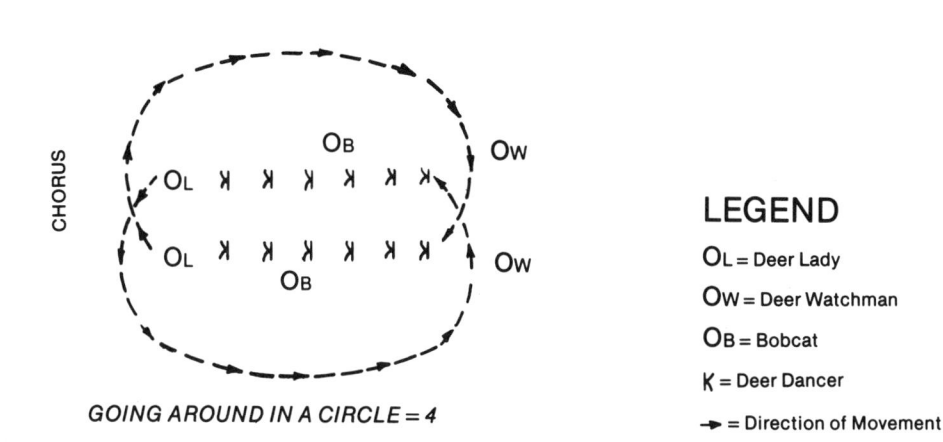

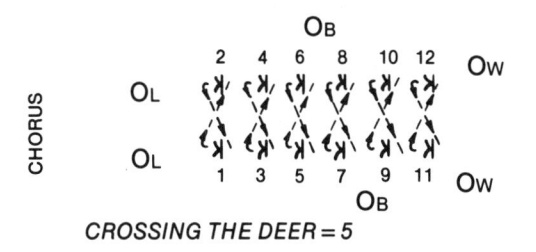

FIGURE 4.1. Picuris Deer Dance patterns

toward the north line of deer dancers and the lead dancer moves into the lead position of the south line, crossing behind the dancer from the south side. In sequence, each of the remaining deer dancers moves to the opposite line in response to the rattling of the Deer Ladies. When the two lines of deer dancers are reversed, the deer dancers continue to dance in place.

6. "Kneeling Song." The deer dancers, facing the singers, kneel on the right knee and move their heads back and forth in time with the drum while the Deer Ladies side-step back and forth in front of the two lines (see fig. 4.3).

7. "Deer stand up and dance lively, turning around." The Deer Ladies continue to side-step back and forth in front of the lines of the deer dancers as the dancers dance in place, occasionally "turning around" in unison (see fig. 4.4).

8. "Deer leave and go back to the mountains." The two lines of the deer dancers cross through one another again, the north line moving in a counterclockwise direction and the south line in a clockwise direction, which reverses the two lines. The deer dancers then exit from the dance area by way of the northeast corner, leaving the Deer Ladies in the dance area.

The Picuris name for the Deer Dance is *pę·pulene*, 'deer dance'. The Deer Ladies are referred to as *pę·tiwene*, 'female of the deer' or *pę·pultiwene*, 'deer dance woman'. The deer dancers are called *pę·siulene*, 'male deer', and the Deer Watchmen are called *pę·helene*, 'deer herder' or 'deer watchman'.

### DESCRIPTIONS OF THE PICURIS DEER DANCE

The following two descriptions of the Deer Dance were tape-recorded at Picuris Pueblo. The first description has been edited in order to provide better continuity. The second description is presented without editing and includes the questions asked during the discussion.[5]

### *Picuris Deer Dance, Pat Martínez (Tape No. 64M8.24)*[6]

We have a special day for the Deer Dance, like after New Year. After the first part of the year we would always put up a Deer Dance. But sometimes they used to have it in the summertime. That is when we have our special day on August 10th. But in the summertime they didn't use the pelts, just in the wintertime they used them. The other way, in the summer,

FIGURE 4.2. Picuris Deer Dancers entering dance area, August 10, 1965. Photograph by the author.

FIGURE 4.3. "Kneeling Song," Picuris Deer Dance, August 10, 1965. Photograph by the author.

FIGURE 4.4. "Deer stand up and dance lively, turning around," Picuris Deer Dance, August 10, 1965. Photograph by the author.

we dance like the way the deer are wandering around in the summertime with light color. Most of the deer are a light color, light red or something like that. So we didn't use a pelt, but we wear the horns.

We got two ladies in that dance. The ladies wear black, sometimes white, but I think they usually use the black mantas. They wear boots, too. They've got feathers, eagle feathers, on their heads and they carry one rattle. And they have evergreen branches in the other hand.

And we have deer, maybe eight on each side or maybe more. It all depends on how many showed up. They wear a kilt around their waist and beads. Their faces are all covered up with evergreen branches. They are tied to the horns [see fig. 4.5]. And then the deer, each dancer has a piece of meat tied around the waist. That shows that the deer always come with meat for the people. If you ever kill a deer that's what you go

FIGURE 4.5. Picuris Deer Dance in upper plaza area by the kiva, ca. 1930. Photographer unknown.

for, for meat. That's why they got that meat tied around their waist so the people will get that meat in order for them to think that the deer still bring a lot of meat to the people there that need it. That's why they got that meat. They wear moccasins and bells and carry two sticks, one in each hand.

We might have one or two bobcats. Sometimes we have a bear, too, with the bobcats. They wear the whole skin.

There are Deer Herders. They come with the deer. They got two of them, one for each side of the rows of dancers.

It takes about four or five singers at least for the ceremonial.

The deer dress out away from the village, way up in the hills. They come in by the old ruins and behind the church. And they pass into the middle of the pueblo. They just come right in on the west side of the church. They come in with more action. When they first start coming in, why they look like they really are wild deers running around all over. As they kind of get up by the church they start dancing. And the Ladies have to go there and meet the deer and bring them in. The Deer Ladies meet them there when the deer are dancing like that with the drums.

Sometimes the bobcats or bear run up and hit the deer, and then the deer falls down. Then the Deer Ladies come over and pat the deer on the shoulder, on the pelt. And then the deer gets up and he can dance again. That means that the deer has been killed by the bobcat or bear, something like that, but as the dancers go on with the Deer Dance they get up and dance again.

When they finish they go back the same way they came in. They dance twice. Later they move their dance up to the kiva. They move up there. They have to dance by the kiva. And then after the dance is over, the deer go back to where they started from. Then the Ladies go back into the kiva and the singers. After they go in the deer dancers come back and go in the kiva where they have special doings.

### Picuris Deer Dance, Ramos Durán (Tape No. 65D8.5)[7]

Now we are going to tell a little what they used to do long time ago. Well, they used to wear a deer pelt with the ears. Of course, that time everybody was agreeable in dancing and enjoyment. They used not to hesitate or have to be bossed around. They used to just volunteer for dancing. They used to dress up nice. And in dancing, keep the time.

There's two ladies dancing. There are two of them. Those are the Deer Ladies, we call them. And they have rattle in their hand in order to cross the deer.

And the Deer Herder which is now kept up until today. They carry their bow and arrow, quiver.

We go dressing way up there in the hills, instead of the kiva, because the deer come from the mountain.

So before we come to dance, first there was the Corn Dance. Those that didn't take part in the Deer Dance used to go down into the kiva, the ladies, the War Captain, all dressing in Indian costume. And soon they come up from the kiva. They start to dance the Corn Dance.

And when the deer heard the drum up there, the Deer Herder or any deer taking part in the Deer Dance, well, they used to hear the drum and they used to hurry up. Hurry themselves to come off in order to get there by the time the Corn Dance Songs are over.

When they are coming over here close, the deers, they don't

*Dance as Experience*

come in a line. They come scattering, acting just like deer, scratching against the wall with their horns on and the deer pelts. And they coming now the Corn Dance Song is all over.

So now the two Deer Ladies, they are with the Corn Dancers first dancing. And they got their feather, they got the looks that they were the Deer Ladies, what we call them. Well, those two now begin to dance. Both Ladies been crossing each other, dancing, dancing, keeping time. Now they go way out there where the deer are coming, to meet the deer, to call them in, call them by rattle, shaking the rattles. From there with the Deer Herders, they are dress in their costume, too, with chaps and beaded and feather in their head. Then they come dancing until they get over here to a dancing place where they usually dance out here in the yard.

So now they come dancing. They cross them, the north side, the others. And it goes way around until you get in a line. Now they begin. The Deer Ladies take their part in the cross dancing. And the deers dance in a line, keeping time all the time, listening to the song of the Deer Dance, the Deer Dance Songs, and finish. They cross the deer one by one until they get through crossing the deer. When crossing the deer, the line from the north side and the line from the south side. When they get through crossing, now they kneel down, moving their head, turning around until the song is now over of the Kneeling Dance, keeping time so. Then they start a song again. Then they begin to stand up. They use bells, too, you know. Long time ago they didn't use to use bells. They didn't have no bells. But now we use them jingling bells. But the dance I saw they didn't use bells yet. But lately they do.

[Question: Is there a special deer dancer who leads, or are all the deer just the same?] Just the same. Just the leaders are ones who know how to dance so others could follow.

[Question: Nowadays they just wear the horns?] Now they wear the horns with the palms [evergreen branches]. Of course, they used to wear the horns with palms. They didn't use pelts. And sticks, those sticks representing the front feet.

[Question: Is there a ceremony that goes on when they get dressed, before they come into the village?] No. They just go out there dressing, paint themselves. They use the white paint, those that want to be summer deer. They also paint red, whatever color they want, whether black, dark. Course the deers are different, winter deers and summer deers.

[Question: When they come into the village and dance do they go into the kiva at all?] When the dance is over they pretend they went away, ran away scared. But after the Corn Dancers and singers, and all the principal goes into the kiva, when everybody get down there, that's the time the deer come. Without dancing, just themselves to the kiva.

[Question: Do they come individually or as a group?] Just a group, the way they are. Then they take their horns out and put them away in the kiva. So the War Captain said they could take those palms out, take them to the river. Just the horns are left there, so they could take them up to the hills for future use.

[Question: Is there a special place in the hills where they are left?] They used to, but now they put them anyplace. Just so they up in a tree. But sometimes people takes them, so they put them in different places like that.

[Question: Are there special songs that are sung at the end in the kiva?] Yes, just Petting Songs.

[Question: Do the deer dance in the kiva?] No, they don't dance anymore. They just sit, you know, just sit. And the ceremony is over.

[Question: Do the boys go down to the river then and wash after it is over?] They used to, not now anymore. It's forgotten now. They used to after the dance, yes. Those that want goes, but those that don't want they don't.

[Question: Does anyone bring food to the kiva?] Afterward, the ladies bring food after they get through taking the horns outside, after they get through undressing. They didn't let us go with pants, just with chaps. Everybody had chaps. See, they was strict long time ago. I remember that. But now everybody go with pants. Can't help it as long as they obeying the War Captain.

[Question: Is there anyone in the village that owns that dance?] Nobody. Well, the War Captain calls a meeting in the kiva, and then he turn it over to everybody, to the public inside, from children to grownup, whichever dance they want to put up certain day, like August 10, see. They didn't use to have nothing long time ago, just the foot race, that was all (on August 10). Lately they put up dance because people used to stay.

An additional comment by an elderly Picuris resident during another discussion of the Deer Dance indicates that before the dance the dancers are lectured by the officers of the Pueblo. "We tell them to dance right, to dance good. That's what we tell them. We tell them to do like Picuris Indian long time ago. To dance good. That's what we tell them" (Tape No. 64Me7.13).

The purpose of the Deer Dance is stated by Pat Martínez to be the following:

According to the legend, the Deer Dance being danced so

*Dance as Experience*

that we'll have our deer, the game. There might be times that the deer won't be living close to our place anymore if we don't dance. So for that reason we use the dance to remind the game that we would like to have them around, for the use of the meat and all that (Tape No. 64M8.24).

Ramos Durán provided another perspective: "This dance is for Mother Nature that gave us the deers, for we don't just treat them any old way. We treat them nice in the dance so they could be plentiful for us, for our children to have plenty of meat" (Tape No. 64M8.24).

Another statement by Ramos Durán relates the Deer Dance to the deer hunting activities at Picuris Pueblo. This statement was in response to my question about the disposal of deer bones at two special trash areas west of the pueblo.

They have to be careful, not throw away. Because they were food, just like taking care of food. That was the ceremonial way. They used to drop cornmeal (on the killed deer) and pat them, just like patting. We want them not to run away from us, to be friendly. It's a nice ceremony, Animal Dance. They don't just go ahead and dance it. They keep it kind of holy like, superstitious like. But now the deers don't show up anymore. At that time the deer used to be around here. When they do that dance, they use the horns. The deer used to be around where the deer horns are. You advise them that they are to take care of the horns, to take care of everything of the Deer Dance. Not to abolish and not to forget it. It's a nice dance (Tape No. 65D8.18).

AN ANALYSIS OF "UNDERSTANDING"

The three dimensions of form, meaning, and function have been used in an analysis of Taos Dance (Brown 1976). As defined by Linton (1936:403), "form" refers to "something which can be established objectively and through direct observation," while "meaning" refers to "the associations which any society attaches" to the activity. He adds: "Such associations are subjective and frequently unconscious. They find expression in behavior and therefore cannot be established by purely objective methods" (1936:403–4). Function is defined as "the sum total of its contributions toward perpetuation of the social-cultural configuration" (1936:404). Each of these dimensions is determined through observation and analysis of behavior patterns by an outside observer.

A fourth dimension which can be added is understanding. This dimension is based on an analysis of the experience of a participant in the cultural system. While it may be closely related to the dimension of meaning, it approaches its subject matter with a different question. Rather than asking "What does it mean?" which requires an explanation and interpretation, the question here is, "What is your understanding of it?" The response is phrased in terms of symbols shared within the community and personal experiences of participants in the cultural system, rather than in terms of explanations and interpretations for the outside investigator. Understanding also includes the affective and qualitative aspects of an activity (Mills 1957). These aspects are culturally specific and are discovered through an analysis of both statements about participation in the activity and symbols associated with the activity.

This approach to the analysis of dance emphasizes dance as participation rather than as a means of communication. To dance is to participate in shared symbols and feelings, symbols and feelings shared not only by the other dancers, but also by the resident observers, for both are members of the cultural community. It is not an attempt to communicate ideas or emotions to outsiders. It is the "work" which the community was given to do when the world was established, the "work" which must be continued if the world is to be maintained (Brown 1976:216).

For ritual activities the analysis may be diagrammed as in figure 4.6.

### I.A. *General Symbols*

When dealing with a dance which is only a part of a larger ritual activity, some general symbols may be associated with the overall ritual activity while others are associated only with the dance. Also, the dance, itself, may be associated with either single or multiple symbols.

The Taos Buffalo Dance provides an example of multiple general symbols. On January 6, 1978, the Buffalo Dance was performed at Taos Pueblo. In discussions with residents of the pueblo, three general symbols were recognized. A male ceremonial leader stated: "The men from here used to hunt buffalo down around Oklahoma in the old days. They would bring back the hides and dry meat,

```
                    UNDERSTANDING
                   /            \
                  /              \
          I.  SYMBOLS          II.  FEELINGS
```

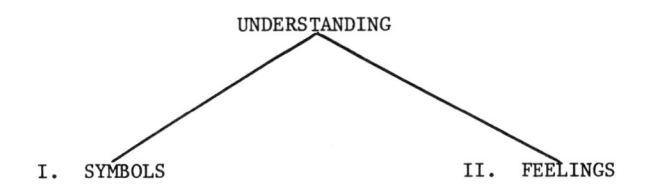

A. <u>General</u>: Symbols associated with the overall ritual activity.

B. <u>Specific</u>: Symbols associated with details of the ritual activity.

A. <u>Interests</u>: Feelings expressed as special attention to specific details.

B. <u>Sentiments</u>: Feelings due to specific thoughts about the activity.

C. <u>Disposition</u>: The attitude toward the ritual activity.

FIGURE 4.6. Analysis of understanding.

jerky, no fresh meat. When they would get near the village, they would stop and dress up in the hides and sing the Buffalo Dance Songs as they came into the village." From this perspective, the Buffalo Dance is a reenactment of a historical event. A married woman who frequently participates in the Taos ritual dances recognized a second general symbol: "We do the Buffalo Dance to honor the buffalo, to thank them for bringing their meat to us, to show them we take only what we need." This second perspective views the dance, and the ritual which accompanies it, as a recognition of the importance of the buffalo in traditional Taos life. The third perspective was expressed during a discussion of the Matachina Dance which is also performed frequently during the winter dancing season. Another Taos woman criticized the Matachina Dance because "it doesn't bring the snow as much" as the Animal Dances performed during the New Year season (Brown 1976:218). The third perspective views the dance and ritual as symbolizing a traditional winter activity which influences the weather for the benefit of the pueblo. Parsons (1936b:94) also noted this relationship between the winter Animal Dances and the weather.

In the statements about the Picuris Deer Dance two general sym-

87

bols can be identified. Ramos Durán stated, "this dance is for Mother Nature." This is similar to the second perspective mentioned above concerning the Taos Buffalo Dance. The Deer Dance honors the creative force which provides the deer. It could also be considered as honoring the deer which provide meat for the pueblo.

The second general symbol, recognized by both Ramos Durán and Pat Martínez, relates to the availability and fertility of the deer in the area of the pueblo. As stated by Ramos Durán, "so they could be plentiful for us, for our children to have plenty of meat." Pat Martínez adds, "We use the dance to remind the game that we would like to have them around, for the use of the meat and all that."

### I.B. Specific Symbols

A number of specific symbols can also be identified in the statements about the Deer Dance. Examples of these include the following:

1. The animal dancers represent the deer as they would appear at the season of the dance performance, i.e., summer deer or winter deer.
2. The animal dancers dress in the hills and return to the hills after the dance because the deer live in the hills.
3. The movements of the deer entering the dance area represent the movements of "wild deer."
4. The meat tied at the waist of the deer dancers represents the food obtained from the deer.
5. The actions of the bobcats and bear in striking down the deer represent the cycle of life, death, and rebirth in the natural setting.
6. The horns used in the Deer Dance are kept in the mountains as a sign of respect for the deer and as recognition of the importance of the deer to the residents of the pueblo.

### II.A. Interests

Four interests can be identified from the statements:

1. The importance of costume is indicated by the attention paid to details of costumes for each of the dance roles. The seasonal variations in the costume of the deer, attention to paraphernalia carried

*Dance as Experience*

such as the rattles, bow and arrow, and sticks, and descriptions of body paint also suggest this interest.

2. The specification of the various dance roles—deer dancers, Deer Ladies, Deer Watchmen, bobcats, bears—suggest a second major interest. Each of these roles is identified and care is taken to indicate what each of these roles is to do in the dance.

3. A third interest which appears in the description by Ramos Durán is the importance of the dance patterns. He is very specific about these patterns and the sequence of patterns.

4. The consistent reference to the north-south orientation of the dancers suggests a fourth interest, one reflecting the dual organization structure found in the traditional ceremonial organization of Picuris Pueblo. All individuals who lived in the pueblo were members of either the North-side group or the South-side group. These directional terms did not signify a geographical pattern of residence for these members, but rather indicated on which side the members were placed in ceremonial activities. The north line of deer dancers was drawn traditionally from the North-side group, and the south line of dancers, from the South-side group. This orientation was also of special importance for the annual foot race run on August 10.

### II.B. Sentiments

A series of specific sentiments can be identified in these descriptions of the Deer Dance:

1. Participation in the dance is a means of identification with Picuris Pueblo. It is one of the "special Picuris Indian dances" which are to be performed only at Picuris Pueblo.

2. The dance provides a sense of continuity with the past, or traditional, Picuris culture. The dancers are lectured "to do like Picuris Indian long time ago."

3. The dance is an activity involving the entire community. Individuals who do not participate in the Deer Dance can participate in the Corn Dance. If they do not dance in one of these dances, they can provide food for the dancers in the kiva after the dance. It requires the efforts of the entire community for the dance to be successful.

4. Finally, there is a recognition of change, change within the

dance and in attitude toward the dance. The addition of bells to the deer dancers is pointed out as a change. "Long time ago they didn't use to use bells." A change in attitude toward participation in the Deer Dance is also stated. "They used not to hesitate or have to be bossed around."

### II.C. Dispositions

As noted above, there appears to be a change in attitude toward the Deer Dance by some members of the community. There is a hesitancy on the part of some residents to participate in the dance. Traditionally, however, three attitudes can be identified from the dance descriptions:

1. The dance is important. It helps to maintain life within the pueblo through insuring availability of deer for food.
2. Participation in the Deer Dance is enjoyable; "everybody was agreeable in dancing and enjoyment."
3. The Deer Dance is entertaining for the dancers, for the other residents of the pueblo, and for the visitors to the pueblo. "It's a nice dance."

## CONCLUSION: SOME OBSERVATIONS FROM THE OUTSIDE

This chapter presents what I believe to be a useful approach to the analysis of cultural behavior. Its focus is on the experiences of participants in the cultural system rather than on abstractions and generalizations drawn by an outside observer. Although the categories chosen for the analysis may change as other interests develop or as new questions are asked of the data, the approach remains useful. Including the verbatim statements by Ramos Durán and Pat Martínez adds a further useful dimension to this approach. Researchers interested in other topics can refer to the baseline data as a source of basic information.

This analysis of a specific ritual dance illustrates the continuing dual processes of continuity and change in which both tradition and innovation are recognized by the participants in the cultural system. The Deer Dance continues to be an essential ritual for the purpose

## Dance as Experience

of maintaining a valued resource, the deer, even though the resource is less significant in the economy of today than in the past. Only the traditional songs are used, and the traditional roles in the dance continue to be filled. Yet the dance is now performed on August 10 to accommodate visitors to the pueblo for the feast day activities. On one occasion (August 10, 1969) the dance performance was shortened to only a single sequence of songs because the primary singer had been seriously ill and pueblo officers feared that repeating the songs would be too tiring for him.

From this outside perspective, the Picuris cultural system is seen not as a static fossil form inherited from the past, but as a dynamic force which has allowed the residents of the pueblo to adapt and survive in a continually changing social and natural environment. Ritual dance remains a vital activity; drawn from tradition, it makes life possible today.

### NOTES

1. This approach is closely related to the phenomenological approach. As stated by Bidney (1973:136):

> The Concept of the Life-World, introduced by Husserl, links together the natural and historical sciences by providing a universal object for all subjects. The life-world is the world as given in experience prior to critical reflection, the world as experienced by man in society and in a given ecological environment, and it includes his experience of the world of nature as well as the world of his culture. The cultural anthropologist or ethnologist studies and records the cultural life-worlds of human society and in the name of "ethnoscience" attempts to reconstruct the cognitive maps of their symbolic modes of experience, such as their art, rituals, and systems of belief and logic. A phenomenological approach to the study of human culture is at the same time an existential approach, since the anthropologist records the lived experiences of given subjects at a given moment of their history. The task of the anthropologist is not merely to give an objective account and to record the traits and artifacts abstracted from a given culture, as one writes a catalogue of merchandise, but to describe and interpret the intentional meaning and the intersubjective symbolic meanings of the behavior and the interactions of the members of a given society.

In a study of *The Phenomenology of Dance*, Sheets (1966:4-5) vividly describes the phenomenological approach to dance research.

In anthropology, Sapir's (1949:576) comments also suggest the usefulness of such an approach:

> It is only through an analysis of variation that the reality and meaning of a norm can be established at all, and it is only through a minute and sympathetic study of individual behavior in the state in which normal human beings

find themselves, namely in a state of society, that it will ultimately be possible to say things about society itself and culture that are more than fairly consistent abstractions.

2. The Picuris Deer Dance was most recently performed on Sunday, April 2, 1978.

3. This two-part classification is similar to that at Taos Pueblo which classifies dances in terms of "Ours" and "Not Ours" (Brown 1961).

4. The Picuris Deer Dance Songs were sung by Ramos Durán and Pat Martínez and tape-recorded in Mr. Martínez's home at Picuris Pueblo. The tape recording was then played back and each segment of the dance was identified and discussed by the two singers. Sketches of the dance patterns were also made in order to follow the discussion.

5. No attempt has been made to alter the transcriptions of the tape-recorded sessions into "correct" English. The descriptions are presented as transcribed directly from the recorded tapes.

6. Mr. Pat Martínez was born in 1914. He has served as governor of Picuris Pueblo a number of times. He is well known throughout the Rio Grande Pueblo area as a dancer and singer.

7. Mr. Ramos Durán was born in 1896 and died in 1975. He was a respected elder in Picuris Pueblo and widely known as an outstanding musician.

# 5
# Motion Pictures of Tewa Ritual Dances

## GERTRUDE PROKOSCH KURATH
Ann Arbor, Michigan

*PRELUDE*

Motion pictures provide a haven midway in the journey of the ritual dances of New Mexican Tewa to the printed page, from live motion to hieroglyphics.

Photography cannot completely capture the aura of the ceremonies, but it can show visual aspects. Even stills can show the color, costumes, setting, postures, and the rapt expressions. Movies can show kinetic formations, steps, rhythms, and slow or fast episodes. Potentially, still and motion photography can aid dance research in the same way as tapes aid musicology. If reality is still far from the ideal, that is due to costs, cumbersome mechanisms, and requirements of special skills. The visual record can be so valuable as to merit photography when possible, especially if the dances are complex achievements by trained groups.

Various scholars agree:

> Film has often been suggested as an alternative to notation. Film, however, presents many difficulties which often make notation the only feasible means of recording a dance. . . . Film would be valuable in use as stimulus materials, or in large-scale analyses of movement styles (Royce 1974:73–74).

A musician says:

The value of sound-track film for the study of ethnic dance can scarcely be overstated. Even the most highly trained and experienced field worker cannot possibly observe and write down all the details of a dance, during or after a performance. Recorded film, synchronized with sound, enables the scholar repeatedly to play back dance sequences for detailed and isolated observation of every facet of body motion. Good color film enhances the spectacle of native costumes and environment. The sound track enables him to observe the relationship between music and dance (Miller 1970:315).

An anthropologist says:

Many of the skills dependent upon neuro-muscular coordination, including those of gesture as it affects communication, are better studied from cinema records than from observation (Sorenson 1967:450).

Few investigators concerned with this problem now seriously dispute the theoretical value of motion pictures and still photographs in the documentation and study of the visual data of passing events such as these. However, the vast potential of film has not been fully realized, partly because of (1) the distortion of film research efforts by dependence on methods and facilities of the entertainment motion picture industry; (2) the lack of adequate financial support for the preparation, storage, and use of research films; and (3) the lack of a generally accepted method for the production of research films (1967:443).

## PURPOSES

The diversity of methods is in part due to the various functions of dance research photography. An eminent dancer-photographer (Snyder 1965) discusses three categories: (1) documents of dances for their historical value; (2) a record for analyses and reconstruction; and (3) ciné-dance, an art form. The two factual categories include many purposes, such as documentation, education, formal analyses, ethnological interpretations, therapy, and the elicitation of background information from native viewers.

Kenneth Foster recorded the entire Navajo Night Chant to preserve this great ritual drama. Nadia Chilkovsky and her associates created films of ethnic dances for teaching in secondary schools.

## Motion Pictures of Tewa Ritual Dance

Joann Kealiinohomoku filmed Hopi dances and a festival at Gallup as an enrichment of her analyses.

A film can serve more than one purpose, for the photographer or another viewer. Rosalie Jones's motion picture of the Blackfeet Sun Dance provided material for a Master's thesis (R. M. Jones 1968) and for an original composition, which was also filmed. Joann Kealiinohomoku (1976:179) examined many films of diverse origins for her analyses of African and jazz dance. Irmgard Bartenieff (1974) studied films, from travelogues to research records, for a cross-cultural comparison of movement styles and effort expenditures.

My Tewa films were intended for dance analysis, but they have also entertained many viewers, from children to scholars.

### PERSONAL PROCEDURE

After the requisite preparations to mitigate my ignorance, the production of the Tewa films involved four steps: the acquisition of equipment, the activity of photography, the inspection of the films, and deductions.

#### EQUIPMENT

I used a 16 mm silent Bolex movie camera with Kodachrome II film; for stills, I used a Leica and a Pony Kodak. Hugh Miller, with whom I collaborated after 1963, had 8 mm sound equipment.

> The equipment used for this project was a Fairchild Cinephonic 8 mm camera which has a synchronized sound track, together with a three-lens turret head comprising 13 mm (standard), 36 mm (telephoto), and 8.5 mm (wide-angle) lenses. (This model was discontinued around 1964.) Accessories included a view finder, exposure meter, microphone and stand, double earpiece headset (for monitoring sound), 85B filter for outdoor filming, and a tripod. The projector has a separate speaker and a microphone for overlay recording, used occasionally for spoken commentary. The film used was Kodachrome II with prestriped double fifty inch spools, ASA 12 artificial light, and ASA 10 natural light. The camera runs at twenty-four frames per second, 2¾ minutes per side, and 5½ minutes per spool.
>
> The advantage of such a camera is, of course, its portability. It can be operated by one person, although an assistant would be advantageous. There are, however, numerous disadvantages.

A two-and-three-fourths-minute run is not long, and rethreading the film between shooting sequences is time consuming, even with practice (Miller 1970:315–16).

PHOTOGRAPHY

Efforts at filming Algonquian Powwows in 1954–56 showed the error of the fragmentary technique in travelogues. I lengthened exposures within the possibility of rewinds. I adhered to a consistent focus, within the possibilities of group movements. So, by 1957, I worried chiefly about mechanical settings and shifting light in a catch-as-catch-can situation.

My first attempts at Santa Clara must have amused the residents. I toted tripod and camera from plaza to plaza and struggled with the leveling of the three ornery legs. Surprisingly, the Game Animal Dance on March 3, 1957, turned out fairly well, perhaps because of consistent overcast, as did the Buffalo Dance on Easter Sunday, when a dust storm blacked the sky and tore at the trees and the dancers' costumes.

However, all this flurry interfered with my enjoyment of the spectacle and with my memorization of the patterns. Thereafter I decided on several practical measures, for example, to omit the tripod and to film motion during the later repeats of a dance, after relaxed viewing and after shooting some stills. In the pueblos there are usually many repeats during a day. At Puyé Cliffs each dance had one appearance, with four repeats, at the cardinal directions. I sought a steady, inconspicuous location. Hugh Miller tried for coherence by shooting a phrase with each rewind. He used this device in several movies during my absence. At the Puyé Cliffs public performances we found a suitable location on one of the towers east of the plaza, with support for our cameras and a slight elevation above the great plaza.

At Puyé Cliffs the admission fee included permission to photograph these sacred dances. Some "eager beavers" crawled among the dancers for close-ups. On one occasion a team of men placed a stepladder in the center of the plaza, and used it as a perch for bird's-eye-view shots. The dancers ignored them with magnificent dignity. Perhaps by now the Tewa have regulations for the behavior of spectators, and may have suggested telephoto lenses for close-ups.

# Motion Pictures of Tewa Ritual Dance

ANALYSIS

For the notation of the plaza dances, the value of film projection varied according to the complexity. For the earth-pounding male line dances, films were an eloquent reminder rather than a necessity. For dances of medium complexity, like the Corn Dances (Xoxeye) with opposing male and female lines, they were a great help, a confirmation of memory. For newly created, complex dances like the Game Animal Dances, they were indispensable.

Many viewings produced the choreography of the Santa Clara Game Animal Dance (Kurath and Garcia 1970:Figs. 108,109,110). The order of inspection was something like the following:
1. General effect of countermovement between two main groups, of buffalo and antlered animals.
2. Straight-lined spatial progression of buffalo and buffalo maidens.
3. Circlings and meanderings of deer.
4. Body movements of buffalo—pawing, pivoting.
5. Loping of deer, tripping of mountain sheep, runs of antelope.
6. Combination with music from a separately recorded tape, including recognition of metric shifts, t'a.
7. Total pattern of countermovements.
8. Temporal structure.

Needless to say, the coordination of dance and music posed no problems during the study of Hugh Miller's sound films. It was even possible to choreograph dances he photographed in my absence, since the style was familiar.

All too few films by others were available. "Southwest Indian Dances," a film by Portia Mansfield, though silent, provided the stimulus for the choreography of an unusual Eagle Dance, the Tesuque performance by four men.

These sources combined produced classifications of ground plans, Corn Dance (1970:Fig. 79) and Buffalo Dance (1970:Figs. 99, 100).

DEDUCTIONS

The study of the motion pictures confirmed my impressions about the integrity of the Tewa ritual dancers and singers. They adhere, even at Puyé Cliffs, to the standards of moderation and precision. As Garcia (Kurath and Garcia 1970:35) says, "In general, the individual should be part of the group and conform to the style, not try to stand out."

A comparison with my Powwow films revealed the contrast of the dignified Tewa style with the competitive frenzy of the male "Pan-Indian" war dancers. The Tewa do not admire these "Kiowa" dances.

The personal observations and motion pictures reveal meaningful interactions of dance groups, of dancers and singers, of performers and spectators, that is, the aspects that are usually perceivable in the plaza. These phenomena are dramatic and artistic. They do not tell the whole story of the ritual dramas. Like the visible parts of an iceberg, they conceal important parts of the ritual dramas—the kiva preludes and postludes (Garcia and Garcia 1970:38–43). It is not likely that these activities will ever be available for photography. They must remain hidden, dedicated to deities.

## PROSPECTS

Since the personal explorations, conditions have improved for motion picture photography of Tewa dances. A team with the requisite skills would benefit from the Tewa attitudes, from improved technology, and new repositories.

Permits are still available on many occasions. At the same time the dances have retained their meanings. They are more numerous than in 1957. The dance lines are longer and are attracting young performers. The Puyé Cliffs programs are flourishing and offer dances from several pueblos. Some Tewa artists are willing to work on explanatory films of steps, gestures, and symbols.

The mechanics of photography have become encouraging (Mannheim 1974). Cameras range from Mount Palomar's giant to instamatic dwarfs, with numerous sizes and qualities of film, even to the visualization of infrared energy rays (Gore and Blair 1978). For motion pictures, the professional and amateur technology serves fact and fantasy (Mertz 1974).

It would be possible to use 16 mm sound equipment in the plazas, but it would be conspicuous and costly. The field photographer should settle for compact equipment like Ektasound 8 mm with Super X film, equipment that eliminates the worry of settings and yields good results. Videotape is also practical—$38 an hour.

## Motion Pictures of Tewa Ritual Dance

Nevertheless, the process is not automatic. It requires ingenuity to achieve a reasonably complete, coherent, and clear record. Field photographers have tried several devices. Joann Kealiinohomoku and a partner ran their 8 mm cameras in alternation, to eliminate gaps. Independently, Don Brown and the Sweets found the bird's-eye-view from a rooftop excellent for formations, though this angle does not show body movement as well as a level position (See figs. 5.1, 5.2). The Sweets found time-lapse photography inexpensive and practical for certain purposes, though this technique cannot show continuous motion.

> Elevated time-lapse data collection involves one or more small movie cameras with single frame capability. These are secured in elevated positions, each focused on a main activity area. The cameras remain stationary throughout the event. Ideally these cameras should have an intervalometer so they can be set to automatically take one still frame every 10, 20, or 30 seconds. Cameras which do not have an intervalometer can be used manually with a long cable release and a watch with a second hand.
> This data collection method is inexpensive since shooting single frames can record changes throughout several days on one roll of film. It is relatively unobtrusive since the cameras are small and elevated out of the way of the action. If the camera has an intervalometer it can even be left unattended.
> Obviously, this method is not possible where photography is prohibited. Fortunately, at San Juan I was permitted to have one movie camera stationed at each of the four plaza areas. One frame was taken every thirty seconds throughout the two day event, resulting in a total of 3,300 photographs.
> The concept of public display and the method of elevated time-lapse data collection aided greatly in analyzing the San Juan fiesta. It provided a record of where the participants and observers were throughout the event. It made possible the construction of an aerial view of the village architecture in relation to the spatial arrangements of the people at any particular time during the fiesta (Sweet 1976:6-8).

Another favorable circumstance is the recent development of specialized repositories. There are numerous commercial distributors of dance films from all parts of the world, as well as private collections (Feld 1976:318,320,324). The listings include a few Amerindian items, nothing on the Tewa.

FIGURE 5.1. Santa Clara corn (harvest) dance, with men and women in opposing lines. Photographed from kiva roof by Donald Brown, 1958.

FIGURE 5.2. Santa Clara corn dance. Photographed on a level at Puyé Cliffs by Gertrude Kurath, 1961.

## Motion Pictures of Tewa Ritual Dance

Now the Tewa films may become accessible. E. Richard Sorenson directs the National Anthropological Film Center in Washington, D.C. Steve Feld is associated with the Anthropological Film Center in Santa Fe, where, in cooperation with Carroll and Joan Williams, he is locating and indexing audio-visuals in the state of New Mexico for the Southwest Foundation for Audio-visual Resources in Santa Fe. The staff members of the Center range from American Indians to eastern academicians. Fortunately, they have the support of a CETA Title VI Special Projects grant, and are able to advise field photographers on finances.

These repositories can guide researchers to films of the past and future, though they may not necessarily store copies of documents or have the facilities to convert field originals into educational reels. They can help dance researchers with diverse objectives and perhaps they can prevent retreading of old paths.

### POSTLUDE: TEWA DANCE FILMS[1]

1. Donald Brown, 16 mm silent, August 13, 1958, Santa Clara Feast Day Corn Dance.
2. Gertrude Kurath, 16 mm silent, deposited with the sponsoring Wenner-Gren Foundation, copy in Kurath collection.
    a) Santa Clara Sun Basket Dance (b/w), February 10, 1957.
    b) Santa Clara Game Animals, March 3, 1957.
    c) Santa Clara Buffalo, Easter, 1957.
    d) Puyé Cliffs, July 22–23, 1961
       Buffalo, Rainbow, Bow and Arrow, Buffalo and Deer, Yellow Corn, Butterfly, Cloud, Fertility Bull, Blue Corn, Eagle, Comanche, Harvest.
    e) Puyé Cliffs, July 25–26, 1964
       Buffalo, Basket, Buffalo and Deer, Blue Corn, Dog, Ange'ing.
3. Hugh Miller, 8 mm sound, deposited at Wenner-Gren Foundation.
    a) Tesuque Corn Dance (b/w), June 13, 1964.
    b) San Ildefonso Bow and Arrow, Eagle, August, 1964.
    c) Puyé Cliffs, July 25–26, 1964
       Buffalo, Basket, Buffalo and Deer, Blue Corn, Dog, Ange'ing.

4. Hugh Miller, 8 mm sound, deposited at University of New Mexico.
   a) Puyé Cliffs, assorted, July, 1963.
   b) San Juan Deer Dance, February 9, 1964.
   c) San Ildefonso Snowbird, March 29, 1964.
   d) Santa Clara Corn, June 13, 1964.
   e) San Ildefonso Rain Dance (*Kwanshare*), June 13, 1964.
   f) Nambé Eagle, Snake, Round, July 4, 1964 (filmed by Don Roberts with Miller's camera).
   g) Puyé Cliffs, July 25–26, 1964.
   h) San Juan *Matachine*, Christmas, 1964.
5. Hugh Miller, 8 mm sound, in Kurath collection.
   a) San Juan Deer Dance, February 18, 1964.
   b) Santa Clara Sun Basket, July 25, 1964.
   c) San Juan Rainbow, Dog, July 26, 1964.
6. Jill and Roger Sweet, 8 mm silent, Sweet Collection.
   a) San Juan, 1973
      Yellow Corn, Parrot, Corn Maiden, Buffalo, *Matachine*, Comanche.
   b) San Juan, June 23–24, 1976, time-lapse. Buffalo, Comanche.
7. Portia Mansfield, 16 mm silent, n.d., available for rent from Perry-Mansfield Camp, Steamboat Springs, Colorado.
   *Southwest Indian Dances* – Tesuque Eagle, fragment Santa Clara Sun Basket, other fragments (Acoma, Cochití, Taos).

*NOTE*

1. All films are in color except where black and white (b/w) is specified.

# 6
# A Calendar of Eastern Pueblo Indian Ritual Dramas

### DON L. ROBERTS
*Music Library*
*Northwestern University*

## INTRODUCTION

The Pueblo Indians have a very active and complex ceremonial life. The underlying purposes of their ceremonies are to maintain harmony with nature and to insure good life. Many Pueblo rituals are elaborate and colorful and can be observed by the general public while others are restricted to Pueblo Indians, members of a particular village, or those affiliated with a specific religious society. This chapter is primarily concerned with the public ceremonies of the Eastern Pueblos.

After the Advanced Seminar on Southwestern Indian ritual drama, the author attempted to identify those Eastern Pueblo ceremonies which could be designated as "ritual dramas." (See page 3 for a definition of ritual drama.) It is difficult to address this topic adequately. Not only do ceremonial production and participation vary from village to village, but also, within a given pueblo, differences exist in the attitudes and approaches of various ceremonial groups.

Another problem in ascertaining whether or not a specific dance can be considered a ritual drama is the fact that outside investigators know relatively little about the intricate details of Eastern Pueblo ceremonial activities. Pueblo residents, especially those in the Keresan villages, rarely reveal ceremonial information to non-Pueblo people. There are many reasons for this, some of which date back at least to the period of early European contact when the Spanish Roman Catholic priests prohibited most native rituals. Pueblo religious leaders were thus forced to perform their ceremonies in secret. This attitude still prevails, and, as a result, most Pueblo people have a limited view of the ceremonial activities of their village.

Several other factors make it difficult to obtain adequate and accurate data on ritual drama. Some important religious practitioners feel that no one can be trusted with their esoteric knowledge; when they die, this information is irretrievable. Linguistic difficulties cause further complications. Very few researchers have become fluent in a Pueblo language, and those who have are often stymied by the fact that many ceremonial texts contain archaic and/or unknown words.

Perhaps the best way to discuss Eastern Pueblo ritual drama is by dance type. Pueblo dances can be categorized according to function, choreography, costumes, origin, accessibility, and season. Dozier (Kurath and Garcia 1970:24), Brown (1962), and D. L. Roberts (1964) are among the various writers who have suggested ceremonial classifications. Dozier (Kurath and Garcia 1970:24) divides Tewa dances as follows:

> 1. Big Dances with limited participation and supervision of sacred societies. . . . 2. Big Dances with communal participation, arranged by social divisions, moieties, as well as societies. . . . 3. Big Dances with limited participation by men and women, less sacred but still under the supervision of secret societies. . . . 4. Little Dances with sacred connotations but less importance than the above. . . . 5. Dances of Spanish derivations, for limited participation . . . with a vaguely ceremonial significance. 6. Secular dances for social occasions . . . with no ceremonial connotation. . . .

Brown (1962), primarily on the basis of costumes, groups Pueblo ceremonies into Kachina Dances, Society Dances, Animal Dances, Corn Dances, and Foreign Dances. D. L. Roberts (1964) separates

## Calendar of Eastern Pueblo Ritual Drama

Rio Grande Pueblo dances into seven categories: "Secret Dances, Semi-Secret Dances or 'Maskless Kachina' Dances, Corn Dances, Animal Dances, Borrowed Dances, Social or Round Dances, and dances with jazz or popular music."

Eastern Pueblo Kachina Dances, which are secret with limited participation under the supervision of sacred societies, are ritual dramas. Although relatively little is known about Rio Grande Pueblo masked ceremonies, they are extremely sacred and, often, very dramatic productions. Laski (1958:42-50) chronicles the intense rise in dramatic anticipation, and the subsequent joyous release experienced by those in the kiva as the clowns describe the approach of the Kachinas from the sacred lakes to their arrival on the kiva roof.

Except for the absence of masks, "Maskless Kachina" Dances closely resemble Kachina ceremonies. The choreography, music, costumes, and texts of Kachina and "Maskless Kachina" ceremonies are practically identical. It is generally assumed that "Maskless Kachina" rituals utilized masks before they were condemned and forbidden, on grounds of idolatry, by European settlers. Some "Maskless Kachina" dances are borrowed from Laguna, Acoma, Zuni, and Hopi; others are public versions of secret masked performances. Most "Maskless Kachina" ceremonies are ritual dramas and consist of a single line of self-accompanying male dancers singing songs with an A A B B A form. "Maskless Kachina" ceremonies include the Bow and Arrow Dance, the Turtle Dance, the Deer Dance, and the Antegeshare (Footlifting Dance).

The Basket Dance, as performed at Santa Clara, San Juan, and other Pueblos, can be considered a "Maskless Kachina" ritual even though women participate. The choreography is similar to the Hopi Hemis Kachina Dance. In the middle section of the dance, the Eastern Pueblo female dancers kneel in front of the men and accompany the songs with notched rasping sticks; at Hopi, the Hemis Kachinmana (Kachina maidens impersonated by masked male dancers) perform in a like manner. Another choreographic parallel exists between the Hopi Bean Dance and Eastern Pueblo ceremonies known as the Parrot Dance in the Keresan villages or the "Going in the Middle Dance" by the Tewas. In the Keres version of this beautiful ritual, dancers in the two side lines, one of men and one of women, face inwards and slowly move, shoulder-to-shoulder, to the back of the dance area. Upon reaching the end of the line, the male and female meet in the middle, forming a center line of couples. The man places his hand on the woman's shoulder and they pivot in each direction while dancing toward a native priest standing at the front of the middle line. When the couple reaches the priest, he hands the woman a basket containing a brightly decorated, carved bird with feathers. The woman, still accompanied by the man, presents the bird to each cardinal point. After the bird is given back to the priest, the couple separates and each person returns to his/her respective side dance line. Although the Hopi Bean Dance does not have the priest, the bird, or women dancers, the overall choreographic pattern closely resembles the above description.

Game Animal Dances, which are among the most elaborate Pueblo dramas, occur in many forms but the most common consists of two buffalo dancers, one or two buffalo maidens, and a hunter, all of whom dance as a unit, plus a supporting cast of deer, antelope, mountain sheep, and elk. These ceremonies are for the propagation of game and successful hunts. Most Game Animal Dances take place during December, January, and February. Since the Pueblo people had relatively few agricultural responsibilities during the winter, this was the major hunting season. Most game animal ceremonies are ritual dramas.

The better Game Animal Dances are complex dramatic productions. In the predawn darkness, the animal impersonators are rounded up from the hills near a pueblo and led into the plaza. During the predawn portion of the San Juan Deer Dance, the deer are herded into the village by two San Juan hunters called "Apaches." Their identification as "Apaches" suggests that San Juan respects the Apaches' hunting ability. The texts spoken by the "Apaches" include many Apache words.

During the course of the day, the Game Animal Dancers will appear several times. Each cycle begins with a slow Entrance Song as the dancers move into the plaza. Next, there is a slow dance followed by a period when the animals meander around the plaza to the accompaniment of a drum tremolo. The circuit is then completed with a fast dance. At some villages, the entire cycle will be repeated before the dancers leave the plaza to rest. In certain villages, the dance terminates when the animal impersonators suddenly disperse and attempt to escape to the hills. The dancers are pursued by townspeople and hunters shooting guns into the air. If

## Calendar of Eastern Pueblo Ritual Drama

an animal is caught, it is carried to the hunter's house and must provide meat for the captor's family. This part of the ritual symbolizes the successful hunt.

Most mixed Game Animal Dances are performed in the Keresan Pueblos, at Jemez, and at San Ildefonso. The February 2 San Felipe Game Animal Dance is renowned for being an outstanding presentation with beautiful costumes. San Ildefonso often does the Game Animal Dance on January 23. Other performances can be found at San Felipe, Santo Domingo, Cochití, Jemez, Zia, and Santa Ana from late December through February.

The Corn Dance is, perhaps, the best known Eastern Pueblo ceremony. This is primarily because, being a summer dance, it is performed at a time when tourists are in the area. The term *Corn Dance* is a misnomer because in addition to prayers for corn, the ceremony is concerned with weather control, good life, and fertility in the broadest sense. When the Corn Dance is given in the fall, it is often called the Harvest Dance.

The Corn Dance is divided into two parts. During the Entrance Song, the dancers circle around the plaza. For the main dance, there are two dance lines normally arranged by height in an alternating pattern of males and females. From this basic pattern, a series of cross-overs, circles, and other similar patterns are derived. The choreographical and musical forms of the main dance are A A B B A.

Corn Dances are especially popular in the Keresan Pueblos and often occur on Feast Days. Corn Dances will normally be found at San Felipe on May 1, at Sandia on June 13, Cochití on July 14, Taos on July 25–26, Santa Ana on July 26, Jemez on August 2, Santo Domingo on August 4, Zia on August 15, Isleta on September 4, Laguna on September 19, and Jemez on November 12. Other Corn Dances usually take place at Santo Domingo on January 1–4 and December 26–28, at Cochití on January 1, and at Zia on December 27–28.

It is reasonably safe to state that most Corn Dances are ritual dramas. However, an observer can sense that they are, as a rule, less sacred than Game Animal ceremonies and "Maskless Kachina" performances. Certain Corn Dances, especially those danced only by young children, probably are not ritual dramas since they do not provide a variety of multisensory, multilayered experiences.

There are a number of Borrowed Dances performed by the Eastern Pueblos. These can be derived from other Pueblos, non-Pueblo tribes, and non-Indian sources. Certain of these presentations, especially those borrowed from other Pueblos, will often be ritual dramas. Most of those borrowed from other tribes, for example, the Comanche Dance done at San Juan Pueblo, cannot be considered ritual dramas. The enigma surrounding certain dances based on non-Indian sources prohibits a definitive statement as to whether or not these are ritual dramas. The Matachina, when accompanied by the violin and guitar at San Juan Pueblo, does not contain the complex layers of ritual drama. However, the "Pueblo version" (accompanied by a drum and chorus) of the Matachina as performed at Santo Domingo and San Felipe seems to possess most of the elements required for ritual drama.

Pueblo Indian Social Dances are primarily secular events. These are not ritual dramas although they function as a release from the intensity of participation in ritual drama.

In conclusion, it can be stated that most Eastern Pueblo ceremonies, with the exception of Social Dances and certain Borrowed Dances, are ritual dramas requiring a great amount of preparation, participation, and sympathetic observation.

## CALENDAR

One of the primary purposes of this chapter is to document Eastern Pueblo ritual drama by citing the performance dates of specific ceremonies in individual villages. The calendar concentrates on the period 1963–68, when the author was privileged to observe and study all basic categories of public Pueblo rituals. This calendar records the existence of ceremonies within an identifiable time-span and, since many Pueblo rituals are not performed on set dates, provides data for scholars investigating ceremonial activity and change.

Previous attempts to compile calendars of Pueblo ceremonies have not been entirely successful. General schedules, such as Dutton's (1975:265–69) "Calendar of Annual Indian Events," are useful, though not always accurate, and are limited to dances which occur on, or near, a specific date. Goggin's (1937, 1938a, 1938b, 1939) detailed calendar of Eastern Pueblo rituals is, unfortunately, confined to two years. Lyon's (1975) "A Calendar of Indian Fiestas" provides

## Calendar of Eastern Pueblo Ritual Drama

detailed information about annual, fixed-date fiestas. A comparison of published Pueblo calendars indicates that there has been relatively little change in ceremonial activity during the last 100 years.

Most Pueblo rituals occur at a specific or predictable time of the year and are based on solar and lunar observations (Parsons 1939b:493), on an annual cycle which is "tied to nature's basic rhythm and to the Tewa's attempts to influence that rhythm for his well-being" (Ortiz 1969:103), or on the liturgical calendar of the Roman Catholic Church, where the celebrations of ecclesiastical feast days include Christian elements, but feature indigenous Pueblo rites. Ceremonies which deviate from the above patterns tend to be secular in nature. The intricacies of Pueblo ceremonial cycles are described by Ortiz (1969:98-111), Parsons (1939b:493-549), Kurath and Garcia (1970:23-27), and R. Rhodes (1977:8-13).

Observers of Pueblo dances have long been puzzled by performances of native ceremonies on Christian Holy days which apparently honor elements of the Roman Catholic liturgy. Although certain portions of these activities are tied to the Catholic Church, the basic underlying power is directed toward the native religion. For many years, European settlers forced the Pueblos to accept Roman Catholicism. Accept they did, but not at the expense of ignoring their traditional religious beliefs and practices. A strange duality has evolved and, as one of my Pueblo friends asserts, it is now possible for a person to be a good Indian and a good Catholic, a good Indian and a bad Catholic, a bad Indian and a good Catholic, or a bad Indian and a bad Catholic. The Mass preceding a Corn Dance is a Catholic ritual, but the Corn Dance, even if there is a shrine for the santo, is an indigenous ceremony. In sum, it can be stated that there are many gods in the Pueblo pantheon and one of them just happens to be the Christian god.

The following calendar of rituals is by no means complete but does present a reasonably comprehensive overview of Eastern Pueblo ceremonial activity. Emphasis has been placed on the public ceremonies of the Tanoan and Northern Keresan villages. Since most Rio Grande Pueblo ceremonies have been chronicled by other researchers, the narrative portion of the calendar is limited to general observations, comments on unusual features, and references to published descriptions of the rituals. Throughout the calendar, ceremonies observed by the author are marked with an asterisk (*).

Other entries are based on information supplied by fellow students of Pueblo culture.[1]

CALENDAR FOR EASTERN PUEBLO RITUAL DRAMAS

*January—Fixed Dates*

January 1. There are usually ceremonies in most of the Keresan Pueblos and in several of the other villages.

*Cochiti:* 1962, Buffalo Dance. Lange (1959:322-23) states that a Corn Dance is usually performed on January 1 in honor of the new officers.

*Jemez:* 1962, Game Animal Dance. 1963, Rainbow Dance; Eagle Dance; and a Corn Dance for the young children. The Rainbow Dance consisted of one male and one female dancing in a circular pattern. The female wore a white ceremonial dress and her face was painted white. She carried a rainbow in each hand and wore a rainbow-shaped tablita with many feathers, including parrot and peacock, on the back. 1965, Matachina—completed the December 12 ceremony which had been suspended by an epileptic seizure. 1966, War Dance and "Maskless Kachina." 1967, Hopi Dance (?) and Corn Dance for the young children.

*San Felipe:* 1966, "Maskless Kachina."

*Santa Ana:* 1962, a pageant, with an altar and santo, by 13 men and women costumed as a Catholic priest, 2 nuns, a Negro boy, a blind Negro with a cane and guide, 2 Negro men, 2 Negro women, a Plains Warrior, and 2 Mexicans (1 had a guitar) who were performing mock miracles for the blind man. 1966, Corn Dance. 1967, "Maskless Kachina."

*Santo Domingo:* Corn Dance—1962, 1965, 1966, 1967\*. The 1967 ceremony was a typical Corn Dance with 190 dancers, a chorus of 125, and the long decorated pole. This Corn Dance usually lasts for four days.

*Taos:* 1961 and 1977, Turtle Dance.

*Zia:* 1962, Crow Dance. 1963, "Maskless Kachina" with 16 male dancers, 11 of whom wore headbands of eagle and parrot feathers and 5 of whom had deer heads. 1965, Apache *Gahan* Dance. 1966, Game Animal Dance. 1967, the children did poor performances of a Plains Dance and an Apache *Gahan* Dance they learned at school.

## Calendar of Eastern Pueblo Ritual Drama

January 6. Most Pueblos dance in honor of their newly selected secular officials. Animal or Hunting Dances are usually performed, but no village repeats the same ceremony each year.

*Cochití:* 1962, Eagle Dance; Elk Dance. 1964, Buffalo Dances*. 1965, Eagle Dance; Buffalo/Comanche Dance. 1967, Buffalo Dances. 1968, Eagle Dance; Elk Dance. These rituals synchronize with the three-year cycle of January 6 Animal Dances reported by Lange (1959:324-28).

*Jemez:* 1962, Game Animal Dance of 2 Eagles, 2 Buffalo, 3 Mountain Sheep, 1 Hawk (?), and 50 Deer. 1964, Buffalo Dance. 1968, Game Animal Dance.

*San Felipe:* 1968, Butterfly (?) Dance.

*San Ildefonso:* 1978, Game Animal Dance.

*San Juan:* 1964, Buffalo Dance*. 1968, Bow and Arrow Dance*. 1977, Buffalo Dance (moved to Sunday, January 9). 1978, Hopi Buffalo Dance (moved to Sunday, January 8).

*Sandia:* 1962, Eagle Dance. 1964, Butterfly*. 1967, Eagle Dance; Buffalo Dance. Sandia will often dance in the church during the evening of January 5. Night Dances follow which are not open to the public; these are partially repeated in the plaza on January 6.

*Santa Ana:* 1968, Game Animal Dance.

*Santa Clara:* 1964, Buffalo Dance*; Sash Dance*. 1968, Matachina (Indian version).

*Santo Domingo:* 1962, Buffalo Dance. 1964, Bow and Arrow Dance*. 1967, various dances were held in houses at night. Lange (1951) gives an illuminating description of the 1940 Night Dances.

*Taos:* 1968, Corn Dance*; Deer Dance*. 1978, Buffalo Dance. In contrast to other Pueblo Deer Dance costumes, which utilize only the antlers or head of a deer, the Taos impersonators wear the entire deerskin (Fergusson 1931:36-40; Parsons 1939b:844-47).

*Tesuque:* 1968, Hopi Buffalo.

*Zia:* 1968, Crow Dance.

January 23. San Ildefonso Feast Day. Ceremonies are held each year. 1965, Game Animal Dance* (North plaza); Comanche Dance* (South plaza). 1966, Game Animal Dance* (South plaza); Comanche Dance* (North plaza). 1968, Game Animal Dance (South plaza); Comanche Dance (North plaza). 1978, Deer Dance. The Game Animal Dance is described by Whitman (1947:138-39) and

Anonymous (1928), and the Comanche Dance, by Kurath and Garcia (1970:233–34).

*February—Fixed Dates*

February 2. Candlemas Day.
*San Felipe:* 1964, Game Animal Dance. 1965, Navajo Dance*. 1966, Game Animal Dance*. 1967, Navajo Skip Dance*. 1968, Navajo (?) Dance. 1969, Game Animal Dance*. 1978, Game Animal Dance. The San Felipe Game Animal Dance is considered to be the best rendition of this ceremony. Details are available in Fergusson (1931:40–44), Parsons (1939b:834–36), Roediger (1941:190–93), and White (1932:56–60).

*January–April—Irregularly Scheduled Ceremonies*

Many of the more important and impressive Eastern Pueblo dramas occur in January and February. From the ceremonial viewpoint, it is the busiest time of year and there are rituals almost every weekend in at least one of the villages. Many types of dances are performed, but most are Animal/Hunting Dances or "Maskless Kachina" Dances. The latter category includes some of the most sacred rites a non-Pueblo observer can witness.

Except for Easter dances (see below), public ceremonial life noticeably decreases in March and April. Most activity after mid-March is concentrated in the Tewa villages. With the possible exception of March 27, there are no fixed dance dates in March and April.

The following ceremonies were observed in January, February, March, and April and are not performed on a regularly scheduled date:

*Acoma*

February 12–13, 1966—Governor's Dance*. There were 9 dance groups: Eagle, Deer, 3 Buffalo (1 typical and 2 with "modern" headdresses), 2 similar to the September 2 Feast Day dancers, Shield (?), and Goat (?) or Sheep (?).

*Cochiti*

February 7, 1965—Buffalo Dance. Densmore (1957:82–87) and Kurath (1959:539–45) give descriptions and transcriptions of this ceremony.

## Calendar of Eastern Pueblo Ritual Drama

February 14, 1965—Buffalo Dance.
February 16, 1964—Game Animal Dance*.
February 18, 1968—Buffalo Dance.
February 20, 1966—Game Animal Dance*.
February 21, 1965—Game Animal Dance*.
February 25, 1968—Game Animal Dance*. A typical ceremony except during the fast dance when one Buffalo would leave his rattle and bow on the antlers of a Deer and the other Buffalo would retrieve them. There were 2 Buffalos, 1 Buffalo Maiden, 1 Hunter, 10 Deer, 2 Mountain Sheep, and 3 Antelope.

February 26, 1967—Game Animal Dance*. The dancers consisted of 2 Buffalos, 2 Buffalo Maidens, 1 Hunter, 3 Antelope, 6 Deer, and 2 Mountain Sheep.

*Isleta*

February 6, 1966—Evergreen Dance.
February 21-23, 1964—Turtle Dance*. There were plaza dances on the 21st and 23rd. A rabbit hunt was held on the 22nd.
February 24-27, 1966—Turtle Dance*. There was a Night Dance in the kiva on the 24th and a rabbit hunt on the 26th. Plaza dances were on the 25th and 27th.
April 5* and 12, 1964—Ceremonial races.

*Isleta (Laguna Colony)*

January 6-10, 1966—Dances.
January 13-17, 1965*—Dances planned, but postponed for one week due to deaths in the colony.
January 14, 1968—Dances.
January 21, 1968—Dances.
January 27, 1963—"Maskless Kachina" Dance. A line dance with 12 male performers.
January 28, 1968—"Maskless Kachina" Dance with 30 men and 1 woman in honor of the Village Governor.
January 31, 1965—"Maskless Kachina" Dance by 15 self-accompanying dancers with no drum or chorus.

*Jemez*

January 7, 1968—Game Animal Dance (two groups)*.
January 15, 1967—Kiowa Shield Dance*; Navajo Dance*. The latter was very amusing with a hilarious couple dressed as Navajos.
February 4, 1968—Bow and Arrow Dance.

*Laguna*

January 7-9, 1962—Dances.

February 14-15, 1964—Eagle Dance; Buffalo Dance.

*Picuris*

February 21, 1965—Butterfly Dance.

*San Felipe*

January 8, 1967—Hopi Dance*. While the ceremonies were in progress, 5 boys with whitened faces and hair visited with spectators in the plazas and in various houses. It is assumed they were mimicking Hopi albinos.

January 9, 1966—Eagle Dance*; unidentified Line Dance*.

January 10, 1965—Matachina.

January 15, 1967—Navajo Dance*.

January 26, 1969—Navajo Dance.

January 29, 1967*—Unidentified creatures, who appeared to be masked, were walking on the mesa west of the village.

February 5, 1967—Buffalo Dance*; Matachina. It was reported that an accordion was used during the Matachina.

February 12, 1967—Game Animal Dance*.

February 14, 1965—Green Corn Dance*; Mexican Dance with bull impersonator*.

February 16, 1964—Game Animal Dance*.

February 20, 1966—Buffalo Dance*.

February 21, 1965—Parrot Dance*. One of the most beautiful and unusual Eastern Pueblo ritual dramas. It is one of the very few ceremonies where the women sing. Seven female and three male Koshare were present. The choreography resembles the Hopi Powamu. Fergusson (1931:45-49) describes a similar ceremony at Santo Domingo.

February 24, 1968—Parrot Dance.

February 25, 1968—Mexican Dance*. It is difficult to comprehend fully the meaning of many Pueblo ritual dramas as this ceremony, which apparently is a historical pageant about Mexican contacts, illustrates. Both the costumes and the dances are Mexican. On this day, a large black bull, impersonated by a man, ran around, mooed, clacked his movable mouth, and chased children. Parsons (1939b:811-12) provides additional data.

February 26, 1967—Koshare Society Dance*. This was probably the public portion of an initiation rite.

February 27, 1966—Mexican Dance*. Similar to February 25, 1968 with the addition of two tents pitched in the plaza.

## Calendar of Eastern Pueblo Ritual Drama

February 28, 1965—Parrot Dance*. Parallel to the February 21, 1965 ceremony with Kwirana replacing the Koshare.

March 1, 1964—Koshare Ceremony*.

*San Ildefonso*

March 15, 1964—Belt Dance*. A secular pleasure dance described by Kurath and Garcia (1970:237-38).

March 16, 1968—Women's Dance.

March 20, 1966—Antegeshare (Footlifting Dance). Kurath and Garcia (1970:133-35) and Whitman (1947:138-39) describe this ceremony.

March 21, 1965—Snowbird Dance.

April 20, 1966—Antegeshare.

April 28, 1968—Basket Dance (women only). A satire by the women about the ineffectiveness of San Ildefonso men.

*San Juan*

January 23, 1966—Pogonshare*. Also called Corn Maiden Dance, Squash Blossom Dance, and Rainbow Dance. An uncommon feature of this ceremony is the zigzag choreography of the two female dancers. Kurath and Garcia (1970:150-51, 164-65) supply additional details.

January 24, 1965—Pogonshare*.

January 26, 1964—Basket Dance. The middle part of this dance is similar to the Hopi Hemis Kachina Ceremony; the women kneel and scrape notched sticks while the men dance next to them. Thus, a masked origin is suggested for this ritual.

January 29, 1978—Basket Dance.

January 30, 1977—Cloud Dance.

February 5, 1967—Deer Dance*. There were 85 Deer Dancers. Kurath and Garcia (1970:117-30) document this popular ceremony.

February 6, 1966—Yellow Corn Dance. During the first section (*wasa*) of this ritual, all dancers zigzag into the plaza.

February 9, 1964—Deer Dance*.

February 13, 1966—Transvestite Dance. Done by the women as a preliminary event to the Butterfly Dance performed one week later.

February 14, 1965—Yellow Corn Dance*.

February 18, 1968—Deer Dance.

February 20, 1966—Butterfly Dance*. This is a rare example of competition in Pueblo ceremonial life. Each of the 20 couples attempted to dance better than the previous one.

February 26, 1978—Deer Dance.

February 27, 1977—Deer Dance.

February 28, 1965—Deer Dance.
April 12, 1966—Bow and Arrow Dance.
*Sandia*
April 21, 1968, and April 23 and 30, 1966—Closed to the Public for Kachina Ceremonies.
*Santa Ana*
January 15, 1967—Closed to the Public.
January 29, 1967—Game Animal Dance*.
February 18, 1968—Buffalo Dance.
*Santa Clara*
January 29, 1978—Basket Dance.
February 5, 1978—Deer Dance.
February 7, 1965—Pogonshare.
February 8, 1964—Kachina Ceremony (closed to non-Pueblo people).
February 13, 1966—Antegeshare.
February 21, 1965—Deer Dance*.
February 27, 1966—Matachina.
February 28, 1965—Matachina.
*Santo Domingo*
January 15, 1967—Hopi Dance*.
January 19, 1964—Matachina*.
January 22, 1967—Game Animal Dance. Densmore (1938:143-66) and Lange (1954) give good accounts of this ceremony.
January 23, 1966—Paiute Dance* and unidentified Circle Dance*.
January 24, 1965—Matachina*.
January 25, 1965—Sandaro; probably included a Mexican Dance. See Densmore (1938:176-80) and White (1935:149-55) for descriptive information.
January 29, 1967—Acoma Dance*.
January 30, 1967—Mexican Dance.
February 5, 1968—Game Animal Dance*.
February 7, 1965—Game Animal Dance.
February 9, 1964—Buffalo Dance.
February 12, 1968—Matachina.
February 16, 1964—Game Animal Dance*.
February 18, 1968—Buffalo Dance.
February 23, 1966—Matachina.
February 27, 1966—Comanche Dance*. All dancers and singers were female. Their antics were hilarious.

## Calendar of Eastern Pueblo Ritual Drama

March 1, 1964—Parrot Dance*.
March 3, 1968—Closed to the Public.
March 5, 1967—Navajo Dance*.
March 6 and 7, 1965—Eagle Dance*.
March 12, 1965—Navajo Dance.
March 28, 1965—Closed to the Public.
*Taos*
January 29, 1978—Hand Dance.
*Zia*
March 12, 1967—Closed to the Public.

*Easter*

Many Pueblos have ceremonies on Easter. These are sacred Pueblo rituals and do not incorporate Christian or Penitente elements.

*Cochiti:* It was reported that kick-stick races were held in 1965. Evidently this ancient ritual has been revived in spite of predictions to the contrary (Lange 1959:334-35). A Corn Dance was performed in 1968. Bandelier gives an interesting description of the 1882 Easter Corn Dance (Lange and Riley 1966:258-63).

*Jemez:* Jemez presented Corn Dances in 1965 and 1968*. In 1968, the two groups of dancers, and their choruses, simultaneously performed their final dances. Each moiety had its own song and the result was a marvelous atmosphere of contrapuntal unity.

*San Ildefonso:* San Ildefonso usually dances on Easter. In 1964, the Snowbird Dance* was given in the North plaza (Kurath and Garcia 1970:174) and the Antegeshare*, in the South plaza. Although vastly different, the ceremonies each contain an uncommon characteristic: the Snowbird Dance is done in a circle and the Antegeshare features a perfectly paced accelerando and ritardando. These gradual tempo changes are similar to those found in certain Zuni and Hopi Kachina Songs. The clowns did a most amusing burlesque of the Catholic Church during the final Antegeshare appearance (Kurath and Garcia 1970:133-35). In 1965, the North plaza presented a Basket Dance* while there was a Turtle Dance* in the South plaza. Two deaths in the Pueblo resulted in the cancellation of the 1966 dances. The North plaza had a Bow and Arrow Dance* in 1967 and the Antegeshare was danced in 1968.

*San Juan:* There was a Green Corn Dance* in 1967.
*Santa Ana:* The Corn Dance is usually given (1965 and 1968*).

*Santa Clara:* There were Buffalo Dances in 1966\* and 1968. In 1968, all of the dancers were female.

*Santo Domingo:* A four-day Corn Dance always commences on Easter at this Pueblo. On Sunday, the dancers are usually children (1965\*, 1967\*). The fourth day of the ceremony was viewed and eloquently described by D. H. Lawrence (1924).

*Zia:* In 1965, there was an unidentified Social (?) Dance and in 1968\*, a ceremony which apparently was a planting ritual.

## May Ceremonies

May 1

*San Felipe:* A Feast Day Corn Dance is presented annually at San Felipe (1964\*, 1965\*, 1968\*). In 1968, one group numbered 150 dancers and 60 singers; the other, 180 dancers and 55 singers. Three Santiagos ("horses") accompanied the santo from the plaza shrine to the church.

May 3

*Taos:* Ceremonial races (1964\*).

*Cochití:* A Corn Dance with the appearance of "River Men" is usual (Lange 1959:337–38). An informant reported that the "River Men" were present in 1966.

There are also a few noncalendrical ceremonies in May. In 1966, Jemez performed a Laguna Corn Dance on May 15 and the women of San Ildefonso danced on May 8. Santo Domingo usually has a Corn Dance on Corpus Christi (May 28, 1964 and May 25, 1967\*).

## June, July, and August Ceremonies

Most Eastern Pueblo summer ceremonies occur on annual Catholic Feast Days. The dances are often preceded by a Mass in the village church and a procession, sometimes noisily accompanied by a drum, bugle, and gunfire, bringing the santo from the church to a covered shrine erected for the occasion in the dance plaza. Even though the dancers may enter the shrine to pay respect to the santo, the dances are indigenous Pueblo rituals.

June 13. Feast Day at Sandia, where a Corn Dance is held (1966\*, 1967\*). Other villages may also have ceremonies. In 1964, Cochití,

## Calendar of Eastern Pueblo Ritual Drama

San Ildefonso*, San Juan*, Santa Clara*, Santo Domingo, and Taos all performed Corn Dances. In 1965, San Ildefonso and San Juan* did Corn Dances while Santa Clara presented a Comanche Dance. San Juan had a Corn Dance in 1977.

June 24. Feast Day at San Juan, where the Comanche Dance is usually performed (1964*, 1967*, 1968*, 1976, and 1977). In addition, the Buffalo Dance was done in 1976 and 1977.

July 14. The Corn Dance is performed at Cochití for Feast Day (1964*, 1968*). This ceremony is well documented by Densmore (1957:90-92) and Lange (1959:341-53).

July 25. Feast Day at Taos where the Corn Dance is performed (1965*, 1966*). There were no men in the 1966 Corn Dance. Other Pueblos sometimes dance on this day.

July 26. Feast Day at Santa Ana which does a Corn Dance (1965*, 1968*). Corn Dance at Taos (Brown 1976:227-33).

August 2. Feast Day of the Pecos people who abandoned their pueblo in 1838 and moved to Jemez. A Corn Dance, also known as the Pecos Bull Dance, is performed (1964*). Further information is available in Fergusson (1931:61-65), Keech (1934a), and Parsons (1939b:848-52).

August 4. The August 4 Corn Dance at Santo Domingo is probably the best known Eastern Pueblo ceremony. A festive, but sacred, atmosphere prevails. Each kiva has over 300 dancers and approximately 125 singers. Thousands of visitors, mostly tourists, pass through a carnival on the village outskirts to view the spectacle. The perfection and immensity of the ceremony have inspired many writers, among the more interesting of whom are Buttree (1937:149-57), Densmore (1938:92-110), Fergusson (1931:56-60), Hewett (1913), Huebener (1938), White (1935:159-60), and Anonymous (1929).

August 10. Feast Day at Picuris. Performances include the Corn Dance and Deer Dance, 1965; Basket Dance*, 1966; and the Mountain Sheep Dance, 1968.

August 12. Feast Day at Santa Clara.

August 15. The Corn Dance is performed for Zia's Feast Day. This ceremony parallels other Keresan Corn Dances and is described by Keech (1934b) and White (1962:269-74).

There are relatively few noncalendrical summer public ceremonies. An unidentified Santo Domingo ritual was reported on June 16-19, 1967. In the main part of this dance, the dancers moved in a counterclockwise circle. The chorus sat in the center of the circle while three men, playing long flutes, moved in a counterclockwise pattern between the chorus and the dancers. Santo Domingo did a Basket Dance on June 28, 1964. There is also evidence of closed ceremonies: Acoma was closed to the public July 10–13, 1968 and Santo Domingo was off limits to visitors on June 13, 1967.

Tesuque performed Corn Dances on June 6, 1964 and June 12, 1965. Picuris had a Corn Dance on July 26, 1966. At Santo Domingo, the Corn Dance was performed on Corpus Christi (June 17, 1965* and June 9, 1966).

Mention should be made of two dance festivals sponsored by Tewa Pueblos. On July 4, Nambé Pueblo presents a variety of dances at Nambé Falls. There are also dance groups from other villages. In late July, Santa Clara has many interesting performances at the Puyé Cliff Dwelling, an ancestral Santa Clara ruin. Both festivals provide a good overview of Tewa dances.

*Autumn Ceremonies*

Between September 1 and Christmas most public rituals occur on the fixed dates of Catholic feast days. It is not unusual to find a Pueblo closed to the public during the fall and, when this happens, it can be assumed that a secret ceremony is under way. There are very few known non-feast-day fall dances. San Juan performed the Harvest Dance on September 20, 1964*, September 18, 1966*, and September 25, 1977. This Harvest Dance is infrequently done and differs from most other public Pueblo rites. The dancers move sideways in a clockwise circle while the chorus sings 10 songs, 1 for each religious society and 1 for the elected secular officers (Kurath and Garcia 1970:186–97). There was a Corn Dance at San Ildefonso on September 18, 1966*.

The following ceremonies appear annually on a fixed date:

September 2. Feast Day at Acoma. In 1965, two choruses took turns singing, but there were no dancers.

September 4. Isleta's Feast Day. A Corn Dance is performed (1964*).

September 19. Feast Day Corn Dance at Laguna. In 1965*, there was also an Eagle Dance and an Aztec Dance. The latter was sponsored by the Albuquerque Inter-tribal Dancers.

## Calendar of Eastern Pueblo Ritual Drama

September 29/30. The Fiesta of San Geronimo at Taos. On the evening of September 29, there is a simple, brief Sundown Dance. There are ceremonial races early next morning followed by the attempts of the sacred clowns to climb a tall greased pole (1964*).

October 4. Feast Day at Nambé. In 1964 an Elk Dance* was performed. The Game Animal Dance and the Comanche Dance are also done on this date.

November 12. Feast Day dances at Jemez and Tesuque. Jemez performs the Harvest Dance (Corn Dance) each year (1965*, 1966*, 1967*, 1969*).

December 12. To be in Jemez Pueblo on December 12 is a unique experience. One can observe the Matachina, a drama of Moslem and/or European origin which was conveyed to the western hemisphere by Spanish missionaries and is now found throughout the Spanish-American world in various forms with different names. Two versions are found in the Pueblos. Although the choreography of each is practically identical, one is accompanied by a drum and a chorus singing Pueblo-style songs and the other, by a fiddle and guitar, sometimes an electric guitar, playing Spanish-American tunes. Except for Jemez, a pueblo will do either the "Indian" or "Spanish" rendition. At Jemez on December 12, the alternating versions provide a fascinating glimpse of a historical pageant (1964*, 1965*, 1966, 1968* which was moved to December 13). For further details, see Kurath (1957) and Kurath and Garcia (1970:257-78). Santo Domingo often dances on December 12; a Buffalo Dance was performed in 1964 and a Hopi (?) Dance*, in 1965. San Felipe performed a Game Animal Dance* and Bow and Arrow Dance* in 1965. It was reported that Cochití did a variety of dances on December 12, 1965 at a ceremony honoring the construction of the Cochití Dam.

### Christmas

The greatest concentration of Pueblo dance activity occurs during the Christmas season. Almost every village has at least one ceremony between December 24 and 28. Several pueblos have sacred native dances inside the churches on Christmas Eve or very early Christmas morning. The dirt floors of the churches enable the ceremonial participants to maintain direct contact with "Mother Earth."

*Cochití*
December 24, 1963—Buffalo Dance.
December 24, 1964—Two Buffalo Dance groups.
December 25, 1964—Buffalo Dance.
December 25, 1966—Two Game Animal groups*.
December 25, 1970—Two Game Animal groups*.
December 25, 1976—Two Game Animal groups*.
December 26, 1967—Eagle Dance*; Comanche Dance*.
December 26, 1967—Eagle Dance*: Comanche Dance*.
December 27, 1963—Game Animal Dance; Navajo Dance.
December 27, 1964—Eagle Dance; Comanche Dance.
December 28, 1964—Laguna Rain God Dance*; Deer Dance*: an informant stated the lead animals in the two deer lines were Moose. If true, this would be most unusual, to say the least.
December 28, 1967—Eagle Dance*; Navajo Dance*.
December 29, 1964—Buffalo Dance.
December 29, 1967—Buffalo Dance.

*Isleta*
December 25, 1966—"Christmas Dance"* (Parsons 1932:303-5).
December 27, 1963—"Christmas Dance."
December 27, 1967—"Christmas Dance*."

*Jemez*
December 25, 1961—Basket Dance.
December 25, 1968—Two Buffalo Dance groups*.
December 26, 1963—Two Buffalo Dance groups.
December 26, 1965—Buffalo Dance with the Buffalo blowing small, eight-inch flutes.
December 28, 1963—Game Animal Dance.

*San Felipe*
December 24, 1961—Game Animal Dance; Buffalo Dance; Hunting Dance.
December 24, 1963—Bow and Arrow Dance; Two Buffalo Dance groups.
December 24, 1964—Mountain Sheep Dance; Two Buffalo Dance groups.
December 24, 1965—Two Buffalo Dance groups; unidentified group.
December 24, 1966—Game Animal Dance; Eagle Dance.
December 24, 1967—Two Game Animal Dance groups*; Kiowa Dance*.

*Calendar of Eastern Pueblo Ritual Drama*

December 24, 1968—Navajo Dance*; Plains Butterfly Dance*; Kiowa Dance*.

December 24, 1970—Two Game Animal Dance groups*; Hunting Dance* (may have been an unmasked version of a Hopi Kachina Dance).

December 25, 1976—Basket/Plaque (?) Dance*; Game Animal Dance*; Bow and Arrow Dance*.

December 26, 1963—Bow and Arrow Dance; Two Game Animal Dance groups.

December 26, 1964—Game Animal Dance.

December 26, 1967—Game Animal Dance*.

December 27, 1963—Corn Dance.

December 28, 1963—Corn Dance.

December 28, 1967—Corn Dance*.

*San Ildefonso*

December 25, 1964—Matachina (Spanish version)*.

*San Juan*

December 24/25, 1964—San Juan performs the Spanish version of the Matachina* every year on Christmas Eve and Christmas Day (see Parsons 1939b:852-55 for a report on the 1927 performance).

December 26, 1964—The Turtle Dance* is performed every year on December 26. A prelude is given the evening before. LaVigna (n.d.) has thoroughly analyzed the Turtle Dance Songs.

December 26, 1976—Turtle Dance*.

*Sandia*

December 24, 1963—Matachina.

December 25, 1967—Butterfly Dance. A Sandia resident stated that the Butterfly Dance is performed every Christmas morning.

*Santa Ana*

December 25, 1961—Buffalo Dance.

December 25, 1967—Game Animal Dance*.

December 25, 1968—Buffalo Dance*.

December 26, 1963—Game Animal Dance.

December 26, 1964—Corn Dance.

December 26, 1965—Game Animal Dance; Corn Grinding Ceremony.

December 26, 1966—Buffalo Dance.

December 28, 1963—Corn Dance.

December 28, 1967—Corn Dance.

*Santo Domingo*

December 24, 1963—Buffalo Dance; Hopi Dance; Navajo Dance.

December 24, 1964—Supai (?) Dance; unidentified dance.
December 24, 1965—Navajo Dance; unidentified dance.
December 24, 1966—Hunting Dance; Ute (?) Dance.
December 24, 1967—Horse Dance*; Navajo Dance*.
December 25, 1966—Hunting Dance*.
December 25, 1970—Unidentified dance*.
December 26, 1965—Corn Dance—children dancing.
December 26, 1967—Corn Dance*—children, ages 2-8.
December 26, 1976—Corn Dance*—children, ages 2-8.
December 27, 1963—Corn Dance.
December 27, 1964—Corn Dance.
December 28, 1961—Corn Dance.
December 28, 1963—Corn Dance.
December 28, 1964—Corn Dance*.
December 28, 1967—Corn Dance*.

*Taos*

December 25, 1964—Deer Dance.
December 25, 1967—Matachina (Spanish version).

*Tesuque*

December 25, 1964—Pogonshare*.
December 26, 1964—Bow and Arrow Dance*.
December 27, 1964—Buffalo Dance; Deer Dance (?).

*Zia*

December 25, 1967—Game Animal Dance*.
December 25, 1968—Buffalo Dance*.
December 26, 1963—Game Animal Dance.
December 26, 1964—Buffalo Dance; War Dance.
December 26, 1965—Buffalo Dance.
December 26, 1966—Game Animal Dance.
December 27, 1964—Corn Dance.
December 28, 1961—Corn Dance.
December 28, 1963—Corn Dance.
December 28, 1964—Corn Dance.
December 28, 1967—Corn Dance*.

## NOTE

1. I would like to thank Bill Robertson, Antonio Garcia, Maria LaVigna, and many others for generously providing information which substantially increased the comprehensiveness of this calendar.

# 7
# Singing for Life:
# The Mescalero Apache Girls' Puberty Ceremony[1]

### CLAIRE R. FARRER
*Department of Anthropology*
*University of Illinois at Urbana-Champaign*

## INTRODUCTION

> All our actions are based on our religion—if that goes, we go as a people.
>
> Bernard Second[2]

The Mescalero Apaches have increased from fewer than 500 people (by the Army's 1873 census) to over 2,000 formally enrolled members on the tribal rolls (1975 tribal figure). Within the last 20 years they have moved to an enviable position of prestige and relative wealth. These people, who were hunted, beaten, decimated, and finally incarcerated, have—within 100 years—more than quadrupled their population and raised their standard of living almost beyond imagination. What caused the rejuvenation?

Whenever the question was asked, the same answers were given: "our feast" and "tribal leadership." This chapter concerns the former, the "feast," as the Girls' Puberty Ceremony is often called in English. It is the Singers who have sung the tribe back to viable existence.

History, in the form of census records, supports the folk explanation that the Girls' Puberty Ceremony contributed to tribal increase, since the population did not increase substantially until after 1912, when ceremonial activity resumed following the government-enforced hiatus from 1873 to 1911.

Similar ceremonies have captured the interest of anthropologists. M. E. Opler (1965:82–134) wrote in detail of the Chiricahua version; he also described the Jicarilla practices (1942:25–38 and 1946:105–15). The homologous Cibique Apache rite has been the subject of a monograph (Basso 1966), while Clark (1976) has described the San Carlos Apache version. The full Mescalero Apache rite has yet to be discussed, although portions of it have been considered by Breuninger (1959) and Nicholas (1939), both Mescaleros.

At Mescalero the Girls' Puberty Ceremony is an annual event celebrating the initial menses of selected girls, as well as the perpetuation of the tribe. During the event, the Singers recount tribal history from the time of the beginning by the shores of a big lake far to the north.

While the Ceremony celebrates womanhood and focuses on women, it is conducted by men; not just ordinary men, but powerful holy men who are beyond reproach. Each Holy Man/Singer (*Gutąął*, One Who Sings) must be intelligent and able to memorize and interpret songs in a special form of Mescalero Apache. Each must sing 64 different songs on each of the four nights of the Ceremony. Additionally, the Singer must memorize long stories of the people, their travels, and accounts of tribal interactions from the beginning to the present. The Ceremony is thus a reenactment of events from the beginning of cosmological time and a recitation of ethnohistory.

The Ceremony and its attendant rituals are seen by the Mescaleros as *the* crucial factor in their ethnicity and their success in coping with the rigors of survival as a people in a pluralistic society not of their making. The Singers sing women into their adult roles, sing tribal history, and sing the people into their concerted existence.

> Our Ceremony, the puberty rites, is the most important religious rites that we adhere to today . . . . The female - - - - the woman of the tribe, when she reaches womanhood, this elabo-

rate Ceremony is held over her. Not, not because she has reached puberty, but because she is a *woman*. And, then, everything is done - - - - for her that a people might live. That a people will *always* live. Every year we have this to regenerate ourselves as a people. - - - - - - - - That we will make her strong, and generous, and kind, and proud so that she will bring forth *strong* warrior child that . . . will protect the people. - - - - - - This is the way a people perpetuate themselves.

Not only do the rites celebrate the achievement of womanhood for girls, but also they serve a sociability function. Each summer the parking lot adjacent to the Ceremonial grounds boasts cars with license plates from several states, attesting that friends and relatives from across the country have arrived.

At the same time, the Ceremony is a reunion with the primary life force, the Creator God (*Bik'egudindé*, Because of Whom There Is Life), and his consort, Mother Earth or White Painted Woman (*Isdząnatł'eesh*, Woman Painted White).

CRF: Tell me when you first had this.
BS: When we were created as a people and we became a people . . . in order for us to return respect for our Mother, we organized this ritual. We, as men, organized this religion to give thanks back and also to our hopes and aspirations in this life. . . . [We say,] "Give us strength to live on this earth - - that we will live as strong and good and holy people and that our womenfolk will continue to bring forth strong and healthy children and that we will continue to live as a people.". . . This is a reenactment of our creation as a people.

The Girls' Puberty Ceremony, then, is a ritual drama, a reenactment of creation. The Ceremony is also a cultural performance (Singer 1958, 1972) during which time those things of value to the people are displayed for themselves and for outsiders.

. . . my . . . friends—and perhaps all peoples—thought of their culture as encapsulated in . . . discrete performances which they exhibit to visitors and to themselves. The performances . . . had a definitely limited time span, or at least a beginning and an end, an organized program of activity, a set of performers, an audience, and a place and occasion of performance (Singer 1972:71).

Cultural performances communicate what is of importance to a people; however, that communication is not always readily grasped, as Singer observes:

... these were the kinds of things that an outsider could observe and comprehend within a single direct experience. I do not mean that I could, even with the help of interpreters, always understand everything that went on at one of these performances or appreciate their functions in the total life of the community (1972:71).

The difficulty in understanding is compounded when the cultural performance spans several days and includes various performance genres. The interpretative task is facilitated by following a base metaphor through its many guises or transformations and recombinations during the cultural performance.[3] Balance, circularity, directionality, the number 4, and sound/silence are all components of the Mescalero Apache base metaphor.

The various subsystems constituting a culture are unified through a shared set of organizing principles, or a base metaphor. Such sharing produces the patterns that allow recognition of particular kinds of behavior and beliefs as being characteristic of a culture. For the Mescalero Apaches the components mentioned above produce patterns that begin to make the cultural performance of the Girls' Puberty Ceremony intelligible. What the patterns and their significance are form the burden of what follows—the singing for life.

## THE CEREMONY

### THE FIRST DAY

The few spectators who have braved the predawn chill sit on the north side of the ceremonial area directly opposite the large cooking arbor. Several Singers and Painters (*Anaagu'łiin*, One Who Makes Them) emerge from behind the cooking arbor. They have been singing and praying near the girls' quarters while each Godmother (*Naaikish*, They Who Direct [the girls]) begins to dress her charge from the left, the side of the heart and, therefore, the side closest to the Creator God. First comes the left moccasin, then the right. Next comes the soft buckskin skirt made heavy with its fringe, each strand of which ends in a handmade tin cone. The buckskin overblouse with its elaborate beading and more tin cones follows. Finally, the scarf is added, attached at the shoulders and falling down the back. Finishing touches are provided by jewelry: beaded work, porcupine quill work, turquoise, and silver (see fig. 7.1).[4] The proc-

FIGURE 7.1. Ceremonial girl.

ess is reversed and the girls are undressed from the right toward the end of the four days and nights of the public ritual.

As the final items (scratching stick, drinking tube, pollen bag, and sometimes a medicine bundle) are put in place on the dresses, the Singers come to the northwest side of the Ceremonial grounds and stand near the spectators. The Painters array themselves behind the Singers. The lead Singer begins to chant a prayer to the Powers.

Strong, young men assemble the poles for the holy lodge (*Isąą-nebikugha*, Old Age Home), inside which the actual ritual will take place. The 12 evergreen poles are arrayed in a circle, bases toward the center, behind the Singers. Grasses are tied to the tops of the four primary poles, the Grandfathers; they are then blessed with cattail pollen (*tełí, Typha latifolia*). The circle opens to the east and has a basket at its center. The Singers pray as they sprinkle pollen from the base to the tip of each Grandfather.

Prayers continue as the mothers, grandmothers, and Godmothers of the girls join the Singers. As the Singers chant to each Grandfather, the women "send forth a voice," a high-pitched ululation of reverent praise and pride. Meanwhile, the young men who are raising the poles pause four times, once for each cardinal direction, before bringing the poles to their full upright position.

The first Grandfather represents the moon and the stars; he stands in the east. The second Grandfather represents the sky elements (wind, rain, lightning, clouds, thunder, rainbows, mountains) from his position in the south. The third Grandfather represents the animals; he stands in the west. And the fourth Grandfather represents man, humanity; he stands in the north. "And since man is a frail being, it takes all the other three to hold him up." The four Grandfathers remind the people of creation.

CRF: Tell me about the beginning time. What happened then?

BS: When my grandparents started off these stories, they started it off with the word '*niaguchilaada*', when the world was being made. At that time there was nothing in the universe except - - for the Great Spirit God. And He - - *He* made the world in four days. First came Father Sun and Mother Earth; then the sky elements and Old Man Thunder and Little Boy Lightning. Next came animals and on the fourth day came man, the Apaches.

*Singing for Life*

When the 12 evergreen poles are in place and lashed together at their tops, a young man climbs up the frame to secure the lashing and then cover the top third with white canvas.[5] Other men cover the bottom two-thirds with freshly cut oak branches. Soon the holy lodge is completed on the outside. At the very top are tufts of boughs left on when most of the trunks were stripped of their branches and greenery. In the middle is the white canvas and, finally, the bottom is composed of tightly interwoven oak boughs.

> The main Ceremonial lodge is made of 12 evergreen fir tress. These poles . . . represent eternal life for us. And the 12 represent the 12 moons of the year. . . . The 4 main structure poles . . . correspond to the 4 directions of the universe, the 4 seasons, the 4 stages of life - - for in the natural world everything is based on 4. . . .
> These 12 poles that form the tipi, to us represents the balance of Power, goodness, generosity; all that is good in this world comes from this tipi, this holy lodge. . . . It says to us, "Come forth, my children, enter me. I am the home of generosity, pride, dignity, and hope." . . .
> The 4 Grandfathers hold up the universe for us. . . . These poles are heavy; it takes many men to lift them. . . . When these poles are being raised, the mothers of the daughters put their hands on the poles. And that signifies that the home is not a home without the woman; and even though this Ceremonial structure is going up, it also has to have the help of the woman even though she is physically not able to put it up.

The basket that had been in the center of the circle formed by the poles is now brought out in front of the holy lodge. It is a handmade basket containing gramma grass, pollen, eagle feathers, and tobacco.

> [The] basket represents the . . . heart of a people: it has all the important things. It has grass in there: food for all that we live on, the animals. The feathers represent eagle. . . . We get our authority to live as a people from Eagle. He is God's earth authority. That's why we wear the feathers . . . feathers are our authority and pride. . . . Tobacco is man's hope and his prayers . . . the basket is industriousness.

Activity intensifies as men labor to form a runway of fully boughed evergreen trees, four on the south and four on the north of the east-facing entry to the holy lodge. Other men begin to bring in freshly cut tules (*Scirpus lacutris*) to carpet in front of and inside the tipi. Simultaneously, a fire-pit is dug in the tipi's center.

> The fire-pit . . . signifies the woman and the poles represent the man. Men are the shield; they protect. The woman is the center, being protected. . . . Everything revolves around the tipi . . . it's a people. The cover is men. The fire is woman, warmth, love, and perpetual labor for a family to live. If there's no woman in here, there's no rhyme or reason to it. . . . Everything is male in that lodge except the women and the fire.

Outside the holy lodge the Singers are facing east and praying. The lead Singer slowly raises his left hand as he sings. His palm faces outward; painted on it, in red, is a sun with rays emanating outward to the four directions. The Godmothers lead the girls to their places on buckskin mats placed on the quilts and blankets on top of the tules just as the Singer completes his last song and his arm is fully extended. As if on command, the sun tops East Mountain, striking his upraised palm. It is a moment of breath-taking beauty, requiring an exquisite sense of timing and precise attention to minimal light cues as well as the manipulation of the songs so that the last line of the last song coincides with the sunrise.

> When men offer red paint to the sun - - red signifies male and men. That's the background of the sun. The two basic colors of the universe is yellow and red, yellow for women. . . . And the sun is the physical representation of God. . . . [As the sun rises] goodness washes over you.

The girls kneel, facing east, on their skin mats while a line forms to the southeast of them. The girls' mothers stand behind them holding burden baskets filled with food; their fathers and uncles stand to either side, inside the runway and directly in front of the holy lodge. Each Singer applies the yellow cattail pollen to the girl for whom he is singing: a tiny sprinkle to the east, south, west, north, thence from the west to the east (from the crown of her head to her forehead), to the south (on her right shoulder), to the north (on her left shoulder), and from south to north (across her nose). The movements form a cross, linking the four directions with the girl as the center.[6]

> Pollen is applied to them. They are blessed with pollen. Pollen is the color of yellow. The yellow color represents God's generosity. It also represents the south, from which the warm

*Singing for Life*

winds bring rain that a thirsty land might drink and bring forth its bounty of fruit and meat. And they are . . . blessed that they will be fruitful and bring forth strong sons that they will be mighty warriors . . . that they will bring forth strong daughters that will become the mothers of a warrior race; that they will perpetuate themselves in a good way, a holy way, with the Powers of the four directions.

The Singers step to the front of the line that has formed and are blessed by each of the girls, beginning with the one kneeling on the south and proceeding to the northernmost girl. Then the people in line pass before the girls. As the girls complete the blessing sequence for those kneeling in front of them, they are, in turn, blessed by the person's reaching into the pollen bag and repeating the sequence that the Singers had performed. Babies too small to move their own hands have them moved by the parent or relative bringing them through the line. Those who have specific complaints linger to rub some of the pollen on the afflicted area. Anyone who is sick or troubled will go through the line as will those who seek to remain well and partake of the blessings of God as mediated through the girls.

Singers and Godmothers keep a careful watch for signs of fatigue on the part of the girls, for there is still more strenuous activity to come. Sometimes the line is so long that not all waiting will be blessed in public. Those remaining will go to the homes (tents, arbors, and a tipi) behind the cooking arbor after the morning's public activities, there to be blessed privately (fig. 7.2).

The lead Singer motions away those still in line as the Godmothers assist the girls in going from their knees to their abdomens. Each girl lies face down with her head to the east as her Godmother presses and "molds" her into a fine, strong woman. The hair is smoothed over the girl's shoulders and back before molding begins: first the left shoulder, then the right; next the left and right sides of the back; the left hip and the right hip; the left then right thigh and calf; the left and right foot.

As the Godmothers near the feet, a man takes the basket, that had been present since the morning began, out to the east. While the Singers chant and the Godmothers ululate, the girls run along the north side of the dance arena, around the basket, and back on the south side of the arena. The basket is moved closer to the holy lodge three more times; and the running girls encircle it three more times.

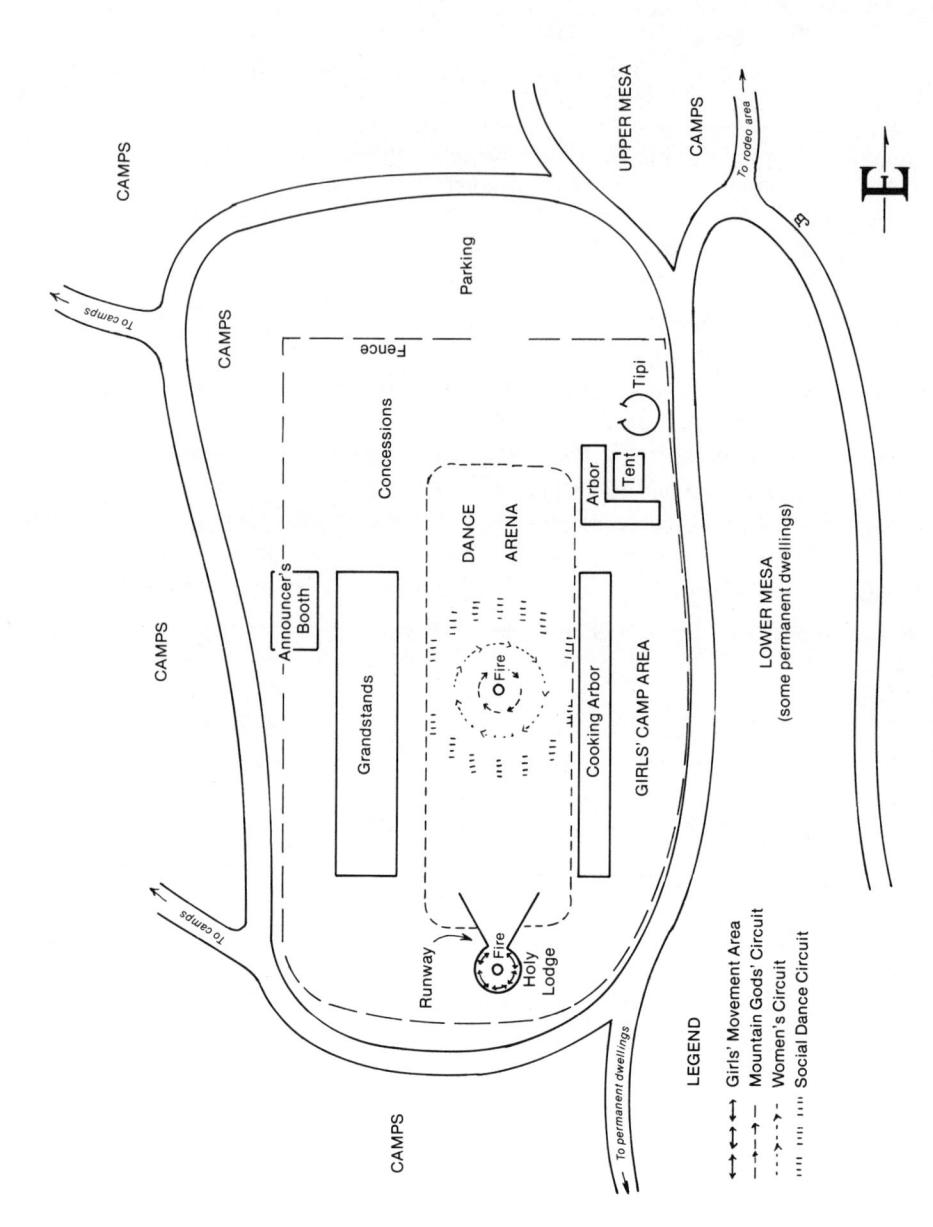

FIGURE 7.2. Ceremonial site plan.

## Singing for Life

The four runs around the basket symbolize the four cycles of life: infancy, childhood, adulthood, and, as the basket nears the Old Age Home in the west again, old age. As the primary characters in the ritual drama, the girls reenact the legendary journey of White Painted Woman who walked to the west as an old woman only to return from the east as a young woman once again.

At the conclusion of the fourth run the girls return to the entranceway of the holy lodge where their uncles or brothers invert the burden baskets, spilling tobacco, candy, piñons, fruit, and money over them.

The spilling from the baskets signals the end of the public rites and triggers massive give-aways by matrilineal members of the girls' families. Relatives throw candy, oranges, apples, and cigarettes from the beds of pickup trucks. People of all ages dash to pick up the gifts, for this is special food and tobacco that has been blessed.

While the assembled crowd, many of whom arrived with the sunrise, scampers for the distributed gifts, the girls return to their camp-out homes. There each girl's Godmother talks to her of sex and her responsibility for motherhood. The Singer gives his "daughter," as he will refer to the girl for the rest of her life, Indian bananas (*husk'ane, Yucca baccata*) and says, "Be fruitful all the days of your life; obtain food and not be lazy." He repeats this, and the feeding twice more. The fourth time, the Godmother feeds the girl; as she does so, she tells her, "May you bring forth in this world strong male children so they will protect your people."

Even before the Singer and Godmother finish, those who were not yet blessed form a line outside the camp-out home. At the conclusion of the feeding, they are admitted. Each kneels in front of the girl, who is sitting on a bed or a chair, and pollen blessings are exchanged.

The cooking arbor is also the scene of lines. Each girl's family has a fire in the arbor where food is cooked for all who come to the Ceremonial. A breakfast of fry bread and coffee is available; some families provide a meat, potato, and chili stew as well. In the camp-out homes, relatives and close friends eat traditional foods blessed by the Singer as well as bread, coffee, and stew.[7] Everyone who comes to a Ceremonial is fed all meals free. It is an embarrassment, and a rarity, to have the food run out before all have been fed. After breakfast participants and spectators alike rest at home;

some go to their year-round houses and others to their campsites on the hills and mesas near the Ceremonial grounds. After lunch is served, preparations are under way for the supper to be served around 6 P.M.

While Ceremonial participants rest in the afternoon, the spectators are entertained by contests. Some members of the audience of the ritual drama become performers in these events. An all-Indian rodeo, with competitors from many states, takes place on a mesa to the northeast of the Ceremonial grounds. Prizes are generous and points are earned for the annual all-around Indian cowboy championship.

> [We had] horse racing and gambling [hand-game] in the old days. - - - Government outlawed it. Now, rodeo takes its place.

Meanwhile, in the dance arena there are dance contests in the pan-Indian Powwow style.[8]

The mounting tension is almost tangible as darkness begins to descend and the huge bonfire is prepared and lit in the center of the dance arena. When the sun no longer colors the mountains and deserts to the west and when the fire is roaring, jingling noises can be heard from the east as the Mountain God dancers (*Gą'he*) prepare to enter the dance arena. Their Painter and his assistants have been busy for the past few hours praying, drumming, and chanting while the entire group of Mountain God dancers (*Baanaaich'isndé*)[9] has been painted and dressed.

The designs that appear on the Mountain God dancers are different each night. Since the men work hard at dancing and stay close to the fire so that they sweat even on cold nights, the design from one night doesn't last until the next. Any parts of the design remaining are simply painted over. While the same design is not repeated, the elements are combined in a different manner for each of the four nights. The combinations follow the precepts given long ago when the first Painters were given their dancers, songs, and symbols, as well as curing power. While the designs appear different to outsiders, they are said to be the "same thing" as the previous night. Thus the designs shown in figure 7.3 are said by Mescaleros to be the same; and, indeed, by making a horizontal cut through the center of 7.3a, 7.3b is produced.[10]

Each dance group is identifiable by its design set, distinctive

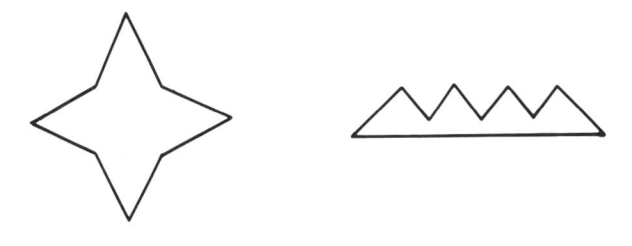

FIGURE 7.3. Two ceremonial body-painting designs.

sashes, and headdresses. The general costuming is the same—kilts, paint, head covering, headdresses, and red streamers with four eagle feathers attached and tied to each upper arm. There is no mistaking a Mountain God dancer or the group to which he belongs.

Each dancer wears an A-line wraparound buckskin kilt that is fringed and fitted with beaded or skin decorations as well as "jingles" cut and shaped from tin cans, which jingle each time the dancer moves. Worked leather belts, often with bells attached, and red sashes hold up the kilts. The mid-calf length buckskin moccasins[11] are decorated with bells either at the top or at the ankle. If there are no bells on the moccasins, leather straps with bells are worn around each leg.

A head covering of black fabric (canvas, heavy cotton, dyed buckskin, or heavy doubleknit), with round openings cut for each eye and the mouth, is topped by a bilaterally symmetrical headdress[12] made of yucca and wood. The headdress of each group member is the same and is painted with designs matching or repeating an element of the design painted on the dancers' bodies. Thus, with the exception of the palms of the hands, a dancer is completely covered with clothing or paint from the top of his head to the soles of his feet. He becomes the anonymous personification of a Mountain God (see fig. 7.4).

Usually there is a dance set (four Mountain God dancers and one or more clowns) for each girl, although at times two girls will share a set of dancers. Sharing is most apt to occur when the girls are sisters or first cousins.

The spectacle is awesome as the fully costumed Mountain God dancers converge on the dance arena, jingling rhythmically as they move, their headdresses piercing the darkness above them. The dancers pause from a trotting step just outside the dance arena. There the lead dancer gets the others in step by striking the sticks he carries in each hand against his thighs. The clown (Libayé) mimics each movement of the lead dancer, but always a bit late.

FIGURE 7.4. The Mountain God.

*Singing for Life*

All being in step, and all noises from the bells and the tin cones—as well as the strident note from the cow bell slapping against the clown's derrière—being in synchrony, the lead dancer moves his group into the dance arena. They raise their arms and sticks (see fig. 7.5a) as they approach the fire and emit a hooting sound resembling that of an owl or a turkey. They are said to be praying as they make this noise. Their movements and vocalizations are said to be "blessing the fire." When the lead dancer is within a few feet of the fire, he lowers his arms and sticks and bows his head before the line steps backward still facing the fire (see fig. 7.5b). The approach, hooting, lowering, and retreating sequence is repeated three times. On the fourth approach the dancers dip their bodies first to the left, then to the right as they approach the fire; they move so quickly in their four dips to each side that their arms seem like windmills. This time as they retreat the lead dancer again slaps the sticks on his thighs as he guides the group once around the fire to the south side of the dance arena. The blessing sequence is repeated again from here, thence from the west and north each time with one complete circuit of the fire between stops for the cardinal directions.

FIGURE 7.5. Arm positions —blessing sequence.

After the fire has been blessed, the group moves to the holy lodge where the sequence is repeated from each of the directions in order (east, south, west, north).

When the blessings are completed the Painter begins his drumming and chanting from a position in front of the holy lodge. The Mountain God dancers and their clown now dance with dramatic posturing, stamping, and gesturing around and around the bonfire, always moving in a clockwise direction. Even when there is no singing or drumming, they keep moving; they are never still the entire time they are in the dance arena.

As the Painter begins his drumming a large cardboard is placed on the ground in front of the benches where he and the chanting men sit. Young boys congregate around the cardboard carrying evergreen sticks they have gathered from near the holy lodge. They join the adult drummers and chanters by beating in rhythm with their sticks and, occasionally, also join in the singing of one of the choruses of a song. Once again, a part of the audience becomes performers.

The regular dancing of the Mountain Gods signals the women to join in the dancing as well. Their dance path is several feet away from the bonfire and the path of the Mountain Gods. Some of the first women to dance are the girls for whom the Ceremony is being held; they are accompanied by their Godmothers who dance in front of them. Their mothers and close female relatives dance behind them: ". . . while the men are dancing, the women dance around them. There again, we can't separate the male from the female in our religion."

The girls for whom the Ceremony is being held wear their Ceremonial attire. All other women wear everyday dress without jewelry that might make noise. Only the Mountain God dancers, the clowns, and the girls make noise in the dance area; those sounds are perceived as music. Added to the everyday dress is a shawl, a piece of fabric approximately two yards long that is worn folded in half lengthwise and draped over the shoulders in such a fashion that the hands are covered and the 12–14-inch fringe hangs down on the sides and in back. Only the women's legs move in performing the dance steps used; however, the execution of the steps moves the body toward, then away from, the fire; and that movement produces a swinging motion of the fringing on the shawls: it is said to be beautiful.

The girls make only a few circuits of the fire before retiring to their arbors to rest before their strenuous dancing begins. As they retire, other women begin to dance "in support" of the Mountain Gods. Mothers encourage their very young (four- and five-year-old) daughters to dance, too. The women dance in groups of matrilineally related kin. Women of all ages dance, although those who dance longest are those between 15 and 50.[13]

While the Mountain Gods and the women dancing in support of them hold the attention of the spectators, the girls are led into the holy lodge by their Godmothers. During the leading-in portion of

*Singing for Life*

the Ceremony, the girls are said to be inviting in life and magnanimity for their people and for themselves.

Cowhide dance mats are awaiting the girls around the inside periphery of the holy lodge. The Godmothers spread blankets for themselves and the girls to sit on while resting; it is here that they await the arrival of the Singers.

Before recounting the tribe's history through chants accompanied by the deer hoof rattles, the lead Singer offers smoke to the Powers. The other Singers follow his lead. As soon as the Singers begin to chant, the girls rise to dance.

Two dance steps are used by the girls. The more common one involves keeping the body rigid while only the feet move. By pivoting alternately on the balls and heels of their feet they take four "steps" to the left, then four to the right. The cowhide on which they dance is just wide enough to allow four lateral movements. They hold their arms in front of them by bending their elbows, raising their forearms, and making their hands form relaxed fists with the palms outward while the knuckles rest lightly on the shoulders. The position and step create movement of the girls' clothing and cause the tin cones to strike one another, adding another sound to that produced by the men's voices and the percussion of the rattles. The other dance step the girls use is designed as a rest; it, too, however, is strenuous. Again the body is held still while the feet move. With their hands on their hips and while standing in place, they kick one foot and then the other straight out in front. Between songs the Godmothers will massage the girls' shoulders, backs, or legs if it appears they are showing signs of fatigue. Alternating the two steps with short rest periods, the girls will dance for several hours while the Singers chant.

> They're dancing . . . it used to be buffalo hides but now it's beef hides. They are dancing on it, gliding. They glide back and forth on these hides, shuffling. The . . . men sing to them and tell them, "These sounds that you make on this hide are the songs of a people walking and living. Dance on this hide - - for it is your home. It is your food." The sound that it makes as a girl dances back and forth on it, it says, "This is the sound that a people will make on this earth. It is a pleasant sound, a good sound. Abide by it."

The girls dance while 64 songs are sung. During rest periods the Godmothers interpret the meaning of the Singers' "classical" language songs.[14]

The girls dance from about 10 P.M. to midnight before retiring to their camp-out homes. Social dancers replace the Mountain God dancers between 11 P.M. and midnight. Sometime between 2 A.M. and dawn the social dancers leave the dance arena. The first day ends.

### THE SECOND THROUGH FOURTH DAYS

There is no morning ritual on these days. Afternoons are filled with Powwow-style dance competitions and the rodeo.

After supper, but before the bonfire is lit for the Mountain God dancers, the war dancers appear in the Ceremonial arena. They carry rifles loaded with blanks or bows and arrows. Their hair is usually long, held in place with a plain headband. They wear loose shirts or are bare chested; each wears moccasins and a long G string, often over Levis. In the old days, I am told, they wore only buckskin and carried weapons. They danced in front of the girls' tipis to protect them. Now they dance in the dance arena and seemingly take delight in frightening the audience by aiming at the people with their arrows or shooting them with blanks, thus again giving the audience a performer role.

The bonfire, several feet in diameter, is lit at dusk in preparation for the Mountain God dancers and the social dancing that will follow them. Around 10 P.M. the girls will again dance for two hours or so in the holy lodge as the Singers continue their chanting recitation of tribal history, keeping track of the songs with sticks placed in a circle around the central fire-pit.

### THE FIFTH DAY

Since time is reckoned from sunrise to sunrise and since the fifth day's activities begin when the fourth day is almost complete, the activities are considered to be a part of the fourth day: this despite a fifth sunrise coming in the midst of the fourth day's final activities.[15] They may also be viewed and indeed are, as the beginning of the second four days when the girls will remain on the Ceremonial grounds with only close female relatives and their Godmother—when the public aspect of the ritual is over and the private aspect begins.

Again, people assemble before dawn for the final ritual activities just as they did for those on the first day. This time there are many people present for some of the social dancers have been there dancing all night, as was the custom in the old days. The girls' families distribute presents (cloth, dippers, knives, tobacco) to the dancers just as the sky begins to lighten. The presents are a tangible reminder of the endurance of the dancers and their dedication to tradition.[16]

*Singing for Life*

The jingling of the girls' dresses and the percussion from deer hoof rattles are also heard just before dawn on the fifth morning, for the girls have been dancing all night while the Singers sang and the Godmothers counseled.

> These girls have been dancing for four nights. On the fourth night they dance from when it gets dark to daylight with a break around midnight. It is a physical ordeal for them. But they must go through it.... It is a sacrifice they make ... their physical contribution that they make that a people can be strong and healthy.

On the previous three nights the lead Singer placed song tally sticks in a circle around the fire; this morning the sticks make a pathway (see fig. 7.6a), replicating the form of the holy lodge and its runway.[17] As the last stick is planted, the Singers rise, signaling the Godmothers to take the girls back to their living quarters where their hair and bodies will be washed in yucca-root suds, repeating the actions of the first day when the girls were cleansed and dressed. This ritual foreshadows activity which will take place at the end of the eighth day.

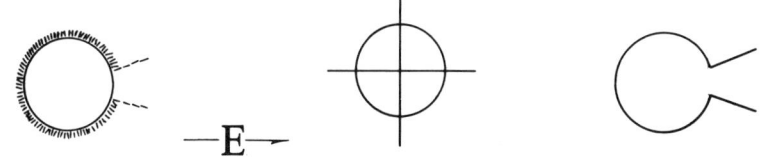

FIGURE 7.6. Tipi, runway, and counting sticks; depiction of the universe; tipi and runway.

All tules are taken out of the holy lodge and replaced with fresh ones. The folding chairs for the Singers are placed so they face east and are behind the girls, whereas previously they had faced west toward the girls.

Before the girls reappear in the holy lodge they will have their faces painted with white clay by the Singers. Their arms, from fingertips to elbows, and their legs, from thighs to feet, will also be painted.

> The girls' faces are painted white signifying that they have achieved; they have done their ordeal. They have lived four good days and they will be running. Running signifying a physical effort that they must do in order to prove themselves that they are worthy mothers.... That white paint is the sign of

143

> purity and of the Mother Earth. . . . They are called White Painted Woman, because white is the color of purity, these four days.

But before their final ordeal, that which was given form by the males must be destroyed by them.

The young man who had placed the white covering on the holy lodge once again shinnies up the poles to disengage the lashings and lower the covering. While he is working, other men on the ground take away the oak boughs that had covered the bottom of the lodge. Meanwhile, inside, the girls are being blessed and sung to. People crowd in, even though the poles are beginning to fall. As the last of the poles falls, save the Grandfathers, the girls are revealed sitting on the ground, each with her Singer and Godmother kneeling in front of her. People form lines in front of one or another of the girls; the Singers take seats to the left of the girl for whom they sang while the Godmothers stand to the right. The girls sit with their eyes downcast as the Singers bless each one in line; this time there is no hurry—all who so desire will be blessed. Rather than pollen, the blessing is performed with white clay and red ochre. Each Singer paints the faces of those in line a bit differently from the other Singers. Males are painted on the left side and females on the right side of their faces; each Singer uses his own marks. When all have been painted and blessed, each girl is led out of the holy lodge with an eagle feather by her Singer.

> Now they have been brought out of the tipi after the four days of religious functions. - - - - They have been brought out. They have been brought by an eagle feather. They tell them,
>> Four days you have walked your land and done good.
>> Now hold this eagle feather, the symbol of authority
>> And walk out of your home.
>> Go forth into the world.

The girls are escorted to a white buckskin that has been placed on the ground in front of the runway, now lined by their fathers and close male relatives. Four crescent moons, painted with colors evoking the directions and said also to represent life's stages, form the stepping-stones each girl walks on, left foot first, before her final run. As the girl under the tutelage of the lead Singer steps on the first crescent, the first song is sung; one additional song is sung for each of the other three crescents.

*Singing for Life*

>And she will be told,
>>Now you are entering the world.
>>You become an adult with responsibilities.
>>Now you are entering the world.
>>Behold yourself.
>>Walk in this world with honor and dignity.
>>Let no man speak of you in shame.
>>For you will become - -
>>The mother of a nation.

At the end of the final song, she is pushed off the buckskin by her Singer and Godmother. The other girls follow the first one by quickly stepping on each of the four crescents and, like her, running to the east around the same basket that was used on the first day's run.

>They are singing to them as [they are] running and they are telling them,
>>You will be running to the four corners of the universe:
>>To where the land meets the big water;
>>To where the sky meets the land;
>>To where the home of winter is;
>>To the home of rain.
>>Run this! Run!
>>Be strong!
>>For you are the mother of a people.

Three times the girls run around the basket; each time it is placed farther from the frame of the holy lodge (the four Grandfathers).[18] On the last run, each girl takes from the basket the eagle feather with which she was led into and out of the holy lodge, and, instead of returning to the holy lodge as she had on the three previous runs, she runs to her quarters behind the cooking arbor. Simultaneously, the four Grandfathers crash to the ground.

>During their last run they are running to their destiny; they are running into the hard world of adulthood . . . the hard world of a hunting world, a war world. . . . When the last run is completed, food will be thrown out that a people might be fruitful and multiply to many.

What began five mornings ago with the erection of a holy lodge and the distribution of food, ends with the destruction of the holy lodge and the distribution of food. In between have been goodness, holiness, the affirmation of the essential rightness of the world, and the place of humans in it. As the last of the Dance Songs states,

In your country
In your plains and green mountains
You have lived four days
In holiness and goodness.

In your country
In your plains and green mountains
You have existed four days
In holiness and goodness.

In your country
In your plains and green mountains
You have walked four days
In holiness and goodness.

In your country
In your plains and green mountains
You have danced four days
In holiness and goodness.

Naaishá.
I have done this.
Here
It ends.

## DISCUSSION

A Puberty Ceremony, by definition, is a ritual recognition of sexual maturity. Were it only that, it might be exotic, but would be rather uninformative. Among the Mescalero, however, the physical event of puberty forms a nucleus around which many attributes—believed to be essential for describing and defining what constitutes Mescalero Apache ethnicity—coalesce. Native exegesis, such as that provided by Bernard Second, is necessary for insight into the meaning of the Ceremonial, but is insufficient for outsiders to understand fully the ramifications of the total event. But modesty prevents Mr. Second from stating what becomes obvious through observations spanning several years: the Singer orchestrates the various segments that form the recognizable society.

The Ceremony may be thought of as possessing several layers; each layer is complete in itself, each has its own integrity. Yet recognition of the totality as a Ceremony depends upon the layers being in proper relationship to each other. The Singer provides the inte-

*Singing for Life*

grative force to bring together those things that allow the label "Mescalero Apache."

> . . . the four laws of our people are honesty, generosity, pride, and bravery. And a great people, they cannot be great if they have no sense of generosity about them. For it is out of generosity that a man sees the world and what a man is worth in this world. He cannot be proud if he is not generous, as he has nothing to be proud for and brave for. He cannot be honest, for honesty has no basis if it is without generosity. So generosity, at the end, is the most important law that we have. It is the value we have cherished from the day we became a people to today.

And generosity is certainly in evidence at the Ceremonial, from the massive food give-aways through the altruistic self-sacrifice of the girls, as they run for strength and endurance for their tribe, to the generosity of the Creator God.

The laws and values rest upon a layer I call the base metaphor; this layer is characterized by the number 4, balance, circularity, directionality, and sound/silence.

The Singer integrates the layers through his recitations of tribal history; in song, explicitly and implicitly, he forges the union which ensures that Mescalero Apache life will continue as it has in the past. This is achieved through attention to laws, values, and the underlying principles that permeate and define life. The girls, who impersonate White Painted Woman in the ritual enactment of her life-giving mysteries, are the vehicles through which life is continued; therefore, the songs are directed to them as audience, *not* to the spectators.

Directionality seems to have primacy in Mescalero Apache life. It underlies both circularity and the number 4. Following "the natural order of the universe," we go from east to south to west to north to east, and so forth, thus describing a circle with four named points.[19] As the girls bless themselves and others, they sprinkle pollen, following the directional circuit, and create patterns of circles within which are contained crosses, thus duplicating the visual form of the base metaphor. The erection of the holy lodge, a tipi, with its four Grandfathers, one for each direction, again underscores the importance of the cardinal directions in describing a circle and orienting the Ceremony.

Directionality gives rise to both the concept of "four" and its related concept of balance. Together the latter two may be said to establish the harmony essential to existence. The Creator God created the world in four days; examination of the creation sequence reveals that not only did he *call* entities into being, but also that balance was present. Two days were devoted to the creation of the inanimate (sun, earth, sky elements, and earth elements) and two days to the animate beings (winged insects, crawling things, four-legged animals, humankind). Four sets of entities occur within each of the two sequences, as balance is further present in the juxtaposition of the above and the below.

Creation is recapitulated in the holy lodge as the Singers sing the first night to the first Grandfather and what he represents, the second night to the second Grandfather, and so on. The singing is structured to bring together male principles (the structure itself, the dancing hides, the Singers) with female principles (the fire-pit, Godmothers, those impersonating White Painted Woman)—balance again. Within the holy lodge, then, is the visual and verbal manifestation of balance and four. It is a visual and oral transformation of the base metaphor.

Both concepts are given further visibility in the costuming of the portrayers of both White Painted Woman and the Mountain Gods. The girls' costumes consist of an overblouse and a skirt. Each item of clothing has two areas, front and back, on which decorations are placed. Thus, there are four fields; blouse front, blouse back, skirt front, skirt back. The beaded designs balance: that is, what appears as decoration over the left shoulder will also appear over the right shoulder. What is painted on one side of a girl's face will be painted on the other side. Similarly, the designs on the moccasins balance each other and, most of the time, they are composed of four elements. When not composed of four elements, balancing each other in sets of two, the design is composed of two elements, each of which is seen to balance the other.

The Mountain Gods provide an even more striking reminder of the importance of balance and the number 4. A Mountain God is quadrilaterally symmetrical both above and below the waist. The design, in evidence by facing him forward and dividing his painted areas on both midsagittal and lateral planes, can be replicated four times to reconstruct his image front and back. Likewise, by so dividing his costume from the waist down, he can again be seen to present a quadrilaterally symmetrical picture. His back is perceived as

*Singing for Life*

being in balance with his front, as each side of his front and back balance each other. Each of his arms balances the other. His sash, headdress, and even his kilt and moccasins present a balanced picture. It is number and arrangement that create this balance rather than area, just as it was number and taxonomic equivalence that provided the balance in the creation.

The basket around which the girls run contains four items: grass, pollen, tobacco, and eagle feathers. Both grass and pollen are earth items while feathers and tobacco are sky items: that is, they mediate between the below and the above in that both eagle and tobacco are viewed as communication channels to the Powers. Thus, the four items in the basket are seen as being in balance and hence contributing to the harmony and rightness of the world.

The girls take four steps on the painted skin before running around the basket. Each step represents a stage of life with the first (infancy) and the last (old age) balancing the two in the middle (childhood and adulthood). Infancy and old age are seen as times of dependence when one must rely on others to fulfill needs and often to help one move about. Childhood and adulthood, in contrast, are times of free movement, independence, and self-reliance.[20]

Eight evergreen trees balance each other as four line each side of the runway/entrance for the holy lodge. The lodge itself is balanced with the four powerful Grandfather poles balancing the other eight poles.

The Ceremony abounds in additional examples of four and balance: activity spans four days with the two middle days presenting the "same" picture and the two days on either end balancing each other, partially by reversal. Four varieties of dance are performed with the dancing of the Mountain Gods (and the women dancing in their support) balancing that of the girls; the two kinds of social dancing provide balance to the two kinds of ritual dancing. Even the physical site is balanced in that the dance arena for the girls is balanced by the dance arena for the other dancers; and the girls' camp area balances the general camp area.

While directionality, four, and balance permeate the entire system, the other set of components, circularity and sound/silence, are less apparent. Of the latter two, circularity is more easily recognized and has already been discussed in regard to the cardinal directions.

Dancing provides the most obvious instance of circularity during the ritual drama. The primary dance pattern is circular and follows a "sunwise" circuit, clockwise, beginning in the east.

Traditional dwellings (tipis, arbors) are also circular. Today the rectangular pattern of a commercial tent is often appended to a more traditional camp-out home. But all ritual activity occurs either in a traditional, circular structure or outside in the world that is also perceived as being circular.

Perhaps the most pervasive aspect of circularity during the Ceremonial is time—cyclic and endlessly circular. Human existence has been so short in terms of time in general that we are unable to comprehend fully the magnitude of the wheel of time, it is believed. The girls provide a visual reminder of the circularity of time by running around the basket four times to symbolize infancy, childhood, womanhood, and old age. Simultaneously, this indicates human existence through time and time's ever constant cycle. Although each girl will die, she allows the tribe to live through her and her offspring: the tribe endures through the cycling of time as White Painted Woman herself endures by ever cycling from east to west and by ever appearing as an aspect of each girl participating in the ritual. The cyclical nature of time is said to be represented through the daily circuit of the sun, from which is taken the "proper" movement while in the holy lodge, or any ceremonial structure where entrance is from the east. Movement should properly follow the sun's circuit: east, south, west, north.

Circularity is engendered and maintained by following the "natural" order. Even salt sprinkled on food during the meals at Ceremonial time is distributed in a circular, clockwise motion.

Time is collapsed into symbols during the Ceremony. The girls are both symbol and icon of White Painted Woman. As it was with her in the beginning of time, so now it is with the girls in contemporary time. White Painted Woman had twin warrior sons who saved the people from all manner of tragedies; the girls are exhorted to be good mothers and bring forth strong sons, sons who will be the future saviors of the tribe. The girls' four days of exemplary existence and their journey through the four stages of life are emblematic of White Painted Woman's journey through the eons.

Of all the components of the base metaphor, sound/silence is the least accessible and the most difficult to discuss. During the Girls' Puberty Ceremony many distinctions are made between sound and its absence. In general, sound is for the Powers while silence is for humans during ritual times.

## Singing for Life

In words and in silence there is power. The Creator called the world into existence through the power of words. The Creator God communicates through the power of thought in dreams. People can utilize this channel through *'inch'in'di* [roughly, 'communicating without words']. *'Inch'in'di* characterizes the conversations of old friends or those married a long time who seem to "read" each other's minds without verbalization. It also describes the communication between humans and animals. To think a thought during *'inch'in'di* is often all that is necessary for action to occur, so it is not surprising to find great importance attached to the sound/silence continuum.

Mountain Gods vocalize only in prayer; their costumes "speak" for them. The rhythmic sounds produced by their movements are thought of as music; beautiful structured sounds are produced by the sticks they carry, the tin cones on their costumes, and their movements while dancing. In contrast the clown produces noise, albeit holy noise, by his clanking cowbell. His costume has few or no jingling bells or tin cones. Because he is so vastly powerful, however, he automatically makes a powerful statement; he is so powerful that he need not produce structured sounds as must the Mountain Gods. His communication is also through *'inch'in'di*.

Women dancing in support of the Mountain Gods produce no sound. Even noisy jewelry is removed before they dance. Their dance steps, in contrast to those of the Mountain Gods and the girls, are executed in silence. Women make their statement through their presence and their participation. In the realm of ritual sound/silence, the place of humans is to be silent while Power's is to invoke sound.

The most holy ones present, save the clowns, are the girls impersonating White Painted Woman. Even when they are not dancing, their slightest movement produces organized sounds perceived almost as music. But again the sound is holy sound; the girls themselves speak little in public. The Power filling them is responsible for the noise; they, as humans, remain almost completely silent, as is proper when a human confronts Power.

Those who "speak" the most during the Ceremonial are the Singers. Their form of "speech" is chanting and percussion, both of which are music; music, by this contexting, is sacred. Whether it is the music of the Painters, the Mountain Gods, the costumes, or the Singers, it is holy and beautiful.

Sounds produced by the Mountain Gods' hooting and the Godmothers' ululations are sacred prayer. When the Godmothers speak, they do so only in whispers and only to individual girls. And while in their costumes, the Mountain God impersonators do not speak, nor are they spoken to. It is not necessary to verbalize to Power.

Once uttered, words seem almost to take on a life of their own. Bad words, or thoughts, are avoided because your "words can come back on you." Good words and thoughts can also come back on you. Hence strategic manipulation of the sound/silence continuum during the Ceremony is another way of creating, or recreating, the inherent goodness, beauty, balance, and harmony of the world through the power of words, thoughts, and sounds as sanctified by uncounted repetitions through the generations and travels of the people.

Orally, aurally, visually, and kinesically a metaphor is proposed that links the Mescalero Apache people to their beginnings and to their future. On a very basic level the message is a sexual one, but it is sex in perspective and with respect for all life. As Bernard Second explicitly states:

> The four Grandfathers are the home; in the center is the hearth, the woman: this is completion. Neither is anything without the other. That is what our life is about.

The Ceremony accomplishes much more than the bringing together of the two biological elements; the Ceremony orders life as well.

The Ceremony is high context.

> A high-context communication or message is one in which most of the information is either in the physical context or internalized in the person, while very little is in the coded, explicit, transmitted part of the message.... The level of context determines everything about the nature of the communication and is the foundation on which all subsequent behavior rests (including symbolic behavior) (Hall 1977:91–92).

Observers not familiar with Apache culture easily misinterpret intended communications. Misattribution is exacerbated by local newspapers referring to the girls as "debutantes" and the Ceremony as a "Rain Dance," or the dancing of the Mountain Gods as a "Devil Dance."

The Ceremony can be appreciated by those who do not know the code, since the dancing alone is spectacular in form, movement, use of time and space, and setting. But in order to understand fully the cultural performance with its manifold messages, one needs to know the presuppositions which give rise to the performative statements being made. These presuppositions, or the base metaphor, are given oral, aural, visual, and kinesic currency during the Ceremony so that the code can be perceived by astute observers. The keys to the code are presented repeatedly.

Turner (1967:19–20, 93–111; 1969), working from Ndembu native exegesis and building upon van Gennep's (1960) tripartite schema, developed an elegant model termed "the ritual process" wherein the subject(s) of a ritual event passed through states of separation, liminality, and reincorporation (cf. Turner 1969:94) to emerge into a new status. Before having spent a sustained time in the field, I believed the Mescalero Apache data confirmed Turner's expansion of van Gennep. Accepting native exegesis, I must conclude that the Ceremony is a rite of confirmation and a rite of intensification (Chapple and Coon 1942). This does not deny that it occurs at a life crisis; but a girl is said to *be* a woman immediately upon menstruation. She does not *become* a woman through the Ceremony; she already *is* one. Girls become women whether or not they have a Ceremony. It is possible to have a Ceremony several years after the initial menses, since a Ceremony makes one a better woman.[21]

My data suggest that a ritual drama image works better than does a rite of passage. Girls are characters in a drama—a life-giving drama. Costuming and behavior contribute to the message that a Mescalero Apache is good, kind, generous, proud, brave, and dignified. One gives of oneself by playing a demanding role for the betterment of the group. And the roles are indeed demanding for all participants: for the girls through a physical ordeal; for the Singers through prodigious feats of memory and performance; for the families through resource sharing,[22] to say nothing of the energy expended in food preparation; for the Painters and dancers who maintain a state of ritual purity during the four days and nights; and for the audience whose focused energies are essential whether as "good thinkers," partakers of the blessings, fearful targets of the war dancers, or as vital life forces in social dancing.

Rather than a rite of passage, then, it seems more accurate to consider the Ceremony a rite of confirmation and a rite of intensification. It is a rite of confirmation in that the main characters are already women—menstruation has made them so while the Ceremony publicly confirms the status of woman. It is a rite of intensification in that participants are viewed as having the potential of being better women for having experienced the good, holy, and proper and for having fully learned the vital importance of the woman's role: to become a mother and thereby perpetuate the people. Through song the participants are shown their relationship to the first woman; their role is sanctified through time and publicly acknowledged. Each learns the enormous power she controls through the proper use of her body.

The primary participants are never in a liminal state; they are children until the onset of menstruation when they become women. While impersonating White Painted Woman in the Ceremony, they are enacting a role. A girl does not become White Painted Woman; the girl *is* White Painted Woman, as is any woman who allows her body to be the vessel through which her people are continued. She does become infused with White Painted Woman's healing power while she impersonates her during the four days of the public Ceremony and the four days of the private one. As Schechner (1977:2) states, "Theatrical techniques center on transformation." This obtains whether the theatre is in an urban center or a Southwestern mesa. The girls comport themselves well not because their faces will wrinkle prematurely if they smile [this is just-so logic], but because they are playing a character who was/is omniscient—White Painted Woman knew the result/end—and so need not worry or become distraught. Calmness characterized her. For the course of the drama the girls are transformed into White Painted Woman by playing her part.

Similarly, a man in a costume is not the Mountain God he plays. Each character is an icon of the supernatural being and each is temporarily infused with the power of the Powers. The actions each displays were determined in the beginnings by the actions of the first Mountain Gods and the real White Painted Woman. But the contemporary messages are every bit as arresting as were the original ones. The Ceremony states, "We are a proud, generous, dignified, and holy people. We have plumbed the structure of the universe and live in harmony with it. We demonstrate this to ourselves, the Powers, and to you, the audience, through our Ceremony."

In a very literal sense, then, as long as there is the Ceremony, there will be the Mescalero Apache people, Ndé. The Ceremony can occur only when the people live right, operate by and understand their philosophical system, and have respect for the Creator and all Power.

The Ceremonial activities constitute a cultural performance directed to two groups simultaneously: themselves and their audience

## Singing for Life

of outsiders. If cultural performances do, indeed, communicate not only what the essentials of being Mescalero Apache are but also about other aspects of culture as Bauman (1976) indicates for a variety of cultural situations, then we can reasonably expect to find manifestations of these messages in other areas of social life as well. They abound at Mescalero. The stress on activities occurring in their appointed spaces in the Ceremony is evident daily in adult and children's activities.[23] The politeness-decorum system lays stress on not wasting words: this leads to an economy of speech that strikes outsiders as being conversation punctuated by silences. To a Mescalero it is conversation punctuated by time for reflection, framing the next statement, being sure that the previous speaker is finished, and showing proper respect for language. Formal meetings are arranged into four spatially distinct sections; speeches have four parts. When entering a tipi, even one raised alongside a house to provide guest quarters, a polite person always makes a sunwise circuit to her/his place.

Thus ritual—even a complex, many-day ritual—economically provides insight into the workings of everyday life and provides a template for organizing that life. When the ritual is cast in the form of a drama, individual society members have the opportunity to become personally involved in the affirmation of life as it should be. No matter what terms are used to describe this particular series of events, a rite of passage, of confirmation, or affirmation, the activities are seen by Mescaleros as being the essence of their uniqueness as a people.

As a ritual drama, the Mescalero Apache Girls' Puberty Ceremony celebrates (and ensures the perpetuation of) the existence of the Mescalero people through the balanced juxtaposition of the female and male forces that are seen to exist in the world. Simultaneously, the ritual dramatizes the essential rightness of life by its reaffirmation through chants, dances, music, use of space, and sharing of food. Concomitantly, the rules for proper existence and the ordering of the universe are given form. The daily social order is legitimized through its recreation in the Ceremony. Girls learn how to be better women by playing the part of the "perfect woman." The society is presented with a complex drama reinforcing ethnicity.[24] Mescalero Apache life is dissected, explained, reaffirmed, and celebrated. In both literal and figurative senses, the Singer is singing for life.

# NOTES

1. Intensive fieldwork from September 1974 through September 1975 was supported by the Whitney M. Young, Jr. Memorial Foundation and the Mescalero Apache Tribe. Time to think and write was made possible by Dr. Douglas Schwartz and a Weatherhead Resident Fellowship at the School of American Research. Grateful acknowledgment is tendered to all.

2. All quotes are from field notes and tapes made with the cooperation of Bernard Second, my friend and "brother," a holy man and one of only five Mescalero Apache Singers. All were made at Mescalero, New Mexico at various times between 1974 and 1978. The 1976 material was recorded in Washington, D.C., and Harpers Ferry, West Virginia. The Harpers Ferry material was "elicited" by slides, when Bernard Second and I presented a seminar to National Park Service employees and townspeople utilizing slides I'd made of Ceremonials. Those slides provided the visual stimulation for his extemporaneous commentary, which I recorded. Material gathered using standard field methodology is indicated by being preceded by my question; this style of reporting is what Barbara Tedlock termed "dialogic anthropology."

Permission to present the material contained in this chapter has been granted by Mr. Second who has followed its progress from idea through finished product. However, I retain responsibility for any errors.

In the quoted material ellipses [. . .] indicate omissions while dashes [ - - - - ] indicate pauses. Each dash approximates one second of time.

The orthography used for Mescalero Apache words is that approved by the Mescalero Tribal Language Committee in 1975. It corresponds to Hoijer's (1938) symbols as follows:

| Hoijer | Language Committee | Hoijer | Language Committee |
|---|---|---|---|
| a | a | c' | ts' |
| a· | aa | ɬ | ł |
| e | e | l | l |
| e· | ee | λ | dl |
| i | i | ƛ | tl |
| i· | ii | ƛ' | tl' |
| o | u | y | y |
| o· | uu | š | sh |
| b | b | ž | zh |
| m | m | ǯ | j |
| t | t | č | ch |
| d | d | č' | ch' |
| t' | t' | k | k |
| ⁿd | nd | g | g |
| n | n | k' | k' |
| s | s | x } h } | h |
| z | z | | |
| ʒ | dz | γ | gh |
| c | ts | ' | ' |

3. I use "transformation" in its geometric sense (see Goffman 1974:41 and Basso 1979:13, 97). The term should not be equated with its use by structural anthropologists after Lévi-Strauss or by those linguists who follow Chomsky.

The base metaphor concept is given extended treatment in my dissertation (Farrer 1977).

*Singing for Life*

I am indebted to Leanne Hinton, who pointed out to me that the drawing I received depicting the universe (see fig. 7.6b) is a visual representation of the base metaphor. Perhaps it is this conception of the structure of the universe that is the genesis of the base metaphor. But regardless of which preceded which, the depiction inherently encompasses circularity, balance, four, and directionality. The sound/silence component is, I believe, analytically demonstrable; however, my data are insufficient to demonstrate sound/silence as a primary component of the base metaphor.

4. Figures were prepared by Richard W. Lang, staff archaeologist, at the School of American Research. His interest in the Ceremony and in rendering accurate representations are most appreciated.

5. The first Grandfather, the east pole, has a long rope secured to it immediately below the greenery at its top. As the pole is raised, a man pulls the rope taut. When the four Grandfathers are upright, they are pulled in, one at a time, until they lean against the east one. They are fastened together by throwing and wrapping the rope. The process continues for all 12 poles. Finally, a young man climbs the tipi frame both to tighten and check the lashing and to attach and secure the fabric cover.

6. Note that this produces another rendering of figure 7.6b.

7. Traditional foods eaten at this time include mesquite beans (*Prosopis glandulosa*), Indian bananas, mescal (*Agave parryi* or *A. neomexicana*), various wild berries and seeds, nuts, dried meat, and the flowers from Spanish bayonet (*Yucca elata*). It is as though there were an intermission in the performance of the ritual drama. Yet, it is also a logical extension of it, since mothers, including White Painted Woman who the girls represent, not only give life, but sustain it as well.

Preparations for lunch begin shortly after breakfast is served. The girls' tipis are used primarily for food storage and preparation prior to cooking while the tents and arbors are living areas; some final food preparation also takes place in the family arbors, although most of it is done in the large cooking arbor. There stews are cooked in new 20, 30, or 40-gallon trash cans that are placed in fires, next to them, or on grates over them. Male family members of the girls butcher cattle daily to provide the meat. Fry bread browns in bubbling lard inside cast iron pots on the fires. While some women tend to the cooking fires, others prepare salads in the tipis and family arbors.

Lunch and supper menus are the same: meat, potato, and chili stew; salad (usually potato or macaroni—occasionally tossed); fry bread; beans (pinto, rarely mesquite); coffee; Kool-Aid; fruit, either fresh (watermelon, apples, oranges) or canned (fruit cocktail or peaches). People are served as many times as they choose to be; but, since portions are generous, seconds are seldom sought other than for fry bread, coffee, or Kool-Aid. Sometimes people ask for, and receive, raw meat. They take it to individual campsites where they cook and eat it.

8. That is, straight dance and fancy war dance categories for men, buckskin and cloth dress categories for women as well as a junior (9–15 years) division, a tiny tot (1–8 years) division, and a division for men and women over 50. Dance prizes range from a minimum of $20 to a maximum of $200 (1975 levels). The master-of-ceremonies as well as the head singer and his drum and chant group are usually invited from other areas—most often the Plains.

9. Collectively their formal term is *Baanaaich'ishndé*; colloquially, they are termed *Gą'he*. An individual dancer is referred to as *Gą'hi* colloquially even though each dancer has his own individual term. In order from the lead dancer back to the clown their names are as follows: *Gą'hidziłihitlin*, *Gąhidziłigan*, *Gąhidziłitsulin*, *Gą'hidziłchilin*, *Łibayé*. *Łibayé*, the clown, is said to be the most holy, although he is the youngest and always trails the others in dance formations during the Ceremony.

10. It is interesting to note that both of these figures, as well as most of the others

157

painted on the Mountain Gods, can be generated from the depiction of the universe in figure 7.6b. Paint is first applied to the lead dancer, the first one in line. He forms a living template from which the other dancers are painted. On the one evening I was allowed to watch the painting, each man was painted with a yellow four-pointed star on a green field over his heart and a green crescent moon on a yellow field over his right pectoral. The back of the body was painted to represent a mirror image of the front. The front of the right arm was painted with a green lightning bolt on a yellow field that extended to the back of the arm. The left arm echoed the right with a yellow lightning bolt on a green field. I was not allowed to watch the painting of the clown. It is this group of Mountain God dancers that most people will say is painted "wrong" since the colors used are other than black and white; also, it is to be noted that these dancers cannot be bisected quadrilaterally—theirs is a bilateral symmetry.

11. A turned-up toe, or toe guard, on the moccasins indicates that the wearer is Chiricahua; the Mescaleros have no protrusions on their moccasins.

12. The elaborate headdress with its "horns," as the upright projections are sometimes called, gives rise to the English colloquial names for the Mountain God dancers: horn (var. horned) or crown dancers.

13. These dances are discussed in detail elsewhere (Farrer 1978).

14. According to Bernard Second, "The real stories are told in classical language and you have to stop and explain the language. The classical language is full of allusion so that each word stands for a series of related concepts and it needs strict interpretation. The classical language is the root words of my language. Even a girl who speaks good Apache . . . has to have it interpreted; that's what that woman [the Godmother] is there for: my job is to sing - - *she* interprets and tells them what I'm singing."

Singers train the Godmothers in terms of verbal instructions and how to dress the girls. Physical movements (for example, the molding) learned by observation and interpretation are transmitted from a woman to woman, from a Godmother to her apprentice, the woman who assists her during a Ceremony. Most often, the apprentice is a daughter or niece of the Godmother.

15. These are five days of ritual time. And, since time and space are collapsed in ritual drama, time is both here/now and then/ago while the space in which the drama occurs is both of this and the other world. Thus, days can be, and often are, cancelled. If, for instance, it rains during the day and the Ceremonial grounds become a sea of mud, the evening's activities will be postponed until the next evening. Or, if the sun does not visibly rise, due to fog, rain, or overcast conditions, on one of the days when it must wash over the girls, that day will be cancelled. The Ceremony consists of four full days of ritual events regardless of the number of times the earth spins around. Since days are reckoned by sunrises, there can be no day unless the sun rises over East Mountain; at least, there is no ritual day. On occasion, due to rains, days have been cancelled when people return to their jobs in the midst of the Ceremonial; when the weather is right again, they go to the Ceremonial grounds once again to resume the ritual events.

16. In the old days the men would pay the women for the honor of dancing with them all night; payment was money, a shawl, a blanket, or even a horse. As one old man said, "It was the gentlemanly thing to do."

17. The tally sticks and the fire form a variant of the depiction of the universe: the pattern shown in figure 7.6c rather than that in 7.6b.

18. On this final day, however, the basket is placed by a woman rather than by a man as on the first day.

19. It is worth noting that while the Apache directional system generates a circle, the Anglo-American system of north-south and east-west generates a grid.

## Singing for Life

20. This provides at least a partial understanding of the freedom accorded Mescalero Apache children. They are free to choose with whom they will live (usually a mother's sister if not mother herself), whether or not they will behave as is socially acceptable, and so on. They are at a time of life when they are expected to be responsible for their own behavior.

21. In the summer of 1977 a young woman, several years past initial menses, requested and had a full, but private, Ceremony. She felt that she was not behaving properly, a situation she attributed to her not believing in the Ceremonial when she was younger and having refused to participate in it. She felt that, having attained a measure of wisdom and having seen a bit of the world, her earlier judgment was incorrect. In order to put her life in balance and to allow her better self to emerge, she felt a Ceremony was in order.

22. In 1974 a Ceremony cost a minimum of $1500. This is a prodigious amount of money in an economy where most workers earn only slightly more than minimum wage.

23. For a detailed look at spatial, kinesic, verbal, and nonverbal manifestations of the messages sent in the Ceremony, see Farrer (1977).

24. I am indebted to Norman Whitten, Jr., for suggesting I consider ethnicity within the Ceremonial.

# 8
# Ritual Drama in the Navajo House Blessing Ceremony

### CHARLOTTE J. FRISBIE
*Department of Anthropology*
*Southern Illinois University at Edwardsville*

*INTRODUCTION*

The Navajo House Blessing Ceremony, *hooghan da'ashdlishígíí*, traditionally is held to bless newly constructed dwellings or those about to be reinhabited. As such, it is one of several ceremonies belonging to the Blessingway, *Hózhǫ́ǫ́jí*, which is viewed as the cornerstone and backbone of Navajo religion.

Unlike the curing ceremonials (Holyway, Ghostway, or Lifeway), Blessingway is prophylactic or preventive in nature. It is held to invoke positive blessings and simultaneously to avert potential misfortunes. As such, it ensures peace, harmony, good luck, health, success, order, good fortune, and general well-being for the People, their relatives, flocks, and other possessions, and by extension, the whole tribe. Variously described as a one-, two-, or four-night ceremony, Blessingway includes the ritual components of hogan consecration, bathing, body blessing, breathing in the dawn, myth, song (all night on the last night), prayer, and sometimes, dry painting.

Kluckhohn and Wyman (1940:184-85) classified Blessingway as including five possibilities distinguished by differences in legends and songs: Talking God Blessingway, Enemy Monster Blessingway, Chief Blessingway, Mountain Peak Blessingway, and Game Way Blessingway. Related to Blessingway, in a manner perhaps best described as a derived subceremony are the Kinaaldá (Girls' Puberty Ceremony), the House Blessing Ceremony, the traditional wedding, and the seemingly obsolete Seed Blessing and Rain ceremonies. In addition to the uses suggested by these taxonomic labels, Blessingway serves to bless departing and returning travelers and members of the Armed Services, pregnant women before delivery, ceremonial paraphernalia, newly trained ceremonial practitioners, and livestock. It can also be used to counteract bad dreams, remove contamination of the dead from the living, and for a multitude of other purposes, such as to locate lost children. Finally, Blessingway, either in whole or part, is added to curing ceremonials to negate performance errors or omissions which may have occurred.

Blessingway has been the subject of comment by many Navajo scholars through time, including Aberle, Adair, Bailey, Brugge, Coolidge, E. Curtis, N. Curtis, Fishler, the Franciscan Fathers, Frisbie, Gill, Haile, Hill, Hoijer, Klah, Kluckhohn, Lamphere, Leighton and Leighton, Matthews, McAllester, Mindeleff, Newcomb, Ostermann, Reichard, Sapir, Schevill, Stephen, Tozzer, Wheelwright, Witherspoon, and Wyman. Among their perspectives have been the questions of origin; form, use, and function; relationship to the rest of Navajo religion; classification of internal variants and native taxonomies; description of specific subceremonies; analysis of specific songs, myths, and prayers from a variety of theoretical perspectives; and analysis of the meaning of Blessingway's central concepts, $sq'ah\ naaghéi, bik'eh\ hózhǫ́ǫ́$.[1]

The main reference, however, is Wyman (1970b). This source provides a scholarly introduction and analysis of the meaning and use of Blessingway, deities involved, mythology, dry paintings, and ceremonial procedures. A major portion of the study is devoted to annotated presentations of three versions of the Blessingway myth recorded by the eminent Father Berard Haile, O.F.M., from Slim Curly, Frank Mitchell, and River Junction Curly. The myths include a great variety of Blessingway songs and prayers, and since the Navajo texts are available to serious scholars (Wyman 1970b:xxvii),

## Ritual Drama in the Navajo House Blessing Ceremony

the work continues to represent a challenge to all interested in the ceremony.

Since the publication of this work, there have been only a few publications which advance Blessingway studies. One which will undoubtedly prove to be of importance to Navajo scholars, once it becomes more accessible, is Gill's (1974) dissertation on Navajo prayers. This theoretical work is based on an analysis of published and unpublished ceremonial prayers, including some from Blessingway. It analyzes Navajo prayer style, structure, and classification; considers the basic goal of Navajo religion; reviews the classification of Navajo ceremonials (and supports, on the basis of the proposed theory of prayer acts, the earlier work by Wyman and Kluckhohn); briefly discusses Navajo symbolism; and reconsiders the history of Navajo religion, suggesting that Blessingway is, in fact, a development upon, if not a reassertion of, Athapaskan hunting religion ideology (1974:517). Most important, however, is the "theory of Navajo prayer acts" it proposes, which challenges, for the first time, Reichard's (1944) view of Navajo prayer as "the compulsive word."

Witherspoon (1974, 1975a, 1975b, 1977) has augmented our theoretical knowledge through his careful linguistic and philosophical analysis of the concepts *sǫ'ah naaghéi, bik'eh hózhǫ́ǫ́*. These "sacred words" have been the subject of countless translation attempts and numerous discussions through the years. Witherspoon (1977:17–46) provides a cogent, far-reaching analysis which relates these concepts to the Navajo view of the universe, its animating powers and ideal environment, the relation of thought and speech, and the relationship between language and reality. He also considers the arts among the Navajos by reacting to earlier studies by Mills (1959) and Hatcher (1974) and the analysis of a Shootingway Snake Song by McAllester (n.d.).

The life history of a Navajo Blessingway Singer, Frank Mitchell, has also become available (Frisbie and McAllester 1978). In addition to a wealth of autobiographical and ethnohistorical information, this source includes much material on the training of Blessingway singers and actual ceremonial procedures, and affords opportunities for comparative analysis and study.

Other recent publications have less relevance for Blessingway studies, but are important to scholars interested in Navajo ceremonialism. Among these is the volume dedicated to Clyde Kluckhohn (Taylor, Fischer, and Vogt 1973), which contains an assessment of Kluckhohn's contribution to Navajo studies (Aberle 1973), and Lamphere and Vogt's (1973) reanalysis of the Navajo ceremonial taxonomy proposed by Wyman and Kluckhohn (1938) and Kluckhohn and Wyman (1940). Two works by Luckert (1975, 1977) consider Huntingway and traditional religious preferences in the Navajo Mountain and Rainbow Bridge regions respectively. Included in these are information on the use of Blessingway Hogan Songs in sweathouses, a further consideration of Brugge's (1963) ideas about the origin of Blessingway, and comments on regional differences in Blessingway. Lamphere (1977) considers cultural and social bases for cooperation in a number of cultural spheres, including ceremonialism, and Blanchard (1977) explores the relationship between religious change and economic behavior, focusing on Christian missions among the Rimrock Navajos.

## HOUSE BLESSING RESEARCH

Unlike the literature on curing ceremonials and even Blessingway per se, that on the House Blessing is limited, despite numerous comments by many on the style, history, and significance of the Navajo house or hogan. Among the earliest sources on the ceremony are Mindeleff (1898, 1900) and Ostermann (1917:20–30). Haile devoted further attention to it in his 1937, 1942, and 1954 publications. The author became interested in the ceremony during fieldwork with Blessingway singers in the early 1960s. It later became the topic of her dissertation research[2] and of a short, general paper for a Navajo issue of *El Palacio* (Frisbie 1968). The dissertation (Frisbie 1970) used a cultural change perspective. Based on field, library, and archival research, its objectives included: documentation of the historical development of the ceremony, discovery and contextual description of its two extant versions (public and private), consideration of the question of origin, evaluation of its present status, and discussion of theoretical implications. While ritual components were identified, and in the case of myths, analyzed thematically, the ceremony, at that time, was not considered from the perspective of ritual drama. The School of American Research Advanced Seminar afforded an opportunity to do so, over a decade

## Ritual Drama in the Navajo House Blessing Ceremony

after the initial fieldwork (1964–67). Since that time, literature on Navajo architecture has increased, thanks mainly to the efforts of Spencer and Jett (1971) and Jett and Harris (n.d.). The present author has witnessed one additional public house blessing and kept track of others, but no further concentrated fieldwork on the ceremony has been possible. The present comments, therefore, represent an update of earlier work, especially that on the public version and cultural change, but, more important, a consideration of the ceremony from the perspective of ritual drama.

### FOCUS OF THE CEREMONY

The emphasis in the House Blessing Ceremony is on the hogan, the single-room dwelling which has been traditionally and exclusively Navajo for centuries. While variations in shape and building materials have been characteristic over time and in specific regions of the reservation, the ecologically sound concept of the hogan continues to endure despite cultural change.

Its tenacity appears to derive mainly from the fact that the hogan is an all-purpose structure, one that has a dual meaning and function; it is both a dwelling place or traditional home, and the only appropriate place within which Navajo ceremonials may be conducted. According to a variety of origin myths, the hogan was first conceived, planned, and constructed by specific Holy People near the Rim of the Emergence Place, after the emergence into the present world. This event is documented in myth, prayer, and song (Chief Hogan Songs). This hogan was the site of many plans for the future and the creation of many elements in the present world. Later, Changing Woman, the only all-benevolent deity in the Navajo pantheon, instructed the Navajos in its construction, maintenance, and preservation. Her instructions continue to be cited as reasons for the many rules which surround contemporary hogan construction: choice of site, orientation of structure, interior design, building materials, care of structure, etiquette of usage, and abandonment upon death or repeated misfortune.

Like our dwellings, the hogan is a home, a place of security, the scene of daily living and learning. In a somewhat similar sense, having one's own hogan is equated with maturity, settling down, a willingness to discuss and plan for the future. "Without a hogan you cannot plan. You can't just go out and plan other things for your future; you have to build a hogan first. Within that you sit down and begin to plan" (Frisbie and McAllester 1978:244). But unlike our houses, hogans are important mythologically and are personified both as deities and as living entities. Symbolically, the hogan is associated with Water Woman, Mountain Woman, Wood Woman, and Changing Woman (the deities mentioned in myths, songs, and prayers), and also with the Sun, in shape and required directional movement within it. Its individual components, such as beams, earth, and fire, and its complete entity as a phenomenon are addressed in song and prayer. Likewise, hogans are personified in ordinary conversation—they are alive; they need to be fed, cared for, spoken to, and shielded from loneliness.

As discerned by Leighton and Leighton (1949:92), the hogan "is the theater for many religious activities and its structure plays a part in ceremonials." As Haile (1942:5) noted, the Blessingway itself is responsible for identifying the hogan as the proper place for traditional ceremonials by "supernaturalizing the various spaces of the hogan interior. . . . [Curing] ceremonials have followed the lead, both in borrowing Blessingway hogan songs and in selecting the hogan as the center and starting point of their liberation prayer." As the author stated earlier (Frisbie 1970:28), the hogan can be and is sanctified by every ceremonial occurring therein. It alone answers every requirement of Navajo religion, including problems raised by

> the ritual of the emesis, raising the door curtain, exorcising evil, greeting the sun through the smoke hole, recognizing the four directions and performing the fire ceremony. Its eaves and crevices offer places where ceremonial paraphernalia, plants, and other protectives against and remedies for witchcraft can be kept, and its dirt floor offers a suitable base for the sandpainting associated with various curing ceremonials (1970:28).

## HISTORICAL DEVELOPMENT AND PURPOSE OF THE CEREMONY

A study of the origin and development of the House Blessing Ceremony (Frisbie 1970) has suggested that the ceremony now exists in two versions, a private one, whose ritual procedures are minimal

## Ritual Drama in the Navajo House Blessing Ceremony

and exoteric or shared as common knowledge among traditional Navajos, and a public one, which is esoteric in its performance, since it involves a ceremonial practitioner. Comparative analyses of Plains, other Athapaskan, and Pueblo data have suggested that the private ceremony has numerous Pueblo parallels and may, in fact, ultimately derive from Mesoamerica (1970:114-47). The public version appears to be a twentieth-century development encouraged by such tribal leaders as Chee Dodge and based on architectural developments and models in the bureaucratic and religious procedures of the dominant Anglo culture. Its emergence serves as a clear-cut example of revitalization efforts in Blessingway ceremonialism and of the vitality of traditional Navajo religion, which since 1969, has received additional support from training programs for ceremonialists, the Navajo Health Authority, and most recently, the Medicine Men's Association constituted in December 1977.

The private version continues to focus on newly constructed or reoccupied dwellings, although some Navajos believe that the ritual procedures may be modified to be applicable to sweathouses, summer ramadas, corrals, certain hunting structures, caves used as shelters, and *kin* (or houses). The reasons for the ceremony are commemorative, preventive, and protective. The ceremony commemorates the building and blessing of the original hogan and implements instructions from the Holy People for future generations to continue the procedures, thereby maintaining the balance, peace, and harmony between humans and Holy People necessary for the orderly functioning of the world. Through the ceremony, the hogan becomes blessed and is recognized as such by the ever-present, ever-watching Holy People who then continue to bless it and its inhabitants.

The ceremony is also believed to prevent general misfortune, bad dreams, illness, hardship, wind and fire destruction, and visitations and harm from ghosts and evil spirits. It concurrently brings happiness, safety, holiness, a friendly spirit, permanency, and protection from evil to the hogan. It also serves to feed the house, show proper treatment and respect to it, prevent timber breakage, and remove the hogan's loneliness. The inhabitants of the house also benefit in that the ceremony brings them blessings, peace, happiness, security, good luck, health, prosperity, general good life and welfare, successful planning, and protection from evil. In essence, the ceremony brings about *sǫ'ah naaghéi, bik'eh hózhǫ́ǫ́*, the central values of the Navajo world, in all of their ramifications as articulated by Witherspoon (1977).

The public version of the ceremony has the same purpose but extends the blessings and benefits to all Navajos and even others. It focuses on public buildings and other locations, their aims, and those who use them. The structures may be new or remodeled, but in most cases they are already being utilized by the time of the official blessing. Historically, the earliest known examples, at present, are the off-reservation dedication of the Fred Harvey Hotel El Navajo in Gallup in May 1923 and the 1930 blessing of the Kinlichee Chapter House on the reservation (Williams 1970:Plates 1–2).[3] Among the structures dedicated before 1970 were schools, chapter houses, hospitals, trading posts, supermarkets, civic or community centers, museums, and Navajo homes. Other structures not so frequently dedicated included post offices, clinics, banks, arts and crafts shops, motels, inns, restaurants, Tribal Council Chamber, General Dynamics plant, Western Navajo fairgrounds, EPI/Vostron plant, and a hot springs pool. In addition, before 1970, ceremonies had been held for such off-reservation buildings and events as factories, a stadium, subagency office, car dealer's garage, hotels, skating rink, Girl Scout camp, fair exhibits, art shows, Navajo hogans, and houses belonging to both Navajo and Anglo people. While anything seemed possible, most collaborators felt that jails and courthouse structures were inappropriate recipients of the public House Blessing Ceremony, and a few also felt this way about non-Navajo houses.

The tribal newspaper, the *Navajo Times*, has continued to report dedications regularly, including those sponsored by churches, government, and industry as well as the more frequent ones involving the services of a Navajo ceremonial practitioner. While coverage varies in detail[4] and amount of accompanying illustrations, much can be learned from it. Since 1969, the House Blessing ceremony has been variously termed a "dedication," "blessing," "a special Navajo ceremony," "a Navajo Blessing," "a traditional Navajo ceremony," "a Blessing Ceremony," and "the Blessingway ceremony." Some 1973 reports elaborated, referring to it as "the ancient way of blessing a hogan" or "one of the most ancient sacred ceremonies." Occasionally there is recognition of the recency of the public ver-

*Ritual Drama in the Navajo House Blessing Ceremony*

sion, such as in the label, "the now traditional blessing ceremonies" (*Navajo Times* 7/31/75), and occasionally the Navajo procedures are called "traditional" and separated from missionary involvement, which is referred to as "the modern way." In the 1970-77 period, coverage seems most extensive in 1971, with full pages being devoted to illustrations of various dedication activities. This was also the year of the caption, (*Navajo Times* 9/2/71), "Would you believe, a dedication of a livestock corral?"

Newspaper coverage suggests that the public version is not only viable but still expanding in scope. In addition to the structures named above, since 1969, the public version has been applied to many new phenomena including a nursing home, an alcoholic rehabilitation center, Powwow, livestock corral at an auction yard, political barbeque for a United States Senatorial candidate, auto parts store, football field and electric scoreboard, fire-police station, several bridges, and the laboratory and office of the Rough Rock Navajo Mental Health Program ("school for medicine men"). Likewise, it has been used to bless a variety of tribal buildings such as a radio network studio; mobile optical unit; community college and its branch campuses; multipurpose buildings which house career development, rehabilitation and opportunity centers, craft shops, and sheltered industries; and most recently, a judicial building (*Navajo Times*:3/9/78, A-2). Schools continue to be the most frequently blessed structure, but in addition to new ones and additions, the ceremony is now being used for day care centers, preschools, kindergartens, a variety of schools and learning centers for the retarded and handicapped, and adult education centers. Many such structures are hogan-shaped in response to increased interest in the Navajo side of bicultural education programs.

There are also several other developments worthy of mention. The *Navajo Times* has reported the application of the ceremony to a 1973 Conference for Eastern Navajo Educators by a medicine *woman*,[5] and the participation of Navajo medicine men in several, pan-Indian blessings of public buildings, such as those held in 1973 for the Newberry Library Center and the Cultural Center at the Chicago Circle Campus. Thus, vitality continues with expansion in scope being stimulated both by the new directions of tribal concerns, development, and programming, and also by an apparent willingness to use the House Blessing Ceremony for just about anything.

CHARLOTTE J. FRISBIE

# RITUAL DRAMA IN THE NAVAJO HOUSE BLESSING CEREMONY

### PERSPECTIVE

In identifying and discussing the components of ritual drama in the Navajo House Blessing Ceremony, it must be made clear at the onset that the author is doing so from an etic perspective. To date, despite the amount of literature on Navajo ceremonialism, no work exists that illuminates any Navajo semantic equivalents for "ritual drama" or perception of its sources, varieties, and criteria. An outsider, particularly a cultural anthropologist, immediately turns to specific elements, such as myth or story line, song, prayer, dance, dry painting, personnel and their actions, and all costuming and paraphernalia involved when dissecting the drama, viewing the combining, sequencing, patterning, symbolic associations, and unfolding of the phenomena as the drama per se. While the author prefers a combination of emic and etic approaches, lacking information on Navajo taxonomies for ritual drama, the current approach is one of the few options presently available.

Using such an approach suggests that the amount of, options for, and variability in House Blessing ritual drama differs greatly in the two versions, with the public one having the more highly developed possibilities of the two. The extent of these differences and some of the reasons for them will become obvious in the discussion which follows, wherein the options in each version for specific ritual components are compared.

### STORY LINE

The House Blessing Ceremony is rationalized and founded in Navajo mythology, particularly the portion of the Blessingway myth that concerns the Emergence and Creation. According to many but not all Navajo collaborators, the first hogan was built at the Rim of the Emergence Place and was blessed so it could be used by the Holy People as a meeting place in which to implement the Creation.

A review of the literature reveals 15 published versions of the myth (cf. Frisbie 1970:75, n.118, n.119; Frisbie and McAllester 1978:170–75). The author has been able to add another 13 from

## Ritual Drama in the Navajo House Blessing Ceremony

fieldwork and a final one from the notes of the late Odd Halseth.[6] A comparative analysis of this corpus suggests that House Blessing myths are extremely individualistic in most details and motifs. Over 170 themes are identifiable, but only 6 are mentioned by more than 50 percent of the collaborators. These include most of the essential features of the ceremony: its origin in the present world, its conception by the deities, the anointing of the hogan timbers in four directions, the use of cornmeal for anointing, and the use of songs, specifically Hogan Songs. Slightly fewer than 50 percent also mention two other features: the use of a prayer or prayers, and the directional progression of east, south, west, north for the anointing.

An explanation for this significant variation is required, especially since it is atypical of the Blessingway myth corpus or that related to another subceremony, Kinaaldá (Frisbie 1967). At present, several factors rather than a single one seem to be involved; among them are the variation caused by the oral transmission process, the Navajo tendency to avoid excess, the strong cultural emphasis on individualism, and the unverified but likely possibility that some of the variation represents regional differences. However, since all of these factors would also be involved in Blessingway and Kinaaldá myths, which do not show such limited core elements, another approach seems required. One possibility is that the House Blessing Ceremony is newer than Kinaaldá and has not progressed as far as the latter in the process of being integrated into Navajo culture. The latter proposition, based on Anderson's (1960:50-62) work on the reduction of variants, received support from earlier analysis (Frisbie 1970:57-60).

While essential to an outsider's understanding of the ceremony, the House Blessing myth is rarely part of the verbalized ritual drama, for unlike other ceremonies, in the House Blessing the myth is not recounted. Reference to the original events may occur in songs and/or prayers, but these are considered by many as optional rather than necessary. In the public version, the singer, in a speech, may or may not refer to the myth, but if he/she does, it is usually in one or two sentences, such as "These procedures were done for the original hogan at the Rim of the Emergence Place and it has been decreed by the Holy People that all future generations continue them. That is why we are here to do this today."[7] While such references anchor the proceedings in the past and provide reference to the story line, the dramatic effect is hardly comparable to that achieved by the detailed recounting of relevant parts of myths during other ceremonials.

## A COMPARISON OF RITUAL DRAMA IN THE PRIVATE AND PUBLIC VERSIONS

As stated earlier, the private version is exoteric; knowledge of its procedures and ability to perform it rest with a number of Navajos rather than solely with ceremonial practitioners. The private version is short and includes building a fire, marking the hogan, possibly the use of song and prayer, and rarely, dry paintings. In the public version, these procedures are altered and often expanded; therein, the Navajo House Blessing is part of a "program" which involves a ceremonial practitioner and a number of other people, many of whom participate as audience onlookers. Ritual drama is heightened in the ceremonial part of the program accordingly by the possible addition of a speech by the practitioner, the use of costuming, "props," and assistants, and possible changes in the execution of the marking, song, prayer, and other ritual components. As such, the public version is a perfect example of what Singer (1958) and Bauman (1976:36) have termed a "cultural performance."

The information that follows is based on fieldwork interviews (1964–67), available literature, other anthropological accounts (cf. Frisbie 1970:190–95 for one of a 1930 public ceremony), and the author's observation of three public versions, two of which involved schools (1965, 1967) and a third, the first on-reservation extended care facility (1971).[8] Data have been ordered according to ceremonial position of the ritual drama components; discussions have been organized to present private version materials before the public ones for each component.

### PERSONNEL AND PREPARATION OF THE HOGAN (PRIVATE)

The private version emphasizes the household unit, although by extension its effects radiate outward to all Navajos. Unlike other ceremonies, it is not an occasion for a large gathering of kinfolk and friends, feasting, and an all-night sing. Instead it may be and often is conducted by one person, without an audience, or at best, in the

# Ritual Drama in the Navajo House Blessing Ceremony

presence of those who will actually inhabit the hogan. Collaborators agree that it is the household head who usually performs the procedures. This often is the oldest male, but may also be his wife, oldest female, or one of the children. In other words, anyone can do it as long as he/she knows how to do so properly.

If a new hogan is being blessed, it is usually the female who removes construction debris before the fire is built. If the blessing is for a hogan about to be reoccupied, the door is unlocked upon return and the fire, built. The fire symbolically represents, among other things, annihilation of evil (Reichard 1963:554).

### DECISION MAKING AND SPONSORSHIP (PUBLIC)

Although neither the *Navajo Times* nor personnel involved in the public performance refer to it, the process of decision making is one of the most interesting aspects of the public version and one that directly affects the type, amount, length, and ordering of ritual drama components. While one might think that in Navajo ceremonialism, the ceremonial practitioner who performs the ceremony controls its content, such is true only to a limited degree (Frisbie n.d.:16–29). In the public House Blessing the practitioner's input is even more limited than usual; in many cases, the ideas and wishes of the whole community or specific officials sponsoring the event carry more weight.

During interviews, singers stated that the people in the community usually decide whether or not to have a public ceremony for a particular building. Often this happens during a regular chapter meeting; sometimes the decision occurs naturally and sometimes, only after the urging of a Tribal Council member, tribal administrator, or school principal who attends the meeting for that purpose. Sometimes community leaders will approach a trader or store operator and suggest that the person have it done because the community wants it. Occasionally a school prinicipal or other person just decides to have the ceremony without going to the chapter meeting to discuss it. When this happens, it is never viewed as a negative event, despite the loss of "decision-making power."

The general attitude is that while the public House Blessing Ceremony is common, it is neither necessary nor required. "The community decides. If the local people decide they don't want to go through with it, then they don't. They just invite people to say their piece on what use the building is for and then they feed them. It's not required to have that ceremony." When the idea is rejected, it is most often because of the type of building involved, the unavailability of appropriate practitioners, or the desire of local people not to bother with something that may be long and cause them to get restless. In such cases, they may ask a missionary to offer an invocation and/or benediction. In at least one instance (Roessel 1967:33), a community decided that the public ceremony was Anglo-oriented and only represented compliance with the white people's wish to see a Navajo sing. Therefore they did not have one.

It should also be noted that while many public ceremonies are planned beforehand, sometimes the desire for the ceremonial part is expressed as the program begins. In such cases, a singer who is present will be asked to perform the procedures or someone will be sent to bring such a person to the gathering.

When the event is preplanned, the community often identifies what singer should be asked. Bauman's (1976:36) work suggests that cultural performances feature accomplished performers in a community. According to Navajo practitioners, the one chosen should be a person who is from the community, well known, respected, qualified, reliable, dependable, and who will thus do the ceremony carefully. It is understood that the person will be experienced in the Blessingway ceremony. A person's performance record is also considered; if he/she did it once, he/she is responsible for dedications of future additions to the building. However, if the community was dissatisfied with that person's performance, then a different singer will be asked next time.[9]

The local people also often express definite ideas about length, preferring the ceremonial side to be short (under an hour's duration). This often leads to a request for "just one song" rather than a series, or for no songs or prayers, but just the cornmeal marking. Occasionally, communities also identify the kind of song preferred.

Input from singers also affects the ritual drama, but even this input does not yield uniform results from one community to another, singer to singer, or from one occasion to the next in the case of the same singer. Practitioners' ideas about appropriate content are based on a number of sources: their own training in how to perform the public version (which only three had), their observations of and critical reactions to other singers performing it, their own commitments and schedules,[10] physical abilities, and their own feelings about a number of variables. Included in the latter are how they feel about offering sacred songs and prayers in settings which include non-Navajos in the audience; the type, location, purpose, and significance of the building; the expectable compensation; the size and nature of the crowd; and the possible presence of photographers, reporters, and anthropologists. In general, the individual decides whether or not to do it, and then decides, through discussion with others, whether songs and/or prayers should be used, and if so, how many.

As the above suggests, nothing is standard. As several collaborators said, "We medicine men are not united on that. We use whatever we think would be appropriate." "It's your own privilege to do it the way you want. You go according to your own ideas." "It's sort of a new way of doing things with education coming in. . . . We adopted that from white man's way. There are many ways of doing it. It depends on what area you're in and how ceremonially minded the people are there, how much white influence there is there." "The bigger the building, the more important it is and the more people you expect, the more impressive your program has to be. You must dedicate that building in a big way; you need to add a little more ceremony to it to look more impressive."

In any case, the singer is always approached and asked to do the job; "the community has to come to us; we don't go around looking for jobs."[11] The compensation which often affects the use and number of songs and prayers "may be just 'eats,' unless you're doing it for non-Navajos." In most cases since the 1930s, however, a set cash fee has been agreed upon beforehand or donations for the singer's services have been acquired by "passing the hat" during the nonceremonial part of the program. "There's no set fee for that, but you have to give the medicine man something. They don't do anything for nothing. If you don't pay them, the ceremony isn't really effective and it doesn't carry through the meaning of the ceremony." Research (Frisbie 1970:240–45) suggests fees ranging from $10 to $1,000, with $10 considered the minimum, and the highest fees expected for performing the ceremony on off-reservation buildings for Anglos.

## PROGRAM POSITION AND PERSONNEL INVOLVED (PUBLIC)

Unlike the private, the public version is one of several events which constitute a "dedication program." Daytime scheduling is preferred, although two programs have been held after dusk. In most cases, the Navajo ceremonial part is first on the roster of events, usually after a brief introduction by the Master of Ceremonies, instructions to the People to quiet down, rearrange their seating, or whatever. The ceremonial component is followed by a variety of speeches from appropriate community, school, tribal, state, and/or Washington officials. Then a meal is served, often buffet style and featuring traditional Navajo food. Tours of the facility or a general open house may follow, as well as other entertainment, such as flag raising, the National Anthem, performances by school musical or dance groups, drill team maneuvers, student art shows, ribbon cutting, award presentations, and games before the conclusion, which may be a missionary benediction.[12]

The personnel involved in the public program are more numerous and varied than those in the private counterpart. In addition to the Master of Ceremonies, speakers, and all other scheduled performers, there is an audience which often ranges from several hundred to over a thousand. Among the many Navajos are others from distant places. While some Navajos say people "only show up for the eats," a dedication is a community event, and the People brave all kinds of weather for a chance to witness it, share in the resulting blessings, and exchange news.

The Navajo ceremonial component also involves more people. The practitioner often has one or more assistants. About half of the public dedications now reported are following this trend, and the highest number of assistants recorded to date is 21. The person chosen is most often a relative of the singer, although it can be someone else, such as an official's daughter, the Corn Pollen Queen, or Miss Navajo. While most prefer to use women or girls, some prefer a boy and others, one of each. In the latter cases, there is some preference for "young virginal assistants." Mature women are relatives of the singers in all known cases, but adult male assistants are often associated with the building, in the role of owner or manager. In one case, a female singer and her family assisted a male singer. Whatever their number and identity, these individuals usually help with the marking and may also assist with the singing or other activities.

## Ritual Drama in the Navajo House Blessing Ceremony

### COSTUME AND PROPS (PUBLIC)

Another way to be "impressive" is to be dressed in *full* traditional regalia, or "your union suit." Most singers and their assistants do just that for a public House Blessing Ceremony. The dress includes earrings, headband and armbands (for males), necklaces, bracelets, rings, concho belt, sash (females), cotton or velvet shirt, trousers or skirts, and moccasins or shoes. Additional items may include a shoulder pouch, Pendleton blanket, buckskin vest, suitcoat, and a deerskin or fox skin. The singer also usually brings a pollen pouch, a Navajo basket which contains the cornmeal and possibly some other items from his/her medicine bundle, and occasionally other items such as one or more purses, old style hats, and rugs, buffalo robes, deerskins, or Pendleton blankets if he/she is going to work from a ceremonial spread on the floor. Some also use Pueblo-made ceremonial bowls. Many singers recognize that the props are often more numerous, and the costumes more traditional, than those accompanying other Navajo ceremonials. They view these differences as another way of responding to audience expectations and increasing the effect of their performances.

### SPEECH BY THE SINGER (PUBLIC)

In many public versions, the singer begins by making a speech, often from a stage. In it is explained the purpose and meaning of the ceremony, its origin (in brief and with reference only to the private version), and often why the singer is about to do it the way he/she is. These comments rarely, if ever, refer to the decision-making process which has already occurred on the part of the community and singer, but instead focus on "my teacher said to do it thus" or "although I do 'x' in private, I do 'y' in public." The singer may also verbalize thanks for the privilege of performing and possibly instruct the audience to be careful in utilizing the structure. Seven examples of such speeches are available; two occur in Frisbie (1970:182–84, 228–29), two in the *Navajo Times* (4/21/77:1; 11/29/73:A–11), and others (by BY, 1971; DT, 1958; and ChC, 1950) are available from the author. Sometimes the speech follows the ceremonial procedures and sometimes it represents all that occurs, as in the case of DT's blessing of a museum in 1958.

### MARKING

The main feature of the ceremony is the actual marking of the hogan or the process of putting the chosen substance on predetermined locations within the structure. In the public version, the marking usually follows the speech, if there is one; in both versions, the actions may be synchronized with a song or formalized prayer text.

Although in pre–Fort Sumner times, hogan blessing practices utilized arrowheads, rock doorslabs, and/or precious stones (Frisbie 1970:89–91), and a *Navajo Times* report (7/29/71:26) suggests that at least one singer continues to use arrowheads, most prefer other substances. Various kinds and colors of cornmeal and corn pollen are most favored for both versions; other alternatives include ashes in the private version, and mirage stone (aragonite), and/or "sacred water from a bubbling spring" in the public version. The marking substance is usually put in a ceremonial basket, although it may be carried in a ceremonial bowl or in the individual's buckskin pollen pouch. In the public version, the singer's assistant often carries the basket and sometimes does the marking according to the singer's instructions; occasionally both the singer and the assistant perform the marking. One of the most elaborate versions to date is that of FS, wherein the singer uses a mixture of white and yellow cornmeal and is followed first by a young boy, who sprinkles sacred water from spruce boughs tied with yucca, and then by a young girl, who marks with corn pollen.

Individual preferences exist for what should be marked; these include the main hogan timbers, posts of the cardinal points, foundation poles, main roof logs, the walls, and the position of the fire, smoke hole, doorway, and floors. In a public version for a multiple-room building, the singer may opt to perform the marking in the largest or most central room, or in each room. Occasionally, special features, such as a cash register in a restaurant, are also blessed.

Most people mark one pole in each of the four cardinal directions, although some prefer to differentiate between the two doorway poles and mark five. The marks are made in an upward direction at the highest, naturally reachable point, although in the public version, singers will occasionally climb ladders or bleachers to extend this point. All follow the east, south, west, north order, and

## Ritual Drama in the Navajo House Blessing Ceremony

then return, counterclockwise, to the east and sprinkle the substance sunwise in an incomplete circle. Sometimes the substance is also tossed upward, "out the hogan's smoke hole." While most people just mark the inside of a hogan or other structure, in the public version, occasionally the procedures are carried outside to exterior walls, fences, or a sports field. Many collaborators regard this latter practice as a straight imitation of missionary blessings with holy water.

The person doing the marking and assistants in the public version usually bless themselves with the substance upon completing the job. In three known public cases (the blessing of the El Navajo Hotel, a PHS clinic, and the Tribal mobile optical unit), the sponsors or main medical figures were anointed with or "fed" corn pollen at this time. In several other instances, reported between 1971 and 1973, the singer's pollen pouch was passed around the audience, with the invitation to all to offer their prayers.

Much of the ritual drama in the marking derives from the symbolic associations the act has for the Navajos. The emphasis on the cardinal points, using an upward motion, and sprinkling the substance in a circle are all related to directional symbolism. Collaborators, both in recounting the myth and in conversations, suggested multiple meanings for these activities. For example, the east is associated with Gobernador Knob, dawn, white shell, soft goods of all kinds, Mother Earth, Sun, and Talking God. Additionally, the directions are viewed as living persons who have "inner forms" or personalities (cf. Haile 1934:91; 1943:70–71). The upward motion recalls the direction of ritual growth and life, or the progression from "butt to tip" (Matthews 1892). Circles are incomplete in order to leave a path for good to enter and evil to exit (Reichard 1963:164) and to avoid excess and completion (Kluckhohn and Leighton 1951:225–26).

Other symbolism includes number symbolism, focusing on both the original hogan and cultural preference for four, and that associated with the marking substances. Of these latter, corn is the most important symbol. Like the earth and several other things, it is called "mother" (Witherspoon 1975b:126). For the Navajos, it stands for food, fertility, life itself. It "is more than human; it is divine" (Reichard 1963:540). By eating it in its pollen form, one identifies "with the supernatural and the desirable fabrics and jewels which the supernatural can provide" (Wyman 1970b:31). It guards against abuse (1970b:30) and represents control. The application of it to a person or object is the "most general . . . means of asking for blessing" (Reichard 1963:509).

PRAYERS

The phrase "individual variation" best summarizes collaborators' thoughts about the necessity, type, and number of prayers in both versions of the House Blessing Ceremony. While some believe that a prayer or prayers are not necessary in either version, 34 use them while marking their own hogans and many also use them in public. In private versions, 20 preferred "free or individualistic prayers," those created by the person blessing the hogan and spoken in that person's words. Eleven preferred formalized prayers, and the others said that either type was applicable. In public versions, one-third of the collaborators opted for individualistic prayers, sometimes because they felt that none of their ceremonial prayers was appropriate for the structure or because they had been taught not to expose ceremonial knowledge before non-Navajo audiences. Another third opted for formalistic prayers, and the final group, for either. Some used both types in public,[13] or varied their choices depending on their time, the potential fee, composition of the audience, and the importance of the occasion.

Most believed that if prayers were needed, one was sufficient although many said that in public, one could do more if the situation so warranted and one was so inclined. To date, reports suggest that the most ever used in public were six, at the blessing of a chapter house. The singer involved later used no prayers when blessing a hospital, because of the "mixed audience."

The prayers that are available for analysis are listed in table 8.1; "type" refers to the taxonomic label given to the prayer by the collaborator.[14]

*Individualistic Prayers*

While Gill (1974:171–74) questions the use of individualistic prayers in Kinaaldá and suggests that FM described them as such to avoid giving the prayer texts, both he and Reichard (1944) recognize

## Ritual Drama in the Navajo House Blessing Ceremony

the existence of such prayers. Reichard (1944:9) notes that pollen strewing "is a prayer for well-being, whether accompanied by words or not." Among her types, in addition to formalistic prayers, are silent prayers, songs, the common prayer of laymen—"a muttered may it be beautiful, may it be beautiful again," and "extemporaneous prayers," in which people ask for what they need, "praying in their own words" (1944:13). As she continues, "even the extemporaneous prayers are cast in the formal mould."

Gill (1974:184-88) identifies that formal mold as "Unit V," where the basic constituent is a desired state of blessing and where the emphasis is on the reinstatement of a petition or "that it has come to be again." When this V unit is used by itself, it takes a petitionary form and results in prayers that are brief, frequently accompanied by

> a ritual act such as pollen application or strewing and . . . not uttered in the formal manner common to major prayers. These short prayer formulas appear to be very important to the ritual process and may be an important way in which a ritual process is channeled toward a specific situation. The importance of these prayers has often been overlooked and they remain unrecorded throughout most of the ceremonial descriptive literature (1974:187-88).

Collaborators described these prayers as "short," "small," "your own," "whatever you want to ask for," "whatever you have in mind to say in your own words." Some said they were addressed to the hogan; "you speak to the hogan just like a human being." "The hogan itself is the foundation for what you are praying; you have to do it carefully." Others said they were really to Holy People (never specifically addressed, perhaps because they are ever-present and ever-watching).

A content analysis of those used in the private version suggests that most are concerned with the occupants of the hogan. Requests made include those for immunity from sickness and misfortune, peace with relatives and friends, beneficial plans for the future, prosperity, and sǫ'ah naaghéi, bik'eh hózhǫ́ǫ́. Specific requests for the hogan include those for its happiness, stability, strength, and blessedness. The individualistic prayers used in public always refer to the specific structure, ask that its purpose be fulfilled, and often that blessing, health, and happiness accrue to its users. The indivi-

TABLE 8.1.
HOUSE BLESSING PRAYERS

| Collaborator | Year | Type Prayer | Individual-istic (I) or Formal (F) | Appropriate Version of Ceremony | Field-worker |
|---|---|---|---|---|---|
| Dlb | 1966 | — | I | Private | Frisbie |
| BS | 1967 | — | I | Private | Frisbie |
| PJ | 1967 | — | I | Private | Frisbie |
| PJ | 1967 | — | I | Private | Frisbie |
| PJ | 1967 | — | I | Private | Frisbie |
| JY | 1967 | — | I | Private | Frisbie |
| FM | 1964 | — | I | Private | Frisbie |
| CS | 1963 | — | I | Private | Frisbie |
| TM | 1964 | — | I | Private | Frisbie |
| DK | 1965 | — | I | Public | Frisbie |
| JY | 1967 | — | I | Public | Frisbie |
| Dłc biye | 1967 | — | I | Public | Frisbie |
| [*Navajo Times*] | | | | | |
| KC | 1972 | — | I | Public | ? |
| X | 1971 | — | I | Public | ? |
| Male | 1972 | — | I | Private | ? |
| Female | 1972 | — | I | Private | ? |
| HT | 1965 | Chief Hogan or Talking God Hogan Prayer | F | Either | Frisbie |
| BN | 1965 | Chief Hogan | F | Either | Frisbie |
| JM | 1967 | Blessingway Prayer | F | Either | Perrine |
| JS | 1940 | Prayer for Hogan Blessing | F | Public | Reichard |
| Hhb | 1956 | Prayer for White Corn Boy | F | Public | Foster |
| Hhb | 1956 | Prayer for Depositing Bear Image and Prayersticks | F | Public | Foster |
| FM | 1964 | Hogan Prayer | F | Public | Frisbie |

## Ritual Drama in the Navajo House Blessing Ceremony

dualistic prayers from both versions follow, with the 11 from private house blessings preceding the 5 from the public version.[15]

My home, I'm back again in your interior. May I have a healthy life. May no harm come to me or my family. May future generations multiply in a good way and prosper here within you. (Dłb)

This home, my home, shall be surrounded with *są'ah naaghéi, bik'eh hózhǫ́ǫ́*. This fire shall be for the good of the family. And the children that may be born in this hogan will all be in good health. Any plans we make in this hogan will be for the good of the family. (BS)

May this be a happy place for the family that will inhabit this hogan. (PJ)

May this be a good place for us to live again, may it be happy in this home; may our lives be long and happy in this home. (PJ)

May this be a good place, may this be a blessed place, and a good place for the family to live in there. (PJ)

As long as this home is standing may there be good living in here. May all the people who live in here live in a good, decent way. (JY)

May I have *są'ah naaghéi bik'eh hózhǫ́ǫ́*; may all the people who live here be immune from sickness; may we be at peace with our relatives and friends; may this be a friendly place. (FM)

May I live in this home happily and peacefully and with respect. May I have a happy life in this hogan. Myself, my wife, my children, my relatives, whoever may come into this hogan, may they relax peacefully and rest up. May all of us have no sickness, no misfortune. (CS)

May I live in this home with good health. May my family, my children and I have no sickness, nor misfortune in it. (TM)

The two individualistic prayers reported in the *Navajo Times* (Benninger 1972:C-1) for the private version of the ceremony include one "chanted" by a man during the marking and another, by his wife.

May my house be in harmony; From my head, may it be happy; To my feet, may it be happy; Where I lie, may it be happy; All above me, may it be happy; All around me, may it be happy; May my fire be well-made and happy; May the sun, my mother's ancestor, be happy for this gift; May it be happy as I walk around my house; May this road of light, my mother's ancestor, be happy.

183

> Then his wife said in a subdued voice [!] while sprinkling meal: May my fire be happy; May it be happy for my children; May all be in harmony; May it be happy with my food and theirs; May all be well; May all my possessions be in harmony; May they be made to increase; May all my flocks be well; May they be made to increase.[16]

The individualistic prayers reported by the newspaper for public versions are from the blessing of a new home and a hogan-shaped school building, by two different practitioners. In the former, the singer reportedly "asked that all good things come to the house and that evil spirits stay away" (*Navajo Times* 7/29/71:26). In the latter,

> Keel Clitso, reverend Navajo medicine man came to consecrate the hogan with songs from the Blessingway Rites. He intoned the rituals and smeared sacred corn pollen along the hogan poles and offered up this petition: 'Let this be assurance that the place will be happy' (*Navajo Times* 6/8/72:B-3,B-5).

The three individualistic prayers recorded by the author as examples of those used in public versions included one by DK, used at a chapter house dedication, a second by JY, used at a school, and a third, by Dłc biye, which was used at the blessing of the Window Rock Lodge.

> In my own words I started out the prayer mentioning Mother Earth—Mother Earth we have this structure set on you for our use, and the purpose for that is for the best benefit of the people. The supreme holy being should oversee us so we discuss things wisely. Then I mentioned the four mountains, the east mountain, the south mountain, the west mountain and the north mountain, and besides that the two that are in the center, Huerfano and Gobernador. I pleaded with the holy beings who inhabit these mountains as their homes that they would be supernaturally present in our discussions, in our meetings and give us some wise ideas to discuss our problems. Washington who is our overseer—that they would be wise people, open minded people, and that you holy beings, supernatural beings, enlighten their minds so that they would give us the best ideas for the welfare of our people. That is what I said.
> Then I also mentioned that the roads in the country were kept up and maintained in the best way for the people to use safely and generally and that also the children, whenever they come of age to go to school, reach six years of age, that they would all be wise enough to go, to enter schools and to learn things and that they would become wise. Then I used the gen-

## Ritual Drama in the Navajo House Blessing Ceremony

eral conclusion of our prayers—it has become beautiful, it has become beautiful, it has become beautiful, it has become beautiful. This is not any set prayer; it's just a prayer of my own, my own ideas (DK).

I asked that things be done right and in a good way and that during the educating, the children would be blessed that they would be in good health and that they would learn a lot. That all the people there would be blessed, be in good health while here on earth, live and breathe the fresh air in the Blessingway, be blessed from the outer atmosphere, that the sun would shine on them in the day in the Blessingway, and the moon would shine on them in the night in the Blessingway. That was the end of my prayer (JY).

I just thought about that public ceremony for a long while. I didn't have any Navajo ceremonial prayer that was right for that so I just decided to pray in the Catholic missionary way. So I did that. We're kind of particular about our ceremonial prayers in those kinds of places. I prayed like this: that people would come in here and eat here, that people would come in here and sleep here, that the people operating this building would have all the food needed for them so that they will be happy when they go out from eating, when they go out (Dłc biye).

As is obvious, most of the individualistic prayers uttered in both the private and public versions consist solely of Gill's Unit V, with variations focused on what all is to be blessed, and no use of the concluding formula, "it has become beautiful again." That of DK is more expansive, however, including what Gill (1974) terms unit A (place designation), B (name mention), G (association with the Holy Person), V (desired state of blessing), and the concluding formula. This prayer, although not a formal, ceremonial one, comes very close to it; as such, it is a good example of the range of variation in individualistic prayers and the fact that while "free," they are built on a formal mold, or identifiable, predictable constituent units.

### Formal Prayers

Several of the collaborators who preferred formal prayers in the private version stated that this really was an option which one employed if he/she knew such a prayer or "was not in a rush." One other stated that the entire family should be assembled before beginning such a prayer. All collaborators specified that a Blessingway Prayer should be used; the most frequently mentioned type was a Hogan Prayer, with people equally preferring the Chief Hogan and Talking God alternatives within this group. Other options mentioned included: Prayer of the Earth, Prayer of the Sky, Monster Slayer's Prayers, Traveling Prayer, Sạ'ah naaghéi Prayer (described as used in Blessingway after the bath and drying on the last day and as having 12 verses), and a Gobernador Knob Prayer (described as the original Prayer of Talking God).

While some collaborators refused to record the formal prayers, saying these could not be repeated out of context or to a tape recorder because they were too sacred and too important, as table 8.1 indicates, seven are available for analysis—four used in the public version, and three, in either. In only one known case, the dedication of El Navajo Hotel in 1923 (Frisbie 1970:188–90), were the formal prayers recited in typical ceremonial litany fashion, with the sponsor or one-sung-over repeating phrases uttered by the singer. Spatial restrictions limit examples to the one which follows:[17]

JS—Prayer for Dedication of Gallup Stadium, 1940
"First of the Prayers of the Hogan Blessing" (Reichard—fieldworker).

With trails of corn pollen leading into it, by means of that my home will be beautifully situated,
With dark colored clouds leading into it, by means of that my home will be beautifully situated,
With male rain leading into it, by means of that my home will be beautifully situated,
Horses of all kinds, those will I accumulate,
Sheep of all kinds, those will I accumulate,
All kinds of soft goods, those will I accumulate,
All kinds of hard goods, those will I accumulate,
According to this being beautiful, I will acquire good crops of food,
In that way beauty from all directions surrounding me, the talks to me will consist of corn pollen,
In this way, my young people will now disperse for their homes beautifully and then we shall live in beauty,
We shall journey along on the corn pollen trail with beauty surrounding us and in that way we shall live beautifully,
Earth people shall increase on the earth,
Old men shall increase on the earth,
Old women shall increase on the earth,

# Ritual Drama in the Navajo House Blessing Ceremony

Young men shall increase on the earth,
Young women will increase on the earth,
Children will increase on the earth,
The Earth Chiefs will increase on the earth,
Those who have no mercy on their fellow beings will live happily,
    I am the Child of White Shell Woman,
    I am the Child of Changing Woman,
    I am the Child of White Shell Woman,
    I am the Child of Changing Woman,
Below the east, Talking God, Hogan God,
At the hogan made of dawn,
At the hogan made with square blocks of dawn,
The dawn trails along on those blocks,
Talking God's foot has become my foot,
Talking God's leg has become my leg,
Talking God's body has become my body,
Talking God's mind has become my mind,
Talking God's voice has become my voice,
Talking God's headplume has become my headplume,
The corn pollen with which he breathes, with that, I breathe;
    therefore I am talking,
The corn pollen with which he speaks out, that I use to speak with
    as I am talking,
The corn pollen with which his mouth is beautified, my mouth is
    also beautified with it as I talk,
By means of these I am talking as I go along,
With beauty before me,
With beauty behind me,
With Sạ'ah naaghéi, bik'eh hózhǫ́ǫ́, that is what I am as I go along,
By means of that my home will be beautifully situated,
From all directions, trails of pollen,
    they will travel on them in beauty,
My male elders will be living happily,
My female elders will be living happily,
My young men will be living happily,
My young women will be living happily,
My children will be living happily,
The chiefs on the earth will be living happily,
Before them it will be beautiful,
Behind them it will be beautiful,
Sạ'ah naaghéi, bik'eh hózhǫ́ǫ́, that is what they shall be as they live,
Before me it will be beautiful,
Behind me it will be beautiful,
Sạ'ah naaghéi, bik'eh hózhǫ́ǫ́; we shall be that,
That is what I am saying,
It has become beautiful,
It has become beautiful.

SONGS

The wide individual variation characteristic of collaborators' views on prayers is also typical of their views on the necessity, type, and number of songs. Many felt songs were optional at best and that their usage was a matter for individual decision. In private versions, a few felt that singing made the procedures "more holy" and "showed that the individual was doing the ceremony more carefully." In public, the decision-making process and other variables already identified affected the practitioner's decision.

Most felt that for both versions, one song was sufficient but that a person could do more if so inclined. Data suggest that while most use just one song, public versions have included 2, 4, 5, 6, 10, 11, and 13 (which two singers said should have been 14).[18] Many but not all coordinate the marking with the singing.

Unlike prayers where either individualistic or formal types may be used, in the songs there is no freely composed option. Blessingway Songs were specified by all as the only kind appropriate, although there has been one known exception in a public version.[19] Hogan Songs were most frequently mentioned, with individuals equally preferring the Chief and Talking God options within this group (Frisbie 1967:99–209), depending on the situation and structure. For example, some felt that Chief Hogan Songs were appropriate for chapter house blessings, and those of Talking God, for hospitals and schools. Many specified the last song in the set (the longest and textually most inclusive) as the most appropriate choice in either group.

Two others preferred Corn Songs. One used one yellow and one white Corn Song, but only in private; the other said any of the set of twelve Corn Songs were appropriate and that these could also be sung while planting corn. Another specified using the Blessingway Song "that refers to Monster Slayer and Born-for-Water thrilled by the sight of Gobernador Knob." One preferred a combination of a Hogan Song in the evening and a Dawn Song in the morning in private, but eliminated the latter in public. Another used a Good Luck Song which he classified as belonging to Blessingway, but "not the ceremonial Blessingway" (?). Two opted for unspecified Blessingway Songs. Another mentioned that the Blessingway Song pertaining to sleep would be his choice if blessing a cave shelter. Another suggested that the Twelve-verse Song he used concerned

## Ritual Drama in the Navajo House Blessing Ceremony

the building of the original forked-stick hogan for First Man and First Woman. Initially he denied that this was either a Hogan Song or a Blessingway Song. Later he said it was a Blessingway Song but refused to elaborate further.

Finally, one collaborator spoke of a special song, *sin banadeełii* ("The Foundation of the Songs") which he used for house blessings as well as in conjunction with searching for a lost child, encouraging safe return from travels or military service, or at the end of singing the Hogan Songs in a ceremony, to erase any errors. He said the song was long and while its use was not compulsory in the private version, to use it made the blessing of the hogan "more holy, more substantial." He further stated that the song was from Blessingway, but was not used in "regular Blessingway." He denied that it was associated with Chief Hogan Songs and did not answer the same question re Talking God Hogan Songs. Stating he was physically too weak to sing it, he described the song's content as follows: "The song has a lot of words. Of course you start from the center of your hogan and you go all around inside the hogan. Then you go out and go to your farms and wherever you may go in doing your chores. Then you turn back and come back into your hogan again."

Not all the singers who said songs were necessary were, of course, willing to record them, although there was more willingness to tape songs than prayers, which were generally considered more important. The total corpus of House Blessing music presently recorded and available[20] is shown in table 8.2.

The tapes of these songs are in the author's possession and have now been transcribed and translated. The musical and textual characteristics of many of these songs can be compared with the discussion of Hogan Songs in Frisbie (1967:99–209) and Blessingway Songs in general, in Wyman (1970b). For example, BN's song is closely parallel in music and text to FM's Chief Hogan Song #7 and HT's is textually comparable to FM's #10, instead of #14. Of particular interest is the song by MK which he labeled a Hogan Song, but would not classify further. Musically it is similar to Chief Hogan Songs in range, contour, and structure. However, the opening chorus lacks the characteristic *holaghei* formula, the singer uses a number of downward slides but not at the end, the final formula is ♫ , and the song has nine verses rather than the characteristic four. Textually, it translates as follows:

TABLE 8.2.
HOUSE BLESSING SONGS

| Collab-orator | Year | Type Song | Appropriate Number | Version | Field-worker |
|---|---|---|---|---|---|
| BN | 1965 | Chief Hogan Song | 1 | Either | Frisbie |
| JS | 1940 | Talking God Hogan Song | 4 | Either | Reichard |
| FM | 1964 | Hogan Prayer Song | 1 | Public | Frisbie |
| | 1964 | Set #3, Song #3[1] following Chief Hogan Songs | 1 | Public | Frisbie |
| HT | 1965 | Last Chief Hogan Song | 1 | Either | Frisbie |
| ChC | 1950 | Chief Hogan Songs | 13 | Public | Halseth |
| AP | 1960 | Hogan Songs [?] | 2 | Public | Foster |
| CC | 1967 | Blessingway—concerns original forked-stick hogan | 1 | Public | Frisbie |
| MK | 1967 | Hogan Song | 1 | Either | Frisbie |
| JM | 1967 | Yellow Corn Song | 1 | Either | Roberts |
| | | White Corn Song | 1 | Either | Roberts |
| Hhb (JF) | 1956 | "Beauty and Mountain Chant Meeting Together Song" | 1 | Public | Foster |
| | | "It is Blessed" | 1 | | |
| | | "Beautyway" | 5 | | |
| | | Corral Dance – Sheep Song | | | |
| | | Magpie Song [?Mountain Sheep] | | | |
| | | Corral Dance – Sun Song | | | |
| | | Talking God Song | | | |
| | | Butterfly Song | | | |
| | | "5 Beautyway Songs" | 6 | | |
| | | Bluebird Song | | | |
| | | Mountain Song [Blessingway] | | | |
| | | Corn Beetle Song [Blessingway] | | | |
| | | Corn Song | | | |
| | | Mountain Song [Blessingway] | | | |
| | | Earth Song | | | |

## Ritual Drama in the Navajo House Blessing Ceremony

*haiye ne yaŋa*
It is placed, it is placed, it is placed,
It is placed, it is placed, it is placed,
Now at the Rim of the Emergence Place, it is placed, it is placed,
At the hogan, blessedness is placed, it is placed,
At the rear, Turquoise Boy, it is placed, it is placed,
At the rear, White Shell Girl, it is placed, it is placed,
Truly at the center of the abalone hogan, it is placed, it is placed,
Truly at the center of the hogan of White Shell Girl, it is placed,
   it is placed,
At the center of the hogan of soft goods, it is placed, it is placed,
At the hogan of all kinds of jewels, it is placed, it is placed,
Now *są'ah naaghéi*, now *bik'eh hózhǫ́ǫ́* below the hogan, it is placed,
   it is placed,
It is placed, it is placed,
It is placed, it is placed, *neyowo*.

### OTHER CEREMONIAL COMPONENTS

Ritual drama in the House Blessing may be further enhanced by the use of at least two other ceremonial components, dance and dry painting. The evidence for dance is restricted to public versions and is both limited and unclear. "Dancing" has been reported twice by the *Navajo Times* for public dedications which also included "chants and prayers," but no further details were offered. The descriptions of the El Navajo Hotel dedication (Frisbie 1970:188-90) refer to arguments over a dance step seemingly Navajo and possibly used in a procession. All other references make it clear that dancing is separate from the Navajo ceremony, occurring usually as part of the secular entertainment for the audience. Herein, dancing is mainly pan-Indian in style and performed by groups, although square dance exhibitions are occasionally used.

Although no collaborators mentioned either dance or dry paintings, two sources and reports of two public dedications suggest the latter are also possible. Both Newcomb (1964:179) and Villaseñor (1963:30,40) refer to dry paintings which may be used for house blessings. While Wyman's (1970b) study of Blessingway does not identify any dry paintings used specifically and solely for House Blessing ceremonies, should they occur, they would undoubtedly be small, simple meal and pollen paintings of Pollen Boy, Changing Woman's house, or something comparable. During the 1923 El Navajo Hotel dedication, two meal-pollen dry paintings were made on buckskin, and during Hhb's blessing of the Museum of Navajo Ceremonial Art in 1956, two were also made. The first of Hhb's, made on day two of the three-day event, was of a Blue Corn Person, and the second, made on day three, was of a Blue Squash Plant (Frisbie 1970:229-31).

When the blessing procedures have been completed, a meal is often prepared and shared, both in private ceremonies for a new home and in public versions. This meal, which meets both biological and social needs, is typical of Navajo ceremonials and is symbolically associated with plenty, "the success of a ceremony, strength, endurance, and transformation" (Reichard 1963:557).

## CONCLUSIONS

The Navajo House Blessing Ceremony offers a challenge to scholars from a variety of perspectives. In this ceremony, one is dealing with a ritual drama wherein many factors crucial to a non-Navajo's understanding are implicit rather than explicit. For example the story line, familiar to traditional Navajos, is abbreviated in performance, if acknowledged at all. The tension, conflict, or struggle obvious in many other ritual dramas is also implicit. Analytically, it derives from the opposition of unblessed and blessed states and the need to prevent identifiable, potential misfortunes, as well as the juxtaposition of the Navajo and Anglo worlds.

The ceremony, especially in its public version, clearly exemplifies the role of creativity in ritual drama at both individual and group levels. Singers can not only compose prayers in their own words, but also have a voice in deciding what combination of procedures will be "appropriate" for particular buildings, events, and audiences. The larger group also participates in decision-making dialogues before the event, and in evaluative ones during and after its completion.

Analysis of these dialogues, however, suggests that while flexibility and individualism remain characteristic of this ritual drama on one level, an element of secularization has been introduced by the public setting and a process of standardization is occurring. The actual development of a public version early in the present century was the harbinger of such a trend. Throughout the decades people have become increasingly familiar with the version, its potential components, and their ordering. Expectations of communities, officials, and audiences have narrowed, resulting in a reduction of variation and a clarification of the parameters of the ceremony and the boundaries within which individualism and creativity can be expressed. Certain options, such as dry painting and dance, have become infrequent whereas others, especially those of elaborate traditional costuming, and numerous props and assistants, have become popular. Overall, it has become possible to predict core components of the ritual drama and in some settings, even their ordering. Among these components are traditional dress and paraphernalia, use of at least one assistant, marking in four directions with cornmeal or corn pollen while perhaps singing one Blessingway Song, the potential use of one individualistic or formal Blessingway Prayer, and one short speech, explanatory and appreciative in nature.[22]

This standardization process is exemplified by numerous other social changes on the reservation, perhaps the most relevant of which is the apparent trend toward centralization in traditional ceremonialism. Moving from roles initially characterized by strong individualism through an unsettling period of flux precipitated by the introduction of numerous non-Navajo religions and the Western medical system, ceremonialists now seem to have entered a new period wherein the key concepts are organization, certification, evaluation, and licensing. The Medicine Men's Association, as now constituted with charter and by-laws, is designed to control the content and transmission of ceremonial knowledge and to protect its performance and paraphernalia from defamation.

While retaining the original purpose, both versions of the ceremony continue to expand in applicability, incorporating appropriate adaptive modifications in the process. Obviously, the impetus for, and direction of, some of these changes derive directly from outside influences, as did the historical origins of both versions. Just as Anglo models were central in motivating the initial development of the public version, response to Anglo expectations of length, staging, props, theatrics, speeches, costumes, "show," remuneration, and publicity through media coverage are obvious in contemporary performances and Navajo dialogues. Likewise Anglo expectations are obvious in evaluation criteria which, for the House Blessing, are somewhat different from those normally employed in assessing Navajo ceremonials (Frisbie n.d.:19–29).

It is true that some Anglos have become "Americanized White

Men" in Cohen's (1952) terms as witnessed by their ability to understand the reasons behind the ceremony and their expectations of its inclusion on reservation dedication programs. But Anglo influence on Navajo performance content and criteria appears to have been much stronger than Navajo influence on Anglo understanding, and to have led to the usual response which anthropologists through time have variously termed the Navajo ability to "be flexible," "adapt," "absorb," "borrow," and "incorporate," always with the idea of taking the best from all worlds and making it Navajo. The result in this instance is a ritual drama which features Changing Woman as the unspecified heroine in an implicit story line, and which is applicable to Navajo or non-Navajo structures and events both within and outside the reservation. The drama, particularly its contemporary public version, represents a new kind of merging of the two worlds in its components, procedures, evaluations, potential use of Miss Navajo or Corn Pollen Queens as assistants, and its potential colleagueship of singers and missionaries on the same dedication program!

The House Blessing Ceremony as ritual drama is also interesting from other perspectives. The historical development of the public version and its continuing expansion and standardization offer an intriguing example of the process of "becoming traditional." Within this ceremony, a new version focused on public phenomena was developed, introduced, and accepted as "traditional" all within a fifty-year span. No other traditional Navajo ceremonial known to the author has a comparable history. New ceremonials per se have been introduced in Navajo history; more recently, shorter versions of traditional ceremonials and new combinations of traditionalism with other religions, particularly Peyotism, have emerged. Likewise, composition continues in those ceremonials, such as Enemyway and Nightway, which include portions wherein such is allowed. But Blessingway alone appears to have the resilience and flexibility to sanction the development, in one of its subceremonies, of a new version in response to changing models and worlds and then to facilitate and achieve it in a way that can be perceived as traditional. Perhaps this very ability to channel and incorporate new things into ritual drama while maintaining the traditional is one of the reasons Blessingway continues to be viewed as the backbone of the traditional Navajo religious system. And, perhaps the House Blessing

## Ritual Drama in the Navajo House Blessing Ceremony

Ceremony continues to maintain its popularity primarily because of a similar ability to merge two worlds in a way that can be perceived simultaneously as a statement of the importance of traditional culture and Navajo ethnicity, as well as an expression of how to be Navajo in today's world.

As a viable, dynamic, traditional ceremony, the House Blessing deserves further study, particularly from a longitudinal perspective to allow further documentation of change and understanding of the sources influencing this process. Of particular interest is the question of how the People will limit both the process of standardization and the historically valued expression of individual and group creativity with reference to new definitions of the importance of each in the contemporary Navajo world.

As ritual drama, the ceremony affords numerous challenges to those interested in developing methodological and theoretical approaches which answer all of the questions relevant to both Navajos and outsiders, and which facilitate understanding at both the emic and etic levels. While no work to date has illuminated Navajo perspectives on "ritual drama,"[23] the present study does further exemplify the need for an ethnography of Navajo ceremonial performance (Frisbie n.d.), and the necessity of studying ritual drama from a variety of perspectives. In this ceremony, ritual drama content is defined by a decision-making process based on past and present ideas of many people, including some who are non-Navajos. Thus, comprehension of the resulting drama cannot rest solely on etic analyses of the individual components, such as story line, marking, song, prayer, dance, or dry painting. Instead, the approach must be broader, including collection and analysis of ethnographic data on the entire context of the drama, from the moment of the initial idea for such and the ensuing dialogues through to its termination, as defined by the cultural system and the critical discussions about the event after its completion. If such a contextual perspective were added to ethnographic, ethnohistorical, and cognitive ones, and the more specialized ones of ethnomusicology and dance ethnology, it seems possible that an understanding, not just of ritual drama in the Navajo House Blessing Ceremony or among Southwestern Indians, but of ritual drama everywhere would be facilitated.

CHARLOTTE J. FRISBIE

## NOTES

1. These words, *sạ'ah naaghéi bik'eh hózhọ́ọ́*, have been left in Navajo throughout the present study. As Witherspoon (1977:21, 23) states, *sạ'ah* "expresses the Navajo concern for and emphasis upon life and their attitude toward death of old age as a goal of life. . . . completion of the life cycle through death of old age." *Naaghéi* refers to "the continual reoccurrence of the life cycle" (1977:23); *bik'eh*, "according to" (1977:23) and *hózhọ́ọ́*, to "the positive, ideal environment. It is beauty, harmony, good, happiness, and everything that is positive, and it refers to an environment which is all-inclusive" (1977:24). In summary, the "goal of Navajo life in this world is to live to maturity in the condition described as *hózhọ́ọ́* and to die of old age, the end result of which incorporates one into the universal beauty, harmony, and happiness described as *sạ'ah naaghéi bik'eh hózhọ́ọ́*" (1977:25). For examples of pictorial representations of these concepts, see Fishler (1956:66–67, 70–71, Plates 4, 11).

2. The author is grateful for research support provided by a National Science Foundation Cooperative Fellowship (1965–1967) and a Shirley Farr Fellowship from the American Association of University Women (1967–1968).

3. In earlier works by the author (Frisbie 1968, 1970), the first on-reservation use of the ceremony was believed to be the 1938 dedication of the Fort Defiance PHS hospital. This dedication is well remembered by collaborators and believed by many to be the first. Its importance was reemphasized at the 1977 dedication of an addition to the facility (*Navajo Times* 4/21/77).

4. The tribal newspaper rarely reports reasons for the ceremony. There are only several such examples in the 1970–77 period; through them one learns that the ceremony was held to bring good things to the house and to keep evil spirits away, to "bring good fortune to a business," and "to unite the community behind the school."

5. This is the first reported incident of a female ceremonial practitioner for the public version; she employed one male assistant (*Navajo Times* 3/22/73). The focus of *Navajo Times* reporting is usually on the male participants, with the exception of any females who may assist the male singer. Occasionally, however, photographs will also show women preparing the meal served during the event. (For additional coverage of the latter, see Gilpin 1968:225–227.) Such information awaits consideration in work on the statuses and roles of Navajo women.

6. These are available in Frisbie (1970:49–51, 323–37).

7. The spoken words of collaborators have been preserved verbatim throughout this chapter.

8. Although the author has seen a variety of hogans under construction, she has never been "in the right place at the right time" to witness the private version of the ceremony.

9. In blessings of chapter houses, a person's status is also considered. If the chapter president is a Blessingway singer, it is considered appropriate to ask that person to do the blessing. Likewise, as Brugge (personal communication, 1978) indicates, if an appropriate singer is employed at the structure to be blessed, an obligation is felt toward asking that person.

10. One singer did a public House Blessing and then apologized for its brevity (10 minutes), explaining he was in the midst of conducting a Blessingway in another community.

11. Occasionally, however, singers do advertise their services; see, for example, Luckert (1975:18).

12. The ordering of program events is highly flexible. Occasionally the Navajo ceremony is preceded by a missionary invocation, speeches, and a meal and is fol-

## Ritual Drama in the Navajo House Blessing Ceremony

lowed by entertainment and a benediction. Williams (1970:46) describes chapter house programs. The Navajo Community College program included a morning seminar led by the Navajo and Hopi Chairmen and a memorial rodeo. Certain events, however, are predictable, as the following description of a bridge dedication in the Red Rock Chapter suggests:

> Among those attending Saturday were a Navajo medicine man and a Catholic priest for the now traditional blessing ceremonies. With the completion of more and more of the new bridges in Western New Mexico, the bridge blessing has become standard practice and is usually followed by a meal for dignitaries and community residents and guests (*Navajo Times* 7/31/75:A–11).

13. For example, FM sometimes added an individualistic prayer after the formal one, in order to call the attention of the Holy People to the specific structure being blessed, and to its use, "so that it would really benefit the People."

14. In the three public House Blessing Ceremonies witnessed by the author, one singer used a single Hogan Prayer; another, a formal Blessingway Prayer and a prayer in his own words inside, plus another of the latter type outside; and the third, a single prayer in his own words. Recording permission was refused in the first instance; in the second, the singer's prayers were barely audible since he turned his back to the microphone and was already far away from it on stage. The third was drowned out by crying babies and chugging pickup motors.

Formal prayers were used in the El Navajo Hotel dedication in 1923. In the public blessing of the off-reservation Etsitty hogan in Pueblo Grande witnessed by Odd Halseth in 1950, ChC and his three assistants each offered an individualistic prayer at the conclusion of the 13 Chief Hogan Songs and asked Halseth to do the same (Frisbie 1970:225). None of these prayers, the individualistic and formal ones used in the blessing of Wyman's hogan (1970:190–95), or the "simple prayers of benediction for the use of the building and the blessing of those who participate in its activities" used at the dedication of a new school in Crownpoint (Gilpin 1968:224) are available for analysis.

15. Although the tribal newspaper rarely reports the use of prayers in public House Blessings, two in each category are from the *Navajo Times*. None of those recorded by the author were recorded in ceremonial context.

16. These two prayers appear to be slight retranslations of those given in Mindeleff (1898:505).

17. Prayers and songs in this chapter were translated by the author with the assistance of the late Albert G. (Chic) Sandoval, Sr. The prayer collected by Reichard is probably that which is the source of her Figure 2 diagram (Reichard 1944), for which no text is given in her analytical work on prayer. This prayer and the four songs JS used with it were located in the Wesleyan University collection of "Reichard-Navajo Song Records." The other six are available from the author, who hopes that some day, someone will study all of them from Gill's perspective. Four verses (#1, 4, 7, and 12) of FM's Twelve-verse Hogan Prayer have been published (Frisbie 1968:29–30). The translations of Hhb's prayers were done by McAllester, whose interpreter found these prayers to be "fragmentary" and "full of errors."

18. The use of songs is rarely reported in *Navajo Times* coverage of public dedications. The few examples tell readers that "songs were sung," "the Navajo Blessing was sung," or that "the building was blessed with traditional Navajo blessing songs," "songs from the Blessingway rites," or songs "from the medicine man's happy ways."

JS told Reichard (1963:565) that "four songs are required, twelve may be sung." There was no objection to using House Blessing songs at the 1940 dedication of the stadium for the Gallup Indian Ceremonial because these songs "belong to everyone" (1963:290). Mindeleff (1898:507-8) provides texts of two House Blessing songs and mentions a total of twelve.

19. During his 1956 blessing, one of the many held during the years for the Museum of Navajo Ceremonial Art (now the Wheelwright Museum) in Santa Fe, Hhb used some Corral Dance Songs and others from the Beautyway curing ceremonial, in addition to some Blessingway Songs.

20. In the three public versions witnessed by the author, AB used one song which could not be recorded; BS used no songs, and BY used two Talking God Hogan Songs, the recording of which is too faint for analytical work. In the early public blessings at the Fort Defiance Hospital and the El Navajo Hotel, songs were used but no information is available as to their genre. In the blessing of Lee Wyman's hogan, Blessingway Songs were also used (Frisbie 1970:186-94).

21. This song has been published in Frisbie (1967:151-58). It is the author's hope that some day the total corpus of House Blessing Songs and Prayers may be made available through publication.

22. Seminar discussions raised the question of whether such a core will eventually include one particular song and/or one particular prayer which would serve as "base metaphors" for the event and be generically derived from the original, private version. At the present time, there is no evidence for such a trend, and on the basis of the importance of "bounded individualism" to the Navajos, the author doubts that such will occur.

23. Earlier work on ethnography of performance exemplifies the need for such an investigation; therein, it was determined that there is no exact semantic equivalent for our concept of "performing" (Frisbie n.d.:9).

# 9
# Shootingway, an Epic Drama of the Navajos[1]

### DAVID P. McALLESTER
*Department of Music*
*Wesleyan University*

## INTRODUCTION

In the late 1950s I had a Guggenheim year in the Sun's House in the sky. I was conducted there by three Navajo ceremonial practitioners (singers) by means of an epic pageant entailing some ninety hours of music, prayer, graphic arts, dramatic staging, movement, and costume. Along with the singer, the one-sung-over (the protagonist), and the other participants, I assumed many roles of deities and other sacred beings. In this mythopoeic world my stage ranged from the snake country in the underworld to the water land of the fish people, to the sky domain of the Sun, Moon, and Winds, and back to earth again. I married four snake girls and poisoned their jealous father, I slept with four buffalo women and fathered a buffalo child, I laughed at the antics of the trickster Coyote, and I witnessed the first coming together of all the sacred beings of earth, sky, and water when they created the Shootingway[2] ceremonial for the well-being of humankind.

My first introduction to these adventures was by Ray Winnie of Lukachukai, Arizona, who devoted 20 days in October–November

1957 to a recitation of the 9 nights and 8 days of the Sun's House phase of the Male Shootingway, as he performs it. His narration, songs, and commentaries filled 36 hours of tape recording and 150 pages of notes. The tape and written documents record 454 songs and six long prayers as well as the accompanying description of the ceremony and information on the Shootingway myth behind it. Still, it became clear that only by witnessing an actual performance of the ceremony could I begin to grasp the complexities in the structure of this massive work of religious art.

Albert G. Sandoval, Jr., was my interpreter in the recording and transcribing of this material into Navajo and English. He informed me that his father, Albert G. Sandoval, Sr., was eager to have a performance of the nine-night version of Shootingway. He had undergone the first of the series some years before and the nine-night version would complete it for him. He and the singer he had chosen, Denet Tsosie of Lukachukai (Johnson 1969), were both interested in the preservation on tape of this rare ceremonial. By these fortunate circumstances I was able to attend an actual performance as recorder/participant.

The event took place on June 2–10, 1958, at Lukachukai. Denet Tsosie's older brother and teacher, Red Moustache, was a cosinger as was Ray Winnie. Ray also provided the Sun's House screen, an essential property. Albert G. Sandoval, Jr., continued to interpret and explain songs, prayers, and ceremonial procedures and also explained my needs and actions to the Sandoval family and the many others who helped with dedication and hard work to recreate the myth of Shootingway and bring about the protection and blessing invoked by the ceremonial. Twenty more hours of tape and 80 more pages of notes were added to the record of what transpires in Shootingway. The outlines of the House Chant became clearer but I also learned the deep truth of Denet Tsosie's remark, "Fifty-four years ago I began learning some things about this, when I was 12 years old. But though I am always finding out more I will never know it all—and there is much that I have forgotten."[3]

The House Chant is understood on at least three different levels by the Navajos. First, it is the actual ceremonial being performed over a person or persons in need of restoration to normal life after suffering certain kinds of traumata. It is also a recapitulation of the first time the ceremonial was given on earth by the Holy People. In

## Shootingway

a third dimension, it is an enactment, in many symbolic media, of a complex myth. To communicate the form and content of this religious drama it is easiest to start with the story. A synopsis of how Ray Winnie told it follows.

### MYTH OF THE SHOOTINGWAY

#### EPISODE AMONG THE SNAKE PEOPLE

There was a man who wanted to know about sacred things. The winds mocked at him for trying to become a holy person and called him "Holy Young Man" for his presumption. He became determined to find out how to see the winds and answer them and he set out on a quest to learn this and what other knowledge he could. His journey led him to the underworld and four snake girls brought him to their home. His new father-in-law pretended to be friendly, but made several attempts on his life and finally gave him poisoned tobacco. Thanks to a supernatural warning, the tobacco was switched and the old man died instead. The Snake People begged for the restoration of the old man's life and in return gave their power to Holy Young Man.

#### THE SKY AND WATER EPISODE

In quest of further power the young man resumed his wandering. He slew a mountain sheep at Mountain-around-which-traveling-was-done and was, in turn, attacked by the Thunder People and carried up into the sky. The Sun befriended him, gave him sky powers and four sacred arrows. He was shown the homes of the Sun, the Moon, Dark Wind, and Yellow Wind and, in the first House Chant in the sky, was shown how these sacred places could be brought together in the future House Chant on earth. When he returned to earth, trees, plants, water, and earth itself danced in the rain that accompanied him.

During the episode in the sky, Holy Young Man, in another embodiment known as Holy Boy, had an adventure in the fish world. He fell into a river, was swallowed by a fish, and finally cut his way out again with magic flints. He cured the wounded fish as it lay dying on the bank and in return was rewarded with the powers of the water world. As is made clear in the songs, Holy Young Man is a Quaternity: he is also Holy Young Woman, Holy Boy, and Holy Girl. At appropriate points in the myth he may take any of these forms. Persons undergoing the ceremonial identify with the appropriate embodiment depending on their age and sex.

### AMONG THE BUFFALO PEOPLE

Still seeking power, Holy Young Man pursued some shadowy figures into the buffalo country. He caught up with the shadows and found that they were Buffalo People. Again he found four wives, but the buffalos moved so swiftly over the vast plains of their country that Holy Young Man found it increasingly difficult to keep up with them. In desperation he killed many of them with his sacred arrows, but he was persuaded to bring them back to life. Finally one of his wives gave birth to his buffalo child; the songs reflect Holy Young Man's feelings as he gets a first glimpse of the baby's dark feather tail and dark flint hooves. When the little buffalo stood up and was able to move, the herd turned away from Holy Young Man and galloped across the plains in a cloud of dust and body steam. As he gazed after them, Holy Young Man was told by Talking God that he must return to Mountain-around-which-traveling-was-done and console himself with the knowledge that he had learned the buffalos' names and so had acquired their power.

### THE FIRST PERFORMANCE ON EARTH OF THE HOUSE CHANT

The story comes back to Mountain-around-which-traveling-was-done. As the Sun had promised when Holy Young Man was carried up into the sky, a great assembly of the Holy People took place: Sun, Winds, Stars, the Night People, Lightning, Water, Coyote, Jackrabbit, birds of all kinds, all came together bringing their songs. They helped put together their separate knowledge and rituals into one great bulwark for the protection of humankind. The focus of it all was the Sun's house. A replica was built banded horizontally with the colors of Sun, Moon, Dark Wind, and Yellow Wind, representing all of their houses, as the ceremony represented the bringing together of all the powers of the Holy People. As this knowledge was given to Holy Young Man, Coyote spoke for them all when he sang:

*Shootingway*

> Holy Young Man, with the eagle feathered arrow,
> you are truly holy, more so than I am!

A discussion of the ceremonial performance itself will show how directly it is a dramatic presentation of the story. After this discussion I will conclude with some thoughts on how the ceremony, both in its ideational content and in its form as a work of religious art, exemplifies certain premises of Navajo religious and philosophical thought.

## OUTLINE OF THE MAIN FEATURES OF SHOOTINGWAY

Despite the risk of oversimplification, I will introduce the reader to the ceremony by means of a greatly reduced outline of some of the main features. Except where noted, the description and explanations of meaning were given by Ray Winnie, Denet Tsosie, and Red Moustache.

Outline of Sun's House Phase of Male Shootingway

| | |
|---|---|
| 1st Night | Short singing: Snake Songs—assumption of snake power, exorcistic ritual: snake unravelers |
| 1st Day | Fire and purification rites, snake offerings made, Snake Prayer, offerings deposited |
| 2nd Night | Short singing: Thunder Songs—hero carried to sky, exorcistic ritual: thunder unravelers |
| 2nd Day | Fire and purification rites, thunder offerings made, Thunder Prayer, deposition |
| 3rd Night | Short singing: Holy Young Man Songs—magic arrows received, exorcistic ritual: arrow unravelers |
| 3rd Day | Fire and purification rites, Holy Young Man and Buffalo offerings, prayer, deposition |
| 4th Night | Short singing: Sun's Songs—Holy People at ceremonial, exorcistic ritual: Holy People unravelers |
| 4th Day | Fire and purification rites, Holy People offerings, prayer and deposition |
| 4th afternoon | Blessingway bath, Sun's house raised, Snake sandpainting, shock rite |

| | |
|---|---|
| 5th Night | All-night singing: Blessingway, Holy People's Songs |
| 5th Day | Outside singing and Snake Prayer/construction of Sun's house, identification ritual on Snake sandpainting |
| 6th Night | Short singing: Snake Songs |
| 6th Day | Outside singing and Thunder Prayer/construction of Sun's house, identification ritual on Fish and Thunder sandpainting |
| 7th Night | Short singing: Fish and Thunder Songs |
| 7th Day | Outside singing and Holy Young Man Prayer/Sun's house, identification ritual on Buffalo sandpainting |
| 8th Night | Short singing: Buffalo Songs |
| 8th Day | Outside singing and Holy People Prayer/Sun's house<br>Blessing Prayer<br>Blessingway bath<br>identification ritual by body painting<br>identification ritual on Earth and Sky sandpainting<br>Cattail Songs, cattail garment |
| 9th Night | All-night singing<br>First Songs—all Holy People present<br>short prayer<br>songs of all deities—recapitulation<br>mixed meat ritual<br>Dawn Songs<br>Blessingway conclusion<br><br>After dawn: cattail garment deposition, Blessing Prayer, Protagonist returns for last pollen blessing |

## Shootingway

### THE FIRST HALF OF THE CEREMONY

The outline brings out how the Shootingway myth is a scenario for the progression of ceremonial acts. The basic story about snakes, thunder beings, magic arrows in the sky, and ceremonial instruction back on earth is recapitulated in the song groups, the prayer offerings, and the long prayers of the first four consecutive night/day periods. At the end of each such period the "one-sung-over" in the role of the protagonist, Holy Young Man, goes out with offerings of jewels, the feathers of beautiful small birds, pollen, and other precious things, made alive ("lighted") by a ray of sunlight and given energy by accompanying small hoops. The offerings are left at an appropriate place—those to Thunder might be deposited at the foot of a lightning-struck tree, for example. The offerings are invitations to these beings to be present at the ceremony now being enacted. In the songs the protagonist is identified with the various beings. The Wind describes Holy Young Man as a snake in the Third Snake Song:

> I went to Holy Young Man,
> His tail was vibrating,
> His scales were menacing. . . .[4]

In a later song the Sun takes on the persona of Holy Young Man in his four embodiments:

> Now that I am Holy Young Man within the sky boundaries,
>   I travel in a sacred way,
> Now that I am Holy Young Woman, all over the earth,
>   I travel in a sacred way,
> Now that I am Holy Boy, over the water boundaries,
>   I travel in a sacred way,
> Now that I am Holy Girl, over the open plains,
>   I travel in a sacred way.

In the exorcistic rites, these are the beings who drive out all disrupting forces. In the prayers, the powers of these same beings are invoked for protection. As the night/day sequence goes by, the roster of allies summoned to the aid of the protagonist grows until it includes Sun, Moon, Earth, Waters, snakes, buffalos, mountains, and deities such as Enemy Slayer, Talking God, Spider Woman, and many others.

DAVID P. McALLESTER

THE PIVOTAL AFTERNOON AND NIGHT

The afternoon of the fourth day and the entire fifth night, taken together, constitute the midpoint of the ceremony. Here a dramatic change takes place. From a focus on exorcism and protection the emphasis shifts to the opposite processes: invocation and blessing. The invited deities have arrived.

One indication of this is the performance of a Blessing rite: the protagonist is bathed and dried with sacred cornmeal and pollen with the appropriate songs from the Blessingway ceremony. Next comes the raising of the house foretold by the Sun when Holy Young Man was carried up into the sky by the Thunder Beings. The blue home of the Sun, the white home of the Moon, the black home of Dark Wind, and the yellow home of Yellow Wind are combined in one structure. The deities themselves are seen at doorways near the ground and again at the top of the house. Over their heads are clouds and beautiful small birds flying and singing. Beside the deities in the doorways, snakes slowly issue forth and then draw back.

The house is a stage set painted on a screen some six feet long and five feet high. It is made of perpendicular wooden rods bound side by side. The clouds are sets of inverted wooden triangles and the deities are represented by painted wooden discs. The small birds have bodies of yucca root and wings and tails of thin wood, carved and painted and inserted in slots in the bodies. They are suspended by threads from the roof and move about when connecting threads are pulled from behind the screen. Helpers blow reed whistles with the tips held under water, producing a canary-like chirping and trilling, and they also move the carved and painted wooden snakes.

In front of this elaborate and beautiful assemblage a large snake sandpainting is laid out on the ground by several assistants under the direction of the singer. When it is completed, the protagonist comes in and sits in the middle, the focus of the Shock rite. From hiding places behind blankets at the north and south sides of the hogan, two actors dressed and painted as a black bear and Holy Young Man, rush out suddenly, stand threateningly over the protagonist, and drown out the singing with loud yells. They represent "the dangers and suffering encountered by Holy Man," and the shock is "intended to eliminate fear and inspire confidence" (Reichard 1950:717).

*Shootingway*

Now the protagonist leaves; the Sun's house, the sandpainting, and the costumes of the impersonators are all dismantled and nightlong singing begins. First there is a sequence of the songs of the Night People and then songs of Blessingway continue until dawn.

THE SECOND HALF OF THE CEREMONY

After the fifth night the progression of the ceremony switches from night/day to day/night. The presence of the deities invited with the prayer offerings is now indicated in the construction of a large sandpainting on the floor in front of the Sun's House screen which is rebuilt each morning. The deities are represented in the design and also in the texts of the songs being sung during the making of the sandpainting. The protagonist is identified with these sacred beings in the texts of the songs and also in the sandpainting ritual itself. Though not allowed to be present while the design is being constructed, the protagonist is called in, once it is completed with a special high-pitched call, "Hataaaahiiiiiooooeee!" (hatááłí—"one-sung-over"). If, for example, there were two protagonists, a man and a young female relative, they would come in answer to the call and seat themselves on the appropriate parts of the sandpainting. If it were the Buffalo sandpainting, the man would take his place on the black buffalo figure identified with Holy Young Man and the girl would be on the yellow figure identified with Holy Girl.

Colored pigments from the figures' feet, knees, front, back, shoulders, and head (Kluckhohn and Wyman 1940:57-58) are applied to the corresponding points on the protagonists' bodies. After this, coals from the fire are placed by their feet and a pinch of incense is sprinkled on the coals. A puff of fragrant smoke arises and the protagonists draw this toward themselves with their hands and rub it on their faces and bodies. The incense is made of various sweet and pungent substances to which are added minute bits of feather from the small birds whose singing symbolizes happiness and blessedness. This act is a "benediction and anodyne" (1940:49) and creates the feeling of happiness associated with the birds.

On the fifth day the sandpainting is of snakes and the singing is of snakes both when the sandpainting is being made during the morning, and in the short singing of the following night. The sandpainting of the sixth day is often a double scene showing Holy

Young Man being carried to the sky by Thunder Beings and also Holy Boy swallowed by fish (Wyman 1970a:58–66). The singing alternates Thunder Songs with songs of fish and ducks.

Another doubling takes place all through the second half of the ceremonial. As the Sun's house is being raised inside the hogan, the singer and protagonist seat themselves, facing east, before an altar a few yards from the door of the hogan. This is a mound of earth upon which are placed the symbols of Shootingway. Many of the darts, arrows, and prayersticks are standing erect in the earth of the mound. Others are lying on it in a prescribed order (Haile 1947a:68).

This set-out ritual begins before dawn. In early June at Lukachukai it began at about 3:30 A.M. and continued while the stars faded and the first light of dawn began to appear in the sky. The outside song was a Coyote Song, very long, in which the trickster vaingloriously claims that all the Night Songs are his, that he understands all the forces of nature (which he lists in detail) and, indeed, that he *is* these forces and that all the world is impressed by the beauty and holiness of his power. The first prayer of the first day was then repeated.

During the Coyote Song and the many sections of the prayer, House Raising Songs were sung inside the hogan as the laborious work of preparing and putting up the screen took place. This involved freshening up the painting on the house itself, on the figures of clouds, deities, and birds, and assembling the whole complex. Supports about five inches thick were set firmly in the ground and a crossbeam was lashed into place. Posts and beam were then completely covered with spruce twigs tied in overlapping tiers. Next came the songs for the sandpainting. Thus the prayers outside as well as the songs inside were a reprise of the first four days but with the augmentation of the Sun's house and the sandpainting and its ritual.

The sandpainting of the seventh day was of the Buffalo People, as were the songs that accompanied its construction. These were also the songs that were performed in the short singing that night. Each day the Sun's house was raised and then a new sandpainting was laid out on the floor before it. Each day the whole assemblage was dismantled when the one-sung-over went out after the incense rite that concluded the sandpainting ritual. When all this activity was over and the hogan had been tidied up and the dust settled, there

*Shootingway*

was a grateful period of peace and serenity when all the participants took time to rest, doze, or converse quietly.

The ceremony approached its second and greater climax on the eighth day. After the singing outside and the last raising of the Sun's house, a Blessingway rite was again given, preceded by a prayer similar to the one at the beginning of the ceremony. The chief difference was that the emphasis had now turned from pleas for protection to statements that with the help of the supernatural beings the protagonist's energy had now been restored.

The Blessingway bath and drying "cleaned the one-sung-over" for the painting of the symbols of Shootingway on his body (see fig 9.1). His face was banded with the colors of the four houses in the sky, snakes were drawn on his arms and legs, ending with heads at the thumbnails and great toenails. The black-tipped yellow snake tongues were realistically carried under on the balls of the digits. At the same time the last great sandpainting was drawn. In Ray Winnie's version he mentioned a design showing the four embodiments of Holy Young Man as appropriate for this day (Newcomb and Reichard 1937: Plate XIV). A. G. Sandoval, Sr., requested the sandpainting of Earth and Sky (Reichard 1934:194–95). As the body painting and sandpainting proceeded, identification between protagonist and sandpainting was established at frequent intervals by gesture and application of pigment. Similarly, when the dressing of the protagonist in a cattail garment (bandoleers and wristlets of braided cattail leaves) took place, each item was applied to the sandpainting before it was put on the one-sung-over.

The long singing of the last night of the ceremony began late: considerable care was taken to see that it did not start before 11:00 P.M. After First Songs and Night People Songs, there was a break at about 2:30 A.M. Among the songs that followed were Holy Young Man Songs. When a Coyote Song came in the sequence, care was taken to see that everybody present was awake. One hundred and thirteen songs had been performed by the time a mixed meat stew had been prepared. This contained, symbolically, meat from every kind of food animal. So many animals had been killed and restored in the enactment of the legend it was necessary for all of us who had participated to partake of the stew before we could eat meat again in ordinary life.

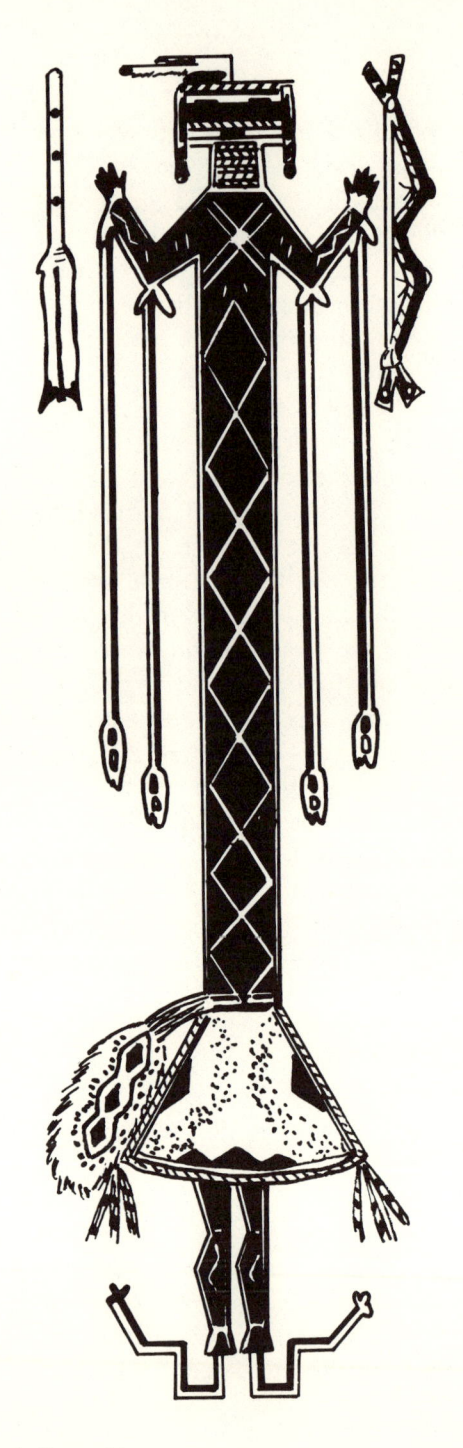

FIGURE 9.1. Holy Young Man.

# Shootingway

The last song was the one hundred and twenty-fifth of the night. At the close the basket drum, used on the last four nights, was put away and a period of quiet ensued in the early light while the protagonist and singer went out to dispose of the cattail garment. It was removed from the protagonist and placed on a small tree in such a way that the tree was dressed as the one-sung-over had been. The feather from the protagonist's head was the last item to be removed and was then attached to the tip of the tree.

The ceremony closed with a Blessing Song back in the hogan. The protagonist was given pollen to eat and his body was blessed with pollen. The pollen pouch was then handed around the hogan, sunwise, and everybody present gave a pollen blessing in turn: a pinch to the tongue, another to the top of the head, and then the last few grains sprinkled out to the world. Usually each participant accompanies this act with a brief prayer in his/her own words ending with the formula:

> Hózhǫ́ǫ́ nahasdlį́į́',
> Hózhǫ́ǫ́ nahasdlį́į́'!
> Conditions of beauty have been restored,
> Conditions of beauty have been restored!

## DETAILS OF THE FIRST NIGHT

Though the minimal outline given above was sufficient to suggest the ritual dramatization of the myth, it gave little indication of the wealth of artistic imagination in an actual ceremony. Yet it is important to understand the sheer mass of the ritual in order to appreciate its quality. To give the reader a sense of this detail I will give a fuller account of the first night and the first day of the House Chant.

### PREPARATIONS

These included the collection of the plants to be used with the unravelers and the fine chopping of other plants used in the emetic. The woolen strings to be unraveled, colored sand and other pigments for the sandpaintings, and yucca strips for tying were all laid by, ready for use.

DAVID P. McALLESTER

CONSECRATION OF THE HOGAN

A helper stuck twigs of oak in the crevices between the lowest roofbeams inside the hogan, first over the door, then in succession at the west, south, and north sides. Cornmeal was then rubbed on each beam in the same order, just below the sprig of oak. These actions were to let the Holy People know that a ceremony was about to take place and the oak twigs also commemorated the oak posts of the first hogan (Kluckhohn and Wyman 1940:77).

PREPARATION OF MEDICINES

The protagonist's bed and resting place was at the west side of the hogan just north of that of the singer. East of the beds a blanket was spread and, just east of this, the singer made a tiny mound of earth on which he set a large shell, like a clamshell with a pink nacreous lining. To the east of the shell, on another little mound he placed a glass dish. He poured water into each of these with a gourd dipper, moving it as he poured: east to west and back again, south to north and back, and then around the container in a clockwise ("sunwise") direction. A powdered medicine specific to Shootingway was added to the water in the shell and a general "chant lotion" (1940:51) to that in the glass dish. A feathered wand about a foot long was laid pointing east across the shell. This was to protect the medicine.

Next, an orange cloth, folded into a long strip about a foot and a half wide, was laid south to north on the blanket near the front edge and the Shootingway properties described above, the wands, darts, arrows, snakes, and other items that were set out on the outside altar, were laid on it. Four unraveler strings were tied to the carved wooden snakes in such a way that each held a small bundle of herbs against the snake. The strings were tied in knitting knots so that a single pull would release the entire binding.

SINGING AND UNRAVELING

The protagonist got up from his resting place, adjusted his blanket toga fashion, and walked sunwise around the stove. When he resumed his seat the ceremony had officially begun. "It shows the Holy People who the one-sung-over is."

# Shootingway

*First Snake Song*

Now Holy Young Man, now Holy Young Man,
   Is carrying the great snake,
Now Holy Young Woman, now Holy Young Woman,
   Is dangling the great snake,
Now Holy Boy, now Holy Boy,
   Is carrying the great hoop,
Now Holy Girl, now Holy Girl,
   Is rolling the great hoop.

The song is a poetic identification of the various embodiments of Holy Young Man with the Snake People and it also indicates a progressively more manipulative assumption of snake power in the form of the garments (the bodies) of the snakes. During the song the protagonist got up from his place, removed his clothing, and sat on the strip of cloth, north of the unravelers. When asked the reason for undressing, Denet Tsosie replied, "It is not the clothing that is being sung over, it is the person."

*Second Snake Song*

His body is dark, he came to us,
   It is edged with white, he came to us,
"My child!" he came to us
   In a sacred way, he came to us . . .
Her body is white . . .
   It is edged with black . . . etc.

The song describes the colors of the snakes' bodies as they are depicted on prayer offerings and in sandpaintings. The word "sacred" (*dighiin*) has the connotation of immunity to danger conferred by the presence of the snakes. The identification motif is conveyed by the snake saying to the Holy Young Man group, "My child."

*Third Snake Song*

I went to Holy Young Man,
   "The tail is threatening," he was saying,
I went to him, I went to him,
   "The scales are threatening," he was saying,
I went to him.

It was the winds who mocked Holy Young Man. They could blow on him from all directions and he could not see them. Here the wind is singing and he has changed his tune. He is impressed by Holy Young Man, now that he has the power of the Snake People. Again we see the identification of Holy Young Man with the Snake People.

> *Fourth Snake Song*
> Walks-with-his-body, here's where he went,
>   I am following behind, looking down;
> He is dark like the night, he is light like the dawn,
>   Warning at his tail, warning at his head,
> A warning sound at either end!
> Slender-body . . .   See-through-his-body . . .
> Pollen-body . . .

The progression of degrees of identity moved another step further in this song with the enunciation of the Snake's names. In Navajo usage, names are seldom used and to do so is to deal with great power.

> *Fifth Snake Song*
> Now Holy Young Man came to us here,
>   The rattle behind him, the rattle before him,
> Both ends are rattling . . .
> Black-all-over came to us here . . .
> Walks-with-his-body came to us here . . .

The text describes the Holy Young Man group as snakes sounding their rattles. The description is repeated in the second verse, but the names are changed to the colors of the snakes. In the third verse the names are changed once again to the increasingly specific and personal names of the Snake People. During this many-layered song of identification the singer put the beaver fur strip around his neck and took his position before the protagonist. This is the companion piece to the smooth otter fur that caused lightning to glance off when Holy Young Man was attacked by the Thunder Beings.

> *Sixth Snake Song*
> Now Holy Young Man, you've started singing
>   my songs, I heard you, I know it,
> Now Holy Young Woman, you've started . . . etc.

This song was by the leader of the Snake People, Holy Young Man's

## Shootingway

father-in-law. The old man urged his son-in-law to learn some of his songs, and here he observes that his advice has been followed. During this song the unraveling rite began with a body blessing by the snake unravelers. The singer picked them up and pressed them to the one-sung-over's body from feet to head, as he sat on the strip of orange cloth. Then the singer put the bundle down except for one which he unraveled at the protagonist's right foot. The string was unknotted with a smooth, sweeping pull that ended with a gesture, with the unraveled string, towards the smokehole. The singer gave a high trill: "Brrrr, brr, brr!" with lips and voice as he pulled the knots out of the string, and he blew his breath towards the smokehole at the end of the gesture. The herbs, untied, fell to the ground and were quickly put aside. They symbolized the falling away of evil or any difficulties, as did the unraveling of the knots. The gesture and the blowing sent the bad influences out of the smokehole.

The second unraveler was used at the left foot, the third was pressed to the protagonist's back, then unraveled at his breast. The fourth was pressed to his head and then unraveled at his face. The trill is the call of the Sandhill Crane who was helped by human beings when his child was ill and gave his song in return. Like the high flight of the cranes, the one-sung-over was symbolically lifted far above any danger.

> *Seventh Snake Song*
> He is crawling along, head raised,
> He is crawling along, head raised,
> Now Holy Young Man is crawling along, head raised,
> Now the Great Dark Snake is crawling along . . .
> He is crawling in the dust . . .
> He is crawling in the dew . . .
> He is radiating danger . . .
> He is trembling at the danger . . .
>    Living into old age, over and over,
>    Because of this, blessed everywhere . . .
> Now Holy Young Woman . . . etc.

Here the identification seems to be complete. The Holy Young Man group have all the characteristics of the Snake People.

### BODY PAINTING AND PROTECTION

As the song progressed, the singer dipped his finger into the chant lotion in the glass dish and traced on the protagonist's body the outline of the body painting he was to receive on the eighth day. At the center of the breast was outlined the sun. Then the singer went over the shoulders and under the arms, tracing bandolers. Where they crossed in the middle of the back a moon symbol was traced. Next the singer went down the arms and legs in the zigzags of a snake design, trilling as he did so. The protagonist then drank some of the lotion and washed his body with the rest.

Now, protected by the sacred decoction and by the drawings of sun, moon, and snakes, he sat waiting for the further protection of an administration of Shootingway medicine. As the singer stood before him, waiting for the next song, he dipped the tip of the feathered wand into the medicine and put it in his mouth to taste it.

*Song of Protection* (This is not a Snake Song but a song of the weapons that protect the medicine in the shell.)
>The dark bow happens to be my power,
>   The eagle-feathered arrow happens to be . . .
>   The mock-orange bow happens to be . . .
>   The tail-feathered arrow happens to be . . .

As the singer started the song he held the shell of medicine to the protagonist's mouth. At the mention of each of the arrows in the song the protagonist drank. The feathered wand was held across the shell so that the medicine flowed under it. After the fourth swallow, the one-sung-over rubbed what was left on his body and the singer drained the last drops into his own mouth and put the shell away in his ceremonial bundle.

*Eighth Snake Song*
>   The striped racer, his ear loops, one of them,
>   This is his payment, my payment, I am saying,
>   The striped water snake . . .
>   The striped rattlesnake . . .
>   The striped mountain snake . . .

This is one of the many songs referring to the payments the Snake People made to Holy Young Man for bringing their leader back to life. It was used for the last bit of ritual during the short singing—the censing of the protagonist. This took place as described above; the protagonist then sat back in his place and dressed himself. The blanket was taken out after the paraphernalia had been returned to the ceremonial bundle.

*Shootingway*

The strip of cloth went to the singer as payment for this part of the ceremony. The last ritual act of the one-sung-over was to put on his blanket, walk outside, and then return. Once again the identity of the protagonist was declared to the watching Holy People. The evening's ritual took little more than an hour, after which the singer and protagonist and a few of the other participants slept in the ceremonial hogan while everyone else went home for the night.

## DETAILS OF THE FIRST DAY

### FIRE RITUAL PREPARATIONS

Firewood, cedar bark for tinder, pokers, and other materials were brought in and the stove was removed to make room for the sudatory fire. A fire drill was prepared by lashing a beargrass point to a three-foot shaft of lightning-struck oak. The four pokers were cut from the east, then west, south, and north side of a lightning-struck cedar tree which also supplied the bark to be used as tinder. Herbs from near the tree were gathered to go in the emetic mixture.

### FIRE STARTING SONG

> You should place one upon the other,
> In the beginning at the very edge of the world,
> First Man and First Woman had them,
> You should place one upon the other,
> You should place one upon the other . . .

Messenger Fly and the Wind People brought fire-making instructions to Holy Young Man at the first performance of the House Chant on earth.

The four pokers were laid in a row in front of the one-sung-over, with their tips to the east. The cedar bark, finely shredded, was placed on top of them and the hearth stick on top of the tinder. The fire drill was set in a notch in the hearth stick and two helpers, taking turns, rotated the drill between their palms, pressing strongly downward. In less than a minute the beargrass tip ground a fine wood powder into the notch and this quickly turned dark, began to give off smoke and then ignited, becoming a glowing coal. The coal was gently tapped out of the notch into the tinder which was then blown into a blaze and the fire was started on the spot where the stove had been. The pail of emetic water was put on the fire to warm and more wood was piled around it.

With several helpers working, four sandpainting snakes, also called "pokers," were drawn about three feet long with their heads towards the fire. The one on the east was crooked and black, on the south, crooked and blue, on the west, straight and white, and on the north, straight and pink and glittering with tiny fragments of mica. One of the wooden pokers was laid to the left of each snake figure.

At the same time a place for the emetic rite was prepared to the north of where the protagonist usually sat. This was a lightning design curved around a basin of clean sand. Short sections of rainbow were made to receive the protagonist's hands and knees as he knelt in front of the basin. A hoop about two feet across was planted at a slant over the sand basin so that the one-sung-over could vomit through it. The principle is that of the valve: evil influences in the vomit could not return through the hoop to lodge again in the protagonist.

The hoop, another locus of Shootingway symbolism, was made of a slender branch of oak; the tip was cut off at a slant, leaving a smooth surface on which was painted a small face in the Shootingway colors: forehead–white, region of the eyes–black, region of the mouth–blue, and chin–yellow. This is the sequence of colors on the Sun's house and the face of Holy Young Man. These colors were also carried on the main body of the hoop in quadrants starting at the butt end: black, white, blue, and yellow. Midway on each quadrant were bands of the opposite color and near these bands were tied spruce twigs except on the blue section which was buried in the sand. The hoop was tied with a strip of yucca leaf and also with an unraveler string where the black butt and the yellow tip came together.

FIRE SONG

I have searched over the earth,
  I was told to do it,
I have searched over the mountains,
  I was told to do it,
I have searched under the sun . . .
I have searched for the fire . . .
I have searched everywhere with water . . .

The song tells of Holy Young Man's search for power. When his wanderings took him up on the mountains he saw the Sun and told him of his quest. The fire represents the campfire of the Great

## Shootingway

Snake. It was seeing this, at night in the distance, that led him to the snake country. The water refers to quenching the fire.

During this song the protagonist came in and undressed at his place. The singer and other participants undressed, also, as the heat from the brightly blazing fire quickly increased.

POKER SONGS

Holy Young Man, thrust him in,
    Sun, thrust him in,
It is frightening to be thrust in,
Old-age-returning, thrust him in,
Because-of-this-blessed-everywhere, thrust him in . . .

Holy Young Woman. . . . Moon. . . .
Holy Boy. . . . Morning Star. . . .
Holy Girl. . . . Evening Star. . . .

Dark Wind, thrust him in,
His dark fire, thrust him in,
It is frightening to be thrust in,
Old-age-returning, thrust him in,
Because-of-this-blessed-everywhere, thrust him in . . .

Blue Wind . . . his blue fire . . .
Yellow Wind . . . his yellow fire . . .
Gleaming Wind . . . his gleaming fire . . .

During these songs the singer added wood from the supply heaped up north of the door and stirred the fire with the poker lying by the north snake sandpainting. Then he added wood from a supply to the south of the door and stirred the fire with the south poker. After this the emetic was prepared and arrowheads were taken from the ceremonial bundle and put at the four points of the compass in the basket containing the emetic. At the end of the second song the protagonist circled the fire, stepping over the snake drawings, and knelt before the basket on the short sections of rainbow.

EMETIC SONG

Water splashing, water splashing,
Female water splashing and gleaming, water splashing,
Medicine gleaming, live medicine, water splashing,
Medicine traveling, medicine talking, water splashing,
    Living into old age, over and over,
    Because of this, blessed everywhere . . .

This was sung by Frog at the ceremony at Mountain-around-which-traveling-was-done. It is his water that causes all things to grow and that quenched the Great Snake's fire. At the time of the ceremony Frog said, "My grandchildren, I would like to have my song put in there."

The protagonist knelt over the sand basin and drank four times from the basket. Using an eagle feather to induce emesis by tickling his throat, he vomited four times through the hoop into the sand basin.

When the emesis was over the one-sung-over was blessed with the hoop while the trilling call of the Crane was made by the singer. At the end of the blessing the unraveler was pulled towards the smokehole by the singer. All this time the fire was blazing from the constant addition of kindling and small dry branches. The protagonist, singer, and all participants were sweating profusely. Because of a curtain-blanket over the door the ventilation was curtailed and the hogan filled with smoke. The singer observed to the coughing participants that this also helped to drive out evil influences, but he did move the curtain aside occasionally, using one of the pokers. Fresh air would rush into the hogan and the smoke would lift.

The final act in the emetic and sudatory ritual was the asperging of the protagonist and participants. After we had all bathed our bodies in the emetic mixture, being careful to scoop up a quantity of the chopped green herbs in the infusion with each handful, the singer dipped an eagle feather brush into a pail of cool water and shook it liberally over everyone. He then went outside with the bull-roarer, a flat wooden stick about six inches long on the end of a leather thong. By twirling this over his head he produced a loud buzzing sound to let the supernaturals know of the ceremony in progress.

After this the one-sung-over went out while the sandpaintings were obliterated with the wooden snakes from the ceremonial bundle. The pigments were collected in a blanket and taken outside. The hoop was dismantled, the remains of the fire removed, and all the warm sand under it also shoveled away. A busy interval of smoothing fresh sand and setting the stage for the making of the prayer offerings ensued. By now it was 8:30 A.M. and a strong shaft of sunlight was streaming through the smokehole and illuminating the

# Shootingway

dense cloud of dust raised by the housecleaning. The call "*Behatá-dłioooooeeee!*" was raised by several voices and the one-sung-over entered and resumed his place in the west side of the hogan.

### MAKING THE PRAYER OFFERINGS

The hogan now became a scene of industrious preparation. Several helpers were seated on the floor cutting four long, jointed reeds into the required lengths with a piece of hacksaw blade. They sat cross-legged using the edge of their shoe soles for a workbench. The short sections were rubbed on pieces of sandstone to make the right surfaces for the painted designs to be applied. Two helpers were given a place on a blanket on the north side of the hogan where they began making small hoops to be offered with the sections of reed. An atmosphere of jovial cooperation prevailed and this increased when breakfast was brought in and work was briefly suspended. Jokes and gossip were exchanged and this continued as the workers went back to the prayer offerings and began preparing pigments for painting them with snake and other designs.

A new strip of cloth, figured this time, was folded lengthwise and laid south to north on the blanket in front of the protagonist. Twelve small squares of cloth were laid in a row, south to north on the cloth.

### THE LEADER PRAYER OFFERING SONG

They are coming, they are coming, they are coming,
They are coming, they are coming, they are coming. . . .

From below the east, they are coming towards us,
Now the Sky People are coming towards us,
The sky is trailing down, they are coming towards us,
With bows of zigzag lightning they are coming towards us,
Now with arrows of zigzag lightning they are coming towards us,
With rain coming down, they are coming towards us,
With dark waters they are coming towards us,
With rain coming down, they are coming towards us,
With dark hoops they are coming towards us,
With dark prayer offerings they are coming towards us,
Hidden in dark mist they are coming towards us,

DAVID P. McALLESTER

Making the Navajo country endure forever, they are
   coming towards us;
From below the west, Water People . . . bows of straight
   lightning . . . blue water . . . blue hoops . . .
From below the south . . . Sun People . . . bows of sunray . . .
   yellow waters . . . yellow prayer offerings . . .
From below the north . . . Summer People . . . bows of rainbow
   . . . gleaming waters . . . gleaming hoops . . .

Ray Winnie's explanation of this song returns to the origin of Holy Young Man's name:

All the people mentioned here are coming in from the four directions to this ceremony that was taking place at Mountain-around-which-traveling-was-done. They wanted to see it. The Sun said, "Listen, my son, they are making fun of you when they call you Holy Young Man, but now I will teach you and you really will be holy. Then all these people will come and see how much you have learned." All these groups of people came to have their songs in this ceremony. That is the reason there are so many. Even the son of the Sun came down. He said, "We are going to be using this ceremony, too." So were the Moon and the Stars. We see them painted on the prayer offerings.

During this first Song of the Prayer Offerings the painting of the hoops and sections of reed began. The next two songs were similar to the first and rapid progress was made in painting snake designs on two groups of four sections of reed about three inches long, and a third group six inches long. Jewels, bits of bright feathers from small birds, native cotton, hairs of turkey-beard, and other precious things were laid out on the cloth squares in front of the protagonist. On the next song they were placed in the hollow reed tubes.

TOBACCO SONG

Holy Young Man, I ask you to prepare it for me,
   Prepare the dark prayer offering for me,
   Prepare the tobacco cloud for me,
   Prepare its broad leaf for me,
   Prepare its dark flower for me,
   Prepare its cool tobacco for me,
   Prepare the sun for me,
Prepare living into old age, over and over,

## Shootingway

> Prepare because of this, blessed everywhere, for me,
>
> Holy Young Woman . . . white prayer offering. . .
>   tobacco water, narrow leaf . . . white flower . . .
>   the moon . . .
>
> Holy Boy . . . blue prayer offering . . .
>   tobacco mist . . . broad leaf . . . blue flower . . .
>   the morning star . . .
>
> Holy Girl . . . yellow prayer offering. . . .
>   tobacco water . . . narrow leaf . . . yellow flower . . .
>   the evening star . . .

Though the song focused on the tobacco it refers to all the offerings being placed in the sections of reed. The next song cites the healing effect of the tobacco.

### SECOND TOBACCO SONG

> He came to the one who was trembling with fear,
> Prepared the tobacco offering for him,
> He prepared it for the one who could not sit still,
> He prepared it and the youth became whole again.
>
> He came to the young woman . . . to the boy . . . to the girl . . .

At this point the offering/deities were given life in a poignant and imaginative way. As each section of reed, from south to north, was filled, the protagonist held a crystal up to the sunlight, then touched the crystal to the open end of the prayer offering. The singer then dropped in a pinch of pollen, moistened the opening with a finger dipped in the glass dish of chant lotion, and then moistened a different finger and dipped it in the pollen pouch. The pollen, adhering to his finger, assumed a pastelike consistency from the moisture and was quickly pressed into the end of the tube, sealing the living sunray in by means of the basic symbol of fertility and life itself.

Though the prayer offerings are so small, they function dramatically in much the same way as the sandpaintings. Not only are they an offering to the deities, they are a portrayal or representation of the deities. They are three-dimensional, like the snake wands carved of wood in the ceremonial bundle, but they are even more lifelike in that they have "insides." As they are prepared for their journey to a location where the relevant deities will find them, the action takes on the dimensions of puppet theater.

The next two songs were of the Snake People. During the first, the protagonist blessed each offering by sprinkling it with pollen from a small brush dipped in the pollen pouch. As the offerings lay on the strip of cloth in a row, the blessing moved from west to east, and then around the small hoop at the base of each one. The singer then did the same, but strewing the pollen in the usual way with his fingers. On the second song the singer stood with the shell of Shootingway medicine in his hand. At appropriate places in the song he administered the medicine to the protagonist, allowing it to flow under the protective feathered wand, as on the night before. He then gestured down the line of offerings from north to south with the wand. After doing this four times he blew his reed whistle, attached to the beaverskin neckpiece, down the line from north to south.

The last song was a Blessing Song. The singer blessed himself with pollen, first on his tongue, then to the top of his head, and then out to the east. Then he gave a body blessing to the protagonist again finishing with a sprinkle of pollen to the east. Next he went down the line of offerings with a sprinkle of pollen and wrapped each one in its square of cloth, folding the small hoop in the last lap. The three groups of four were gathered into three separate piles and then all placed together in a ceremonial basket and put in the hands of the protagonist as he sat in his place.

### THE PRAYER OF THE SNAKES' PRAYER OFFERING

At Tsehot'ahi, at the house made of darkness,
At Tsehot'ahi, at the house made of dawn,
At Tsehot'ahi, at the house made of blue afterglow,
At Tsehot'ahi, at the house made of yellow afterglow;

Dark pollen concealing his body,
  Dark snake young man, leader,
White pollen concealing her body,
  White snake young woman, leader,
Blue pollen concealing his body,
  Blue snake boy, leader,
Yellow pollen concealing her body,
  Yellow snake girl, leader,

Your offering I have made, for you I have made it,
  Today I am your child, today I am your grandchild,

## Shootingway

> Your offering I have made, for you I have made it,
>   Today I am your grandchild, today I am your child,
>
> You will look after me, to defend me,
>   You will extend your hand to defend me,
> You will stand before me to defend me,
>   You will speak to defend me,
>
> Whatever I say to you, you will do it,
>   Whatever you say to me, I will do it.
>
> With every breeze coming towards me from you,
>   There will be blessing there,
> With every rain coming towards me from you,
>   There will be blessing there,
> With every thunder coming towards me from you,
>   There will be blessing there,
> Under plants coming towards me from you,
>   There will be blessing there,
> Under trees coming towards me from you,
>   There will be blessing there,
>
> The dew, let it always take form for me,
> Pollen, let it always take form for me,
>
> With these, before me it will be blessed,
> With these, behind me it will be blessed,
> With these, behind me it will be blessed,
> With these, before me it will be blessed,
>
> Blessed again it has become,
> Blessed again it has become,
> Blessed again it has become,
> Blessed again it has become.

This, in abbreviated form, is the first of four sections of the prayer. Part 2 refers to houses made of plants and pollen at Moving Mountain and Gleaming Mountain and adds the names we have already seen in the Fourth Snake Song. Part 3 specifies the protective snake powers:

> The means by which you breathe,
>   Will be the means by which I also will breathe,
> The means by which you speak,
>   Will be the means by which I also will speak,
> That which is around you,
>   Will also be that which is around me,

> That which flashes out from you,
> Will also flash out from me,
> That which flashes around you four times,
> Will also flash around me four times.

Part 4 identifies additional sacred places, speaks of further protection, and ends with a powerful invocation of blessing:

> Living into old age, over and over,
> Because of this, blessed everywhere,
>   That is what I am,
> Blessed I will be, I am saying it;
>
> With blessing before me I will go,
> With blessing behind me I will go,
>
> With blessing above me I will go,
> With blessing below me I will go,
> With blessing all around me I will go,
> With pollen, truly blessed,
> With these, being blessed, I will go.
>
> Blessed again it has become,
> Blessed again it has become,
> Blessed again it has become,
> Blessed again it has become!

The singer folded a blanket into a low stool and sat on it, facing the patient for the prayer. He spoke in a fast monotone and the protagonist repeated every sacred word, litany-wise, a syllable or two behind.

### PLACING THE OFFERINGS

The last act on the first day was the journey of the protagonist to leave the offerings in a likely place where the Snake People would find them. The singer administered a body blessing, pressing the basket of offerings to the feet, palms, back, etc., of the one-sung-over, trilling with the call of the Crane as he did so. An otter skin with a whistle attached was placed around the protagonist's neck. Carrying the basket and wrapped in a blanket that indicated his role as protagonist in a ceremony, he left the hogan and was driven to the place for disposition of the offerings in a pickup truck. As he left, the last song began:

# Shootingway

SINGING AFTER IT
> With these he goes forth,
> With these he goes forth,
> Now at first light,
>> On the feet of the bluebird he goes forth,
>> With these he goes forth,
> Now his feet, living into old age, over and over,
> Now his feet, because of this blessed everywhere,
>> With these he goes forth.
>
> Now at the lifting of dawn,
>> On the legs of the blue swift . . .
>
> Now just before sunrise,
>> In the body of the yellow tanager . . .
>
> At sunrise,
>> With the voice of thunder . . .
>
> At high sun,
>> With the call of Ripener Fly . . .
>
> With these he goes forth,
> With these he goes forth!

While waiting for the protagonist to return, the singer said a brief prayer and then there was a considerable period of quiet waiting in the ceremonial hogan. When the protagonist returned with the empty wrappers, the singer brushed them out carefully and returned them to his bundle. The ritual was over for the day. When asked, the one-sung-over said that the first four offerings were laid facing the root of a piñon tree. A tree had to be found with roots somewhat exposed. The next four were laid by a living cedar and the last four, by a gray greasewood. He blew the whistle on the otter skin each time he turned away from depositing the offerings to let the Holy People know what he had done.

## CONCLUSIONS

The foregoing has been enough to give the reader an idea of some of the detail with which the story of Holy Young Man is dramatized in the Shootingway. In an impressive number of symbolic media including music, poetry, graphic design, emesis, sudation, and journeys, real and token, the protagonist and other participants stepped into the mythopoeic world of the time when things began, and acted out the adventures of its heroes. By doing so we all received the benefit of protection from harm and invocation of blessing from many potent deities and forces of nature.

In a dramatization employing so many modes of the arts it is to be expected that the world view of the Navajo people would be represented in a variety of ways. I would like to cite some of these, bearing in mind that Shootingway is an expression of traditional Navajo values. The People are a progressive nation and fully aware of the larger world that exists beyond the boundaries of the sacred mountains. There are rock 'n' roll record hops at civic centers and high schools as well as squaw dances that combine social dancing with the exorcism of enemy ghosts. There are some thirty Navajo country and western bands and an estimated three hundred ceremonial practitioners. There are Navajo composers using traditional musical modes to create new songs dealing with such contemporary problems as relocation and liquor. Many Navajos are interested in their traditions and do not see them as a barrier to "progress." Ceremonialism is studied at the Navajo Community College as well as by apprentice singers. Literacy in Navajo is taught in several schools. The old tradition is a vital force and promises to continue so.

Some of the insights provided by Shootingway and other ceremonies are evident in many other aspects of the culture. They have been observed by several generations of scholars of Navajo life, starting in the 1880s. For the reader's convenience I will group my impressions from the House Chant in two sections which I will label "well attested" and "tentative." In the former I will give additional evidence in citations from the literature. The latter are advanced here subject to further confirmation especially by discussion with the Navajos themselves. In each section there is a further subdivision: "ideational," for insights drawn from textual material in myth and songs and from direct discussions with Navajos, and "structural," for elements that seem to me to be embodied in artistic form.

#### WELL ATTESTED (IDEATIONAL)

*It is a world of immanent forces.* Twigs, stones, trees, and almost any living creatures have great power to do harm and to protect one from harm. Earth, air, sky, celestial bodies, fire, water, clouds, lightning, dew, and rainbow are all forces that not only act on, but interact *with* humankind. We saw it in the story of Shootingway, in the properties used in the ceremony and in the poetry of the songs and prayers

## Shootingway

(Reichard 1950:381-505; Haile 1947a:14-74; Kluckhohn and Leighton 1946:227-28; Kluckhohn and Wyman 1940:23-104). One of the most basic methods of interaction between immanent forces and humankind is through *identification*. Instances of how this is achieved were pointed out throughout this chapter (Reichard 1950:xxiv, 5,6).

*The desired state is harmony*, balance, (*hózhǫ́ǫ́*) with oneself, one's family, and all the parts of nature. *Hózhǫ́ǫ́* can be lost but there are ways by which it can be maintained or recovered. This idea is somewhat akin to our idea of good health, but is far more inclusive. It refers not only to sickness in our sense but also to states of mind and to one's relations with the immanent forces. A concomitant of balance is a duality that is all-pervasive. These include night-day, male-female, earth-sky, good-evil, and many others (Witherspoon 1977:201; Reichard 1950:249).

*It is a world with a sharp awareness of kinship*. We saw this all through the Shootingway story. Holy Young Man was himself a family and he became son-in-law, father, child, and grandchild of various beings as the adventure progressed. The assumption of supernatural power often seemed equated with kinship as a symbol of identification. Reciprocity was a principle of interrelationship on the positive side and the most unquestioning reciprocity was that between relatives (Witherspoon 1977:81-120; Kluckhohn and Leighton 1946:225).

*It is a practical world*. The aesthetic, for instance, is functional in the service of harmony, rather than a consideration for its own sake alone. Holy Young Man sought learning not for self aggrandizement but for its usefulness to humankind. "Holy" (*dighiin*) in Navajo is not equivalent to our notion of sacrosanct or elevated but, rather, "immune" to evil forces through knowledge of how to cope with them (Haile 1950a:155-56).

### WELL ATTESTED (STRUCTURAL)

*Duality*. This concept is so ubiquitous a feature of the ceremony that it needs little comment. Pairs, alternations, reciprocals could be seen all the way from minute details in the sandpaintings to the overall structure of the entire nine-nights' performance. The organization of song texts and the stanzas of prayers shows the same features as does the music that accompanies the former (Reichard 1950:147-268; McAllester n.d.).

DAVID P. McALLESTER

*Progression, sequence.* Matthews described the Navajo propensity for arranging songs in cycles and series in 1894. The progression is often in geographical location either mythical or mundane. The concept is evident in ritual acts such as the sequence of applications in a body blessing. It is applied to colors, numbers, jewels, ceremonial costume, and in the order of actions in preparing sacred properties and making sandpaintings. There is plentiful evidence of a universe ordered down to minute detail (Matthews 1894; McAllester 1954:83–84; Frisbie 1967:111; Wyman 1970b:113, n. 97; Reichard 1950:216–36).

*Symbolism of color, position, direction, material, and the like.* Many examples have been adduced in the foregoing pages. They are indications of a system of breathtaking complexity. The most thorough-going discussion of this in the literature is Reichard's monumental *Navaho Religion, A Study of Symbolism* (1950:147–278).

*Repetition.* Even in the partial account of Shootingway given here one can nonetheless see the importance of repetition as a structural principle. It is there in ceremonial acts and gestures, in motifs in sandpainting, song, and prayer. It is of course an essential element in structural devices such as pairing, but the Navajo mind goes much further with repetition than this. Reichard cites it as one of the methods of achieving identification (1950:112) and of increasing ceremonial effect (1950:117–18).

*Mirror image/radial design.* This is an important principle of organization in the reversal from night/day to day/night in the overall structure of the ceremony. It can be seen again in the ninth verse of the Prayer of the Snakes' Prayer Offerings (p. 225), and in the color coding in the second Snake Song (p. 213). Reichard (1950:167) reports its relative rarity in sandpaintings:

> After remarking the rarity of mirror symmetry, especially in the circular sandpaintings, I became acquainted with the paintings of [the Bead Chant] . . . laid out in mirror symmetry, requiring half the picture to be read sunwise, half anti-sunwise.

SOME TENTATIVE INTERPRETATIONS

Matthews and Reichard, more than most other observers, have given the outside world a sense of Navajo ceremony as it is actually performed. As all observers have noted, the apparently limitless and

# Shootingway

bewildering complexity of the ceremonial procedures takes on order with familiarity. We learn that there is a finite sequence of component parts. Thus Kluckhohn and Wyman (1940:76–107) can give a hypothetical outline of ceremonial procedures in general, and Wyman (1963:65–103, 125) can reduce myths and sandpaintings to comparative charts very helpful to the outsider trying to comprehend the whole. Gill (1974:34), analyzing thousands of lines of prayer, found that they all could be subsumed under 22 component prayer procedures.

No other people on earth have been so prolifically studied by anthropologists as the Navajos. Yet new insights such as Gill's from componential analysis of prayer are still possible. The thorough analysis of song form and text has barely begun (McAllester 1954; Frisbie 1967). Navajo myths have been studied for well over 80 years and yet new approaches yield new understanding (Moon 1970). All of this interest is testimony to the richness of the ceremonial arts that the Navajos have built into their lives.

All I would like to add here are a tentative difference of opinion on one point and a matter of emphasis on a structural principle. I have some thoughts on the nature of the persuasion brought to bear on the supernatural by Navajo ceremonialism and on the use of increase, or augmentation, as an elaboration on the principle of balance, pairing, and dualism in general.

### "The Compulsive Word"

In one respect I get a different reading of Navajo relations to the supernatural from the one enunciated in Reichard's *Prayer, The Compulsive Word* (1944), and further developed in *Navaho Religion* (1950:126, 181, 267–76), that requests to the supernaturals via prayer offerings, prayer, and song (and, in fact, all ritual acts) cannot be refused if they are done correctly. This view seems to me to carry overtones of the nineteenth-century separation of "magic" from "religion" and the differentiation of "medicine man" from "priest." It conflicts with Reichard's own category of unpersuadable deities (1950:63–70).

In discussing Navajo participation in ceremonies, Reichard suggests another dimension of persuasion that is much closer to my own experience in Navajo culture and my understanding of the texts of prayer and song. She notes the apparent contradiction of unquestioning conformity to ritual expectations with the individualism that is such a well-known feature of Navajo character. Her explanation is that the conformity does not result from external compulsion but from the high valuation of cooperation and reciprocity within the community, i.e., the " . . . privilege a Navaho individual values in his personal subordination to his group . . . " (1950:xxvii).

As I see it, this is the kind of relationship the ceremonial procedures attempt to establish between the protagonist and the supernaturals. It is not a mere formality when a Navajo addresses a stranger as "my uncle," or "my grandfather," and does the same to the deities in myth, prayer, and song.

The notion of reciprocity is more consonant than that of compulsion with such language as:

> Your offering I have made, for you I have made it,
> Today I am your child, today I am your grandchild . . .

from the third stanza of the Snake Offering Prayer, and the fifth stanza:

> Whatever I say to you, you will do it,
> Whatever you say to me, I will do it.

Denet Tsosie explained the meaning of the prayer offerings:

> The prayer offering is an exchange. It is an invitation to the Holy People and in return they restore the energy of the one-sung-over. When we put out the offerings we leave what is inside the cloth wrapping over there and bring the cloth back. Some of the Holy People might be inside that cloth when it is put away in the ceremonial bundle. We are pleading for them to help the one-sung-over and the singer to perform this ceremony that is to be done.

Gill does not find the element of compulsion in the corpus of prayer material he has analyzed, but finds Navajo prayer:

> . . . an act of communication, a re-enactment of primordial creation events, an act of establishing relationships on the basis of reciprocity, and an act of re-establishing place, which implies the re-establishment of relationships (1974:537).

Witherspoon argues from textual and linguistic evidence for the

## Shootingway

enormous power of the word in the Navajo world. Rather than functioning as we commonly see it as a set of symbols for describing the outside world, "language is the means by which form is projected onto substance" (1977:34). In the chapter "Controlling the World Through Language," he goes on:

> To the Navajo, sound is air in motion, and speech is highly refined and patterned air in motion. To put sound in patterned motion, one must control air. Air contains the supreme power of motion in the universe and the ultimate source of all knowledge. To control air is a process by which man participates in the omnipotence and omniscience of air. Thus the speech act is the ultimate act of knowledge and power, and by speaking properly and appropriately one can control and compel the behavior and power of the gods. This is the ontological and rational basis of the compulsive power of speech (1977:60).

I agree as to the primacy of the word at the time of creation, but here and now the singer in real life is more the *bricoleur* (Lévi-Strauss 1966:17–22) than the master of the absolute word. He tries out every combination that he knows, hoping to hit on the most helpful one. He is well aware that there is much which is beyond the power of words; many a ceremony has been abandoned in mid course because it was not doing any good, and there is a point in illness beyond which no ceremony can do any good. One of the first readjustments I had to make in living with Navajos was to stop thinking of the singer as an all-powerful holy man. I saw that singers were not given the deference I expected for "men of the cloth" and that they were not necessarily community leaders. I became accustomed to the trenchant doubts I heard expressed as to any given singer's authority as a practitioner.

Students of Navajo ceremonialism have been confused about just what illness a particular ceremony will cure. This is because the Navajos are not always sure, themselves. The nature of illness is not sharply defined nor are the means of dealing with it. There is a wide repertory of remedies and singers use something like the "buckshot" technique of the wonder-drug practitioners in Anglo medicine. They lay down a barrage of medico-religious effort—there is no one compulsive word, or even formula of words, but hours and days of prayer, song, and innumerable other symbolic endeavors are enlisted. If it were not for the *uncertainty* in the power of the word the

Navajos might never have created the astonishing edifice of their ceremonial system.

### Increase/Augmentation

Reichard has noted the increase of activity as a ceremony goes on. "On nights two to eight the singing resembles that of the first night, becoming longer as the ceremonial progresses. . . . Generally each rite becomes longer and more elaborate as the ceremony progresses" (1950:xxiv–xxv). In mythic descriptions of the universe she observes: "The worlds are thought of as superimposed hemispheres. . . . Each higher hemisphere is larger than the one below since the characteristics of the lower were imitated and added to, and the whole was magically enlarged" (1950:14).

One is conscious of this increase as the Shootingway described here goes on and more and more is added to it. I would like to stress this increase, noted by Reichard and others, and elevate it into a principle of artistic structure since it adds an important element to the principle of balance, pairing, and duality already so widely attested. In Denet Tsosie's Shootingway there was an increase in activity leading to a kind of climax on the fourth day and fifth night. Thereafter there were two simultaneous rites in progress each morning, with two singers officiating: the singing and praying at the altar outside and the sandpainting preparations inside the ceremonial hogan. This kind of augmentation of ritual activity takes place at any nine-night ceremony and during the latter days and nights of shorter ones (Kluckhohn and Wyman 1940: 76–104; Reichard 1950:349–51, 614–736).

The last day and night of the House Chant constituted another climax, larger than the first since it incorporated ideas from all that went before with the many new developments that took place. Navajo terminology recognizes the importance of this point: the last day is referred to as *"bijį́"* (its day) and the last night as *"bitłʼéé"* (its night) (1950:xxiv). Denet Tsosie also referred to the fourth day and fifth night by those terms.

It will serve to keep structuralist fantasies within bounds to end with Denet Tsosie's response when I asked him if *he* felt there was a high point anywhere in the long ceremony. His answer was not on what he "felt," but related a matter of fact. He did, indeed, know of

*Shootingway*

two high points, but what he revealed left me feeling more like Coyote mixing things up in his song than like Holy Young Man confirmed in his wisdom:

> There were two high points in the ceremony: the second sandpainting [the double sandpainting of Holy Young Man being carried into the sky by Thunder Beings and Holy Boy swallowed by fish] and the White Buffalo sandpainting. These two are the most sacred to make, even though other sandpaintings like Monster Slayer, or Earth and Sky seem as though they ought to be more sacred. But those other two are the ones – I don't know why that is.

## NOTES

1. My deepest gratitude goes to Ray Winnie, Albert G. Sandoval, Jr., Denet Tsosie, Albert G. (Chic) Sandoval, Sr., and Red Moustache for their willingness to share their knowledge and expertise concerning Shootingway with me. I am also indebted to Leland C. Wyman for reading the final manuscript. His keen eye and incomparable knowledge of the history of Navajo studies have been enormously helpful, but any recalcitrant errors are entirely mine.

2. From the time of Washington Matthews' studies, beginning in 1880, Navajo ceremonialism has engaged lively scholarly interest. Shootingway was first listed by the Franciscan Fathers, who also itemized ceremonial properties of this chant, among others (1910:363-65; 402-21). Reichard (1934) published the first detailed account of the ceremony. She had been the one-sung-over herself in two performances and gave an intimate perspective of the ceremony from the point of view of a woman in a Navajo household. Wyman (1936) also reported on his experiences as the protagonist in a Female Shooting Lifeway and concluded his description with an analysis of commemorative, symbolic, and therapeutic motifs in the ceremonial acts.

In 1932 Reichard learned that Franc J. Newcomb, a trader's wife at Newcomb, New Mexico, had recorded some 300 Navajo sandpaintings, 56 of which were from Shootingway. With the consultation of Miguelito, a practitioner with whom she had studied since 1930, and in collaboration with Newcomb, Reichard produced *Sandpaintings of the Navajo Shooting Chant* in 1937, a discussion and analysis of the Bush Collection (purchased from Newcomb) at Columbia University. Reichard had presented a brief version of the Shootingway myth in 1934, but a much more detailed rendition, collected in 1924 from Blue Eyes of Lukachukai by Fr. Berard Haile, was given with the 45 illustrations in the sandpainting volume. The value of the myth was clearly stated: "Without it no satisfactory interpretation of the ceremonial details could be made."

Enough information was now available for the attempt to itemize the complex roster of Navajo ceremonials and create a taxonomy. Two classifications appeared in 1938, one by Fr. Berard Haile and one by Wyman and Kluckhohn. Both are based on Navajo categories but the latter is the more comprehensive grouping. Shootingway appears with Hail Way, Water Way, Red Ant Way, and Big Star Way in a "Shooting Chant Sub-Group."

Another collection of sandpainting reproductions, that of John F. Huckel, is the subject of Reichard's *Navajo Medicine Man* (1939). Huckel had employed Miguelito for some years in the Fred Harvey Hotel Indian arts program and had obtained from him a long version of the Shootingway myth and 47 sandpaintings from the same ceremony. Reichard combined this material with her own personal knowledge of Miguelito in a tribute to the man and his religious art.

In 1940 Kluckhohn and Wyman pooled their systematic observations of ceremonies in the Ramah-Atarque and Pinedale-Coolidge-Smith Lake areas, respectively, in *An Introduction to Navaho Chant Practice*. They provided a basic outline of procedures applicable to most Holyway ceremonials and presented "severely technical" (1940:8) details of four. One of these was a Female Shooting Holy Way (1940:155–68).

The first analysis of ritual poetry in Shootingway was published in 1944 in Reichard's *Prayer, The Compulsive Word*. Her approach was to identify the patterning of repetitions in the long prayers that accompany Navajo ceremonies. She also identified certain standard components of prayer such as invocation, petition, and benediction (1944:41). Considering the importance of prayer in Navajo ritual, it is surprising that no further work was done until Gill's (1974) painstaking analysis of more than 15,000 lines in some 300 prayer texts. He found that all of this material could be subsumed in only 22 "constituent units," such as place designation, plea for assistance, association/identification with a Holy Person, state of safety upon the avoidance of attack, and desired state of restoration/recovery (1974:34). On the basis of this and other analysis he proposed a theory of Navajo religion, a new classification of ceremonies, and other ideas of the meaning behind the ceremonial practice.

Father Berard's next work on Shootingway appeared in 1947: *Prayer Stick Cutting in a Five Night Navajo Ceremonial of the Male Branch of Shootingway* (Haile 1947a). Like Kluckhohn and Wyman's (1940), it presents a step-by-step account of ceremonial acts in a Shootingway prayerstick ceremonial, followed by the Navajo text from which the account derives. The text, recorded from White Singer of Chinle, Arizona, is the first account of the ceremony published in Navajo. Complete with interlinear and free translations this recording of narrative, songs, and prayers adds a new dimension to Shootingway studies. For the first time the native literary art becomes accessible to the reader. This valuable contribution was repeated by Haile (1950b) with Gray Man's *Legend of the Ghostway Ritual in the Male Branch of Shootingway*.

Gladys Reichard's *Navaho Religion* appeared in 1950. Much of its 800 pages of description and analysis is based on Shootingway material. The discussion deals with Navajo dogma, symbolism, and ritual, and there are three concordances: supernatural beings, ritualistic ideas, and rites.

Another dimension of Shootingway, the visual, was made available in *Navaho Means People* by McCombe, Vogt and Kluckhohn (1951). This photographic essay, part of which first appeared in *Life* magazine, gives a comprehensive pictorial coverage of the Navajos of 25 years ago and includes 18 pages on Shootingway. The sudatory, emetic, and a buffalo sandpainting are among the ritual events illustrated.

The Wetherill collection of sandpaintings was analyzed by Wyman in *The Sandpaintings of the Kayenta Navaho* (1952). This collection, notable for its unorthodox colors and designs and containing six sandpaintings from Shootingway, is compared with the relevant material from other collections.

Shootingway was included in Katherine Spencer's *Mythology and Values: An Analysis of Navaho Chantway Myths* (1957). All of the Shootingway myths mentioned above were explored in an overall analysis of Navajo mythology to "see what light it throws on the life views and values of the people whose literature it represents" (1957:1). Such value areas as health and sickness, ritual knowledge and power, and

## Shootingway

family relations occupy a large proportion of the mythic material and are given functional and psychological consideration by Spencer.

Wyman has made typically thorough and knowledgeable analyses of three other collections of reproductions of Navajo sandpaintings. The Huckel collection, described by Reichard in 1939, was bequeathed to the Taylor Museum in Colorado Springs a few years later and Wyman was asked to prepare the handbook (1960). The 111 reproductions (49 are from Shootingway) receive the full comparative treatment. In the Walcott collection (Wyman 1970a) in the U.S. National Museum, 21 of the 28 reproductions are from Shootingway. The comparison here is with 11 different collections, all meticulously documented including six Miguelito reproductions housed in Stockholm! The 10 sandpaintings from Male Shootingway in the Goldwater collection at the Museum of Northern Arizona are described and discussed in Wyman (1972c).

Among the most recently published contributions to the Shootingway literature are two descriptions of medicine bundles associated with this ceremonial (Wyman 1972a, 1972b), and the appreciation and critique of Kluckhohn and Wyman's classification of ceremonials by Lamphere and Vogt (1973). A reanalysis of the classification is attempted based largely on the wealth of data provided in Wyman and Kluckhohn (1938) and in Kluckhohn and Wyman (1940). Using linguistic and structural models, Lamphere and Vogt rephrase the classification. For Shootingway, for example, they question the propriety of including other major ceremonials in a "Shooting Chant Sub-Group" because of similarities in myth and procedure unless there is also support from native linguistic categories.

With so much material already published on Shootingway one might ask for the justification of presenting yet another account. My response is that given the richness of this complex of ceremonies and the relative poverty of any written account, every description and discussion adds a small retranslation, as it were, of an almost infinitely large subject. The present rubric of ritual drama affords a different language and perspective for a task which, by definition, is never done.

3. Quotations in this chapter are paraphrases, not exact renditions or translations of recorded material.

4. I regret the presentation of song texts in such fragmentary forms as are used here. Without the vocables, the full repetitions and, above all, the music, most of the artistic impact is lost. However, restrictions of space work hand-in-hand with ceremonial propriety. Many Navajos would feel uncomfortable if these texts were published in their full song form.

# 10
# O'odham Celkona: The Papago Skipping Dance[1]

## J. RICHARD HAEFER
*Department of Music*
*Arizona State University*

Most Papago ceremonies would lend themselves equally well to a discussion centered on the principles of ritual drama in this culture. The *wi:gita*[2] or Harvest Festival, *gohimeli* or Saguaro Wine Feast, and *wusota* or Curing Rite are the most sacred and most elaborate of *O'odham* rites. Although offering the most potential for the study of Papago ritual drama, they have not been chosen for the topic of this chapter for the following reasons: the *wi:gita* in its most formal state is no longer practiced in that part of the Papago land contained within the boundaries of the United States. Though still celebrated in northwestern Sonora and with a less conventionalized version occasionally presented at Ak Cin, several good summaries of the ceremony have been published to date (Mason 1920; Chesky 1942; and R. D. Jones 1971). The *gohimeli* is the foremost public ritual still regularly practiced by the Papagos. This author believes that sufficient study has not yet been conducted about the oratory, song and dance of this celebration to present a detailed account. The *wusota* has been discussed by Bahr et al. (1974), although this study concentrates on the theory and concept of sickness and only cursorily mentions the ritual aspects of the *wuso*.

Many other *O'odham* ceremonies are practiced with still less frequency (such as the *wuaga* or Girls' Coming-of-Age Ceremony), or have dropped from general ceremonial usage (i.e., the *limhu* or purification rite and various rituals associated with hunting and agriculture). Some of the latter, however, have been recreated in recent years both as a means of teaching the young people about their culture and as vehicles for public dancing at Powwows and other places of entertainment.

The *celkona* has always been connected with entertainment, although this rite is not without religious overtones. It is the purpose of this chapter to present the history of this rite and to offer a portrayal of the *celkona* of the 1970s as a means of understanding the duality of purpose of the dance, the larger ceremonial connotations, the ritual elements, and the survival of the form. The observations are based on a survey of the ethnographic literature; photography, field notes, and interviews with leaders of two *celkona* groups performing from 1968 to the present; and a series of interviews in Papago discussing the philosophy and design of this rite with some of the practitioners.

## THE CELKONA IN PIMAN ETHNOGRAPHY

Though our primary concern is the function of the *celkona* among the *tohona o'odham* ('desert people'[3]—Papago), several ethnographic references suggest a similar practice among their close relatives, the *akimel o'odham* ('river persons'—Pima)[4] and indeed, even joint participation by Papagos with Pimas. Therefore, in the ethnographic survey, it is necessary to discuss the Piman literature as well to determine the extent of participation by the northern River People. In each case, only the general pattern of the ritual is described since the details are considered later.

### A CHRONOLOGY OF DANCE PERFORMANCES

In addition to the ethnographic accounts given below, several calendar stick records have been left by the Pimas. Russell (1975:

## The Papago Skipping Dance

34–66) presents a narrative telling of two such records for the Pimas, and Underhill (1938a) details the events recorded on the calendar stick kept at San Xavier del Bac by the Papagos. The latter is especially interesting due to the preoccupation of the "Keeper" with recording ceremonial dances, especially the *celkona*. Although this record is unofficial and not always accurate (1938a:16), a great deal of attention is given to topics such as Apache raids and Papago retaliations, the lynching of sorcerers, local deaths, and the Skipping Dance.

Data presented in table 10.1, which lists the *celkona* dances recorded on calendar sticks and in ethnographic reports, suggest several possible generalizations: 1) often a reciprocal arrangement, in the same or following year, can be noted between two villages or village groups; 2) sister villages may combine into village groups to host the *celkona*, presumably due to the need for more food to host the challengers; 3) of the recorded dance topics, all are different and apparently localized; and 4) the period of the 1870s, a time of drought, notes no such celebrations in Papagería.

Several additional dances are mentioned in the records. The Piman descriptions are especially difficult to evaluate, since the recorder often uses the term "dance festival" with no further details. Such events occurred in 1883, 1888, 1889, 1892, 1893, and 1894. In 1886, a medicine man "gave" a great dance; in 1888, a "prosperous season enabled the Salt River people to hold a dance festival," and "A Papago who knew the bluebird series of songs sang for the Santan people during the festival held by them" (Russell 1975:61). Although such events do not appear to describe the *celkona* as outlined below, they occupied the minds of the calendar stick keepers as important to the people.

#### THE CELKONA OF THE PIMA

The primary reference to *akimel o'odham* practices is the work of Frank Russell (1975) based on his fieldwork on the Gila River Reservation in 1901–2. Other than in the calendric records, it is only within the broadest context of the term *celkona* (to denote a large scale ritual event involving dance, gift giving, races and games, bet-

TABLE 10.1.
LIST OF RECORDED CELKONAS

| Date | Host Village[a] | Visitant Village | Dance Topic | Name Songs | Comments | Source |
|---|---|---|---|---|---|---|
| 1850 | San Xavier | Santa Rosa | | | | Underhill 1938a:20 |
| 1850 | Santa Rosa | San Xavier | | | a return gesture after a few days | Underhill 1938a:20 |
| 1862 | Arci | Santa Rosa | | | after *wi:ikita*/races held | Underhill 1938a:28 |
| 1881 | Gila Crossing | Casa Blanca | | | | Russell 1975:58 |
| 1884 | Comobabi | Coyote Village | | | organized by a woman with ladies' races (male singer) | Underhill 1938a:45 |
| 1884 | Coyote Village | Comobabi | Eagle Songs | | a return gesture, also by ladies, held a few days later | Underhill 1938a:45 |
| 1885 | Anegam | San Xavier | Wind Songs[b] | | relay race the next day[c] | Underhill 1938a:49 |
| 1887 | Gila Crossing | Casa Blanca | | | | Russell 1975:60 |
| 1889 | San Xavier helped by Coyote Village | Iron Pump helped by Comobabi | | X[d] | races after | Underhill 1938a:52 |
| 1890 | Iron Pump | San Xavier | | | | Underhill 1938a:53 |
| 1894 | San Xavier | Many Ants | | X[e] | a return | Underhill 1938a:56 |
| 1895 | Ak Cin | Santa Rosa/ Quijota/Water Whirl | "newly dreamed" | | relay races 10 days preparation | Underhill 1938a:56 |
| 1896 | Water Whirl | Ak Cin | | | relay race | Underhill 1938a:57 |
| 1897 | Ak Cin | Water Whirl | | | see note[f] | Underhill 1938a:57 |
| 1897 | Akutciny | Rsanikam[g] | | | relay races | Russell 1975:64 |
| 1925 | San Xavier | Sil Nakia | | | races, shinny | Underhill 1938a:62 |
| 1927 | San Xavier | "northern villages" | Morning Star | | | Underhill 1946:121 |
| 1932 | San Xavier[h] | | | | | Underhill 1938a:63 |
| 1938 | Gu Aci | Gu Oidak | Cloud Songs | | races | Chesky 1943:68 |

a. Names of the villages refer to those given by the source cited and are not necessarily the present names.
b. One boy in the middle of the dance circle "leaped about like a whirlwind."
c. The races are described in Underhill (1938a:50).
d. It is stated that the Naming Songs were sung to "cheer up the host as the crops had been bad."
e. These songs were said to have been the same songs as used the year before.
f. No songs are mentioned for this return match.
g. This dance was held to "show the young how it was done and to bring back memories of the old."

## The Papago Skipping Dance

ting, Name Giving Songs, and other associations between two villages explained below) that we find reference in Russell to a part of the *celkona*. While he describes the Name Song as a "social device that accomplishes the ends of organized charity, together with those of the ordinary festival" (1975:171), an explanation of the "ordinary festival" is nowhere to be found. Likewise, the statement, "When there are many participants in the ceremony, nearly the entire day may be consumed in its performance" (1975:171) unfortunately receives no further discussion. Mention is made of the "nomadic Papagos" coming to entertain (i.e., to sing for) the Pimas, while the River People have returned the practice "but twice" in the last fifty years—both visits to "*Suijotos*" [Quijotoa].[5] Later, Russell (1975:285–89) gives 12 *Tcŋtcŋka Nyŋi* [*cecega nen'ei*] 'Name Songs' which he indicates are only part of a large group of such songs.[6]

Luckily, Gunst (1930:47–51) presents a more detailed account of a ritual she calls, "The 'Harvest Ceremony' in December" which is made up of several elements in a patterned sequence.[7] Based on a need by one village for food and the abundance of crops in a second village, the latter becomes the hosts and the former, the visitant participants.

The first element is the "Run in the Middle"[8] (Gunst 1930:48) or "dance of thanksgiving." This appears to be the *celkona* proper with 12–20 participants dancing to a series of songs based on the dream symbol (usually a bird) of a "special singer" chosen by the visitant village. It is noted that in this dance, at a signal, the dancers "pass under the raised hands of two dancers," a type of movement which receives no further documentation in the literature.[9] This part of the ceremony is said to continue for most of the day.

Immediately following this action, a relay race is held for amusement and competition, including betting. The distance run is approximately fifteen miles with each runner racing about three-fourths of a mile. The reward for the winners is the prestige and honor of winning for their village.

The third event is "the call" said to take place at night following the races. Also a means of exchanging gifts and thereby creating or solidifying friendships, this activity seems synonymous with Russell's naming ceremony. The final event is termed the "Sun ceremony," a ritual of singing "thanks to the sun for its graciousness in granting good crops" (1930:50). Although the sun is revered by the Papagos and represented in several ceremonies, this appears to be the sole source for the use of this type of rite for the conclusion of a *celkona*.[10] However, the earlier events do parallel the activities of the Papagos to whom we now turn our attention.

## THE *CELKONA* OF THE PAPAGO

With the exception of the San Xavier calendar record and Densmore's brief account (1929:135-37), the Pima data all predate our Papago information. However, one must bear in mind that the Pimas had been in close contact with Anglo settlers and, since the late nineteenth century, had been subjected to a great deal of missionary pressure to denounce their traditional religious and "heathen" social practices. The Papago people, missionized by the Catholic Franciscans, were not subjected to such strong pressures, and it may be seen that even in the 1930s they retained practices only remembered by their northern neighbors. It is not surprising then, that the most detailed accounts of the *celkona* are found in Papago ethnographies. For a better understanding of the *celkona*, let us first examine the most complete written reports of this event, those by Gunst (1930:21-28) and Underhill (1946:116-34). This will also serve as a reference point for the remaining ethnographic descriptions of this ritual. One must remember that the *celkona* in its broadest definition implies an entire sequence of activities, one of which is the *celkon* or dance, itself.

The possible sequences of events are outlined in table 10.2 for those dances described in the literature. Some kind of prior notification may be assumed since few, if any, public ceremonial activities of the *O'odham* take place without deliberate consultation by the village elders. Only Underhill (1946) indicates a formal 10-day notification by the challengers, mentioning the delivery of a bundle of 10 sticks (one for each day) to the host village. This is a typical method of notification of a pending important event by the Papago. Several other sources mention a yearly alternation of the challenge between two villages which also implies prior notice, although crop failure would force such a pattern to be broken upon occasion.

## The Papago Skipping Dance

The first formal movement is the arrival of the challenging village at a camp just outside the host village. One or more young men, said to be in war dress with black clay covering their faces, enter the host village to announce the arrival of the challengers and to issue a challenge speech. Gunst (1930:23) mentions a formal reply, a welcoming speech which would be the expected tradition. The "black face" then attempts a retreat while the host villagers pelt him (or them) with various crops of the melon variety, a burlesque activity made possible only by abundant harvest. The sequence of events is unclear in both sources at this point, but it is believed that the challengers spend the night camped outside the host village with minimal contact between the two groups.

The following morning several "location finders" enter the host village to determine where the activities will take place. It is at this point that the sequence of events differs between Gunst and Underhill. Gunst implies a series of speech exchanges between the "location finders" and the host elders, followed by the entrance of the challengers to the dance plaza and then the dance. She is unclear as to when the "feed" takes place. Underhill, however, indicates that the challengers enter and eat before going to the dance area. In both cases, it is either clear or implied[11] that after the entrance of the residents of both villages to the dance area, the singers from the challenging village take their place standing[12] either in the center of the plaza or to one side.

Underhill mentions the presence of a dancer called the *ta'iwuni*. This is a solo performer who 'jumps out' over the dance area prior to the entrance of the complete group of dancers. It is said (HAE-PAP-II-C5)[13] that he is "checking the dance grounds to be sure there are no evil or bad spirits around." The crucial event of the morning's activities is the *celkona* dance proper which follows. The dance was dreamed by the lead singer who may, or may not, be from the challenging village. (If a singer who has dreamed a *celkona* does not live in their village, the challengers would have to pay someone to come and teach them the songs and dance prior to the festivities.)

The consensus of prior descriptions of this event is that an entire morning is consumed by the foregoing activities. What follows thereafter varies according to source. Gunst implies that both the

TABLE 10.2.
PAPAGO SEQUENCE OF EVENTS*

| EVENT: | 10-day prior notice | arrive outside village | black face + enters | challenge speech | welcome speech | burlesque retreat | location finders | guests enter host village | guests arrive at dance plaza | singers enter | tá'iwunim | dancers enter and celkon | feed | gifts | races or games | gambling | Name Songs | Bird Songs | other |
|---|---|---|---|---|---|---|---|---|---|---|---|---|---|---|---|---|---|---|---|
| **PAPAGO** | | | | | | | | | | | | | | | | | | | |
| Densmore (1929) | | | | | | | | | | | | x | | | | | | | |
| Gunst (1930) | | 1 | 2 | 3 | 4 | 5 | 6 | | 7 | 8 | | 9 | ? | x | x | x | next day | if longer | |
| Underhill (1938b) | | | | | | | | | | | | x | | | x | | x | | |
| Underhill (1939) | | 1 | ? | 2 | ? | ? | | | | | | | | x | x | x | | | |
| Chesky (1943) Sil Nakia | | | | | | | | | | 3 | | 4? | | | | | | | 1. *waila* 2. set up 5. Circle Dance 6. *waila;* clowns present |

|  |  |  |  |  |  |  |  |  |  |  |  |  |  |
|---|---|---|---|---|---|---|---|---|---|---|---|---|---|
| Chesky (1943) Gu Aci | | ? | | | | | | ? | | x | | x x x | |
| Underhill (1946) | x | 1 | 2 | 3 | ? | 4 | 5 | 6 | 8 | ? | 9 | 11 | 7 | 12 | x | x x x | x or may alternate | 10. speech |
| Haefer (1972) | | | | | | | | | | 1 | (*) | 2 | | | | | 3. other trad. dances & a *waila* |
| PIMA | | | | | | | | | | | | | | | | | | |
| Russell (1975) | | | | | | | | | | | | | | | x | | |
| Gunst (1930) | | | | | | | | | | | | 1 | | 2 | 3 | | "Sun" ceremony |

KEY:
 \* a numeral is used to indicate the order of events where known.
 + black face implies the "war dress" of the Papagos.
 x indicates the event is noted, but the sequence is unknown.
 ? denotes an event that is implied in the literature.
  (\*) used by Tucson group, Spring 1978.

consumption of food and the exchange of gifts follow, while Underhill (1939 and 1946) suggests that the exchange of gifts takes place when the general populations of both villages join in the dance with the hosts paying for the privilege of dancing.

The postdance activities include the races and games, both associated with a great deal of wagering. Implications for other activities, such as "Naming" or "Bird" Songs noted in table 10.2, are discussed later. A completely different setting is implied by Chesky (1943) in her description of the dance at Sil Nakia. Here the *celkona* proper is preceded and followed by a *waila* style dance, this activity taking place in 1942. No mention is made of other traditional activities such as races, games, or betting, although a "feed" may be assumed.

## THE CELKONA AS PRESENTLY PRACTICED

The last ten years have seen a revival of this dance genre by at least two groups, one in the Tucson–San Xavier area and the other from the Gu Aji–Quijotoa villages. In the last two years, under the sponsorship of the Papago Culture Awareness office, some of the students at Baboquivari High School in Sells have learned to *celkon*.

### RECENT PERFORMANCES

The *celkona* is presently used as a means of entertainment for both Papagos and non-Papagos. The dance is often performed as a contest dance for local Powwows, rodeos, or Indian days and upon occasion it is presented to a school or village as a means of self expression of the *o'odham himdag* or 'way'. The following performances have influenced the development of this chapter: May 26, 1968, at San Xavier village;[14] November 22, 1971, at Santa Rosa School; February 15, 1972, at Sells village; May 13, 1972, at Gu Aji village; and one in the spring of 1978 in Phoenix, Arizona. The first and last performances were led by the same singer and are based on his *ce:cki* or 'dream' about the *ko:kod*, 'sea gulls' (HAE-PAP-II-C5). The 1968 version (see fig. 10.1) is said to have been a complete

## The Papago Skipping Dance

enactment of the *celkona* dance proper for the benefit of the residents of the San Xavier area. The 1978 presentation was a shortened version of the same dance presented to the public.

The performances of 1971–72 were given by students of the Papago Club of Phoenix Indian School under the direction of elders from the villages of Gu Aji and Quijotoa. The first two performances were presented while the students were still learning the dance and must be considered incomplete since the entire cycle was not danced.[15] The dance of November 22, 1971, was given at the Bureau of Indian Affairs Boarding School in honor of Papago Culture Day for the benefit of students, parents, teachers, and visitors. The dance in Sells, the following February, was presented as entertainment for Papagos and visiting dignitaries after the inauguration

FIGURE 10.1. *Celkona* dance at San Xavier Village, May 26, 1968. The lead singer is Lorenzo Pablo, standing with the rattle to the basket drummer's left. Photo by James Griffith, 1968.

of a new Tribal Chairman. In each instance, two other traditional dances were demonstrated (the *eḍa wo:p* and *gohimeli*) and a brief session of social round dancing (*keihina*) followed. Only the occasion of May 13, 1972 offered this researcher the satisfaction of witnessing a complete version of the *celkona* dance in a village setting.

THE *CELKONA* OF MAY 13, 1972

The events leading up to the fiesta of May 13, 1972, were in most ways typical. Certain villagers had determined just cause for a celebration, and a dinner followed by an all-night *wailadag*[16] was planned. Unique to this situation was the decision to hold a full afternoon of traditional dancing prior to the start of the now typical dinner and all-night *wailadag* celebration. This decision justified two ends: (a) it gave the Phoenix Indian School students an opportunity to present in their entirety the dances they had been learning for over half a year, and (b) it provided the village community the chance to witness two traditional dances which had not been performed for some time. In addition to the *celkona*, the dancers performed an *eḍa wo:p* of the *gigitwal* ('crisscrossing' of the 'swallows'), a version of the *gohimeli* dance from the Saguaro Wine Feast, and finally, a session of social round dancing. The entire program lasted over three hours on a hot (high 90s) Saturday afternoon.

The dance was held near the *piastakuḍ* ('fiesta thing' or dance grounds) in Gu Aji village. The *piastakuḍ* is located to the southeast of the Catholic church, just off the main road through the village, and the main area for this dance was situated immediately to the south of the dance plaza (see fig. 10.2).

An outer line, about fifty feet in diameter, was drawn with white ash to keep the audience out of the dance area. The audience was seated on benches, chairs, or on the ground, with some people sitting or standing in pickup trucks parked around the outside of the dance area. In the center, an eight-foot *u:saga*, 'wooden pole', was erected with the symbols of a *cewagi* ('cloud'), a *ko:koḍ* ('sea gull'), and a *gigitwal* ('swallow'), on the top of the pole. Around the *u:saga* were 10 chairs for the singers and a pail of water to assuage their

KEY:

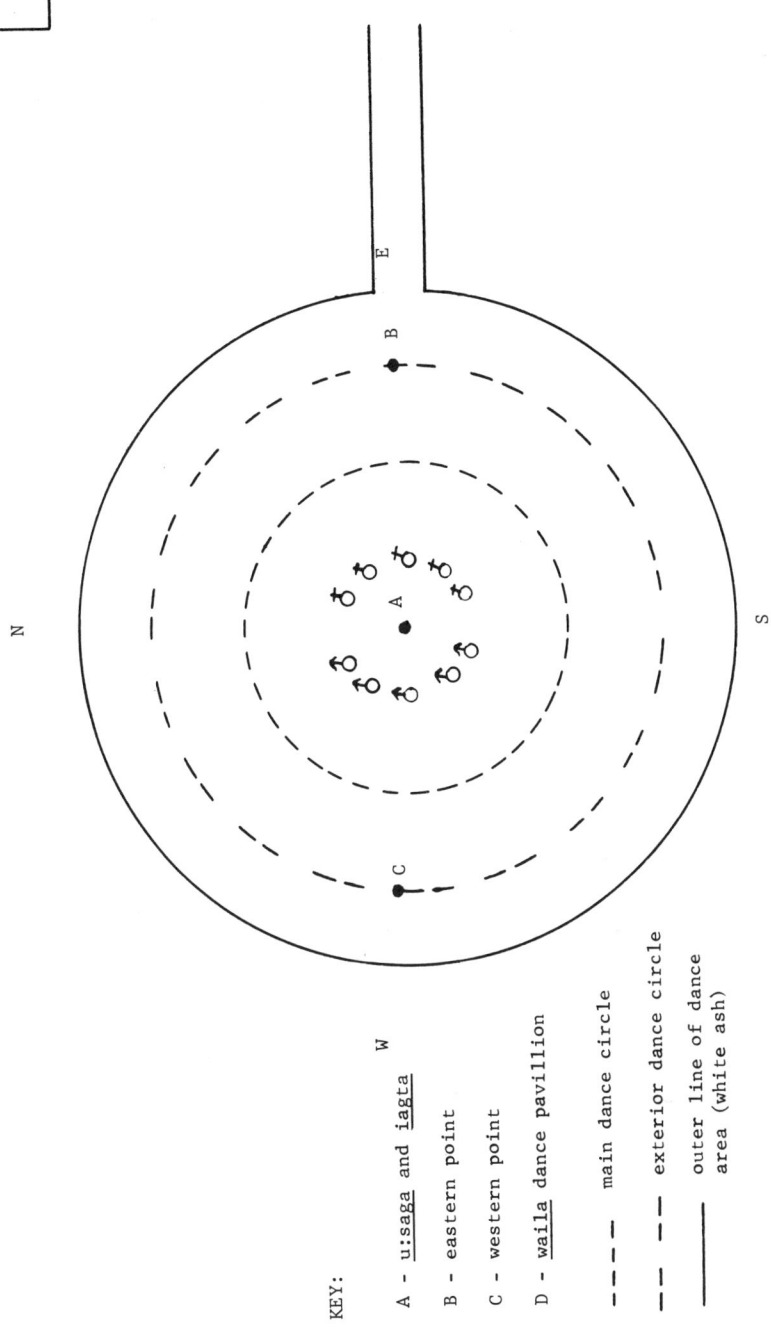

A - u:saga and iagta
B - eastern point
C - western point
D - waila dance pavillion
- - - - main dance circle
— - — - exterior dance circle
———— outer line of dance area (white ash)

FIGURE 10.2. *Celkona* dance circle of May 13, 1972, at Gu Aji Village.

thirst. The dancers entered from the east as the singers began their first song, and danced counterclockwise in a circle of about twenty-five feet in diameter. Near the end of each song they moved either to the east or west side of the dance area and circled around the plaza on a diameter of circa forty feet.

Two dance steps were used: the first, a moderate paced shuffle-walk step, and the second, the 'hop' or 'skip' denoted by the term *celko*. The former step begins each dance and alternates with the latter at a point in each song called the *i-nodag* ('turn'). This corresponds musically to the place where the formal design changes to an incomplete repetition pattern. The two designs, complete and incomplete, normally alternate twice in each song. Not only does the dance step and formal musical design change at the *i-nodag*, but also the musical accompaniment and additional dance movements such as the position of the *iagta*. The sequence of the dance follows.

Preliminary announcements, spoken in both English and Papago but not with equivalent translations, introduced the singing and dancing groups. Spectators were told where to sit, and a general introduction to this particular *celkona* dance was given.[17] The singers moved to their seats during these announcements. There were five male and five female singers. Two of the men played a *hoa*, 'basket', which was inverted and rubbed with a stick at the beginning of the songs and struck with the stick at the *i-nodag*. The remaining three male singers each played a *sawkud* or gourd 'rattle'. The rattle is first played with a circular motion, creating a continuous sound, *i-mu:sigd g sawkud*—'make music the rattle' (HAE-PAP-II-C5). At the *i-nodag* the rattle is shaken up and down, creating a short and a long pulse (♪♩). This action is said to be the *saw*, ('to rattle'). The male singers were dressed in typical cowboy fashion including hats, while the women wore long dresses with scarfs or shawls around the head or shoulders.

The dance formation was led by a single male said to represent I'itoi, a cultural hero of the Papago. Wearing slacks, a T-shirt, and boots, he carried a fan of about two dozen feathers which he held in front of his face and raised over his head at the *i-nodag*.

The dancers (eight male, eight female) were grouped in two lines. They entered with the males on the right (outside) and the female line forming a circle of smaller diameter to the left of the male line

## The Papago Skipping Dance

nearer to the singers on the inside. Each dancer held an *iagta* or ceremonial symbol on the top of a wand. For this dance the symbols were arranged by dance partners, and included two pairs of white sea gulls, one pair of grey geese, two pairs of black swallows, a couple with clouds, and a couple with lightning superimposed on clouds; the final couple carried rainbows. Since the construction, function, and significance of these elements are discussed later, it will suffice to say here that the *iagta* are carried in two positions: the lower position, i.e., in front of the face or at the top of one's head, and, at the *i-noḍag*, the upper position, raised high over the head.

Since the dance movements vary only slightly from song to song, only the formations of the first song are explained. As the singers begin, the two lines of dancers enter side by side from the east led by I'itoi. (The first line of the text states, "Green I'itoi came from the east.") The song begins with the complete formal design, the basket being rubbed, and the rattles shaken circuitously. The dancers move with a shuffle-walk carrying the *iagta* in the lowered position. For each stanza of the song the dancers progress just a little more than one complete circuit of the dance area. The second stanza is sung with no change in the dance movements. Approximately two bars before the end of stanza two, the rattles change to the *ṣaw* movement and the third stanza begins the incomplete formal design. As verse three begins, the basket drum is struck and the dancers move in the *celkon* motion best described as a skip, step, and pause on three fast, consecutive beats. The *iagta* are raised over their heads. The fourth stanza is similar.

This four-verse pattern is repeated with stanzas five and six in complete form (shuffle-step, *iagta* down, rattles shaken in circular fashion) and stanzas seven and eight in incomplete form (with appropriate choreographic and musical changes). Near the end of stanza eight, as I'itoi approaches the eastern portion of the dance circle, he moves to the "eastern point" on the exterior dance circle (see fig. 10.2). During the next two stanzas (numbers nine and ten which retain all the form and relevant characteristics of the incomplete design) the two lines of dancers move toward I'itoi and divide, with the boys crossing left in front of the girls and moving counterclockwise, the girls moving to their right, clockwise. The two lines pass each other at the west end of the dance circle and arrive on either side of the leader forming a large semicircle as the song ends.

(This motion is a reversing device so that as song two begins the boys will be dancing in the inner circle close to the singers with the girls on the outside. This reversal pattern continues to function at the end of each song.)

Only two variations from the above pattern were observed in the rest of the song set. First, the number of stanzas varied from song to song.[18] Each stanza contains four or more phrases with the second phrase a textural repetition or variation of the first. Melodically, the second phrase is a close variation of the initial line. It is this initial phrase which is dropped in the incomplete form. The general pattern, explained above, is for two complete (C) stanzas to alternate with two incomplete (I) stanzas: CC II CC II. Additional incomplete stanzas (as many as four) are added to allow the dancers to complete their reversing movement. The number of these additional repetitions is determined by the position of the dancers in the dance plaza when the paired alternations conclude. However, songs six and eight are shortened considerably when the complete form is used only at the beginning, e.g., CC II plus one or two more I's to complete the reversal.

The second variant is the directional orientation of the dancers. The dancers enter from the east and conclude songs one and two with an eastern orientation. However, at the end of song three, *l'itoi* moves the dancers to the western point of the dance plaza as the song text says, "The ocean lies far away to the west. There they arrive." A western orientation is continued through song seven with the dancers leaving to the east at the end of the dance.[19]

The *celkona* portion of the May 13, 1972, dance lasted a total of 45 minutes. Over 80 percent (36 minutes) of that time was devoted to dancing and singing. Following the exit of the dancers, the singers left the plaza for a brief period of relaxation.

THE SONG TEXTS

Following are an English translation of the songs used in the performance of May 13, 1972, and, for comparative purposes, texts used "when the northern villages 'sang for' San Xavier" in 1927 (Underhill 1946:121-22). It may be speculated that the "northern vil-

## The Papago Skipping Dance

lages" included the Santa Rosa–Sil Nakia area, therefore placing the source of both texts in the same region. Certain unifying devices occur in each text and some are shared between the two cycles, although the subject matter is localized. Brief mention of these devices is made here, although a detailed study must be based on the texts in their original language.

The songs of the 1927 series tell of the morning star which visited the composer in his dream in the form of a woman. The dancers carry *iagta* and the songs mention the things which she showed to the dreamer. The identity of morning star is not revealed to the audience, however, until song six. Natural phenomena such as rainbows, cranes, rain, mist, mountains, and the earth are mentioned in each verse. Directional orientation is from the west, the location of the ocean and the direction from which the lifegiving rains usually proceed. Just as, "From the west they run" to arrive in song one and begin the cycle, so too, do they, "Go back whence we came" after having sung the series (song eight). An interesting feature of song five is the description of a *celkona* including the minimal level of naming (see pages 262–263 below) of the host village—the Hollow Place, i.e., *wa:k* or San Xavier.

The texts of *Celkona* songs of May 13, 1972 are based on the appearance of *I'itoi* who comes to the Children's Shrine near Santa Rosa village bringing the children out of the ground and taking them on a tour of Papageria.[20] Each song of this cycle also mentions or alludes to a bird or a natural phenomenon which is seen or visited by *I'itoi* and the children. The texts appear to be grouped in pairs by sharing such ideas as "running," "arriving," "birds," "remainder people," "mountains," "roads," and the "ocean" or "water." Some of these key terms may be found in several of the song texts.

It is also interesting to note the similarities between the two cycles. Both contain some type of directional orientation with a "coming" and a "returning" respectively at the start and conclusion of the cycle. The idea of the earth becoming green alludes to the grass which grows after heavy desert rains. In both cycles the natural phenomena, although often specifically different, refer to rain indicators such as ocean birds, mountains located near the water, and the ocean itself. The cycles close with reference to the conclusion to the specific story and the end of the songs. The latter concept is typical of Piman song cycles.

*Celkona* Songs, May 13, 1972

Song 1
Green *I'itoi* came from the East.
Little green *I'itoi* came from the East.
And there he stood up and saw it.
Therefore the spreading land got green.

Song 2
Now you come running! The children come running!
Now you come running! The children come running!
They don't know the place where they arrived.
From there they dance zigzagged.

Song 3
The ocean lies far away.
The ocean lies far away.
There they arrive and see
White birds there in [the water side by side].

Song 4
The ocean lies far away.
The ocean lies far away.
Near it they see
The sea birds [making] tracks.

Song 5
Black mountain in front of the water stands.
Black mountain in front of the water stands.
They arrive there and see it.
The "remainder" women come running.
All raise up their arms together rustling.

Song 6
Foam mountain in front of the water stands.
Foam mountain in front of the water stands.
They arrive there and see it.
The "remainder" children spring out
And arrive all carrying foam.

Song 7
There's a big road, there's a big road lying.
There's a big road lying, lying to the west.
Big "gourd carrying" mountain stands there.
From here the wind blew noisily.

Song 8
There's a big road, there's a big road lying.
There's a big road lying, lying to the west.
They arrive there and see it.

## The Papago Skipping Dance

"Remainder" children arrive and
Over *Aji* fields the songs end.

*Celkona* Songs, 1927 (Underhill 1946:122–24).

Song 1
   From the west they run
   To sing for us.
   There I stand and see
   That it is good.
   Yonder I see them run,
   Holding the rainbows high.

Song 2
   Crane birds!
   Side by side, in a row!
   Under you I stand, and look.
   You go a little way and spread out.
   Behind you it is raining.

Song 3
   There, indeed, I stand
   And toward the west stretch out my hands.
   The mist I summon.
   It comes. The earth dissolves.
   Then, as I walk, I sink down deep (in the moist earth):
   I stand in the midst of the land.
   I think it good.

Song 4
   In the night
   The rain comes down.
   Yonder, at the edge of the earth,
   There is a sound like cracking.
   There is a sound like falling.
   Down yonder, it goes on slowly rumbling.
   It goes on shaking.

Song 5
   The fields of the Hollow Place
   Lie in hollow land.
   There came [a village] and sang for them.
   Beside [the dancers] I run,
   Holding out my hands.
   We take our gifts, clutch them and run.

Song 6
   Who is the woman who will lead me?

And where will you lead me?
Morning star woman brings me forward.
When I surprised, have seen her,
My heart is deeply stirred.
This, her glance, shines greatly over the earth.

Song 7
The mist rises
And lies in this direction.
It lies at the base of the Mountains;
It lies deep under them.
Thither I came.
It caught me.
And fine rain sifted over me.
The earth grew very green.

Song 8
Then we, having sung,
Go back whence we came.
Watch! It will not be long
Till the earth grows very green.

## TOWARD AN O'ODHAM THEORY OF THE CELKONA

For some time now this author has been concerned with extrapolating an *O'odham* theory of music and dance from concepts and thought patterns as expressed both verbally and through the actions of various individuals. Linguistic materials have been collected concerning songs, dance, musical instruments, and other aspects of ceremonial life. In addition, the actual use and presentation of songs and dances have been noted in varying situations. Based upon this material, the following observations toward a Papago theory of the *celkona* are offered.

### THE TERM CELKONA

Responses to the question, *"hascu wuḏ hegai mo hab a:ga celkona?"* 'what is the thing that is called a *celkona*?' lead this author to believe that the term *celkona* may be viewed on at least three levels. The broadest and most inclusive use of the word implies a large-scale series of events referred to by Underhill (1946:116) as the "In-

## The Papago Skipping Dance

tervillage Games." These include a ritualized system of greetings, a tributary dance, the exchange of gifts, various races and games with a great deal of wagering, and, perhaps, a series of Name Songs.

The second conceptual level for the term *celkona* is that of the dance proper. Here the term refers to a type of dancing used within the large-scale context and delimited by a particular kind of dance step. It is believed that an unlimited number of different *celkona* dances are possible dependent upon the subject matter dreamed by the creator of each dance. One informant (HAE-PAP-II-C5) speaks of a *ha'ṣuni celkona*, a *ko:koḍ celkona*, and others based on the subject matter of the conceptual dream.

The most specific level for the term is the literal translation of the word, *celko*, meaning 'to skip'. This type of step is said to be present in every dance which may be called a *celkona*. The implication here is that the type of motion used (third conceptual level) determines the generic dance classification while the subject matter (second conceptual level) determines the specific individual dance. This determination is a reversal of the level of specificity from the conceptual levels of definition of the term as just stated. This is not, however, a contradiction and other examples of such interaction of concept levels with broad/specific taxonomic levels in O'odham theory may be found such as in the naming of songs (Bahr and Haefer 1978:89). The intrinsic value of all three levels of the term *celkona* become more apparent as one further examines the theory of the whole.

### THE PURPOSE OF THE CELKONA

The overt purpose of the *celkona* is one of social interaction for fun and friendship. Combined with the frivolity of games, races, feasting, and dancing is the added social measure of intervillage comradeship. It is apparent that some villages may have established biannual patterns of exchange for the *celkona* with each village alternating as challenger and then host (Underhill 1938a, 1938b, 1946). Reciprocation of gift giving is stressed not only on the day or days of the event, but also for the future as well. This creates compadrazgolike ties between the families of two villages; the partners may call each other *nyi owih* [*ni aigo*] 'my opposite' and expect to be treated as a relative (Underhill 1939). These village partnerships might continue for generations and even lead to marriage alliances, though a series of poor harvests could cause both villages to establish ties with different people. It is believed that at times of unusually bad harvest, people from as far south as Covered Wells would travel to the villages of the northern River People (Russell 1975:171) so that they might survive by means of the gifts given to them in payment for dancing the *celkona*.

Although set within the festivities of intervillage rivalries, the *celkona* is not without certain religious overtones. Gunst (1930:21) says the *chilt-ko* [*celkona*] is given in "thankfulness for bountiful crops." Underhill (1938b, 1939, 1946) indicates the ceremony is given to bring rain and crops and, therefore, further blessings to the people. The details of preparation for the ceremony, the learning of speeches, songs, dance, the building of *iagta*, and the training for races all were undertaken with the same reverence and respect given to other ceremonies of specific religious context. The training of the *runners, especially, received the attention of the ma:kai* ('doctor') since almost all available materials would be wagered on the race.

The religious undercurrents of the *celkona* are further complicated by the relationship of some performances to the most important harvest ritual of the *O'odham*, the *wi:gita*. To understand this relationship it is necessary to digress for a moment to discuss the function of the *celkona* within the Papago ritual calendar.

Most early sources say the *celkona* celebration is held late in the autumn, after the harvest, that is, in October or November (Gunst 1930, Underhill 1938b, 1939, 1946). This apparently is the correct traditional time, following the harvest but prior to leaving the summer camp for the winter village. If the harvest was good, this would be the time of most plentiful food supplies. However, as early as 1938 there are reports that the dance was being held on various ecclesiastical holidays (Chesky 1943).[21] This is further substantiated by present-day usage of the dance at any time of the year, although most informants continue to recognize the fall of the year as the proper time to *celkon* in the broadest sense of the word (HAE-PAP-II-C5).

The *wi:gita*, too, should take place after the harvest (Mason 1920, Davis 1920, Hayden and Steen 1937, Chesky 1943, and R. D. Jones 1971). This festival has also been called a "Sun Dance" (Norman 1960:98) and the "Prayer Stick Festival" (Underhill 1946:135). In the northern parts of Papago land, *wi:gita* activities were centered around Aji village with the ceremony held approximately every four years and requiring almost 150 participants. It lasted for several days following

## The Papago Skipping Dance

weeks of preparation. Although still practiced near Quitobac, Sonora, Mexico (on a yearly basis), this ceremony has not been held in the north-central part of the Papago lands for many years. A shorter variation of the *wi:gita* is held frequently to heal those who may have offended a ritual object of the *wi:gita* in earlier ceremonies (Bahr et al. 1974:23). In recent years these reenactments of a "miniature ritual on the patient's behalf," said to be the necessary maximal level cure (1974:298), have taken place in Ge Oidak (R. D. Jones 1971:10) and Ak Cin (personal observation). This "cure" may be held at any time of the year.

The problem concerning both the *wi:gita* and the *celkona* arises with the dance described by Chesky (1943:65–68) at Sil Nakia. This dance is unusual in several ways. First, it was held on May 3, 1942 (for the Feast of the Finding of the Holy Cross), rather than at the normal postharvest time. Second, the *celkona* was preceded by a *wailadag* [Anglo-style Dance] the entire night of May 2 and followed, in the afternoon of May 3, by a brief *keihina* [Traditional Round Dance], after which the *wailadag* began again. The main focus of the ceremony appeared to be directed toward the healing of "two sick people" who were "carried out and set down just outside the ash line." This practice resembles that of the *wusota wi:gita* of Ge Oidak and Ak Cin mentioned above. Two additional dancers dressed "as *Wiyikita* [*wi:gita*] clown dancers," carrying "the customary *Wiyikita* paraphernalia" (1943:66), moved freely in and around the *celkona* dancers and the two sick persons, alternately dancing and "pantomiming, sometimes obscenely." According to Chesky's informant (1943:67), the "clowns took part in this dance for the purpose of curing these people." The rest of the dance description parallels the "true" *celkona* with regard to performers, symbolic paraphernalia, dance steps, staging, and so forth.

Contemporary opinions concerning a relationship between the *celkona* and the *wi:gita* are varied. Initial reactions have been that the *wi:gita* is so sacred, because of the many things represented therein and the fact that one can become sick by not handling the *iagta* properly, that it contains "some things that we can't even do [or see]." Many of the characters and elements, it is felt, should not be represented except within the context of the *wi:gita*. Concern was expressed when at a recent Powwow one dance group was led by a ceremonial dance leader who should, in the opinion of one informant, only participate in the *wi:gita*. However, the question of a close relationship between the two ceremonies has not been satisfactorily resolved since most discussions of this aspect of the *celkona* ended without definite statements either pro or con.

### THE *CELKONA* AS AN INTERVILLAGE FESTIVITY

On its most inclusive scale, the *celkona* would include all or most of those activities outlined in table 10.2. The last such occurrence of a full-scale *celkona*, recorded in the literature, took place in 1938 at Gu Aji village when a challenge was issued by the families living at Ge Oidak village.[22] Chesky's details (1943:68–70) are sketchy, but it is known that a *maka-ha* [*ma:kai*] "instigated the challenge and took charge of training the runners." There was much secrecy surrounding the training of the runners, including the exertion of "various kinds of magic to make the boys run fast."

Chesky (1943) mentions that "several kinds of races for both men and women were staged" without citing specific events. Typically activities are divided by sex with races for the boys including the relay race and kickball race, and similar activities for the females including a type of field hockey. It may be speculated that older people engaged in more subdued activities, such as the various types of stick games.

Less formal activities of the intervillage festivals include the "feed" and the burlesquelike actions carried out against the challengers. It was the duty of the host village to provide food for everyone, presumably following the *celkona* dance and/or after the races. This act may be preceded by the burlesque actions of throwing melons or cooked squash and beans at the challengers or putting "a lot of chili in the [drinking] water" (HAE-PAP-II-C4). These actions were most frequently directed at the singers, dancers, and other performers from the challenging village.

The *cecega nen'ei*, 'Name Songs', were often a part of the intervillage gatherings. Most sources, including the two Piman ethnographers, mention this aspect of the *celkona*. The *cecega nen'ei* are songs which name a person (or a place) and extol his accomplishments such as "enemy slayer," "shaman," or "eagle killer." Again, however, a dichotomy of definition for the term *cecega nen'ei* surfaces. Initial responses to queries implied that the *cecega nen'ei* and *celkona* are the same (that is, different parts of the same large-scale ceremony), yet further conversations revealed that one can *ce:ck* 'name' while one is dancing the *celkona*

## The Papago Skipping Dance

(that is, name during the songs of the *celkona*). Further examination suggests that the principles of *cecegk* 'naming' include: (1) the minimal level of naming—that is, calling the host's village or the name of a nearby mountain, performed as part of the text of the *celkona* dance songs; and (2) the maximal level of *cecegk*—that is, the calling of a series of names of respected men of the village. In each case, the caller(s) is rewarded for calling out the village or personal name because "the people respect their home and their people and they [the hosts] have to pay them [the callers] because they named their mountain [or personal name]" (HAE-PAP-II-C5).

The minimal level of naming is to be expected at any intervillage celebration. It can be accomplished by simply substituting the name of the village, its "field" or summer camp, or a nearby mountain at the appropriate point in one of the first songs of the dance. This level of naming is anticipated and the host villagers collectively reward the visitants. The maximum level of naming involves the *cecega nen'ei* proper. This would probably be a special series of songs designed so that key words—the name and virtues of the one called—can be changed from stanza to stanza. Most reports indicate that the *cecegk* would take place on the second day of the *celkona* with the singers having one night to practice the songs after receiving the names they were expected to call. There is reason to believe that the host villagers would reciprocate by calling the names of the challengers, and in such a case, a return exchange of gifts would take place. This element of the *celkona* has not been practiced for some time and a feeling of hesitancy and doubt was detected in responses to questions about the *cecega nen'ei*.[23]

Other activities, such as the singing of Bird Songs, feats of strength like a tug-of-war between several women and one man, and various forms of social dancing may be assumed dependent upon the length of the ceremony, the amount of food available, and other variables. Many of these events would be impromptu.

### THE CELKONA AS A DANCE

The second conceptual level of the term *celkona* is the dance proper. This activity involves specific performers, music, dance steps, costumes, and paraphernalia and is performed in a specific location. The various elements of the dance are examined below.

J. RICHARD HAEFER

*The Dance Grounds*

Specific territory in or around each village is reserved for certain ceremonial activities. Although the literature provides little detail as to location, most sources agree that the formal procedure of sending one or more "location finders" to the host village was practiced. These "finders" were sent to determine where both the dance and the races were to be held.

Presently each village has a *wailakuḍ* 'dance thing' (that is, dance ground) usually situated near the village Catholic church. Chesky (1943:65) implies the use of such an area when she states that "two old men appeared and set up [for the dance] in front of the church." The *celkona* of May 13, 1972, was danced just to the south of the Gu Aji *wailakuḍ*. The 1968 San Xavier dance was held near a private dwelling.

There is no indication that locations for other traditional ceremonies, such as the *gohimeli*, are ever used for the *celkona*. Nor was the *piastakud* 'fiesta ground' near the Montezuma church in Ge Aji chosen for the dance there. It may, therefore, be inferred that the *celkona* dance, at least for the last 40 years, is properly held near, if not at, the location used for most other social dances in the village—the *wailakuḍ*.

*The Performers*

Table 10.3 lists the presence of various performers in the *celkona*, giving the number of participants, the ages, and the sex, if known. "Black face" signifies the war dress of the *O'odham* and functions as a "scout" who makes the initial contact with the host village. No real data concerning the various speakers from both villages are given, although the implication is that selected elders, perhaps even *ma:kai* would present rather stylized greeting, welcoming, and pregame speeches. The position of "location finders" was also conventionalized. Since there were normally only two such "foreigners" entering the host village, they could expect to be pelted with melons or squash and subjected to other such ludicrous actions.

The singers represent a major force in the *celkona*. Each group of nine or ten singers is dependent upon a "leader." This person (normally a male) is the owner of the song cycle which may be of his

TABLE 10.3.
PERFORMERS IN THE CELKONA*

| Performers: | black face | speakers | location finders | tá iwunim | singers | dancers | age | helpers | dance leader | clowns |
|---|---|---|---|---|---|---|---|---|---|---|
| PAPAGO: | | | | | | | | | | |
| Gunst (1930) | 1 | | | | X | 6B 6G | 10–14 | | | |
| Underhill (1939) | ? | X | X | X | ? | ? | | | | |
| Chesky (1943) S.N. | | | | | 7M 2F | 5B 9G | 7–14 | 2 | | 2 |
| Chesky (1943) G.A. | | | | | | 14 | | | | |
| Underhill (1946) | 2M | X | X | X | ? | 10B 10G | | | | |
| Haefer (1972) | | | | | 5M 5F | 13B 13G | 15–18 | 2 | 1M | |
| PIMA: | | | | | | | | | | |
| Gunst (1930) | | | | | ? | 12–20 | young | | | |

*Numerals indicate the number of performers in each section.
Key: B = BOY
 G = GIRL
 M = MALE
 F = FEMALE
 X = presence stated (no number indicated)
 ? = implied

own creation or borrowed from a relative or friend. The leader is responsible for teaching the songs to the rest of the group and leading the actual performance. He must also teach the dance to the dancers and supervise the building of the *iagta*.

All singing groups identified in this study include both males and females. As many as half or as few as two of the singers may be female. These participants are normally older people (ca. 55–65 years old), although younger men just learning the songs may "sit in." The women are frequently wives or close relatives of the male singers.

The second group of performers are the *celkondim*, 'dancers'. The size of this group may vary from 12 to more than 25 depending upon the available youths of the village. These children range in age from pre- to mid-teens. One lady said that the boys should "really be in good shape" and the girls should "have long hair" (HAE-PAP-II-C4). Dancing in two parallel lines (usually one line of boys and the other of girls),[24] they are arranged according to height, with the tallest dancers first. Although no time indications are given in the literature, contemporary groups spend from one to several months practicing for this dance. One or more "helpers" may be present in the dance circle directing the movements of the youths. In the case of the May 13, 1972, performance, a leader danced with the group, thereby controlling the activity of the lines.

*The Music*

The music of the *celkona* consists of a "set" of songs. The music and texts of these songs and the associated dance movements are usually dreamed by the lead singer. Most cycles are narrative in nature and are based on topics such as "Morning Star's Visit as a Woman" (Underhill 1946:122–24), the swallows, saguaro, or sea gulls (HAE-PAP-II-C5). The examples provided on pages 256–58 are typical of the complete sets recorded to date. All of the three complete cycles available[25] number eight songs per set. Although incomplete performances have been observed, conversations with informants indicate that a complete cycle of eight is the ideal.

The cycle normally begins with one or more directional songs (see pages 255, 256 above) orienting the subject(s) of the song to the O'odham lands. The songs in the middle present, in narrative form, the movement of the subject(s) through the Papago land base. The final song(s) tells of the "return," the "end" of the songs, and often con-

## The Papago Skipping Dance

tains a reference to a "green earth," that is, the coming of rain to Papagería. Musical features often reflect the above text outline with related material at the beginning and end, and contrasting ideas in the middle. Rhythms, especially, are influenced by the text.

### The Ne'ikuḍa

Accompanying the singing for the *celkona* are two or more *ne'ikuḍa*, 'song things' or musical instruments. These are played only by the male singers. The *ṣawkud*, 'rattle' made from a gourd, is the most popular instrument. It is played in two modes, the circuitous and the punctuated patterns explained above. The gourds have normally been boiled and contain many small pebbles so that a quite brilliant sound is produced.

Often a *hoa* or willow 'basket' is inverted and played as a drum. It may be struck with the hand or a stick and two singers may play the same basket. It, too, is played in two modes: the first, a gently rubbing motion and the latter, a sharp striking beat. The third and less frequently encountered instrument is the *u'us hikiat*, 'wood jagged' (notched stick).[26]

Normally the gourd rattle is used with *celkona* songs with as many as five rattles played together at a time. The basket is often played with the rattle. In only one case is it stated that all three were played together: "Two men beat a basket drum with sticks; two others shook gourd rattles. One man played a rasping stick resting on a basket resonator. Two young boys played rasping sticks held with the nether end against their shoulders, rather than on the ground or on a resonator" (Chesky 1943:65).

### The Dance Movements

The reader is referred to pages 250–54 where the general movements of the dance of May 13, 1972, are presented. These movements are typical of a *celkona*, with the circular direction being counterclockwise. Mention is made of occasional movements out into two lines (Chesky 1943:67), circling around the dance grounds (253–54), and other deviations from the round dance position (mention of various bipolar and quadripolar orientations was also made above). In spite of these variations, Papago dance formations tend to be rather simple and stark in their design.

Two different steps have been noted above, the shuffle-walk and the *celko* or 'skip'. Underhill (1946:121) refers to these respectively as the "they hold in" and the "they give out." These phrases have not been confirmed in their Papago equivalents as of the present, but the spirit of the phrase is certainly portrayed in the dance steps. The latter step, the *celko*, begins at the point of the song called the *i-noḑag*, 'turn', where the musical form and accompaniment modes also change. It is during this second part of the song that the dancers may make "mimetic movements from the dream" (Underhill 1946), that is, dance in the movements of the birds through the air or other such movement typical of the subject matter of the songs. The rubrics for the songs given by Underhill (1946:121–23) indicate such a dance formation. Recent dance groups have shown a tendency to change only their step at the *i-noḑag* and not imitate dreams or move in elaborate formations. The two dance steps[27] usually alternate throughout each song and are maintained during any additional line activity such as mimetic movements.

### The Costumes

*O'odham* costumes reflect a development along a continuum from sparse to fairly elaborate. Gunst (1930:27) indicates that both sexes "wore short colored aprons [probably kilts] and paint"; later, long skirts and blouses for the girls, and trousers and shirts for the boys became standard. Underhill (1946:121) states that the boys wore kilts and the girls, wraparound skirts. Chesky (1943:66) describes "customary clothing" with "colored scarfs or ribbons that hung in streamers" tied to wrists and elbows, with hair bands of green ribbons and "red paper flowers" for the girls at Sil Nakia. The dancers at Ge Aji wore "ankle-length white tunics tied with colored sashes" with "downy eagle feathers in their hair and tied to each wrist" (1943:69–70). She further states that they "all wore tennis shoes, though they should have been barefoot."

The dancers of May 13, 1972, wore somewhat more elaborate costumes. The boys dressed in blue jeans or slacks, white T-shirts, and cowboy boots or shoes. Most had a hair band of colorful ribbon over shoulder-length hair. Some had ribbons around their neck and wrists, and white clay paint on their legs. The girls wore floor-length

## The Papago Skipping Dance

white skirts and white blouses. Most were decorated with colorful rickrack in two to five narrow bands near the bottoms of the skirts and some had similar patterns on their blouses. Ribbons hung through their hair and from their wrists.

Some of the dancers wore bright colored sashes and most had a bandolier hanging across the body from the right shoulder. Other contemporary *celkona* dancers wear bright blue or green dresses. Exposed body parts are normally covered with paint in some pattern, geometric or natural. Although colors other than white are mentioned in the literature, white is apparently the most accepted color. The paint is made from natural clays.

The singers dress in "normal" clothing, that is, jeans, shirt, jacket, and cowboy boots and hats for the men, long dresses with a shawl or scarf over the shoulders or head for the women.

### The Iagta

The *iagta* are ceremonial objects found in many Papago rituals. They occur in several forms in the *celkona*. Most *celkona* use a pole called the *u:saga* which is erected in the center of the dance plaza. Chesky (1943:65) speaks of one "painted red, white, and blue." Most have one or more representations of natural objects such as birds, clouds, or mountains attached to the top of the pole.

The most numerous *iagta* are those carried on wands by the two lines of dancers. The exact placement of *iagta* is determined by the dream of the leader, but two basic methods have been observed. One informant (HAE-PAP-II-C5) mentions the pattern of giving one type of *iagta*, such as *ko:koḍ*, to the girls and a different style to the boys. Another method is to present the *iagta* in one or more pairs from the front of the line to the back. The birds are normally first, the rainbows last, with clouds in the middle.

The three basic types of wands have already been mentioned: birds, clouds, rainbows. However, much variety exists within each class. Birds include life-size white cranes made of cotton on wooden twigs with bills and feet painted yellow (Underhill 1946:122), smaller birds of painted wood (1946:118), white birds with a bluish neckband (Chesky 1943:65),[28] and modern representations of the eagle, swallow, and the 'sea bird' (HAE-PAP-II-C5), made from wood, cardboard, cotton, or even styrofoam.

The cloud *iagta* appear in two basic shapes, a triangle and a rounded top cloud. The former is representative of those which pour down the rain, while the latter symbolize those that pass over very high. Therefore, both are needed to bring not only the clouds, but also the rains (HAE-PAP-II-C5). Often a row of black or grey fringe is attached to the bottom of the triangular clouds symbolizing the rain. A red zigzagged line is often painted on the cloud, especially those near the back of the line of dance, representing the accompanying lightning. The clouds were traditionally made of buckskin stretched over wooden poles and painted (Underhill 1946:118), but today, may be made of cotton stuffed in chicken wire or other material.

The final *iagta* in each line (usually only one pair) is the rainbow. Made of buckskin or muslim stretched over ocotillo withes, usually only two or three color bands are painted on the surfaces. All of the *iagta* are carried in two basic positions: (1) just above the head at the beginning of the song; and (2) raised high in the air at the *i-noḑag*. These positions alternate throughout each dance song.

Additional *iagta* such as the saguaro pole, mountain, flower, and less frequently, the sun and moon are also used. The type, size, shape, and number of *iagta* used are dictated by the leader's dream as he learns of the entire setting of the dance. The name of a particular *celkona* dance is usually derived from the type of *iagta* used in the dance and mentioned in the songs.

## CONCLUSIONS

The above discussions of the history and development of the O'odham *celkona* illustrate a complex system of continuity and change. Although many important aspects have changed in the last 50 years, such as the disappearance of the related intervillage games and the place of the *celkona* within the ritual calendar, the significance of the *celkona* proper to the Papago world view is still remembered and respected. In some cases it is used as a vehicle for passing this information on to the young members of the tribe. The symbolism and importance of such dances to a seminomadic desert culture cannot be easily forgotten.

The social purposes for this function have changed little over the

## The Papago Skipping Dance

past century. The celebration of group solidarity through song, dance, ritual symbolism, mock hostility, and food has been apparent throughout the history of the *celkona* although new symbolic milieus have developed for the location of the dance. A special relationship between the *celkona* and the *wailadag* may be seen in that group solidarity is the principal function of each. Also, if a local village does not have the proper *celkona* singers or *wailadag* orchestra, the appropriate people must be brought in from another village. In lieu of the above, Chesky's description of a *wailadag/celkona/wailadag* (page 261) is not so unusual after all. She was perhaps witnessing the time when an important transition from *celkona* to *wailadag* as the primary social event of the *O'odham* was taking place.

Considering both Ortiz's (1972:139) definition of ritual drama as a meeting of religion and world view, and the definition of ritual drama developed in the School of American Research Seminar (page 3), the *O'odham celkona* is an excellent example of ritual drama among the Papagos. Elements of native religion unite with the *O'odham himdag* 'way' through the interaction of humans with other humans and non-humans in a variety of experiences, creating a visible source of spiritual and social resolutions for the Papagos—a process which has been documented for over 100 years and which continues to meet the needs of the *O'odham*.

### NOTES

1. The author would like to thank those who have helped with the development of this chapter, especially Frances Manuel, who has spent many hours patiently answering questions. Initial support was given by the Doris Duke Foundation through the University of Arizona. Thanks also to Donald Bahr for many hours spent discussing Papago song and culture and for help in learning Papago, designing questions in the Piman language, and transliterating the results.

2. The orthography used here is that developed by Albert Alvarez (1969), translated by Kenneth Hale, and recently adopted by the Papago Tribe. The reader is referred to Bahr et al. (1974:1) for a guide to Piman sound. Mention is made here only for the following diacriticals: 1) ' = glottal stop; 2) . = retroflex consonant; and 3) : = preceding vowel is long.

3. Single quotation marks indicate a literal translation.

4. The Pima and Papago speak different but mutually understandable dialects of the Piman subgroup, a part of the Uto-Aztecan language family (Saxton and Saxton 1969:189). Culturally, they are frequently treated as "one" although many subtle variations exist.

5. Through the years, many fieldworkers have developed their own systems for transliterating Piman words. The practice in this chapter is to use the transliterations of the original author with a correction to the adopted tribal orthography given in brackets with the first occurrence of the term.

6. Although the classification of *cecega nen'ei* is valid within Piman concepts of song types, the general classification used by Russell, that of "Festal Songs," is without substantiation both in Piman terminology and present-day thought processes.

7. Unfortunately, Gunst does not present any *O'odham* terminology to identify these events specifically. Her terms, such as "Harvest Ceremony" and "Run in the Middle," are given only as English equivalents. Therefore, their implications for the *celkona* have been assessed, herein, on the basis of a general interpretation of details.

8. Later termed the "Dance in the Middle" (Gunst 1930:49).

9. Indeed, present dancers cannot recall such a step in the history of their dance. This author queries whether the movements have been mistaken for a more common step termed the *eḑa wo:p*.

10. Densmore (1929:135–37) terms the entire *ciwltkona* [*celkona*] a "Dance in Supplication to the Sun" although admitting "adverse circumstances made it impossible to obtain full data concerning it."

11. Underhill (1946:120) speaks next of the *ta'iwuni* [*ta'iwunim*] 'jumping out' which is normally not begun until the singers have taken their places in the dance area.

12. Only on more recent occasions is it stated that the singers sit to perform the *celkona*. Of the two groups presently active, one group of singers stands and the other sits.

13. Parenthetical references in this format refer to field tapes recorded by the author. This particular tape is cassette number five of a second series of Papago tapes.

14. Although I was unable to attend this performance, I would like to thank James Griffith for sharing his color slides and remembrances of the occasion with me. I have recorded the major singers and songs of this dance within a different context.

15. For example, on November 22, 1971, the first, second, and last songs of the cycle were given. Costumes, *iagta* or symbols, and dance movements were simple and elementary when compared with the May 13, 1972, version.

16. From *waila*, 'to dance', the term derives from the Spanish word, *baile*. Pimans, Maricopas, and the general Anglo community use the term *chicken scratch* for this style of dance music, which originated in Mexico and spread through *O'odham* lands as early as the 1870s. By the second quarter of this century, the *wailadag* had replaced the *keihina* as the customary dance for social entertainment.

17. Announcement of the text of each song in English was presented either before or after the individual song for the benefit of the audience, which was about 99 percent Papago.

18. The exact Piman concept of a song is unclear to date. For this discussion, a "song" consists of the total of all the complete and incomplete repetitions of the basic stanza. The songs of this set may be heard on Canyon Records C6098, Side A, bands 1–8 (Haefer 1973).

19. The directional activity on this occasion was limited to the bipolar orientation of east and west. However, some Papago dances do have a quadripolar orientation.

20. Saxton and Saxton (1973:341–46) present a bilingual version of the Children's Shrine myth and earlier (1973:11–19) tell of the appearance of morning star to the *O'odham*.

21. This report is complicated by the fact that Chesky (1943:61–69) discusses collectively those dances which she calls *Koeyihiyna* [*Keihina*]. It is believed that this term

## The Papago Skipping Dance

is used to refer generically to all dances of a social nature (therefore apparently including the *celkona*), and specifically to that social dance termed simply the "round dance." The author has extracted from her discussion those two dances at Sil Nakia and Gu Aji which had the "properties" of most *celkona*.

22. Both of these villages are "centers" producing leaders in the Papago "ways."

23. Some texts for the *cecega nen'ei* are given in Russell (1975:285–89) and Underhill (1938b:154–55).

24. Chesky (1943:65–66) cites two unequal lines: one with six girls and the other with five boys and three girls.

25. One in Underhill (1946:122–24), English text only, and two cycles on personal tapes.

26. This instrument is said to be different from the *hiwculdakuḍ* or notched rasp used in the *wuso* or blowing cure.

27. There are several other dance steps used by the Papago—the *eḍa meḍ*, the *gohimel*, and the *keikon*—each of which is associated with a particular dance genre just as the *celkon* is associated with the *celkona*.

28. Fontana (personal communication 1978) speaks of a black bow tie used as a neckband for a white bird.

# 11
# Vocables in Havasupai Song

### LEANNE HINTON
*Department of Linguistics*
*University of California, Berkeley*

## INTRODUCTION

One widespread feature of North American Indian music, both within ritual drama and in other kinds of musical events, is the notable use of *vocables*—"meaningless" syllables forming part or all of a song text.[1] Few scholars have studied these vocables or paid any attention to them beyond noting their existence; some scholars have even refused to transcribe texts consisting of vocables, choosing simply to write the melody alone. It is, after all, hard to decide what to do with vocables—their lack of linguistic meaning makes content studies impossible; it is hard even to know what questions to ask about them. The one question that is asked frequently is, What is the origin of the vocable in song? I will address myself to that question to some extent, but it is not the focus of this chapter. The question central to the present inquiry is, *What is the function of the vocable in song?* To develop some possible answers to this question, we will enter into a study of the song as a communication event, and also look at the vocables directly, as units of sound created not randomly but according to a certain pattern that functions to enhance sound quality and that can tell us some important things about the aesthetics of song. In fact, far from being unsuitable for study, vocables can provide us some insight into the universals of music.

### PREVIOUS STUDIES

Since this chapter is about vocables in Havasupai songs specifically, I will begin this section with a review of scholarly work on the Havasupais. Leslie Spier was the first scholar to produce a detailed ethnographic account of the Havasupais, and his monograph (Spier 1928) remains the standard anthropological reference for the Havasupais to the present time. The study of music was not his aim, but he discussed dances and musical instruments, and described the use of songs in curing, hunting, and other activities in which music plays a part. Another good ethnographic study of the Havasupais, this one concentrating on women (where Spier concentrated primarily on men), was written by Carma Lee Smithson (1959); this monograph contains scattered references to song traditions. A later book coauthored by Smithson and Robert Euler (1964) provides a good deal of information about Havasupai religion, and gives some detailed accounts of the dreaming of songs, the funeral ceremony, and other musical events. Henry Dobyns and Euler (1967) wrote a detailed historical account of the Ghost Dance among the Havasupais and Hualapais, although they said little about the songs themselves.

Other studies of the Havasupais say nothing about their music, although these works do have some important bearing on the social context and history of Havasupai music. Spier (1929) and Douglas Schwartz (1956, 1959) both address the question of the cultural classification of the Havasupais, with Spier arguing against earlier claims that they are a Southwestern group, and suggesting classification as part of the Great Basin culture area. Schwartz suggests that the Havasupais should not be classified uniquely at all, but recognized as bearing features of Great Basin, Yuman, and Pueblo traits.

In light of these discussions, all of which state emphatically that the Havasupais are not at all typically Yuman in their way of doing things, it is strange that ethnomusicologists—with no musical data—have always automatically placed Havasupai music in the California-Yuman musical style. The California-Yuman musical style was first described by Herzog (1928) in his article, "The Yuman

## Vocables in Havasupai Song

Musical Style." Densmore (1932) provided a detailed description of Yuma music, and Herzog (1933) made a study of Maricopa music. The California-Yuman style has been summarized by H. H. Roberts (1936) and by Nettl (1954).

The Havasupai musical style was not described in print until 1977 (Hinton 1977). In my dissertation I concluded that Havasupai music cannot be placed in the California-Yuman tradition, but instead seems to be most like Great Basin music, with certain interesting traits that link it to some extent with the California-Yuman style.[2] This finding will be no surprise to the ethnologists who have worked with the Havasupais, and I can do little but apologize for the musicologists who seem to have ignored the ethnological literature on this point.

There is a paucity in the literature of in-depth study of American Indian song texts. Scholars such as Herzog and Sapir usually provided good transcriptions and translations of the song texts they collected, but did not do any real analytical or comparative study of them. Such scholars as Densmore (1932) and Merriam (1967) rarely bothered to transcribe them. Basic questions have yet to be answered, such as, How are words fit to music in American Indian songs? What poetic devices are used? In what ways does sung language differ from spoken language?

Nevertheless, the field has been touched on by some scholars. Pioneering forays into the study of song texts were made by Herzog (1934, 1947), List (1963), and Voegelin and Euler (1957). Studies dealing specifically with vocables include Nettl (1953), Frisbie (1967), and Halpern (1976). Recent work by Bahr and Haefer (1978) has advanced the study of sung language considerably. My dissertation on Havasupai songs (Hinton 1977) is also an effort to help close this gap in linguistic and musical knowledge.

### AN OVERVIEW OF HAVASUPAI MUSIC

The Havasupais are a group of about 500 people who live in northern Arizona. Traditionally, they had a somewhat unusual annual cycle: in winter, they were hunters and gatherers living in and around the piñon forests on the Coconino Plateau; in summer, they inhabited Havasu Canyon and did irrigation farming. Their language is Yuman, and they have generally been included as part of the California-Yuman musical area (Nettl 1954). However, their culture does not follow typical Yuman patterns (Schwartz 1959), and in fact, their music is not what could be called typically Yuman at all. They live next to many other groups; they have had extremely close ties traditionally with the Hopis, have interacted positively to a large extent with the Paiutes, and have also traded a fair amount with the Navajos. Their music includes various genres of song either deriving directly from or being influenced strongly by these groups. Those genres of music that have not been adopted from other tribes show more affinity to the Great Basin musical style (described by Nettl 1954) than to the California-Yuman style, although they cannot legitimately be classified as either one. In an earlier study (Hinton 1977), I have shown that nonborrowed Havasupai songs exhibit some characteristics of both musical styles.

Havasupais have very few community-wide ceremonies. Their one traditional ceremony is a late-summer harvest festival (the "Peach Festival"), to which neighboring tribes were traditionally invited, and which was celebrated by feasting, dancing, gambling, and trading. The Circle Dance is the major dance at this festival, and many of the songs sung during the Circle Dance since 1890 were inspired by the 1890 Ghost Dance religion. In the past, a Masked Dance inspired by the Hopis was also performed, and at least a few times, Havasupais remember, a group of men would circle around the dance grounds on horseback singing a group of Horse Songs borrowed from the Navajo Blessingway Ceremony (Hinton 1977).

The only other community-wide ceremonies are funerals and memorial ceremonies. Until about 1910, no singing or dancing accompanied the funeral; however, during a period of severe epidemics that wiped out over half the population, the Havasupais adopted the Yuman mourning practices which they still use, singing the Mojave Bird Songs and Tumanpa, and the Chemehuevi Salt Songs. While several Havasupai singers are able to sing these songs well, Mojave and Chemehuevi singers are often invited to lead the singing of these songs at mourning ceremonies.

Traditionally, no other songs were associated with community ceremonies. The only other group singing was in the sweathouse, where three or four men may sing Sweathouse Songs together. There was a large body of Medicine Songs created through dreaming, and owned and sung individually, and a smaller body of

## Vocables in Havasupai Song

dreamed Rain Songs. Each family had its own special Hunting Songs and Gambling Songs, as well as lullabies (the latter not considered by the people to be real music). There were Story Songs, generally short songs within a long spoken narrative, and always representing a quotation of one of the actors in the narrative, and there was a large body of secular Personal Songs, composed and sung by Havasupais to express their emotions about each other and life in general. Some of these are Love Songs; others express complaints or some grief.

In modern times, most genres of traditional song are disappearing. Very few people play the traditional gambling game of ball hiding, and those few who know it generally know only one or two of the songs associated with it. No one composes the Personal Songs anymore, and only the oldest people can sing any of the old Personal Songs composed before the turn of the century. The last Havasupai medicine man died in 1964, and Medicine Songs are not sung anymore except by a very few old people who have dreamed their own songs to sing over their own illnesses. A few people still sing Hunting Songs, but most say they just pray before a hunt nowadays. There is probably no one alive who knows the Rain Songs; the last known singer of Rain Songs died a few years ago. There are several people who can still tell the traditional stories, so that genre might still be considered viable, although the Havasupais doubt that the young people are learning the stories. The most viable songs at present are the more group-oriented songs: the Sweathouse Songs, the Circle Dance Songs, and the Funeral Songs.

### THE ANATOMY OF THE VOCABLE

Every Havasupai song has some vocables. Even in the fully worded songs, vocables are used as line-end codas and as spacing-out devices to fit the words to the meter. In other genres of song, vocables play a larger role, and in some genres, a text will consist primarily of vocables. Fully worded genres of song include the Personal Songs, Story Songs, Gambling Songs, Medicine Songs, and Hunting Songs; Circle Dance Songs are partially worded, and Sweathouse Songs and lullabies consist almost completely of vocables. Since only one Rain Song was obtained in my study of

Havasupai music, I will not discuss that genre, and for now I will not include songs adopted directly from foreign sources, such as the Funeral Songs and Horse Songs. I will concentrate on Sweathouse Songs as the genre representing the purest use of vocables, Circle Dance Songs for the partially worded genres, and a selected array of fully worded songs from various genres.

### SWEATHOUSE SONGS

Sweathouse Songs consist of a single complex strophe and text sung over several times. While some Sweathouse Songs contain one or two interpretable words, the majority of syllables in all songs are vocables. The most common set of words are [ba hane] (occurring in 4 songs out of our sample of 12) which is translated by Havasupais as "healthy man" ('baa³ "man," han- "good," "healthy"). One song, example 1,[4] is said to contain the word *l'ii g-ta/* "ground weed," the name of a medicinal herb used in curing sores and swellings, which are treated also by sweatbathing. Beyond these, there are other songs containing syllables which are said to be sound effects: for instance, example 2 contains the syllables "ha le ya le ye ya" which is said to stand for the sound of the water as it turns to steam when sprinkled on the hot stones in the sweathouse.

There are also other songs containing unusual syllables which may or may not originate from real words. But, in all cases, including those just cited, most singers do not, in fact, know what words, if any, are in the song. Most Sweathouse Songs at least functionally consist entirely of vocables.

I have listed below (table 11.1) all the syllable types that occur in the 12 songs sampled: the first column is the form of the syllable, the second column shows the number of times this syllable occurs in the sample (counting was confined to a single repetition of the strophe for each song), and the third column shows the number of songs in which the syllable occurred.

We can see that the most common syllables are *ya, ye, ŋa, na,* and *ha*. Patterns become clearer if we coalesce related syllables. As shown in table 11.2, syllables beginning with [y] (V stands for any vowel) are by far the most common; syllables beginning with [ŋ] and [n] are the second and third most common, and syllables beginning with [h] come in fourth.

TABLE 11.1
SYLLABLE TYPES IN SWEATHOUSE SONGS

| Form | No. of Occurrences | No. of Songs | Form | No. of Occurrences | No. of Songs |
|---|---|---|---|---|---|
| ya | 62 | 10 | le | 6 | 2 |
| ye | 46 | 9 | ga | 5 | 2 |
| ŋa | 40 | 6 | ñe | 5 | 2 |
| na | 37 | 10 | ta | 5 | 1 |
| ha | 31 | 9 | do | 4 | 3 |
| 'e | 22 | 7 | ge | 3 | 1 |
| yo | 21 | 7 | yu | 3 | 1 |
| θe | 19 | 4 | da | 2 | 2 |
| ne | 14 | 5 | 'o | 2 | 2 |
| he | 13 | 6 | we | 2 | 2 |
| go | 13 | 4 | θi | 2 | 1 |
| ŋo | 9 | 1 | to | 2 | 1 |
| ba | 8 | 4 | wo | 1 | 1 |
| θa | 8 | 4 | wu | 1 | 1 |
| ŋe | 8 | 2 | no | 1 | 1 |
| de | 7 | 2 | se | 1 | 1 |
| gi | 7 | 2 | 'a | 1 | 1 |

TABLE 11.2.
SYLLABLE TYPES IN SWEATHOUSE SONGS ACCORDING TO INITIAL CONSONANT

| Form | No. of Occurrences | No. of Songs | % of Total |
|---|---|---|---|
| yV | 132 | 12 | 32 |
| ŋV | 57 | 7 | 14 |
| nV | 52 | 11 | 13 |
| hV | 44 | 10 | 11 |
| θV | 29 | 8 | 7 |
| gV | 28 | 7 | 7 |
| 'e | 25 | 7 | 6 |
| dV | 13 | 4 | 3 |
| bV | 8 | 4 | 2 |
| wV | 4 | 3 | 1 |

It is significant that [y] and [h] are *glides* and [n] and [ŋ] are *nasals*. We will see throughout this study that nasals and glides predominate among vocables.

While θV syllables are much less common, they do occur in two-thirds of the songs in the sample, which is notable, because they are not as common in other song types. In fact, it is the predominance of θV and ŋV syllables that is the hallmark of Sweathouse Song texts. yV, hV, and nV are common in other genres as well, but θV and ŋV are common only in Sweathouse Songs. gV, which is almost as important as θV in Sweathouse Songs, also occurs in other genres.

LEANNE HINTON

Table 11.3 shows vowels in Sweathouse Songs (C stands for any consonant). Note that /a/ and /e/ are by far the most common vowels, with /o/ coming in as a poor third, and /i/ and /u/ almost nonexistent.

TABLE 11.3.
SYLLABLE TYPES IN SWEATHOUSE SONGS ACCORDING TO VOWEL

| Form | No. of Occurrences | No. of Songs | % of Total |
| --- | --- | --- | --- |
| Ca | 199 | 12 | 49 |
| Ce | 146 | 12 | 36 |
| Co | 49 | 8 | 12 |
| Ci | 9 | 2 | 2 |
| Cu | 3 | 1 | 1 |

In summary, the typical sweathouse vocable begins, in descending order of importance, with the consonants y, η, n, h, θ, or g and ends in the vowels a or e. (This is diagrammed in fig. 11.1.)

The syllable *ye* in Sweathouse Songs has a special importance as the most common line-final and strophe-final vocable. Eight of the twelve songs in the corpus have a strophe-final *ye*. Sweathouse Songs have relatively rare two-beat syllables within them; these two-beat syllables gain special prominence in the song as a result of their length. Two-beat syllables occur most often as line-finals, but may occur as line-internals in some songs. *ye* dominates the two-beat syllables as well, as shown in table 11.4. (*na* has more occurrences, but these are confined to three songs, whereas *ye* occurs as a two-beat syllable in over half the songs, and is the *only* two-beat syllable in a quarter of the songs.)

Beyond the fact that each Sweathouse Song text has characteristics that are common to all, each song also has its own unique or uncommon characteristics. Thus Text 3 is distinctive in its relatively great concentration on ηV syllables (12 occurrences); Text 1 distinguishes itself by ending every line with [na], and so on. Text 4 is notable for its tendency to transpose syllables in repetitions of lines, as shown below:

a1: baa ga θa *wa yo* nee
a2: baa ga θa *wo ya* nee
b1: *na ya* 'ee
b2: *ya na* 'ee
b1: *na ya* 'ee
b4: *ye na* 'a

TABLE 11.4.
VOCABLE TYPES OCCURRING AS TWO-BEAT SYLLABLES

| Form | No. of Songs | No. of Occurrences |
|---|---|---|
| ye | 7 | 12 |
| na | 3 | 15 |
| ba | 3 | 4 |
| yo | 3 | 3 |
| θa | 2 | 5 |
| ta | 1 | 5 |
| ñe | 1 | 5 |
| ŋe | 1 | 2 |
| 'e | 1 | 2 |
| ga | 1 | 2 |
| le | 1 | 2 |
| ne | 1 | 2 |
| go | 1 | 1 |
| ŋa | 1 | 1 |
| ŋo | 1 | 1 |

This subtle individuation of vocable use is part of the unique quality of each song. The individuated use of vocables will be discussed further in the discussion of other song types.

### CIRCLE DANCE SONGS

Like Sweathouse Songs, each Circle Dance Song consists of a single strophe and text sung over and over. But, unlike the Sweathouse Songs, each Circle Dance Song text has some words in it. These words are most often nouns, usually referring to common events in traditional Havasupai life or to the dance itself. The words lack the various grammatical markers used in speech and in fully worded songs, and are often quite distorted from their spoken equivalents. Content is very sketchy; for example, Song 5 has recognizable words that translate "lie down" and "dance." Since no more information than these agrammaticized words is available to listeners, various different interpretations of the song are possible. One singer explains it as meaning "I am the one who lies still, thinking about songs to make for the Circle Dance." Another interprets it as, "There is an old man laying at his house somewhere—old man, you must come out and start dancing now." All other Circle Dance Songs are also sketchy in content, using just a few words to create a general impression able to be interpreted in several ways unless the composer has passed on the interpretation to the other singers.

Some vocables carry a little bit of meaning, even though they are not words. Just as the vocables "tra-la-la" in English carry the slight connotation of happiness, so do some vocable phrases in Havasupai carry connotations of emotion. In Text 6, the line
*yáŋandŋa héyo ndaá ha yén hdaá*
consists fully of vocables, but carries the connotation of happiness.

When dealing with songs containing real words, it is necessary to distinguish vocable usage from a similar process I will call *vowel insertion*. In all Havasupai songs containing real words, vowels are inserted between consonants. This process is also a normal phonological process in spoken Havasupai: the major distinction between vowel insertion in spoken language and in songs is that while in spoken language a short unstressed [ə] or some variant is inserted, in singing, a full vowel is inserted, often a different one than would be inserted in speaking. Vowel insertion is very closely related to vocable insertion, but a discussion of it would demand more space than is available here. The phenomenon of vowel insertion is analyzed thoroughly in Hinton (1977). We will limit ourselves to a definition of a vocable as being the addition of an entire CV syllable; vowel insertion, which creates CV syllables out of consonantal affixes, is a separate (though related) phenomenon from vocable usage.

Each line of a Circle Dance Song consists, in general, of one word augmented by vowel insertion, accompanied usually by one or more vocables. The vocables most often follow the words, and more vocables may precede the word. Vocables inside a word are rare. We will look first at the more common vocable forms, and then at some devices of vocable choice in Circle Dance Songs.

In a sample of 25 Circle Dance Songs, the most common vocable types are shown in table 11.5. The pattern is slightly different from Sweathouse Songs: $yV$ and $nV$ are still the most common vocable types, but $yV$ does not have quite as strong predominance in Circle Dance Songs as it does in Sweathouse Songs. $yV$ represents 14 percent of all syllable types (including both vocables and real words), as opposed to 32 percent in Sweathouse Songs. $nV$ and $hV$ has about the same representation in both types, but $wV$ has a much more important role in Circle Dance Songs than in Sweathouse Songs—$wV$ represents 9 percent of the syllables in Circle Dance Songs but only 1 percent in Sweathouse Songs. $wV$, then, plays the same role in Circle Dance Songs that $\theta V$ and $\eta V$ play in Sweathouse Songs. (In Circle Dance Songs, by the way, $\theta V$ represents only 2 percent of the syllables, and $\eta V$, only 1 percent.)

## Vocables in Havasupai Song

Looking at vowels in all syllables of Circle Dance Songs, we find the distribution shown in table 11.6. This distribution is much like that of Sweathouse Songs, with the exception that Ci and Cu have slightly greater representation. This is mainly a function of the presence of real words in the songs—Circle Dance vocables consist almost *entirely* of Ca, Ce, and Co syllables, like Sweathouse Songs. Virtually all Circle Dance Songs have line-end syllables with the vowels [a] or [e].

TABLE 11.5.
MOST COMMON VOCABLE TYPES IN CIRCLE DANCE SONGS, ACCORDING TO CONSONANT

| Form | No. of Occurrences | % of Total |
|---|---|---|
| yV | 178 | 14 |
| nV | 164 | 13 |
| hV | 149 | 12 |
| wV | 114 | 9 |

TABLE 11.6.
MOST COMMON VOCABLE TYPES IN CIRCLE DANCE SONGS, ACCORDING TO VOWEL

| Form | % of Total |
|---|---|
| Ca | 44 |
| Ce | 31 |
| Co | 13 |
| Ci | 7 |
| Cu | 2 |

To summarize, the typical Circle Dance Song vocable has the consonant y, n, h, or w, followed by the vowel a, e, or o. (See fig. 11.1.)

Recall that *ye* plays a special role in Sweathouse Songs of being the most common strophe-end vocable and two-beat vocable. That role in Circle Dance Songs is filled by the syllable *we*.

Another vocable with a special role is *ha*, which occurs frequently on the upbeat before the first beat of the line. It will be seen that this vocable plays the same role in fully worded songs as well.

One common device in Circle Dance Songs is that of creating vocables that are either assonant or consonant with meaningful syllables in the line. For example, in Text 7 the word [saw(ə)] (inserted vowels are in parentheses), "eat," is followed by the vocable

Sweathouse Songs: $\left\{\begin{array}{c} y \\ \eta \\ n \\ h \\ \theta \\ g \end{array}\right\} \left\{\begin{array}{c} a \\ e \end{array}\right\}$

Circle Dance Songs: $\left\{\begin{array}{c} y \\ n \\ h \\ w \end{array}\right\} \left\{\begin{array}{c} a \\ e \\ o \end{array}\right\}$

Fully Worded Songs: $\left\{\begin{array}{c} m \\ \tilde{n} \\ ' \\ w \\ y \\ h \end{array}\right\} \left\{\begin{array}{c} a \\ e \\ o \end{array}\right\}$

FIGURE 11.1. Vocable types according to genre.

[*naw*] to produce [*sawənaw*]. As an example of consonance, we find the word [*son(e)wal(a)*] (*wala*, "pines") followed by the vocables *so le*, to produce an echo of the consonants in the main part of the line. We will see the same process more pronounced in the fully worded songs, of using real-word material as the inspiration for the shape of the vocables.

### FULLY WORDED SONGS

Fully worded songs are often very long (as long as thirty minutes) and have through-composed texts sung to a simple strophe. In fully worded songs, the job of distinguishing vocables from meaningful syllables becomes extremely difficult. We find in these songs that certain affixes such as [*-ña*] or [*-ñe*] (a demonstrative suffix on nouns, a tense/aspect marker on verbs), [*-ha*], [*-ya*], and [*-wa*] (all

286

## Vocables in Havasupai Song

demonstrative suffixes) and [-o] (a tense/aspect verb suffix) are used with great frequency in fully worded songs at the ends of lines. There are times when these are clearly part of the sense of the line, and other times when they appear to be semantically empty. The task of deciding whether to count a given occurrence as a meaningful element or a vocable is in many cases impossible. I think it is reasonable to claim that we are in the shady area between meaningful elements and vocables in fully worded songs. A claim that vocables must frequently derive from meaningful elements in these songs is justified by the fact that the [ña] and [ñe] syllables are extremely common in fully worded songs, but extremely rare in the Circle Dance and Sweathouse Songs. We would expect a true vocable to have even more frequent occurrence in vocable-rich genres than in fully worded genres.

It is certainly possible to demonstrate that *some* syllables are true vocables in every sense of the word, either because they do not have the form of any meaningful element in Havasupai (such as [ŋa]), or because they are grammatically impossible (such as [ha] on the end of an inflected verb). But I do not think it is worthwhile to develop a set of criteria for making these judgments, since it would be very complex, sometimes arbitrary, and would not provide much information. For now, then, it does not seem useful to count vocables per se, since we have no ideal way to distinguish them from meaningful segments. For purposes of comparison with other genres, I will show which syllable types are most common, without judging whether a given occurrence is a vocable or not. We will later examine which of these syllables *may* be vocables in some cases and which may *never* be vocables.

We will look first at the consonants. Table 11.7 shows the frequency of occurrence of all Havasupai consonants in a sample of eight fully worded songs (a total of 3,107 consonants were counted).

One's first impression of this chart is that nasals and glides do not show the predominance that they show in songs with more vocables. The fully worded songs show more similarity to spoken Havasupai, in which stops, affricates, and fricatives are extremely common.

On the other hand, when compared to spoken language, we see that nasals and glides in fully worded songs are somewhat more common than in spoken language. Table 11.8 shows this comparison. (A total of 1,792 consonants were counted in a sample of speech.)

TABLE 11.7.
OCCURRENCE OF CONSONANTS IN FULLY WORDED SONGS
(TOTAL CONSONANTS COUNTED: 3,107 in 8 Songs)

| | |
|---|---|
| g | 15.7% |
| m | 10.2% |
| ñ | 10.0% |
| ʼ | 9.6% |
| w | 9.3% |
| y | 9.3% |
| v | 7.4% |
| j | 6.8% |
| h | 5.2% |
| t | 3.1% |
| θ | 3.0% |
| b | 2.8% |
| l | 1.8% |
| r | 1.5% |
| n | 1.3% |
| $g^w$ | 0.8% |
| s | 0.8% |
| q | 0.5% |
| ŋ | 0.3% |
| $g^y$ | 0.2% |

TABLE 11.8.
COMPARISON OF CONSONANT FREQUENCY IN SPEECH AND FULLY WORDED SONGS

| | | Speech | Songs | | |
|---|---|---|---|---|---|
| Nasals | m | 11.5% | 10.2% | *Overall Nasals* | |
| | ñ | 4.9% | 10.0% | Speech | Song |
| | n | 1.1% | 1.3% | 17.5% | 21.2% |
| | ŋ | 0 | 0.3% | | |
| Glides | w | 5.7% | 9.3% | *Overall Glides* | |
| | y | 7.9% | 9.3% | Speech | Song |
| | ʼ | 7.1% | 9.6% | 24.1% | 33.5% |
| | h | 3.4% | 5.2% | | |
| Stops and | g | 17.3% | 15.7% | *Overall Stops/Affricates* | |
| Affricates | j | 7.3% | 6.8% | Speech | Song |
| | t | 6.2% | 3.1% | 45.4% | 30.1% |
| | b | 4.2% | 2.8% | | |
| | q | 0.9% | 0.5% | | |
| | $g^w$ | 2.1% | 0.8% | | |
| | $g^y$ | 0.2% | 0.2% | | |
| Fricatives | v | 8.5% | 7.4% | *Overall Fricatives* | |
| | θ | 5.0% | 3.0% | Speech | Song |
| | s | 1.5% | 0.8% | 15.1% | 11.2% |

## Vocables in Havasupai Song

As table 11.8 shows, overall glides and nasals increase notably in occurrence in fully worded songs as opposed to spoken language, while stops, affricates, and fricatives decrease. Thus, even though glides and nasals are not as predominant in fully worded songs as they are in vocable-rich songs, they are nevertheless dominant in comparison to their role in spoken language.

As for vowels, we find the same predominance of /a/, /o/, and /e/ in fully worded songs that we find in other songs. A comparison of spoken language and vowels from three fully worded songs is shown in table 11.9. This table shows that /a/, /e/, and /o/ increase significantly from spoken to sung language, while /i/ and /u/ decrease, even though /i/ and /u/ are more common in fully worded songs than in other songs.

TABLE 11.9.
VOWELS IN SPEECH AND FULLY WORDED SONGS

|   | Speech | Songs |
|---|--------|-------|
| a | 31.3%  | 39.4% |
| e | 6.7%   | 20.0% |
| o | 5.8%   | 14.3% |
| i | 19.9%  | 14.6% |
| u | 12.5%  | 6.7%  |

On the basis of these findings, we can now describe the most common syllable types in fully worded songs as consisting of a consonant g, m, ñ, ', w, y, v, j, or h followed by the vowel a, e, o, or i. This summary does not describe several important kinds of skewing in the data. First of all, /i/ almost never occurs in line-end or in on-beat syllables—it is always in short off-beat syllables. Secondly, certain consonants—especially /g/ and /j/—are always associated with certain vowels: we find [ga] and [ge] and [je], but rarely, if ever, do we find *[gi], *[go], or *[ja], *[jo]. Thirdly, and related to the second point, syllables with /g/, /v/, and /j/ are *never* vocables—that is, there is never a case where they do not carry semantic value.

On the basis of this consideration, we can return to the discussion of vocables and make a revised version of the syllable type for vocables in fully worded songs as shown in figure 11.1.

Vocables in fully worded songs, then, are distinguishable from those in vocable-rich songs by a predominance of /m/ and /ñ/ nasals (as opposed to /n/ in Circle Dance Songs and /n/ and /ŋ/ in Sweathouse Songs), the predominance of /ʔ/, and the presence of /i/ in off-beat syllables.

Like the Circle Dance Songs, in fully worded songs [hV] vocables occur frequently on the upbeat before the first beat of a line, and [wV] vocables have a tendency to predominate as line-finals.

Which vowel is chosen for a vocable frequently depends on the principle of vowel-harmony discussed for Circle Dance Songs. Out of a sample of 20 fully worded songs, 5 base most of their vocable formation on vowel harmony rules. For example, the Farewell Song (Text 8) has a vocable refrain of [hVŋV] where the vowel usually echoes the vowel of the last syllable of the line preceding the refrain.

As with the other genres, each song has unique characteristics to its vocables. For example, Text 9 (Hank Ward) is unique in that it adds frequent vocables *inside* the line, usually [na], but sometimes [an] or [n] if the meter requires it. Text 10 has a vocable refrain at the end of each line, [he'he ye]; and some songs have one or two verses consisting entirely of vocables at the beginning and near the end of the song.

### SUMMARY OF THE VOCABLE TYPES

To review what we have discussed so far, vocables generally have CV form where C is a *glide or a nasal*, and V is a *nonhigh vowel* (a, e, or o). Beyond these generalities, each song type is characterized by a predominance of certain glides or nasals, and of certain vowels. The three types of vocable usage are shown in figure 11.1.

## SOME MODELS OF VOCABLE FUNCTION

At the outset, we formulated the question, *What is the origin and function of vocables in song?* Previous work on vocables (Halpern 1976 and Nettl 1953) has concentrated on the theory that at least some (so-called?) vocables derive from real words, either in the language of the singer or from a foreign language that the song or song-type was borrowed from. The point of these scholars is well taken. We have seen in the Havasupai songs that in Sweathouse and Circle Dance Songs, real words are present, some of them archaic,

## Vocables in Havasupai Song

and that some (so-called?) vocables represent sound effects or have vague semantic value, usually a connotation of a certain emotion. These corroborate similar findings in the other languages studied. Furthermore, the Havasupais themselves claim that the texts of some songs are archaic language, long forgotten. We have also seen that many—perhaps even most—vocables in the fully worded songs can be interpreted as derivative from meaningful elements.

Nevertheless, at best this theory of vocables as derived from language can be only a small part of the answers we are seeking. Many vocables even in the fully worded songs are clearly not derived from meaningful elements, and in the Sweathouse Songs, even the ones with some words still contain a majority of syllables that no one claims are language-derived. Beyond this, we have seen that vocables are extremely limited in their possible forms, consisting of glides and nasals followed by nonlow vowels. Were these syllables mostly language-derived, we would expect them to look more like language; we would expect them to allow all vowels and consonants present in spoken language, and in fact probably to consist mostly of those vowels and consonants most prevalent in spoken language. Instead, we find that stops, affricates, and fricatives, very common in spoken language, are almost completely nonexistent among vocables. I would like to develop a twofold model of vocable function that begins with the claim that vocables in general are created from the beginning as meaningless syllables. I will discuss vocables first in the context of *communication* in songs and second as a response to *aesthetic goals* in singing.

### VOCABLES AND COMMUNICATION

Lomax (1968) has proposed that a variable he calls "wordiness"—that is, the degree to which a song is nonrepetitive and consists of real words—in songs increases with cultural complexity. He suggests that in smaller, simple societies the communication of information is not as essential as in larger societies, because in the former there is much more shared knowledge, and so less need for further instruction.

I disagree with Lomax for several reasons. I reject the model of a "simple-to-complex" hierarchy of cultures, to begin with, and I consider his sampling methods, which allowed him to come to conclusions about enormous areas of the world based on only a few songs from a few communities, to be shallow. It should be clear from the facts presented here that a musical tradition may, and usually does, include songs all along the continuum of "wordiness."

The question he asked on a worldwide basis should be asked first on an intracultural basis, to wit, why, within a community, do some songs consist of vocables almost entirely, while others have fully worded texts? If that question can be answered, then the question of why some communities specialize in vocable-rich songs while others do not might well be answered automatically as well. Lomax's point is, of course, valid that there must be no need to communicate linguistic information in the songs that have repetitive texts with a large proportion of vocables. It will become clear that vocables are fewest in songs whose function is to communicate information from one human to another, and that those songs consisting primarily of vocables serve other functions than the act of communication.

It is always the function of a fully worded song to convey information to the audience. The Personal Songs were intended to convey a direct description of how the composer feels about some state of affairs; they were often used as a means of social control. For example, Love Songs were, according to Havasupais, sung by women as a way of advertising to the community the man they wanted to marry, thus helping to bring about the desired result. Songs complaining about someone's behavior were sung to change the behavior. Thus the information contained in the song text is essential to the song's reason for being. When asked, "Why do people sing the [Personal] Songs?" singers answered (paraphrase), "in order to let people know how they feel about something."

For the Story Songs, we can make a similar argument. The whole idea of telling a story is to convey content, and the songs are key elements in the story. The Havasupai style of storytelling separates objective and subjective elements completely. The spoken portions of the story objectively describe events, never discussing the emotions or motivations of the characters; the sung portions depict quotations of the characters, always depicting emotions and opinions.[5]

The three Medicine Songs collected are also in first person: one of them (Text 15) describes a dream the medicine man had, and the other two tell the story of an actual curing done by a medicine man for a patient. These songs were sung directly to a patient to help in

## Vocables in Havasupai Song

the cure. By describing clearly the power of the medicine man (through the description of a powerful dream or of a cure), the patient gained the confidence in the medicine man that was presumed necessary for a successful cure. The psychological value of developing the patient's confidence in the power of the curer has been well demonstrated in Western medicine.

In short, communication of informational content of all fully worded songs is an essential part of the song's reason for being, and is the major goal to be accomplished by the song. (The Medicine Songs are slightly more complicated; we will return to them later.) In all cases, too, the songs are sung for an audience who sits and listens; there is no dancing and no group singing with the fully worded songs. The audience's job is to understand the song content, and the singer's goal is to communicate the content successfully.

The vocable-rich songs are a different matter. Looking first at the partially worded Circle Dance Songs, we find that the audience does not sit and listen. Instead, the audience dances, often joining in on the singing at the same time. In fact, when asked, "Why are the Circle Dance Songs sung?" singers answer (paraphrase), "to give people something to dance to." The content of the song is quite secondary to its function, as an accompaniment to group dancing. Most of the songs were composed by converts to the 1890 Ghost Dance religion, and the dance itself, besides enhancing a sense of togetherness, also induced trances. The Havasupais rejected the tenets of the Ghost Dance religion within a couple of years, and stopped doing the Circle Dance for several years. Then it was revived as a Social Dance and is still celebrated today.

The Sweathouse Songs have the function of curing or preventing illness, without the intervention of a medicine man. The sweatbathers usually sing together, although all but the lead singer sing softly. Like the Circle Dance Songs, everyone present during the singing of the Sweathouse Songs is involved in other activities—sprinkling of water on the rocks, and blowing on afflicted parts of their bodies. One singer, when asked why people sing Sweathouse Songs, replied (paraphrase), "So that people won't just have to sit there alone in the dark." So beyond their direct curative powers, the songs also function as a sort of mutual support mechanism for the group in the sweatbath.

For both the Circle Dance Songs and the Sweathouse Songs,

then, communication of informational content is not involved in the song function. However, this does not mean that the songs are meaningless. As stated above, the Circle Dance Songs do have sketchy texts about everyday traditional living or about the dancing. And the Sweathouse Songs, beyond the presence of a stray word here and there, also have specific functions, such as the curing of snakebite. Whenever I ask what a song "means," I am given an explanation somewhat like the following (explanation for Text 3):

> This song means that when the snake bite comes here, the pain goes in every muscle of your body. But we are singing this song for you and it reaches those muscle places and we know already that the pain will be gone when we finish (Hinton 1977:209).

We find that meaning is present in wordless songs in general, but that it is not tied at all to language; it instead becomes fused with function.

When looking at the vocable-rich songs overall, we see two striking aspects of the functions of the musical events that are missing from most of the fully worded songs: the first is the goal of *solidarity*, and the second is *spiritual involvement*.

Recall that the fully worded songs have the primary purpose of transmitting linguistic information, with the ultimate goal of entertainment, moral instruction, eliciting a certain kind of behavior from one's companions, or simply expressing an opinion. The Harvest Festival, on the other hand, along with the dance that is performed at it, has a primary purpose of expressing and reinforcing group solidarity. It has traditionally been performed when members of the community are about to depart from the canyon—in the old days, just before families left the canyon to roam the plateau for the winter, and in recent times, before the children depart for boarding school (Hinton 1977). The communal feast preceding the dance, and the dance itself, where everyone holds hands and faces toward the center of the circle, express solidarity. The song texts themselves, to the extent that they have real words, contrast with fully worded songs in that they mention completely noncontroversial topics, and never contain the first person pronoun. The pronoun differentiates narrator from audience—no such differentiation is made in these song texts.

## Vocables in Havasupai Song

I suggest that fully worded texts are, in fact, anathemas to the direct expression of group solidarity and unification of action. Even in Western culture, most music that is aimed at creating group synchrony and solidarity is either wordless (instrumental music) or scores low on Lomax's "wordiness" scale (such as work songs, marches, and dance music). Group solidarity necessarily involves a suspension of disagreement. By having little or no informational content in a song, it becomes easier for the listeners to suspend the rational faculties that can produce disagreement and thus hinder unified action and solidarity. It is therefore reasonable that vocable-rich songs be used in a ceremony that expresses this solidarity.

As further support for this point of view, I will briefly mention the other major community ceremony, the funerap. I have not included Funeral Songs in this study because they are adopted from foreign sources. Nevertheless, even in the communities they come from, and certainly in the Havasupai community, these songs are also vocable-rich, containing few or no recognizable words. The modern Havasupai funeral is an expression of community solidarity in the face of catastrophe. The funeral, then, is another case of the matching of wordless songs to ceremonies of solidarity.

Circle Dance Songs, Funeral Songs, and Sweathouse Songs also have an attribute of spirituality. The sweatbath, in particular, is an event not designed to create community solidarity so much as to create solidarity between humans and the spiritual power of the universe. It is said that the Sweathouse Songs are not actually sung by humans, but rather by spirits using humans as their medium. A sweathouse singer is inhabited by a spirit, and it is the spirit who sings the songs. The "we" cited by the singer in his explanation of Text 3 (see above) does not refer to humans at all, but to spirits.

Spirit language is known by the Havasupais to be a different language, unintelligible to most human beings, understandable only to medicine men, dying people, and babies (Hinton 1977). Some singers say that the Sweathouse Songs are in spirit language.

This notion that unintelligible texts are associated with spirituality is not particularly foreign to our way of thinking. Religious ceremonies in many cultures are in a language not known to most of the participants. The recent exclusion of Latin from Catholic masses has been both praised and criticized because it removes Catholicism to some extent from the realm of spirituality and places it in closer contact with the everyday secular world. Speaking in tongues, a widespread phenomenon in the United States, is interpreted by its adherents as the speech of God, another example of the notion that spiritual language is unintelligible to humans.

I maintain, then, that another reason for the presence of vocable-rich texts in the Havasupai community is their association with spirituality.

The Medicine Songs appear to be a special case in Havasupai songs. Curing is associated with spirituality as much as the sweathouse and other ceremonies; yet they have fully worded texts. I have already suggested that the texts illustrate the power of the medicine man to increase the patient's confidence. This is the only spiritual event that involves a practitioner serving as a middle man between the people and the spirit world. The songs, then, serve a dual function; they are both spiritual and informational at the same time. Their texts reflect this. Every text, besides having long sections consisting of real words, also has portions consisting solely of vocables—either a short refrain such as the "*he-heya*" of Text 14, or a series of vocable verses, as in Text 15.

In summary, whether a song is fully worded or vocable-rich depends on whether its function is primarily the communication of information or the expression of solidarity or spirituality. For possible future research, I would like to propose the hypothesis that the scale of "wordiness," on a worldwide basis, will have a correlation with these functional factors of information-communication, solidarity, and spirituality.

### VOCABLES AND AESTHETICS

A communication model of music leaves some very important questions unanswered. It explains some of the motivations behind vocable usage, but does not tell us why vocables have specific phonetic forms. Havasupais say that some meaningless syllables represent archaic language, and also that some vocable-rich songs represent spirit language. Beyond this, they also say that some vocables are there just to "fill out the words and make them fit the music." Thus, they are saying some vocables have nothing to do with language at all, either that of humans or of spirits. This brings us into

## Vocables in Havasupai Song

another realm of vocable usage: what do vocables do for a song aesthetically?

It was shown earlier in this chapter that each song type has its own configuration of vocable forms—for example, that [θV] and [ŋV] are diagnostic vocables in Sweathouse Songs, that [we] and [ha] are especially noticeable in Circle Dance Songs, and that [ñV] is important in fully worded songs. One other aspect of "meaning" in vocables, then, is that the vocable form signals the song type. At the same time, we have seen that vocables in all song types have a great deal in common. The vast majority of vocables are of CV shape consisting of either a glide or a nasal consonant followed by a nonhigh vowel. While nasals and glides are well represented in spoken language, they are considerably less prevalent in spoken language than are the stops and affricates, and no more common than fricatives. While the vowel [a] is the most common vowel in both speaking and singing, it is much more common in singing; furthermore, the vowels [i] and [u], which are almost completely absent in vocables, are very common in speaking. The nasal consonant [ŋ], very common in vocables, is not even part of the phonemic inventory of spoken Havasupai. Vocables, then, result in a very different overall sound from that of spoken language. The question that is raised by this observation is, Why is it that vocables have this particular form? Is there a reason for the predominance of nasals, glides, and nonhigh vowels?

Looking first at the vowels, we can find important clues to the answer to our question by looking at the literature on Western art singing. Sundberg (1969) has found and carefully measured a process of vowel lowering that takes place in singing. To state the matter in simplistic terms, this means that high vowels are sung more like nonhigh vowels, a fact which is reminiscent of the predominance of nonhigh vowels in Havasupai. Similarly, Appelman (1967), in his detailed pedagogical work on art singing, describes the mouth positions for sung vowels in a manner that results in vowel lowering. And Vennard (1967) does the same thing in his pedagogical text, adding another key point: in the search for maximum "brilliance" of tone combined with maximum "depth" of tone, relatively low vowels do the most to attain this ideal tone quality. He states, "Fortunately, the vowel /a/ predominates in our literature, and whenever one sings, one can hope to achieve maximum brilliance and maximum depth in the one sound." He goes on to describe vowel lowering for the higher vowels to achieve this goal of ideal tone quality.

Great Basin and California-Yuman singing styles are both characterized by a relaxed, deep voice quality, and Havasupai singing is characterized by the same relaxation. The desired tone quality seems to be deep and strong, unlike the quality in such areas as the Plains, where a more high, piercing quality is the goal. The "depth" described by Vennard is an important aspect of the ideal Havasupai voice quality; the use of low vowels described by Vennard and others helps to achieve this ideal.

As for the consonants, we find that in certain genres of Western song and poetry, as in Havasupai, glides and nasals are predominant. In a study done by a group of my students and me, we found that in lyric poetry, glides and nasals have a much higher rate of occurrence than in either everyday language or nonlyric poetry, e.g., that of Sundberg. The use of glides and nasals allows the uninterrupted flow of vocal resonance, and in songs, allows the continuation of melodic tone. Stops and affricates, in particular, interrupt melody and the flow of the voice. Thus we can speculate that another part of the aesthetics of singing, in some traditions, is this uninterrupted melodic flow, and that the use of nasals and glides is part of the method for achieving this.

I am suggesting, then, that the choice of nonhigh vowels and of glides and nasals in vocable formation is purposeful, not random, and based on aesthetic considerations. To support this, I would also like to point out that in songs containing real words, a series of phonological processes are employed that also result in the increased use of nonhigh vowels, glides, and nasals. We find that underlying high vowels are lowered (/i/ becomes [e]; /u/ becomes [o]). Words containing nasals and glides are used much more often in singing than in speaking. Stops, affricates, and fricatives in songs are sometimes replaced by nasals and glides in the same position of articulation. These processes are described in detail elsewhere (Hinton 1977). This adds supporting evidence to the claim that glides, nasals, and nonhigh vowels are purposefully selected for in songs; the reason for this selection, as I have suggested, is that these types of segments augment an aesthetic ideal of deep voice quality and melodic flow.

This reasoning leads us to another aspect of vocable function; vocables aid in the achievement of the aesthetic ideals pertaining to voice quality and melodic flow. To the extent that a song must be linguistically communicative, these aesthetic ideals must be subordinated to the goal of clear communication. Thus, although we find an increased usage of nasals, glides, and nonhigh vowels in fully worded songs, we do not find them to the degree that they appear in vocable-rich songs. When a song does not need to be linguistically communicative, it is free to concentrate more fully on the aesthetic ideal, and the use of vocables helps achieve that end.

## CONCLUSIONS

In this chapter, I have examined the system of vocable form and function in Havasupai songs, and have tried to formulate a theory about their reason for being. As I pointed out earlier, one theory of vocable origin is that they derive from real language. While this theory is partially true, it obscures some more fundamental principles of vocable formation and function. I have tried to show that linguistic communication becomes less useful in situations where social solidarity is being expressed, and where people are seeking a sensation of spirituality. Language, in these situations, is down-played, and the choice of vocable usage in songs becomes more likely. I have also suggested that when language is down-played, sung syllables are chosen according to their ability to help the singer approach the aesthetic ideals for voice quality and melody flow. If the aesthetic ideal includes depth of tone and an even melodic flow, vocables are formulated using consonants and vowels that help achieve these factors. It is nasals, glides, and low vowels that are preferred for these aesthetic reasons.

Certain hypotheses for future testing are suggested by the findings for Havasupai. Among these, are: (1) if a singing style that prefers a deep tone selects low vowels, we might expect to find a greater predominance of high, tense vowels in singing styles that prefer a strident, tense voice quality; (2) if nasals and glides are chosen to enhance an even melodic flow, we might expect to find that singing styles stressing a strong, quick, choppy beat might select strongly for stops and affricates; (3) on a worldwide basis, we might expect to find that those musical events stressing solidarity or spirituality will be likely to play down the use of intelligible language either through the use of vocables, foreign languages, or a high degree of repetition in texts. It is my hope that comparative data from other scholars can lead us toward a decision about whether the principles of vocable usage that I have described here are peculiar to the Havasupais, or whether they instead represent either areal or universal tendencies.

## NOTES

1. In general, these have been labeled as "nonsense syllables," a term I choose to avoid because of the slightly degrading connotation of the word "nonsense" in common usage.
2. In light of discussions at the seminar that produced this book, I now suspect that a deeper study of Pueblo music may well bring to light some links between Havasupai and Hopi musical styles as well.
3. ['] stands for glottal stop, normally written as [?] in phonetic transcription.
4. See Appendix for examples.
5. As noted in Hinton (1977), this is an interesting parallel to the Personal Songs; when a person wished to express emotions about a situation or person, he or she would do so in a song, just as the character in a story does.

## APPENDIX: Examples

I include transcriptions of sample Havasupai songs, reprinted from Hinton (1977). The fully worded texts are too long to reproduce in their entirety; readers interested in the entire text can consult Hinton (1977). For the fully worded texts, I have reprinted only a page or so of each. The musical transcriptions are also available in Hinton (1977). For Sweathouse Songs, each syllable stands for one beat; two-beat syllables are indicated by hyphens: for example, *na-a*. For Circle Dance Songs, the beat is indicated by accent marks: for example, *ná-a-á*. For texts with words, each line of text is represented by four lines of typewritten material: the first line is a phonetic representation of the line as sung; the second line gives a morpheme-by-morpheme representation of the words of the line; the third line gives a morpheme-by-morpheme gloss; and the fourth line is a free translation into English. Hinton (1977) may also be consulted for an explanation of the grammatical structure of these songs.

# Vocables in Havasupai Song

Abbreviations:  
    contr — contrastive marker  
    dem — demonstrative pronoun  
    di — deictic marker  
    dir — directional marker  
    ds — different subject marker  
    dub — dubitative marker  
    dur — durative marker  
    indef — indefinite demonstrative pronoun  
    irreal — irrealis marker  
    loc — locative marker  
    nom — nominalizing suffix  
    obj — object  
    pl — plural  
    p/r — passive/reflexive marker  
    rel — relative clause marker  
    ss — same-subject marker  
    st — something  
    subj — subject  

## TEXT 1: Sweathouse Song

e gi ta-a ya 'e na-a  
e gi ta-a ya 'e na-a  
e gi ta-a ya 'e na-a  
yo ya ŋe ŋe ya 'e na-a  
yo ya ŋe ŋe ya 'e na-a  
'e gi ta-a ya he na-a  
The singer says the first line can be analyzed as follows:  
   egita na'ena  
   /ii g-ta/  
   /wood rel-grind/.

## TEXT 2: Sweathouse Song

ha le ya le ya ya  
ha le ya le ye ya  
θe na yo θi θe ye yo ŋo  
θe na yo θi θe ye no ŋo  
'e ye ye na ŋa  
ba gi go do ŋo ŋo

he na yo ha ŋa ŋa ye-e
ba gi go do ŋo ŋo
he na yo ha ŋa ŋa ye-e
The syllables "ha leya leyaya" are onomatopoetic, standing for the sound of water as it turns to steam when sprinkled on the hot stones in the sweathouse.

TEXT 3: *Sweathouse Song*

yo ya ŋa ŋa 'e na-a
yo ya ŋa ŋa 'e na-a
yo ya ŋa ŋa 'e na-a
yo ya ŋa ŋa 'e na-a
yo ya ŋe ŋe ya e na-a
yo ya ŋe ŋe ya e na-a
ba-a ha ne θa-a ye-e
ba-a ha ne θa-a ye-e
The second line is said to contain these words:
ba'a hane θa ye
/'baa 'hana/
/man good (healthy)/
A healthy man

TEXT 4: *Sweathouse Song*

ba-a ga θa wa yo ne-e
ba-a ga θa wo ya ne-e
na ya 'e-e
ya na 'e-e
ye yo o ye ey
ye na 'a ne yə
ye na 'a
There are no intelligible words in this song.

TEXT 5: *Circle Dance Song*

é ne yá ge ná-a-á ha
é ne yá ge ná-a-á-a
é ne yá ge ná-a-á ha
é ne yá ge ná-a-á-a
yá-a dó-on sé-e-é he dá-an sé-e-é-e

## Vocables in Havasupai Song

yá-a dó-on sé-e-é he dá-an sé-e-é-e
  (a) éneyágenáaáha
     /yag/
     "lie:down"
  (b1) heyádónsée
     "dance" (loan word from English)
  (b2) hedánséé
     "dance"


TEXT 6: *Circle Dance Song*

só ne wá la só-o lé-e-é-e
só ne wá la só-o lé-e-é na
vá si yó na vá si yó 'u
yá ŋa ná ŋa hé yo ná-a-á ha yén há-a-á o
yá ŋa ná ŋa hé yo ná-a-á ha yén há-a-á-a
  (a) sonewála só léee
     /wala/
     pines [a reference to mountain country]
  (b) naváslyó
     /n:vag/
     come (plural form)
  (c) yáŋanáŋa héyo náaá ha yén háaá
     [not a real word: carries connotation of joy]


TEXT 7: *Circle Dance Song*

mi yá ga yú 'u mát na má-a gá
mi yá ga yú mát na má-a gá
  yá ga yú 'u mát na má-a gá
mi yá ga yú 'u mát na má-a gá
mi sáw ə náw sáw ə náw é-é
ha é mu vá ha é mu vá 'á
ha é mu vá ha é mu vá-á
  (a) miyágayú 'umát namágá
     /myagayu 'mat nəmag/
     /Miyakayu (name) earth leave/
  (b) sawənaw
     /saw/
     /eat/ (?)
  (c) émuvá
     ?

TEXT 8: *Personal Song* (Farewell Song)

1.1 báqe tisbáyvá
/ha:baq t:sbaay-v/
/spring drip (pl) -p/r/
Dripping Spring

1.2 máté 'eyámó
/'mat '-am/
/land I-roam/
Land I used to roam,

1.3 ñévó geyówé héŋé
/ñ-vu g:yo:v/
/di-dem place/
That place,

1.4 gáyáj mu'évəgá
/ga+ya:j m-ev-g/
/indef+talk you-listen-ss/
Listen to what I say,

1.5 wáméjemávugá háŋní
/wa+m-j:mag-g/
/mind+you-forget-ss/
Don't mourn for me.

2.1 báyá'abáygá
/bay+'-bay-g/
/alive+I-be:alive-ss/
(I thought) I would be alive forever

2.2 véñáje 'ámahá
/v-ña-j '-am/
/dem-I-subj I-roam/
(I thought) I would roam (forever),

2.3 véñáje yúwá háŋá
/v-ña-j yu/
/dem-I-subj be/
(But here) I am

2.4 véñáje yújiθó
/v-ña-j yu-j-θo/
/dem-I-subj be-pl-contr/
I (can't) continue on,

2.5 tóyáje há'avá
/tuy-j dav/
/ {false} -pl? {very} /
  {weak}      {weak}
(Now) I am too weak
ETC.


TEXT 9: *Personal Song* (Hank Ward)

1.1 hánkən wódwij
/Hank Ward-wi-j/
/Hank Ward-dem-subj/
Hank Ward,

1.2 hánkən wódwijé
(same as 1.1)
Hank Ward,

1.3 hánkən wódwij
(same as 1.1)
Hank Ward,

1.4 hánkən wódwijé
(same as 1.1)
Hank Ward

2.1 wé gavan'óla
/wii g-v-ul/
/rock rel-p/r-ride/
Williams (lit. "Riding Rock"),

2.2 wé gavan'ólawá
/'wii g-v-ul-wa/
/rock rel-p/r-ride-dem/
Williams,

2.3 ha wé gavan'óla
/ha 'wii g-v-ul/
/dem rock rel-p/r-ride/
Williams

## Vocables in Havasupai Song

2.4 wé gavan'ólawám
/'wii g-v-ul-wa-m/
/rock rel-p/r-ride-dem-dir/
To Williams,

3.1 wása'anádwəm
/wa+s:'ad-wa-m/
/house+sell-dem-dir/
To the store there,

3.2 wása'anádwəmé
(same as 3.1)
To the store there,

3.3 gávuñəñóde
/ga+vu+ñ-yud/
/indef+dem+dem-enter/
That's where he went in,
        ETC.

### TEXT 10: Medicine Song

1.1 máte gənájuwa hé'héye
/'mat gnaa-j-v/
/land point:to-pl-dem/
Our homeland

1.2 həmáte gənájuwa hé'nɨ́m
(same as 1.1)
Our homeland

2.1 vá geyóvuwa hé'héye
/va g:yov/
/dem place/
This place

2.2 vá geyóvuwa hé'héye
(same as 2.1)
This place

3.1 'awé yuhʷátiga hé'héye
/wii hʷat-g/
/rock red-ss/
The rocks are red,

3.2 'awé yuhʷátiga hé'héyəm
(same as 3.1)
The rocks are red,

4.1 ñáosǽməga hé'héye
/ñaa+see:m-g/
/black+greyed-ss/
spotted with brown,

4.2 ñáosǽməga hé'héye
(same as 4.1)
spotted with brown,
        ETC.

# 12
# Epilogue

## CHARLOTTE J. FRISBIE
*Department of Anthropology*
*Southern Illinois University at Edwardsville*

The Advanced Seminar on Southwestern Indian ritual drama was designed to allow time for synthesizing as the group moved from one geographic area to the next, and for discussing results from more general perspectives at the end of the week. The numerous regional syntheses enabled us to assess what features were characteristic of ritual drama for particular groups. As the data base expanded, we began searching for similarities and differences which went beyond information already available in the literature on vocal style, form, body movements, and ground plans (for example, Herzog 1928, 1930, 1936; Kurath and Garcia 1970; Nettl 1954, 1969; McAllester 1961; McAllester and Brown 1962; H. H. Roberts 1936; and others). Fascination with this approach, however, was short-lived, and by the end of the week discussions focused on issues and topics of particular interest to the group: dramatic presentation techniques, dance, backstage activities, the role of singers, role of women in ritual drama, audiences, creativity, transmission techniques and processes, change, and, finally, future directions.

The present chapter is meant to summarize our discussions. It was developed from tapes of our seminar discussions and my own understanding of the significance of the data presented in individual chapters in this volume. Participants have had a chance to react to this chapter in draft form, and I have tried to incorporate as many of their suggestions as possible in the present version. I alone, of course, remain responsible for errors.

## GENERAL COMPARISONS

There are a number of elements which, at the general level, characterize and differentiate the ritual dramas of groups represented in this volume, and a brief summary of these seems valuable.

In the Pueblo culture area ritual drama is considered a necessity by the people. It maintains the orderly universe and validates the system's operating principles; without it, disaster will come to the whole world. Performance of ritual drama is considered to be "work," and performance, to have power intrinsically, thus making it necessary for personae to be purified before and decharmed after participation. Dramas are group-centered, centripetal in nature and direction, and much of the time, calendrical. Moisture, fertility, growth, and group well-being are emphasized. The entire community is involved, many as nonperforming participants who have food-associated responsibilities. Audiences are required to have good thoughts and "good hearts" and to behave in ways conducive to the success of the drama.

Social organization provides both rationale and association for producing the dramas; performers, often called by kin terms, most frequently come from kiva groups and societies whose leaders hold similar roles in ritual drama. In the peripheral areas of Taos and Picuris, however, performers are drawn from throughout the community, except in the cases of clown performances and the Taos Turtle Dance. Performances occur within a kiva and plaza complex, and the spatial arrangement within this arena reflects social organization.

The Pueblos use characteristic dramatic effects that include elements of humor, mimicry, burlesque, and personification conveyed by clowns (who may also be cueing, directing, and providing social control), Masked Dances, Animal Dances, dramatic processions and parades, a Kachina cult (except at Taos and Picuris), and distinctive

## Epilogue

costumes. The latter focus on kilts, belts, fur pieces, and moccasins for males, while off-the-shoulder mantas, capes, and headdresses are common for females. The repeated use of black, white, red, and green for costumes is striking. Singing is carefully rehearsed; male vocal styles emphasize rich, low, deep sounds in contrast to higher pitched female voices. Native participants as well as outsider-researchers recognize a five-part AABBA structure as the basic musical and textual form. Herein, the B is higher in range, syncopated, and often choreographed by increased density of movement which visually suggests increased tempo. All groups have dances for males and females together and for males only. Dance patterns show extreme contrasts between male and female body movement styles. Costumes sometimes serve to inhibit female movement, and masks can affect the clarity of sound, in cases where masked dancers sing. Idiophones, membranophones, and bull-roarers are particularly important as musical instruments in Puebloan ritual drama. Finally, like many of their Southern Athapaskan neighbors, most Puebloan groups structurally emphasize the number 4, asperging, cornmeal and corn pollen, balance, repetition, harmony, order, circularity, and formalism—all important signatures in their ritual dramas.

Southern Athapaskan ritual drama is centrifugal, with the emphasis in many activities being from the center outward. Individualism is also characteristic, with dramas focusing on single-named individuals or places, although, by extension, bringing blessing to all who participate. Among the most characteristic dramas are those emphasizing curing, preventing misfortunes, and rites of passage, or from the Mescalero Apache perspective, rites of confirmation. Initiation rites are nonexistent. Members of this language group do not explain the occurrence of ritual dramas by referring to a sense of cosmic responsibility, nor do they order them calendrically. There are, however, certain seasonal expectations related to occurrence. A historical sense is also characteristic; Navajos restrict its expression to mythological events whereas Mescalero Apaches actually sing tribal history.

Characteristic dramatic techniques include the use of falsetto (which various Pueblos find ugly), a limited number of masked impersonators, and very little dependence on a clown figure as a dance master or trickster. There is very little concern with rehearsal or unified sound, and the typical ritual song format is A, B, B1, B2, B3. . . . A. Unlike the Pima-Papago and Havasupai-Yuman area, songs are not dreamed. Singers are trained and, unlike their Pueblo counterparts, who have public anonymity, enjoy a certain achieved status because of knowledge and ability. However, many differences exist between Mescalero Apache holy men and Navajo singers who are fallible human beings. Dance forms are numerous and varied, and several genres can occur within one ritual drama. Back and Forth Dances, Skip, Circle, Couple, and Line Dances are known, but there are no Bird, Animal, or Plant Dances like those so well elaborated among the Pueblos.

Pima-Papago ritual drama is distinctive from that of Puebloan and Southern Athapaskan peoples in a number of ways. The Papago world view, like that of the Pueblos, implies a balance in the world that can be maintained by humans doing the "work" of performing ritual dramas. At other levels of understanding, however, Papago ritual drama, which historically is less developed than that of the Pueblos, can be viewed as entertainment which includes races, games, wagering, and improvisation. Villages rather than societies instigate and carry out the ritual dramas which are noncalendrical, with the exception of the Summer Wine Feast.

Among other distinguishing features are the strong emphases on plants, animals, and birds, and on the dreaming of songs and holding copyrights to them. Musically, a typical song is fully texted, through-composed in strophic form, and, ideally, performed four times: ABCD, ABCD, BCD, BCD. Vocables and borrowed materials are infrequently used, but song cycles are typical and more prevalent throughout the Southwest than originally thought. Vocal styles are characterized by modest vibratos and little vocal tension. Dramatically, masks are important only during the Harvest Ceremony, but poles, dance wands, baskets and sticks, ribbons, and flowers are prevalent as symbolic elements. Dancing and singing groups are most often composed of both women and men.

Similar to that of the Papagos, Havasupai ritual drama is noncalendrical except for the Harvest Ceremony, and includes games and races. Likewise, there is a concept of ownership of Medicine Songs which may be transmitted by dreaming, teaching, and sale. Havasupais have no known ogres, kachinas, central dance plazas, societies, or centralized villages which are involved in ritual drama. A transhumant

## Epilogue

life style emphasizing individualism is balanced by the Harvest Ceremony and the Circle Dance, which reaffirm group solidarity through ground plans and other proxemic and kinesic features.

Musically, parallels can be drawn between the Havasupai style and those of both the Great Basin and California-Yuman areas, but the Havasupais are musically distinctive from the Yumans despite literature to the contrary. Deep, strong, relaxed voices are valued as is an uninterrupted melodic flow; both of these are facilitated by the choice of particular kinds of vowels and vocables. Song cycles are absent, although long poetic texts are characteristic of contemporary secular music.

### DRAMATIC PRESENTATION TECHNIQUES

Dramatic effects in ritual dramas of Southwestern Indians or any other group are achieved through a variety of mechanisms. In addition to those of costuming and masking (already examined by Haile 1947b, Roediger 1961, Brown 1962, Parsons 1922, and Bunzel 1932b) are others such as vocal style, use of musical instruments, special use of verbal and nonverbal communication, and the inclusion of clowns.

Vocal style includes many features such as the number of voices involved, amount of blending, interaction between leader and group, range, special effects, and degree of clarity. Puebloan people prefer blended vocal sound; groups practice to achieve this and are expected to sing well. Depending on the place and degree of sacredness of the drama, singers and dancers may or may not be one and the same people. For example, these roles are kept separate in the most sacred Animal Dances at Taos and Medicine Society performances at Zuni, but are combined in Taos Turtle Dances and Zuni Kachina performances. Hopis use both techniques, having a Hopi style based on combining the roles of singer and dancer and a New Mexico or Rio Grande style wherein separate choruses, rather than dancers, do the singing. The so-called Social Dances, however, always have a separate chorus.

Navajo and Papago ritual dramas feature a lead voice with others joining in and fading away without attempting to blend in melody, words, or vocables. It is good to help with the singing when one knows the songs and can perform them "correctly" in the Navajo or Papago sense of the term. Havasupai ritual drama entails the use of group leaders, with others joining in softly.

Vocal effects are numerous and are utilized in a variety of ways in the ritual dramas discussed in this volume. In addition to the well-known Southern Athapaskan falsetto, hoots are given by Mescalero Apache Mountain Gods, Hopi Grandmothers in Ogre Dramas, and Havasupais upon completing the Circle Dance. The Hopi Ogres Drama also uses vocal whistles, howls, falsetto, and other effects. The meanings associated with these effects vary; sometimes they are equated with calls of specific deities, animals or birds, or dramatic persons. Among the Mescalero Apaches, however, hooting is equated with praying, and elsewhere, vocal effects may represent cueing techniques.

Musical instruments played by singers, used by leaders, and carried or worn by dancers also serve to increase dramatic effect through their own sounds, and the relationship between these and those of the singing and dancing they accompany. Particularly significant are the changes in percussion patterns which cue information about structural aspects and forthcoming changes in dance patterns and ground plans. The instrument inventory includes a variety of drums; whistles; gourd, hoof, shell, and hide rattles; cone tinklers; ceremonial batons; sticks; and bull-roarers. Ritual dramas include ideas about who should use these instruments, where, and when.

Dramatic effects can also be achieved through the use of special esoteric languages, such as Zuni kachina language or the sacred "classical language" of Mescalero holy men, and through vocables, as demonstrated by Hinton. Dramatic content is affected by verbal communication as well as kinesic and proxemic factors, particularly evident in dance, procession, and the movements of ritual drama leaders and those on whom the dramas focus. Likewise, as Farrer demonstrates, it is possible to make use of a contrast between sound and silence, in dancing styles, use of instruments, and amount and type of speech. Silent communication is also part of ritual drama, whether one is dealing with the Mescalero *'inch'in'di* concept, Zuni singing in the heart, or Navajo silent praying.

Clowns are commonly associated with burlesque, mimicry, and comic relief in ritual drama. In addition to these roles, however, chapters in this volume suggest that clowns at Hopi act as prescrip-

## Epilogue

tive medicine against *kahopi* behavior and as pets of kachinas. At Zuni, they are viewed as grandfathers of kachinas and directors of ritual drama; they serve as part of the audience for kachinas, giving cues, praise, and critical evaluations. At Taos, clowns play an essential role as supernatural hunters in the Deer Dance. The clown has not been a functioning part of Havasupai ritual drama since 1919, nor is it currently viable among the Pimas and Papagos. At Picuris, however, the Clown Society which had been inactive for about 20 years was revitalized in the early 1970s. At Mescalero, the "gray one" is actually the holiest person in the Girls' Puberty drama.

### DANCE

Seminar discussions about dance revealed a variety of genres among the groups represented in this volume. Among these, the Circle Dance received the most attention, being discussed from the standpoint of use and variable execution. This dance is characteristic of Mescalero Apaches, Navajos, Hopis, Zunis, Havasupais, and Papagos, but rare among the Eastern Pueblos except in the Tewa Harvest Dance context and as a social dance at Taos. Havasupais perform it with short, simple, side steps, males and females together, holding hands close to the body. Creativity in posturing is nearly absent, except for some occasional hip swinging, and movements can be described as vertical. The dance, which ends with a characteristic hoot, is accompanied by songs and the total event emphasizes group solidarity. Havasupais also use a Back and Forth Dance, wherein a line of men faces a line of women; this dance is considered to be Mojave in origin and style.

Mescalero Apaches have a variety of dances, all of which can occur in ritual context. Farrer illustrates the different styles, personnel involved in each, and the ground plans typical within the Girls' Puberty Ceremony context. The Mescalero Circle Dance is usually composed of alternating males and females who link arms, although the order is not obligatory. In the Back and Forth Dance, considered to have sexual overtones by the Mescaleros, a male and a female or two people of one sex and one of the other face each other, moving toward and away from the fire. Here, as with all Mescalero dances, the movement is clockwise and sunwise in direction. Individual body movement is basically vertical, although with the Mountain Gods, posturing is extremely rich and varied.

The Papago Circle Dance during the Wine Ceremony features a closed circle, while in other contexts, the basically circular pattern is left open, with participants often moving back to the starting point of the dance rather than completing the circle. Line Dances are characteristic of the girls' puberty rituals and those emphasizing purification.

Lines are extremely important in Pueblo dance. As Kurath (personal communication 1978) states:

> Single and double lines differ in symbolic geometry. The straight, single file survives in the most sacred, ancient Kachina Dances and in other self-accompanied, male rain invocations. It can progress into many designs, as meanders, arcs, or circles (Kurath 1949:290-94). Double files of the Eastern Pueblos suggest European as well as native provenience. The Matachine longways of the Pueblos and Yaqui are of Colonial origin, whether the men move in parallel array or interweave. The interactions of men and women in the Corn Dances suggest sexual-fertility connotations. The double lines sometimes resolve into circles of couples or small groups. The contrapuntal patterns of double files and circlings in Game Animal Dances probably combine ancient prototypes with new, creative ideas for dance dramas.

Hopi Kachina Dances follow the basic pattern of grandfathers who lead in the kachinas for a dance performed on two or three sides of the plaza, moving counterclockwise. Women's Medicine Societies' dances at Hopi are performed by barefoot women, who move counterclockwise, never completing the circle. Traditional Social Dances are viewed by the Hopis as belonging to two styles: the Hopi one which involves groups of two unmarried girls paired with two boys or men and a separate chorus, and the Rio Grande, Tewa, or New Mexico style, wherein two parallel lines face each other and are also accompanied by a separate chorus. Males and females alternate in these lines, with the oldest, most experienced dancers heading the line. At Zuni and in Hopi Kachina Dances, lines are arranged so the dance leader is at the center; to that person's right and left, dancers are arranged by declining height and singing ability. The Tewa people position leading singers in the center of the line. In the Taos and Picuris Animal and Corn Dances, the lines are led by the most experienced dancers.

*Epilogue*

Dances also occur in a variety of genres among the Navajos. Many can be seen during the Enemyway, wherein couples Circle Dance, do Back and Forth Dances, and Skip-Trot Dances holding hands. Processional lines are characteristic of Yeibichai performances, and other ritual dramas provide contexts for such genres as the Corral Dance, Fire Dance, and Feather Dance.

Dance in general is an integral part of Southwestern Indian ritual drama, and while Kurath and Garcia (1970) have made possible a basic understanding of Tewa dance, much remains to be done by scholars interested in this aspect of ritual drama among the other Southwestern groups.

## BACKSTAGE ACTIVITIES

One of the areas the seminar found particularly challenging was that which we labeled "backstage activities." These include events which are part of the ritual drama, but are so often missed when one arrives just in time for the all-night portion of a ceremony or to take a place in the plaza as the kachinas emerge from the kiva. Obviously some of these "behind the scenes activities" such as the praying, singing, and prayerstick-making inside the kivas may not be open to discussion with outsiders; there are others, however, that may be investigated, and the process of so doing reveals the importance of understanding these events when attempting to comprehend ritual drama within its cultural context.

Among the activities is rehearsal, a relatively unstudied phenomenon and one that many Southwestern Indian groups do not feel is especially important, particularly because of varying definitions of good vocal sound and correct performance. Among the Pueblos, however, rehearsals are extremely important, and they consume many an evening before the public part of ritual dramas. As Tedlock demonstrates, at Zuni the song is the most important. Once a song has been composed and emerges from the group editing process, it is then taught to all who will sing it in public. In genres where singers and dancers are not one and the same people, only when everyone knows the song is it rehearsed with the dancers, who can further embellish its rhythms with patterns of body movement. Rehearsals are also times when new songs, dances, and kachinas which will be introduced during the Night Dances are prepared.

Unlike the Pueblos, and perhaps at the other extreme of the rehearsal continuum, are the Navajos. While they emphasize the necessity of correct performance, the onus of meeting that goal falls on the main singer, the one who leads the ritual drama. This person receives assistance from others in the hogan during the all-night singing, but the invariable result is a number of voices expressing typical Navajo individualism rather than perfectly blended, rehearsed sound. The Yeibichai, however, are an exception; teams do rehearse and compete with others from different areas during Nightway performances and in other contexts.

The other groups represented in this volume fall somewhere between the Pueblo and Navajo extremes. Pima-Papagos do occasionally rehearse, but the amount of time spent on this activity varies. Tally sticks, used to indicate the number of days before the beginning of a ritual drama, imply the number of nights available for rehearsals, if such are desired. When these do occur, they involve the lead singer with a small group of from 4 to 12 helpers. In Havasupai ritual drama contexts, the group leader will rehearse a bit before the beginning of the event, but once again, the amount of time spent doing so varies. Mescalero Apaches too, on occasion, will rehearse; an owner of a group of Mountain God dancers may call together 2 or 3 men who regularly sing with him to practice a month or more before a July performance. Small Powwows during the winter provide an opportunity for women to practice their dance steps. But the holy men and other dancers are said not to rehearse.

Another backstage activity which potentially affects the content, order, genre, and length of ritual drama is that of decision making. At Zuni, Dance Talkers decide (within established limits) the genre of Kachina Dance to be performed, and spread the news about future ritual dramas as well as their rehearsal and performance dates. Other examples of decision making include the choosing of Shalako performers for the coming year during the last night of the Winter Solstice Ceremony, and the choices made by kiva groups concerning which dances from the "must" or "optional" categories will be performed. At Hopi, the examples include deciding who can sponsor what drama and whether or not to let one lapse for two years or longer because of a crucial person's stage in training, death, or other variables. At Taos, the Council decides which dances are to be per-

*Epilogue*

formed on Christmas and January 6. At Picuris, as Brown indicates, the entire community decides during a public meeting held inside the kiva which dances to do on certain days. For the Navajos, Frisbie documents a number of decisions made in the context of House Blessing Ceremonies, demonstrating the variable wishes of sponsors, larger communities, and main singers, and how these affect the public performance.

Other examples abound, including all of the decisions related to the rodeo and Powwow contests during the Mescalero Girls' Puberty Ceremony and those involved in the games and races accompanying the Papago Skipping Dance and Havasupai events. Then too, decisions about basic mechanics such as where, when, and how to feed the people gathered for a Navajo Shootingway are also relevant. The importance of a contextual approach to ritual drama is made clear, once the potential effect of these decisions on ritual drama content is realized and once analyses indicate how the mechanics of such decision making relate to the larger social, economic, and political spheres of culture.

## ROLE OF SINGERS

Seminar discussions suggested that while singers are generally viewed as knowledgeable about songs, prayers, myths, and ritual activities, it is hard to generalize about their statuses and roles within the Southwest. Among the Navajos, these men and women act as stage managers, directing the performance of the ritual drama while reciting it. While considered knowledgeable in a culture where knowledge is related to power, they are simultaneously open to suspicion of witchcraft because of this knowledge. Singers are considered to be fallible human beings; one learns through an apprenticeship system, and for a variety of reasons, is always open to criticism. Other colleagues openly challenge singers during and after performances, and many a lively discussion occurs about who was trained by whom, and what is "the correct way" of performing a prayer or song, or arranging sequences in a myth within ritual contexts.

In contrast, the Mescalero Apache singers, who are male only, are equated with holy men. This status, based on both age and ability, implies particular deference behaviors by others in other aspects of life. Apaches are silent in the face of power expressed through the singers and the holy men are not criticized. In essence, as Farrer demonstrates, they bind society together and integrate the past with the present. Also unlike Navajo singers, Mescalero holy men are hierarchically ranked in ways that are visually apparent during the Girls' Puberty Ceremony.

Contemporary Havasupai singers are not highly respected, although in earlier times when curing ceremonies were numerous, medicine men had great power and were feared. In general, these singers are viewed as having a job to do, which includes making the content of textual songs clear to others. At times, they are viewed as being inhabited by spirits which sing through them in spirit language, such as in the Sweathouse Song context discussed by Hinton. In other situations, such as Circle Dance competitions, singers not chosen will actively criticize those who have been more fortunate, and lead singers have been known to get so angry that they go home. More respect, however, is shown toward Mojave singers and their songs by the Havasupais.

Among the Papagos, a singer is one who owns the song cycles and dances which have been dreamed or borrowed. It is that person's job to teach these to others before a ritual drama performance, supervise the building of certain ceremonial objects, and lead performances.

Throughout the Pueblo area, priests who are either in achieved, or more often, kinship-based ascribed roles, lead dramatic rituals. There is no semantic equivalent to "singer" in this area, and while medicine men and women exist, they operate in the sphere of more private curing rituals.

Related to the job of being a singer is the question of compensation. Some Southwestern groups share a belief in the need to compensate particular ritual drama personae for performing their jobs, both to ensure the power and effectiveness of the words and rituals, and to prevent misfortune. Among the Navajos and the Mescaleros, compensation focuses on the individual lead singer and takes the form of food, cloth, jewelry, baskets, skins, animals, blankets, cash, and other items. These are shared by the singer with appropriate kinfolk after the conclusion of the ritual drama and the return home. Navajo singers' attitudes toward expectable compensation vary, but in many contexts, the amount of compensation is directly

*Epilogue*

related to the complexity of the total performance of ritual dramas. Among the Pueblos, it is perhaps more appropriate to view the process as a reciprocal one, wherein items given to performers, particularly food, are collectively shared within the kiva groups involved and the members' families.

## ROLE OF WOMEN

The role of women in Southwestern Indian ritual drama is relatively unexplored. Some of the seminar discussions focused on this topic and led to a number of comments which are worthy of summary and future research.

It is already well known that women are associated with medicine in many Southwestern Indian societies and that these associations are formalized through membership in medicine societies, training, and/or kinship ties with powerful medicine men. It is also known that women have active roles as curers, often traveling to different locations to utilize skills for which they are famous. It appeared, however, at the onset of discussions, that within the total context of ritual drama, women were active mainly in the private sphere, especially since only among the Papagos and the Navajos—after menopause—can one find female leaders of public ritual dramas. Many of these private roles are of an auxiliary, supportive nature, focusing on the preparation and serving of food to participants and guests at public performances, assembling costumes before the event, spreading news of the event's planning through kin and local communication networks, assisting male relatives in various pre-performance purification rites such as hair washing, ritual smoking, asperging with corn pollen, and attending performances. However, once backstage activities, creativity, transmission, and a variety of other issues were discussed, it became clear that a much more active role was typical of women in many Southwestern groups and that in certain places, women were more forward-looking about transmission, borrowing, and reviving lapsed events than their male counterparts.

In many ritual dramas, women participate actively in the singing. Sometimes women sing in voices quieter than those of the men, but often, women's voices are distinct, clear rather than muffled, and in unison or at the octave with men's. Occasionally among the Tewa, when women's voices are thought to be too loud, they are asked by men to sing more quietly. In some areas, such as Taos-Picuris, women are not supposed to sing the ritual drama songs, although they know them. But even in this setting, they have mnemonic roles since they may sit along the edges, humming melodies when male performers forget what comes next. As such, they are active bearers of tradition (Von Sydow 1965).

Women are also active as song composers. At Zuni, one woman, a Hopi-Tewa, is now the most prolific song composer in the Hopi song tradition as well as the inventor of the Olla Maidens. Husbands frequently take songs composed by their wives to kiva groups for further amplification by the group editing process. In earlier times among the Havasupais women were the main composers of Personal Songs, a genre which could be sung at any time of year. Among the Mescaleros, women can and do compose Love Songs.

In many places, women also actively participate in dancing in ritual drama contexts. Many Pueblos have genres performed only by women as well as others for both sexes. At Acoma, there are female kachinas and women in the audience will try and dance with them. At Zuni, women can belong to Medicine Societies, the Kachina Society, and to the Rain Priesthood. At Santo Domingo and San Felipe, they also have roles in Clown Societies which at present are not well understood. Among the Tewa, female burlesques and parodies, particularly of Navajos, are well known.

Women also serve as evaluators and critics of ritual drama. At Zuni, they are the chief critics of kachina dancers, often recognizing individuals by their legs. Among the Navajos, women actively participate in evaluating singers, their dress, mannerisms, qualifications, and total performance; the potential significance of such comments is demonstrated in the life history of one Blessingway singer, Frank Mitchell (Frisbie and McAllester 1978:37).

Women can also serve as sponsors of ritual dramas. Among the Hopis, women have definite ideas about which dances they wish to sponsor, and if they do not get their first choice, they may very well opt not to sponsor any of the alternatives.

Women participate in ritual drama in a variety of other ways as well. Obviously, they are the focus in Girls' Puberty Ceremonies; Farrer's work with the Mescalero Apaches and Frisbie's (1967)

## Epilogue

with the Navajos show the extent and the numerous kinds of involvement typical in this setting. Both groups identify and utilize an ideal woman who molds, instructs, and assists the pubescent girl. Unlike the Navajos, among the Mescaleros these women are the only ones to hear the sacred songs sung by the holy men on all four nights to recount tribal history; the women act as interpreters of these songs, having paid the holy men to teach them the correct interpretation.

In individual curing ceremonies, women can serve as the one-sung-over, or as copatients. In the Navajo House Blessing Ceremony, they may assist the main singer with the pollen-meal blessing and with the singing, if the latter is part of the public performance. Among the Hopis, members of female curing societies are viewed as possessing special characteristics which give them ritual license to participate fully and without restraint in burlesques of men and to retaliate when men do burlesques of women.

It also appears that at least among some Pueblo groups, women are more forward-looking than men. Hopi-Tewa women are actively interested in recording Social and Kachina Dances with machines they keep under shawls, in purses, or in potato chip bags. At Zuni, Olla Maidens not only compose but also take what are considered to be the most sacred parts of songs out into the public world through their performances. Zuni men disavow both their singing and their profaning of the sacred, whether it occurs in song, or in the work of female kachina carvers or female jewelers who include masks in their jewelry designs. Also at Zuni it was a woman who was responsible for the revival of the Buffalo Dance after a 50-year lapse; she provided the nearly forgotten formulae and composed music in this genre.

Not all women, of course, share this outward direction. For example, among traditional Navajos, it may well be a woman who decides that a male singer should not be working with anthropologists or recording sacred knowledge on tape and film, and it is often a woman who cancels such plans or interrupts them as soon as they progress into the sacred domain. The differing attitudes, responses, involvement in the creative process, and participation in ritual drama and its transmission are among the many issues awaiting work by those interested in the further delineation of women's roles in ritual drama.

## AUDIENCES

The consideration of audiences was another aspect of ritual drama which the seminar group found particularly challenging, especially since work on the ethnography of communication by Hymes (1962, 1964) and others has raised so many interesting research questions. Our seminar discussions on this topic, summarized below, suggest that, as was true with the role of women, much remains to be done in comprehending the effect audiences have on Southwestern Indian ritual drama. Unlike Anglo-American audiences which, in many ritual drama contexts, can be characterized as passive receivers who may applaud, native Southwestern audiences are active participants mentally, emotionally, and sometimes even physically in ritual dramas. The idea that one benefits by participating as a member of the audience pervades the Southwest, as does the idea that one supports the intent of the ritual drama by witnessing it. The degree of participation varies from place to place and sometimes from one ritual drama to the next, as do audience roles, spatial arrangements, and the amount of merging that occurs between audiences and performers.

There is no single, shared idea about audience size or composition. While Navajos often emphasize the size of the audience, valuing large ones, Taos people value a large number of dancers rather than large audiences. Among other pueblos, size varies according to the setting of ritual dramas; kivas can hold a limited number of people and only those who are well behaved and qualified in other ways may enter. Plazas, on the other hand, accommodate larger numbers, but even here, at certain pueblos, such as Zuni, the expectation is that audiences will grow during the day. Performers respond by saving their "best" Kachina Songs until late in the afternoon. Audiences grow rapidly once requests are made for repeats of particularly appealing songs. The Zuni Dance Chief, however, prays over the gourd and turtle shell rattles of the dancers and spits medicine on the dancers to help attract larger audiences.

Discussions about audience composition revealed varying ideas about who and what should and should not be present. At times, Anglos will be barred because they are outsiders; in other situations, the definition of outsider is extended to include certain Indians and other ethnic groups as well. The Navajos are particularly concerned

## Epilogue

that dogs be kept out of ritual drama settings, and do their best to shoo them away from the hogan and its immediate vicinity whenever they are spotted. Others have more relaxed attitudes about this, diverting dogs only when there is a danger of their bothering the dancers.

Audiences are also believed by many groups to include the deities directly associated with specific ritual dramas. Among the Navajos, for example, the presence of such other-than-humans is the major reason for the emphasis on "correct performance"; among both the Mescalero Apaches and Navajos, people are identified with these deities through the use of kinship terms and various ritual procedures. Among the Zunis, as Tedlock demonstrates, there is a part of the audience which is viewed as the "raw" audience; this includes both other-than-humans and deceased Zunis.

Spatial arrangements of audiences and performers vary according to ethnic group and particular drama. Pueblo architecture, the Papago Skipping Dance context, and Havasupai ideas permit an arena-type arrangement with audiences surrounding the ritual drama personae. Inside the hogan, Navajo audiences sit to the right and left of the lead singer and one-sung-over, leaving an opening in the east. In other contexts, such as the Yeibichai portion of the Nightway or Fire Dance performances in the Mountaintop Way, people assemble in groups to face the dancers. The latter arrangement is also typical at Mescalero, where during the Girls' Puberty Ceremony, the audience, seated on bleachers or standing by the cooking arbor, faces the dance arena.

A variety of behaviors is expected from audiences of Southwestern Indian ritual dramas. In general, people are expected to be in the right frame of mind and to think good thoughts about the drama and its purpose, the participants, and/or the one-sung-over. Hopis and other Pueblo Indians speak of the need to have a good heart while Navajos speak of the need to refrain from fighting, abusive talk, and drunkenness. Some groups also expect audiences to stay awake throughout the all-night singing or social dancing; while this is more of an ideal than a reality, there are certain critical points, at least in Navajo ritual drama, where it is essential. Mescalero Apaches expect people to stay for the entire event, whereas in other contexts, audience members freely come and go, being bound only by specific ceremonial procedures and times for such movement. Other expectations, such as those restricting recording and photography in certain contexts, are more widely known.

Audience behavior is managed, directed, and supervised by clowns in some places; in others, the audience is subject to the lead singer, particular members of the audience, tribal politico-religious leaders, and/or tribal police. Such managers have variable roles, including those of telling people where to sit and how to rearrange seating if necessary, to remain quiet, to stay awake, and to have a good heart. They also watch for illegal recording equipment, both visual and aural, removing this with the same expediency they apply to those who start fighting, are inebriated, or in some other way profane the event. In general, following guidelines for expected behavior is thought to enhance the efficacy of the ritual drama and to disperse the ensuing blessings to a wider group of "native others."

Audiences have numerous roles, the investigation of which further underscores the variation in degrees of expected participation and the frequency with which audience/performer roles merge. During the Mescalero Girls' Puberty Ceremony, audiences are expected to come down from the bleachers to give blessings to and receive them from the girls, to participate in the give-aways, and to surround the holy lodge as it is dismantled. Likewise, they are encouraged to participate in the social dancing. Interestingly enough, this ritual drama also includes activities of a different nature which entertain audiences. At Mescalero, these include the rodeo and Powwow competitions, while at other places, such as among the Papagos and Havasupais, they can include races, games, and wagering. Among the Eastern Pueblos, booths may be set up to sell crafts, and carnival games and rides may be available. Navajo audiences are expected to join in and help with the singing and to participate in pollen blessings. At Hopi, women stream out of the audience to bless the dancers with cornmeal, and at Acoma and Laguna, women from the audience actually get up and dance with the kachinas on certain occasions. These latter actions, however, are viewed negatively by other pueblos. Among the Papagos, audience members sometimes break into the dance circle to honor the sponsor with yet another dance; such actions are rewarded with a gift.

Audiences also may serve as evaluators, selectors, and critics within the context of ritual drama. The Navajos are seemingly the most critical, voicing differences of opinion during the performance of myths, songs, and prayers, and frequently getting into discussions of the oral transmission process and the allowable range of flexibility that exists within the

*Epilogue*

ideal of "correct, unaltered performance" (Frisbie 1967:48–58,ff.). They also criticize lead singers after the fact and singers criticize audience behaviors and settings when evaluating performances (Frisbie n.d.). As Frisbie's work on the House Blessing shows, this process often serves to define the next occurrence of this ritual drama within the community, if not to alter its present one.

Mescalero Apaches do not criticize the holy men, showing deference to them instead, as has already been noted; in extreme cases of misbehavior, excuses are made for the singers/holy men. At Zuni, audiences evaluate newly composed Kachina Songs, selecting those that are particularly appealing and calling for their on-the-spot repeat. If there are several good songs, a person from the audience will go out and bless the clown and dancers, asking them to return on another day. In addition to this type of evaluation, the clowns at Zuni, as has already been shown, serve as part of the audience for the kachinas, urging them to perform well, criticizing them vocally when they do not, and calling out the names of song parts as performance cues. Other Zunis do not criticize during the performance, but rather leave without asking for repeats, criticizing later in their own homes. At Taos, the effect of the audience can be summed up in the mythological admonition to the dancers: "Dance harder, the people are watching."

Audiences may also assist in other ways during particular portions of ritual dramas. At Pueblos such as Hopi, where clowns or special male accompaniers do not have the specific role of assisting dancers with costume repair and where cultural rules do not prohibit on-the-spot repairs as they do at Mescalero, dancers who lose part of their costumes stop until someone comes forth from the audience and assists in the repair or retrieval. Among the Navajos, men and occasionally women will assist in creating the sandpaintings for curing ceremonies, and in obtaining yucca roots, herbs, or other paraphernalia needed by the lead singer. In public House Blessings, those assisting the lead singer emerge from the audience at the proper time and return to their seats after the portion of the ritual drama in which they are participating is over. Among the Havasupais, in contexts featuring fully texted songs, audiences are basically passive receivers whose responsibility it is to understand the song content. In other situations, such as the Circle Dance and the Sweathouse context, people are doing a number of other things, including dancing and singing, and no difference exists between narrators and audience.

Audience reactions to Southwestern Indian ritual drama also vary according to place and context. At times, the reactions are critical or highly supportive. At other times, as Tedlock notes for Zuni, people may be moved to tears because of thoughts about the raw part of the audience, namely, recently deceased relatives. A wide range of reactions is characteristic of the Hopi Ogres Drama, as Kealiinohomoku demonstrates; an analysis of these suggests that differences in reactions can be related to such factors as age, experience with ritual drama, amount of cultural knowledge or degree of initiation, and roles within the drama itself. In this context, of course, the audience is part of the dramatic personae and many are in league with the performers.

The degrees to which audiences, performers, and performances merge remain in need of study as do so many other facets of audiences, their roles, and their effect on Southwestern ritual drama. One interesting question, based on one of Kurath's ideas and raised by Kealiinohomoku during discussion, concerned the effect of specialization on this merging: is it possible that the more specialized, the more sacred the performers and performances are, the greater the separation becomes between performers and audiences?

## CREATIVITY

Among the more stimulating discussions we had as a seminar group was that concerning the role of creativity in Southwestern Indian ritual drama. Despite the standard view that these dramas are "traditional," unchanging, and constantly performed exactly as they have been for past generations (ideas that natives as well as outsiders verbalize), discussions suggested that creativity is both allowable and even expected within specific contexts. What we set out to identify was not the range of individual choices permissible within ritual drama context (such as the choice of which sandpaintings to use in a Navajo Shootingway), but rather the amount, types, and acceptable contexts for the expression of individual freedom and creativity. What resulted was a deeper appreciation of the role of creativity in

## Epilogue

ritual dramas of Southwestern Indians and a commitment to analyses which reveal both creativity and its cultural boundaries.

Examples of creativity abound and are of several different kinds. One is the more general kind, involving the actual designing of a total public performance. Frisbie illustrates this with her discussion of both the development of a new public version of an older House Blessing Ceremony in response to changing demands, and the actual continuing process of designing total public performances in response to community and individual definitions of what is appropriate for each situation.

Another area wherein creativity may be expressed is that of prayers. While some groups seem to have no place for newly composed prayers within ritual drama contexts, others such as the Navajos, Zunis, Tewas, and Keresans do, at times, give individuals this option. Many things are possible in the free, individualistic prayers offered during a Navajo House Blessing Ceremony; however, content analysis shows that behind the freedom is an identifiable pattern, a mold.

Our discussions showed that the addressee varies in prayers and may include specific individuals, or the people in general, as well as other-than-humans. Likewise, not all newly composed prayers are uttered during the *public* part of ritual dramas, nor are all prayers verbalized. Thus, further work on creativity in prayers should include considerations of dance, song, ritual smoking, the application of pollen, hooting and other sounds as prayer, and the whole realm of silent prayer.

Improvised dialogues, such as those between clowns and others, or among ogres, children, and their relatives in the Hopi Ogres Drama offer other examples of creativity. Likewise, improvised dance movements, such as mimetic movement in the second part of Papago *Celkona* Songs and the ways in which Zuni dancers further embellish song rhythms need attention, as do individual styles in Papago ritual speech and the talks singers give to audiences during Navajo ritual dramas.

Perhaps the most readily accessible kind of creativity is that expressed in the composition of songs. Tedlock defines the process of composing Kachina Songs at Zuni, illuminating the relationship between individual composers and the group editing process, the aesthetic criteria utilized for evaluating new compositions, the skill needed in "breaking the backbone," and the importance of the segue between the A and B parts of the formal structure. She further relates composition to the wider social world, especially ascribed and achieved kiva membership and reputations as song makers and dancers. Her results should stimulate the investigation of compositional processes among other Southwestern groups; to date, the topic has received attention from Garcia and Garcia (1970), Hinton (1977), Haefer (1977), LaVigna (n.d.), R. Rhodes (1977), and Sekaquaptewa (n.d.).

An understanding of formal structure and its complexity is also part of studying the creation of songs. From an analytical viewpoint, this involves identifying internal parts of songs and their interrelationship as Tedlock has done, internal structure of dance as Farrer (1978) has done elsewhere, and internal structures of language and how these relate to song and its purpose within a ritual context, as Hinton has done. The job does not end here, for as the chapters by Farrer, Kealiinohomoku, and Tedlock demonstrate, attention needs to be given to the total phenomenon of sound and its orchestration. Here, as in many other aspects of ritual drama study, comprehension of the native viewpoint is essential. What is music? Is it just the song and its accompaniment, or does it include vocal calls of dancers and sounds made by costumes? What, in contrast, is noise? Does part of the overall form and understanding of the meaning of the drama depend on a perception of the difference between holy noise and silence? The questions are unending, or seemingly so at this stage, but they must be addressed to understand complexity of form and overall dramatic effect.

The identity of song composers and the amount of composition now characteristic of Southwestern peoples also remains in need of work. While Eastern Pueblo groups believe that everyone can be a composer, at Hopi, composing seems to be a male activity, and at Zuni, one needs to have an unusually sharp mind and good memory. While Zunis compose over 3,000 new Kachina Songs each year, Havasupais no longer compose their own songs, but instead, get new ones from the Mojaves. Navajos compose new songs at least for portions of the public part of the Enemyway and the Yeibichai part of the Nightway ritual drama. At present, however, we know very little about their creative processes.

Newly created musical compositions derive from a number of sources. In addition to individual creativity, songs derive from

## Epilogue

dreams among the Pimas, Papagos, Havasupais, and Yumans. According to the Papagos, anyone can dream songs as well as dances associated with ritual dramas, and dramas can also be dreamed in their entirety. Those having the dreams are considered owners of the songs and dances, as is true in the case of Havasupai Rain and Medicine Songs. The owner is responsible for teaching the new material to others. Dreaming can be a source of songs among the Mescalero Apaches, but not of ceremonial songs.

Another source for new compositions is borrowing from others. Herein the real challenge is twofold: how to be different but still maintain continuity with the past, and how to borrow "foreign" material, adapt it to particular native features such as the five-part form among the Pueblos, while retaining enough of the original features so that the material is still "foreign." As such, the process which is identifiable in music today reflects the nature of a large portion of Southwestern history since the time of contact. While the amount and kind of borrowing can be studied in order to gauge acculturation as W. Rhodes (1952) has done, it can also be viewed from the perspective suggested by Tedlock, that of answering the question of how to be Zuni (or any other Native American) but also of the contemporary world. Borrowing can focus on entire song and dance genres, entire ritual dramas (such as among the Havasupais), specific songs, melodic phrases, texts, rhythmic patterns, or other stylistic elements and basic ideas. As such, the borrowing in song and dance mirrors that occurring on broader levels in ritual drama, such as the borrowing of clowns, curers, and singers.

Borrowing exists on many different levels, and the ideas about when it is appropriate as a source for new songs vary with context. For example, at Zuni, Kachina Songs can be stimulated by prayers, tales, recreational events, Pan-Indianism, or world history events. A lot of borrowing is represented in Kachina and Dance Songs, but very little within the sacred Medicine Society Songs. In the former context it is viewed as one way of increasing beauty within the Kachina Songs. Zunis borrow particularly from Hopis, but also from Utes, Anglo-Americans, and Plains groups. At Taos, on the other hand, while borrowing does occur, the borrowed materials, be they words, melodies, or whatever, are kept separate, being perceived dualistically as "not ours" rather than "ours." Haefer (1977:11) documents a similar situation among the Papagos.

Other examples illustrate the following kinds of borrowing: Navajo-Hopi, interpueblo, Pueblo-Plains, Pueblo-Navajo, Pueblo-Havasupai, Havasupai-Mojave, Havasupai-Yuman, Havasupai-Hopi, Havasupai-Navajo, Havasupai-Chemehuevi, and Papago-Yaqui. Examples of Pueblo borrowing from Anglo culture also abound; witness the interpolation of a jazzy episode during a Santo Domingo Corn Dance and kachinas representing Santa Claus, Mickey Mouse, cave men, and the Chipmunks! Kealiinohomoku provided the seminar with a marvelous example of the Hopi borrowing of the Japanese love song, "Shina No Yoru"; the borrowed version was performed as the climax to a Spanish Social Dance at Hotevilla! McAllester traced the spread of this same song onward to the Institute for American Indian Arts in Santa Fe and its arrangement in choral parts as a Hopi Buffalo Song by Mark Romancito for the Bala-Sinem Choir, at Fort Lewis College, Durango, Colorado.

A number of future research questions surfaced during the discussions of borrowing. Of particular interest is the concern with what is being attempted through borrowing. Is it a fossilization of the Golden Age, a restatement of ethnic identity, a response to a felt need to support and identify with Pan-Indianism, or what? Another question was framed as a hypothesis by Kealiinohomoku: is it possible that the closer the borrowing groups are to each other in geographical location or historical contact, the more respectful the borrowing will be, and the further away, the more subject to humorous treatment? These and other questions, such as what happens when a performer lends his/her services to another group, are all part of the research that remains to be done on creativity.

## TRANSMISSION

While the issue of transmission was never specifically addressed by the seminar, many of the other discussions concerned this process, therefore making it worthy of summary comment.

There is varying interest in transmission of ritual drama among the Southwestern Indian groups represented in this volume. Some, such as Mescalero Apaches, offer monetary support from the tribal level, paying what amounts to one-fourth of the expenses related to the Girls' Puberty Ceremony. Navajos are also becoming increasingly involved in politi-

## Epilogue

cally supporting the transmission of ritual drama. Part of this support is represented by tribal endorsements of training programs for future singers at the Rough Rock Demonstration School and Navajo Community College, and the tribally supported Office of Navajo Economic Opportunity (ONEO) Culture Project (1967-69). The latter resulted in the recording of a wealth of songs, myths, and prayers currently inaccessible to outside researchers.

The process of transmitting ritual drama takes many different forms. Among the Navajos, active transmission through the apprenticeship system is still preferred; as one Navajo explained it to Hinton, "While you can learn songs by rote from a tape, you still lack the understanding of the overall structure." Among other groups, the learning is more passive. Papago boys learn by osmosis; they sit in while learning, listen, and sing softly until they know the song. Ideally, they should not sing in public until they know a complete song repertoire; then they "really sing." Havasupais can learn through active teaching, osmosis, or can dream their own songs, as has been noted above. While they hear particular kinds of songs all their lives, it is not until a crisis occurs that they "really hear songs from the ancestors and learn them." Mescalero Apache boys who are learning to be holy men do not sing in public until they have learned the entire repertoire; older men will tell them "not to sing now." But young boys are actively instructed in drumming styles by adult males and are allowed to join in on the chorus of songs sung to accompany the dancing of the Mountain Gods. Among the Eastern Pueblos, people who are learning join in on the chorus if they do not know the rest of the song; here it is all right to sing in public while learning.

Various mnemonic devices facilitate the transmission process. At Hopi, the song is a mnemonic device for dancing; it is the more important and learned first. Among both the Mescalero Apaches and Papagos, tally sticks are used; in the former case these serve to mark the number of tribal history songs sung during each of the four nights of the Puberty Ceremony. In the latter, they help the lead singer remember names of village elders in the Naming Songs. Navajos use drawings of sandpaintings and "picture writing" to record prayers (Newcomb 1956:45-48; Fishler 1956:51-54); songs can be viewed as mnemonic devices for myth recounting (McAllester 1952).

Other kinds of technological devices are now becoming increasingly important in transmission. Foremost among these is the tape recorder, particularly in cassette form. Zunis and Hopis are taping some of their own ritual drama music, and at Zuni, Kachina Song tapes are often played as dinner music. Zuni women also take their tape recorders to Hopi and elsewhere, in the hopes of recording something worth borrowing. Zunis have also used reel-to-reel tape recorders to tape their sacred Medicine Society Songs, with anthropologists serving as consultants about technology and preservation. These tapes have been stored for future use, freeing current performers from worry about transmitting songs to future generations.

Papagos will tape Curing Songs, replaying the tapes very softly and being careful never truly to vocalize the songs until they have been thoroughly learned. Individual Mescalero Apaches, too, have taped a number of sacred materials; tapes made by anthropologists and given to the Tribal Council have been archived by the Tribe and are not played, at least at the moment. Other groups, however, frown on taping and reject offers of use of equipment in order to preserve and transmit their ritual dramas. At Taos, for example, one singer feared that if ritual songs were recorded, someone might steal the tapes and sell them to outsiders.

The different attitudes toward taping suggest that among Southwestern groups, there are varying ideas about the utility and appropriateness of preserving things for the future. The attitude of Lipan speakers at Mescalero sums it up; these speakers believe that if their language is meant to survive, it will without being taped or recorded in writing (Farrer). Mescalero Apaches and Hopis both feel, as do some Navajos, that ritual dramas should pass out of existence, or be taken to the grave with their specialists if they cannot be transmitted to the right person. The problem is, of course, to understand what constitutes the right person from the native perspective.

Havasupais have mixed feelings about preserving and transmitting their ritual dramas through tapes and other kinds of anthropological records. The young people prefer to learn from tapes since by so doing, they are not subjected to critical comments from teachers. But tapes and written works become objects which can be manipulated by others, taken away, sold, and transmitted into the wrong hands for the wrong purposes. Even within the Havasupai setting, when tapes of deceased people are played too loudly, it causes sadness among the remaining relatives.

*Epilogue*

Phonograph records, books, old photographs showing dance costumes and ground plans, and films also have roles in the transmission process. The works of Matilda Coxe Stevenson have been used a number of times by Zunis. Mojaves readily refer to books in order to revive and re-create past ritual activities and designs for facial painting, and the works of Ruth Underhill have formed the basic resource for reviving ritual speeches among the Papagos. Navajos and Zunis actively purchase commercially available records and cassette tapes of their own music. Interestingly enough, sales of recorded Yeibichai and Moccasin Game Songs increase among the Navajos during the winter, when such songs are appropriate. San Juan has recreated ceremonies from tapes when choreographic patterns were still remembered, and other Eastern Pueblos remain interested in making tapes at masked ceremonies in order to preserve ritual drama and facilitate its transmission.

Anthropologists as living human beings also can have direct roles in transmission, both within and between cultures. Sometimes their requests to see a particular ritual drama provide sufficient stimulus for a group to revive it after a lengthy lapse, as in the case of Spier's request to see the Havasupai Peach Festival in 1918. More recently, an anthropologist became the vehicle through which a verbal request could be made to a relative of a deceased singer to continue the role of ritual speech-maker in one Papago village. D. L. Roberts' (1972:255) tape recorder assisted a Hopi Longhair Song in its travels to Santo Domingo, San Juan, and back to Hopi-Tewa, during which time it became an English-worded Turtle Dance Song and then, a Hopi-Tewa Corn Kachina Song. Brown's tape of a two-step, secular song from Picuris traveled to Cochití, where it became a sacred Buffalo Song the following Christmas.

## CHANGE

Ritual drama, like other aspects of culture, remains vital, dynamic, and responsive to the contemporary world. Among the groups represented by seminar research, a variety of changes are occurring, the documentation of which can serve to illustrate the present state of ritual drama in the Southwest, as well as to provide a comparative base for future studies.

In some places, and in certain contexts within one group, ritual dramas are declining. For example, among the Havasupais, most genres of traditional song are disappearing; at present, there are no Rain Songs, few Medicine Songs, and no composition of Personal Songs. Among the Papagos, purification rites, hunting, and agricultural rituals have become defunct as has the Harvest Festival within the United States, and the Girls' Puberty Ceremony is now held less frequently. In other contexts, only certain portions of ritual dramas are held, others having been dropped. Papagos no longer participate in intervillage games nor do they try to include mimetic movements in the second part of *Celkona* Songs. As Haefer indicates, there is also a decline in the maximal level of naming in the *Celkona*. At Mescalero, horse racing and hand game gambling are no longer part of the ritual context of the Girls' Puberty Ceremony nor do men pay women for the privilege of dancing with them all night. Such declines and changes through omission reflect a variety of factors, including effects of missionization, dominant culture legislation, lack of interest among the young in traditional activities, increasing secularization, and deaths of knowledgeable specialists before transmission processes are complete.

Other changes, however, represent adaptations to contemporary situations, and hence, the flexibility and vitality of ritual drama. For example, Mescalero girls now dance on cow rather than buffalo hides, and the costumes of the war dancers and their location within the ritual have changed considerably. At Zuni, sleigh bells and wooden rattles are now included in instrument inventories and all indoor public dances are held in Shalako houses instead of kivas to accommodate larger audiences. Ritual drama calendars are also changing. In some cases, seasonal associations have been dropped, such as in the Papago *Celkona* which is now appropriate at any time of year rather than just at harvest time. The Havasupai Harvest Festival now occurs before the children depart for boarding school. Temporal pressures have been responsible for changes in the Hopi Ogres Drama; now Tewa Village Ogres no longer go to Polacca because "it takes too long and is too much trouble." Acknowledgment of western clock time and boarding school calendars is also obvious among the Navajos, where ceremonies such as the Girls' Puberty one are now sometimes condensed into weekend formats, and shorter ceremonies which do not involve extensive preparations and heavy kinship support are becoming more popular (Wagner 1975a, 1975b).

## Epilogue

The picture is not solely one of decline, disappearance, and condensation, however. Some ritual dramas are being consciously revived after long lapses in performance. For example, at Picuris the Clown Society has been revived and at Zuni, the Buffalo Dance has been reinstated after a 50-year lapse. Among the Papagos, the *Celkona* has been revived during the past 10 years as a way of teaching the young about their culture and as a vehicle for public dancing in Powwows and other situations. *Celkonas* now occur in conjunction with rodeos, Indian Days, and contest dancing, and as such, have become one of the Papago ways of expressing the meaning of being Papago. The Mescalero Apache Girls' Puberty Ceremony, which ceased for 39 years because of government orders, is viewed by Mescaleros as the crucial factor in their ethnicity and their ability to remain strong, to cope as a people in the face of challenges from the outside world.

The history and present state of the Navajo House Blessing Ceremony can serve as an example of another possible response to the challenges of today's world, that of elaboration, expansion, and through these, revitalization. Not only has the original, private version expanded in scope, but also the Navajos have developed, during the present century, a new public version. This latter version continues to expand in scope, and is now appropriate for anything. While core features seem to be emerging, individual options and opportunities for creativity remain high as numerous ideas continue to exist about what constitutes appropriate performance. Already, of course, this public version is accepted as "the traditional way" of blessing particular kinds of structures and events. Part of its popularity undoubtedly derives from the fact that it serves as a statement about being Navajo in the midst of dedicatory programs which include a variety of other events from the outside world.

The response to the Pan-Indian movement and the Powwow circuit is mixed in the Southwest. Navajos, as individuals, have responded rapidly, learning Plains dances and song genres and fancy drumming styles. Girls are learning to Hoop Dance and a number of families are already well-known competitors at the national level. The Hopis neither proclaim ethnicity through their dance nor participate in Powwows as a tribe. Individuals in small groups do participate, however, and are very capable of performing Plains style fancy drumming and competing with others. The Papagos, in general, remain uninterested in Plains style singing although they have now begun to participate in dance competitions and rodeos. Powwows are now considered to be the modern, expected thing to do as an Indian, and Papagos have become particularly interested in the prizes available during such events. However, they dance their own traditional dances and the individual who dances in Plains style is rare. Havasupais do not dance in Powwows, but they do attend them to gamble and to buy and sell things. They have now adopted the Yuman Bird Songs and Line Dance and are interested in performing these, but not for an audience or in a manner that could be said to reflect any incorporation of Plains style singing. At Taos, where there is such a strong emphasis on what is ours and not ours, people willingly participate in the Pan-Indian scene, borrowing or inventing dance forms such as the Horse Tail, Shield, and Hoop Dance to use in national competitions.

Other changes are also noticeable. The increased role of technology in transmission and preservation of ritual drama is one of these which has already been discussed. Another is the rethinking of who should be in audiences, and who should be interested in studying and understanding native ritual dramas. The Red Power movement has encouraged such rethinking, and at some places and for certain individuals, the result has been to label all anthropological research as unwarranted, unwanted intrusion and to close even public ritual dramas to those outside the native culture.

In addition to the numerous kinds of change identified above, any study of change must take into account the problem of varying native definitions of what is "the same." This is especially true in the Southwest, where many people verbalize the thought that the ritual dramas passed along through oral transmission processes have remained "the same" for generations. The problems become those of recognizing that the "same" does not mean frozen exact repetition, discovering how much and what kind of variation is permissible, and learning how much individual creativity can be expressed and when in ritual drama. One also needs to acknowledge and unravel a series of dichotomies which affect definitions of what is "the same," and what is "right." Within a culture definitions often vary between generations, students and teachers, and the trained and the unqualified. Outside a culture, analytically based perceptions of similarity and change often do not mirror the ideas native peoples have about these issues.

# Epilogue

## FUTURE DIRECTIONS

One of the things that happens during an event such as an Advanced Seminar is that particular issues emerge which participants find exciting, intriguing, and relatively unstudied in the extant literature and continuing research efforts of colleagues. In our case, this happened during the first day's sessions and continued throughout the week. Many of the new directions are represented by the topics and approaches utilized by individual authors within this volume. However, for clarity's sake, it was decided to reiterate them in a section devoted specifically to the question, Where do we go from here? Herein, a general rather than an individualistic perspective has been utilized.

Before turning to future directions, the seminar group felt that a discussion of ethics was both relevant and necessary. As discernible in the sections on transmission and change, ritual drama and its components are both extant and viable in the Southwest. Some groups are developing new versions of ceremonies; others are revitalizing earlier practices by reviving them with assistance from photographs, anthropologists' descriptions, and the memories of members of the culture. Simultaneously, some are choosing to let particular ritual dramas lapse for lengthy periods or die altogether, replacing them with other activities on the secular plane and ritual dramas that we would not call traditional or natively inspired. These activities are taking place within a larger cultural setting where there is renewed emphasis on ethnicity—being Indian and being a particular kind of Indian, showing solidarity, and taking pride in traditional culture and one's own language. This reawakened interest in cultural identity expresses itself in ritual drama but also in other activities, such as increased control of tribal education programs. One of the ramifications has been a pulling back from outsiders, a change of attitude toward researchers who want to record, talk, and "understand." In some areas this means that researchers are no longer welcome; in others, it means that tribal groups have begun to sponsor their own research, identify their own projects and researchers, and restrict the use of their results to members of their own culture.

Given this political milieu and the fact that by studying even *public* ritual drama one is automatically treading on sacred ground, it makes professional sense to raise the question of what can be done or what should be done. Seminar discussions led to a reaffirmation of the idea that anthropologists can only work in places where both their presence and their desires to study and understand are acceptable to the people involved. Given the present situation, more careful thought has to be devoted to such questions, even before assembling one's field gear, as Farrer (1976) has so aptly stated. It will undoubtedly become increasingly difficult for new researchers to judge their reception, the accessibility of certain public ritual dramas, and the feasibility of proposed projects. One of the things that can be done is to increase sensitivity to the issues in forthcoming generations of students, and willingly offer advice based on one's perception and knowledge of specific Southwestern groups. Another is to sharpen one's own sensitivity to political issues among Native Americans, staying in touch with individual tribal councils, leaders of ritual dramas, chapter houses, or whatever levels of permission-granting power are relevant to research work.

Another possible response which deserves support is the idea of training native people to do their own research. This implies encouraging them to become exposed to academic training and the use of technological inventions in fieldwork and analysis, and being supportive of their own particular research interests.

Finally, continuing to do research implies an intellectual honesty, where one carefully sorts out the responsibilities one has to the native people involved, the profession, and one's self. Permissions to do research may be restricted to studies of only portions of events. They may also entail agreements on the part of the researcher to provide the people with copies of slides, tapes, or films, or to let them review any and all written words before these are submitted for publication. One must realize these things in advance, and pursue the ramifications well before departure. Likewise, one must remain sensitive to potential changes in the scene during the fieldwork experience, responding with flexibility, sensitivity, and intellectual integrity. Above all else, there must be room in a researcher's understanding for those who do not want to be studied, and for those who choose to let ritual dramas lapse. Such decisions are entirely up to the people to whom the dramas belong; if the ritual dramas die before they are studied and recorded, it is *not* a catastrophe.

Among the topics which we believe should be pursued in future research in order to advance the understanding of Southwestern In-

## Epilogue

dian ritual drama is aesthetics. With the exception of McAllester's work on Navajo and White Mountain Apache aesthetics (1954, 1956), Kealiinohomoku's (1967) work on what constitutes a good Hopi dancer, Frisbie's (n.d.) work on Navajo definitions of a good singer and a good performance, Kurath and Garcia's (1970) discussion of Tewa performance standards, and Tedlock's chapter in this volume, we know little about Southwestern Indian aesthetics. One of the many unanswered questions is, Do all groups have metaaesthetics, a body of theory that can be articulated, or do such theories correlate with certain degrees of cultural complexity as suggested by Kurath (1950)? Tedlock's work suggests that there are areas where the whole notion is inappropriate, such as within the sacred Zuni Medicine Society music. In such research, it obviously is important to remember that not all human activities have a metalanguage.

Other useful approaches involve identifying the range of things considered to be aesthetic and the people within cultural contexts who have the "license" to make such judgments. Also to be considered are questions such as, Are the aesthetic principles applied to music, dance, and ritual drama the same as those applied to other art forms, such as pottery, basketry, beadwork, children's drawings, and bulletin boards, or are they only distantly related, or not at all congruent? What role does language play in aesthetics, especially musical, dance, and dramatic aesthetics? Hinton suggests that vocables among the Havasupai act as aesthetic devices; are there other such devices? The list of questions could continue almost endlessly; suffice it to say that a deeper appreciation of the complexity and importance of aesthetics is clearly needed.

Another issue that needs attention is creativity. Included in considerations of this topic should be further examinations of the compositional process and its sources; native musical theories; identification and analysis of contexts wherein individual and group creativity may be expressed, the forms that it takes, the meanings associated with these expressions, and the cultural boundaries within which these exist. While the seminar, stimulated by Tedlock's work, addressed some of these issues, knowledge about this aspect of ritual drama throughout the Southwest remains minimal.

Hinton's work on Havasupai vocables directly relates to another area which currently suffers from lack of research: the role of language in ritual drama. Her work represents a major step forward, not only in its application to Havasupai ideas and usage of vocables, but also in its identification of a series of hypotheses testable in Southwestern and other cultural settings. We trust that these will stimulate such testing in the future, and that those involved will have both linguistic and ethnomusicological skills. Such a combination could also advance knowledge about other related issues, such as the relationship between sung and spoken language, and the different ideas about the "power of the word" in ritual drama. Farrer's and McAllester's chapters demonstrate that even among Southern Athapaskans, a belief in the power of the word has different implications.

Further work is also needed on the possibility of a perceived sound-silence continuum. Farrer's work in particular delves into this issue, as do the chapters by Kealiinohomoku and Tedlock. Among the relevant issues are native classifications of kinds of noise, definitions of music, and ideas about potential communication through silence, be it through thought, dream, prayer, or singing in the heart.

Work on the role of language in ritual drama should also include considerations of the special languages associated with dramatic contexts. Appropriate topics are numerous and could include studies of archaic and poetic kinds of speech, special kachina languages, the special communications Apache holy men sing in classical language to pubescent girls, the meanings associated with vocalizations often described as hoots and calls, and the spirit language characteristic of the Havasupai Sweathouse genre. A number of chapters in this volume touched on this subject and discussions, stimulated by Hinton's work, revealed the enormous potential this area holds for future research. Among the possibilities are those which could be derived by applying the questions from relevant musically oriented studies to dance and other forms of nonverbal communication within ritual contexts. As Farrer wondered during the seminar, is it possible that there might be something equivalent to the vocables in music in other aspects of drama, particularly dance?

Identification and comprehension of all the backstage activities which affect ritual drama is another direction needing further attention. Frisbie's work illustrates how decision making affects public performance content in the Navajo House Blessing context. Discus-

## Epilogue

sions of this work and the chapters on Pueblo and Mescalero Apache ritual dramas led to identification of other backstage activities such as cueing, rehearsal, costume repair, on-the-spot criticism, and mnemonic devices. Approaching these from perspectives which raise questions about interactions between performers and audiences, performers and performances, and performances and audiences is one way of giving these issues the attention they need in future Southwestern research.

Change in ritual drama is another area which has yet to be exhausted by researchers. As many of the chapters in this volume illustrate, change is on-going, multidirectional, and influenced by a number of factors. Borrowing, incorporating, reviving, and reducing variants are all part of the process, just as are the responses of developing new ritual dramas within the traditional world, in other religious worlds, and in the Pan-Indian scene. While scholars have become more adept at identifying and analyzing individual examples of change as these occur in a variety of settings, we have much to learn about the process as it relates to contemporary ritual drama in the Southwest. Among the relevant questions are, How does something from an Eastern Pueblo become Zuni-ized, and, as Tedlock phrased it, How does one remain a native yet be a part of the contemporary world?

Theoretically and methodologically, seminar participants represented a wide range of approaches including dialectical process, symbolic structuralism, structural-functionalism, ethnosemantics, and preferences for contextual and dialogical analyses. Many participants favored eclecticism, given the strengths and weaknesses of individual theories and approaches, and for that reason among others, we did not endorse any one theory or method as "the way" to approach future research.

Among the theoretical and methodological issues covered in individual chapters and seminar discussions was the dialogical approach wherein all participants' comments are given in toto and in actual speech patterns rather than in rewritten English. Stimulated by Brown's use of extended statements, Tedlock's interest in this approach, and Farrer's (1977) previous work with it, the seminar devoted several discussions to this issue, deciding in favor of preserving actual speech patterns. Such an approach not only records valuable linguistic information, but also makes possible the study of the stimuli which trigger particular responses as well as the separation and fusion occurring in interactions among collaborators, interpreters, and researchers. Brown has been willing to take the first step in this direction, and we trust that others will follow, acknowledging that doing so involves more presentation of self and implies coming to grips with one's own field language patterns and the relevancy of revealing them in print.

One of the themes that binds the chapters in this volume together, despite their diversity, is the importance of native thought. Specific examples of the kinds of understanding that can be unearthed through eliciting native thoughts, feelings, and taxonomies are numerous, particularly in discussions of the multiple levels of meaning in particular ritual dramas and the compositional process. However, discussions of these led us into a reaffirmation of the complexity and multiplicity of native thought. To capture this, researchers must, as Geertz (1974) indicates, abandon the idea that native philosophy is a unitary and unified phenomenon and seek out that thinking as it is represented and understood by a variety of native people, be they intellectuals or lay persons.

The need to combine etic approaches with emic ones was also expressed in discussion. The gaps that exist between insiders' and outsiders' perceptions and understandings have now been well established by ethnosemanticists. McAllester's final example which compares a researcher's perception of the structural climaxes in Shootingway with those of a Navajo singer emphatically underscores the point.

The seminar ended with participants wishing that we were far enough along with in-depth studies and the understanding of the issues enumerated above to attempt to relate our efforts to other anthropological knowledge about the past history and development of the Southwest. With time and effort, interactional-level discussions about ritual drama will be possible. Reaching this level of discussion represents another goal which can be realized once the accumulation of data and their analyses permit moving beyond studies of isolates. For some aspects of ritual drama, such as vocal styles, dance patterns, and musical instrument usage in particular places, such discussions are now possible; in these areas we are ready to move beyond classificatory models and geographic isolates. For others, much remains to be done. It seems possible that team re-

## Epilogue

search might facilitate further work, but not the kind where research teams descend en masse on a field situation. Instead, we envision a number of individuals working on the same problem from different specialized perspectives, converging regularly at nearby field stations or research centers, where intensive discussions similar to those supported by the School of American Research could prevail on a regular basis. Developing financial support for such long-term, coordinated research effort might be the first order of future business.

> Ritual drama, in dealing with life itself, is a process which serves to unite humans with other humans, as well as humans with other-than-humans, the revealed with the unrevealed world, the visible with the invisible. The process is accomplished through a variety of multisensory, multilayered experiences entailing "cultural performances" . . . by actors for reactors. Specific elements of ritual drama, as reflected in the chapters in this volume, include story line, characterization, multiforms, layers of meaning and aesthetic events, and a degree of stylization or formalization that allows recognition and identification of the forms, but does not make impossible the expression of individual or group creativity.

So states our operational definition which was group-authored and derived from research experiences and discussions represented in this volume.

Both in spite of and because of our efforts, ritual drama remains an enigma and a challenge. Southwestern ritual drama continues to be alive and well, dynamic and vital. From the scholarly perspective, it continues to need concentrated attention in ways that are sensitive to changing native perceptions of themselves and others, insiders and outsiders, and the ethical ramifications of these continuing changes. At least part of the work that is ahead can be done by non-native scholars, and perhaps as more Native Americans become interested in their cultural heritage, they, too, will choose to join us in responding to the challenge.

# References

ABERLE, DAVID F.
1973  "Clyde Kluckhohn's Contribution to Navaho Studies," in *Culture and Life: Essays in Memory of Clyde Kluckhohn*, ed. Walter W. Taylor, John L. Fischer, and Evon Z. Vogt (Carbondale: Southern Illinois University Press).

ADAMS, ELEANOR B., AND FRAY ANGELICO CHAVEZ
1956  *The Missions of New Mexico, 1776: A Description by Fray Francisco Atanasio Domínguez* (Albuquerque: University of New Mexico Press).

ALBRIGHT, H. D., WILLIAM P. HALSTEAD, AND LEE MITCHELL
1955  *Principles of Theatre Art* (New York: Houghton Mifflin Co.).

ALVAREZ, ALBERT
1969  "O'odham ne'oki ha-kaidag: The Sounds of Papago," English translation by Kenneth Hale, MS. (Boston: Massachusetts Institute of Technology, Department of Linguistics).

AMERICAN ANTHROPOLOGIST
1954  *Southwest Issue of the American Anthropologist* 56, no. 4, pt. 1, ed. Emil W. Haury (Menasha, Wisc.: American Anthropological Association).

ANDERSON, ROBERT
1960  "Reduction of Variants as a Measure of Cultural Integrations," in *Essays in the Science of Culture*, ed. Gertrude Dole and Robert Carneiro (New York: Thomas Y. Crowell Co.).

ANONYMOUS
1928  "The Animal Dance at San Ildefonso," *El Palacio* 24:119–22.
1929  "The Green Corn Ceremony," *El Palacio* 27:48–50.

APPELMAN, D. RALPH
1967  *The Science of Vocal Pedagogy* (Bloomington: Indiana University Press).

BAHR, DONALD M.
1977  "On the Complexity of Southwest Indian Emergence Myths," *Journal of Anthropological Research* 33:317–49.

# REFERENCES

BAHR, DONALD M., AND J. RICHARD HAEFER
1978    "Song in Piman Curing," *Ethnomusicology* 22:89-122.
BAHR, DONALD M., JUAN GREGORIO, DAVID I. LOPEZ, AND ALBERT ALVAREZ
1974    *Piman Shamanism and Staying Sickness* (Tucson: University of Arizona Press).
BAILEY, FLORENCE M.
1924    "Some Plays and Dances of the Taos Indians," *Natural History* 24:85-95.
BARNES, NELLIE
1925    *American Indian Love Lyrics* (New York: Macmillan Co.).
BARTENIEFF, IRMGARD
1974    "Effort/shape in Teaching Ethnic Dance," *CORD Research Annual* 6:175-92.
BASSO, KEITH H.
1966    *The Gift of Changing Woman*, Bulletin of the Bureau of American Ethnology no. 196 (Washington, D.C.: U.S. Government Printing Office).
1979    *Portraits of "The Whiteman": Linguistic Play and Cultural Symbols Among the Western Apache* (New York: Cambridge University Press).
BATESON, GREGORY
1958    *Naven*, 2d ed. (Stanford: Stanford University Press). First published in 1936.
BAUMAN, RICHARD
1976    "The Technical Boundaries of Performance," in *Form in Performance: Proceedings of a Symposium on Form in Performance, Hard-Core Ethnography*, eds. Marcia Herndon and Roger Brunyate (Austin: University of Texas, Office of the College of Fine Arts).
BEAGLEHOLE, EARNEST
1937    *Notes on Hopi Economic Life*, Yale University Publications in Anthropology no. 15 (New Haven, Conn.: Yale University Press).
BECK, PEGGY, AND A. L. WALTERS
1977    *The Sacred* (Tsaile, Ariz.: Navajo Community College Press).
BENNINGER, GERALDEAN
1972    "Navajo Sacred Places—The Hogan," *Navajo Times*, November 16:C-1.
BIDNEY, DAVID
1973    "Phenomenological Method and the Anthropological Science of the Cultural Life-World," in *Phenomenology and the Social Sciences*, vol. 1, ed. Maurice Natanson (Evanston: Northwestern University Press).
BLANCHARD, KENDALL A.
1977    *The Economics of Sainthood: Religious Change Among the Rimrock Navajos* (Cranbury, N.J.: Associated University Presses).
BREUNINGER, EVELYN P.
1959    "Debut of Mescalero Maidens," *Apache Scout*, June, pp. 2-4. (Same title with virtually the same text by the same author also appeared intermittently in the 1960s and 1970s).
BROWN, DONALD N.
1960    "Taos Dance Classification," *El Palacio* 67:203-9.
1961    "The Development of Taos Dance," *Ethnomusicology* 5:33-41.
1962    *Masks, Mantas, and Moccasins: Dance Costumes of the Pueblo Indians* (Colorado Springs, Colo.: Taylor Museum).
1973    "Structural Change at Picuris Pueblo, New Mexico" (Ph.D. diss., University of Arizona).
1976    "The Dance of Taos Pueblo," *CORD Dance Research Annual* 7: 182-272.
BRUGGE, DAVID
1963    *Navajo Pottery and Ethnohistory*, Navajoland Publications, series 2 (Window Rock, Ariz.: Navajo Tribal Museum).

# References

BUNZEL, RUTH
1932a  *Introduction to Zuni Ceremonialism*, Annual Report of the Bureau of American Ethnology no. 47:467–544 (Washington, D.C.: U.S. Government Printing Office).
1932b  *Zuni Katchinas: An Analytical Study*, Annual Report of the Bureau of American Ethnology no. 47:837–1086 (Washington, D.C.: U.S. Government Printing Office).

BUTTREE, JULIA M.
1937  *The Rhythm of the Redman* (New York: A.S. Barnes and Co.).

CAVALLO-BOSSO, J. R.
1956  "Kumanche of the Zuni Indians of New Mexico: An Analytical Study" (B.A. Thesis, Wesleyan University, Middletown, Conn.).

CHAPPLE, ELIOT D., AND CARLETON S. COON
1942  *Principles of Anthropology* (New York: Henry Holt).

CHESKY, JANE
1941  "Indian Music of the Southwest," *Kiva* 7:9–12.
1942  "The Wikita," *Kiva* 8:3–5.
1943  "The Nature and Function of Papago Music" (M.A. Thesis, University of Arizona).

CLARK, LAVERNE H.
1976  "The Girl's Puberty Ceremony of the San Carlos Apaches," *Journal of Popular Culture* 10:431–48.

COHEN, FELIX
1952  "Americanizing the White Man," *American Scholar* 21:177–91.

CURTIS, EDWARD S.
1926  *The North American Indian*, vol. 16 (Norwood, Mass.: Plimpton Press).

CURTIS, NATALIE
1907  *The Indians' Book* (New York: Harper and Bros.).

DAVIS, EDWARD H.
1920  *The Papago Ceremony of Víkita*, Heye Foundation, Indian Notes and Monographs 3, no. 4:155–77 (New York: Museum of the American Indian, Heye Foundation).

DENNIS, WAYNE
1965  *The Hopi Child* (New York: John Wiley & Sons). First published in 1940.

DENSMORE, FRANCES
1929  *Papago Music*, Bulletin of the Bureau of American Ethnology no. 90 (Washington, D.C.: U.S. Government Printing Office).
1932  *Yuman and Yaqui Music*, Bulletin of the Bureau of American Ethnology no. 110 (Washington, D.C.: U.S. Government Printing Office).
1938  *Music of Santo Domingo Pueblo, New Mexico*, Southwest Museum Papers, no. 12 (Los Angeles, Calif.: Southwest Museum).
1957  *Music of Acoma, Isleta, Cochiti, and Zuni Pueblos*, Bulletin of the Bureau of American Ethnology no. 165 (Washington, D.C.: U.S. Government Printing Office).

DIETRICH, JOHN E.
1953  *Play Direction* (New York: Prentice-Hall).

DOBYNS, HENRY, AND ROBERT EULER
1967  *The Ghost Dance of 1889 Among the Pai Indians of Northwestern Arizona* (Prescott, Ariz.: Prescott College Press).

# REFERENCES

DOZIER, EDWARD P.
1966   *Hano: A Tewa Indian Community in Arizona* (New York: Holt, Rinehart, and Winston).

DUTTON, BERTHA P.
1975   *Indians of the American Southwest* (Englewood Cliffs, N.J.: Prentice–Hall).

EICKEMEYER, CARL, AND LILLIAN W. EICKEMEYER
1895   *Among the Pueblo Indians* (New York: Merriam Co.).

ESTERGREEN, MARION
1950   "When Taos Dances," *New Mexico Magazine* 28:16, 40–41.

FARRER, CLAIRE R.
1976   "Fieldwork Ethics," *Folklore Forum*, Bibliographic and Special Series, vol. 9, no. 15:59–63 (a special issue edited by Steve Mannebach).
1977   "Play and Inter-Ethnic Communication: A Practical Ethnography of the Mescalero Apache" (Ph.D. diss., University of Texas at Austin).
1978   "Mescalero Ritual Dance: A Four-Part Fugue," *Discovery* 1–13.

FELD, STEVE
1976   "Ethnomusicology and Visual Communication," *Ethnomusicology* 20:293–325.

FERGUSSON, ERNA
1931   *Dancing Gods: Indian Ceremonials of New Mexico and Arizona* (Albuquerque: University of New Mexico Press).

FEWKES, JESSE WALTER
1890a  "On the Use of the Phonograph Among the Zuni Indians," *American Naturalist* 24:687–91.
1890b  "Additional Studies of Zuni Songs and Rituals with the Phonograph," *American Naturalist* 24:1094–98.

FILLMORE, JOHN C.
1893–94 "The Zuni Music, as Translated by Mr. Benjamin Ives Gilman," *Music* 5:39–46.
n.d.   *Indian Fantasia*, a musical composition partly based on Zuni themes.

FISHLER, STANLEY
1956   "Navaho Picture Writing," in *A Study of Navajo Symbolism*, by Franc J. Newcomb, Stanley Fishler, and Mary C. Wheelright. Papers of the Peabody Museum of American Archaeology and Ethnology, vol. 32, no. 3 (Cambridge, Mass.: Harvard University).

FRANCISCAN FATHERS
1910   *An Ethnologic Dictionary of the Navaho Language* (Saint Michaels, Ariz.: Saint Michaels Press).

FRAZER, SIR JAMES
1964   *The New Golden Bough*, ed. T. H. Gaster (New York: Mentor Books).

FRINK, MAURICE, AND CASEY E. BARTHELMESS
1965   *Photographer on an Army Mule* (Norman: University of Oklahoma Press).

FRISBIE, CHARLOTTE J.
1967   *Kinaaldá: A Study of the Navaho Girl's Puberty Ceremony* (Middletown, Conn.: Wesleyan University Press).
1968   "The Navajo House Blessing Ceremonial," *El Palacio* 75:26–35.
1970   "The Navajo House Blessing Ceremonial: A Study of Cultural Change" (Ph.D. diss., University of New Mexico).
1977   *Music and Dance Research of Southwestern United States Indians*, Detroit Studies in Music Bibliography, no. 36 (Detroit, Mich.: Information Coordinators).
n.d.   "An Approach to the Ethnography of Navajo Ceremonial Performance," in *Ethnography of Performance*, ed. Marcia Herndon and Norma McLeod (Darby, Pa.: Norwood Editions, in press).

# References

FRISBIE, CHARLOTTE J. AND DAVID P. MCALLESTER (eds.)
1978    *Navajo Blessingway Singer. The Autobiography of Frank Mitchell, 1881–1967* (Tucson: University of Arizona Press).

GARCIA, ANTONIO, AND CARLOS GARCIA
1970    "Ritual Preludes and Postludes," in *Music and Dance of the Tewa Pueblos* by Gertrude P. Kurath and Antonio Garcia, Museum of New Mexico Research Records, no. 8 (Santa Fe: Museum of New Mexico Press).

GEERTZ, CLIFFORD
1973    *Interpretation of Cultures* (New York: Basic Books).
1974    "From the Native's Point of View: On the Nature of Anthropological Understandings" in *Meaning in Anthropology*, ed. Keith H. Basso and Henry A. Selby (Albuquerque: University of New Mexico Press, School of American Research Advanced Seminar Series).

GILL, SAM D.
1974    "A Theory of Navajo Prayer Acts: A Study in Ritual Symbolism" (Ph.D. diss., University of Chicago Divinity School).
1978    "And the Trees Stood Deep Rooted," in *The Religious Character of Native American Humanities*, ed. Sam D. Gill (Tempe: Arizona State University, Department of Humanities and Religious Studies).

GILMAN, BENJAMIN IVES
1891    "Zuni Melodies," *Journal of American Ethnology and Archaeology* 1:63–91.
1898    "Music of the Zuni Indians of New Mexico," *Musical Courier* 37:1–19.

GILPIN, LAURA
1968    *The Enduring Navaho* (Austin: University of Texas Press).

GOFFMAN, ERVING
1974    *Frame Analysis* (Cambridge, Mass.: Harvard University Press).

GOGGIN, JOHN M.
1937    "Calendar of Eastern Pueblo Festivals, September to December," *New Mexico Anthropologist* 2:21–23.
1938a    "Calender of Eastern Pueblo Festivals," *New Mexico Anthropologist* 2:89–94.
1938b    "Notes on Some 1938–1939 Pueblo Dances," *New Mexico Anthropologist* 3:30–32.
1939    "Additional Pueblo Ceremonies—1939," *New Mexico Anthropologist* 3:62–63.

GOLDFRANK, ESTHER S.
1978    *Notes on an Undirected Life*, Queens College Publications in Anthropology, no. 3 (New York).

GORE, RICK, AND JAMES F. BLAIR
1978    "Wondrous Eyes of Science," *National Geographic* 153:366–89.

GRANT, BLANCHE C.
1934    *When Old Trails Were New* (New York: Press of the Pioneers).

GRIFFITH, JAMES
1978    "Southwestern Acculturative Indian Music," paper presented at Arizona Archaeological and Historical Society February Meeting, Tucson.

GROSSINGER, RICHARD
1968    "The Doctrine of Signatures," *Io Magazine* 5:6–14.

GRUNN, HOMER
n.d.    *Zuni Impressions: An Indian Suite* (New York: Carl Fischer).

GUNST, MARIE L.
1930    "Ceremonials of the Papago and Pima Indians, with Special Emphasis on the Relationship of the Dance to Their Religion" (M.A. Thesis, University of Arizona).

HAEFER, J. RICHARD
1972    Notes from Papago fieldwork.

# REFERENCES

1973 "Papago Dance Music," Notes to *An Anthology of Papago Traditional Music*, vol. 2 (Phoenix: Canyon Records).
1977 *Papago Music and Dance* (Tsaile, Ariz.: Navajo Community College Press).

HAILE, FATHER BERARD
1934 "Religious Concepts of the Navajo Indians," *Proceedings of the Tenth Annual Meeting of the American Catholic Philosophical Association*: 84–98 (Washington, D.C.: Catholic University of America).
1937 "Some Cultural Aspects of the Navajo Hogan" (mimeographed).
1938 "Navajo Chantways and Ceremonials," *American Anthropologist* 40:639–52.
1942 "Why the Navaho Hogan?" *Primitive Man* 15:39–56.
1943 "Soul Concepts of the Navaho," *Annali Lateranensi* 7:59–94.
1947a *Prayerstick Cutting in a Five Night Ceremonial of the Male Branch of Shootingway* (Chicago: University of Chicago Press).
1947b *Head and Face Masks in Navaho Ceremonialism* (Saint Michaels, Ariz.: Saint Michaels Press).
1950a *A Stem Vocabulary of the Navaho Language. Navaho–English* (Saint Michaels, Ariz.: Saint Michaels Press).
1950b *Legend of the Ghostway Ritual in the Male Branch of Shootingway* (Saint Michaels, Ariz.: Saint Michaels Press).
1954 *Property Concepts of the Navaho Indians*, Catholic University of America Anthropological Series, no. 17 (Washington, D.C.: Catholic University of America Press).

HALL, EDWARD T.
1977 *Beyond Culture* (Garden City, N.Y.: Anchor Press/Doubleday). First published in 1976.

HALPERN, IDA
1976 "On the Interpretation of 'Meaningless–Nonsensical Syllables' in the Music of the Pacific Northwest Indians," *Ethnomusicology* 20:253–72.

HARVEY, BYRON, III
1972 "An Overview of Pueblo Religion," in *New Perspectives on the Pueblos*, ed. Alfonso Ortiz (Albuquerque: University of New Mexico Press, School of American Research Advanced Seminar Series).

HATCHER, EVELYN P.
1974 *Visual Metaphors: A Formal Analysis of Navajo Art*, American Ethnological Society Monograph no. 58 (Seattle: University of Washington Press).

HAYDEN, JULIAN D., AND C. R. STEEN
1937 *The Vikita Ceremony of the Papago*, Southwestern Monument Monthly Reports, April, pp. 263–83 (Coolidge, Ariz.: Casa Grande National Monument).

HERZOG, GEORGE
1927 A one hour tape consisting of Zuni Social, Kachina, and Corn-Grinding Songs. Pre-54-144-F. Archives of Traditional Music, Indiana University, Bloomington.
1928 "The Yuman Musical Style," *Journal of American Folklore* 41:183–231.
1930 "Musical Styles of North America," *Proceedings of International Congress of Americanists* 23:455–58.
1933 "Maricopa Music," in *The Yuman Tribes of the Gila River*, by Leslie Spier (Chicago: University of Chicago Press).
1934 "Speech Melody and Primitive Music," *Musical Quarterly* 20:452–66.
1936 "A Comparison of Pueblo and Pima Musical Styles," *Journal of American Folklore* 49:283–417.

# References

1947 "Some Linguistic Aspects of American Indian Poetry," *Word* 2:82-83.

HEWETT, EDGAR L.
1913 "The Corn Ceremony at Santo Domingo," *El Palacio* 5:69-76.

HIEB, LOUIS A.
1972 "Meaning and Mismeaning: Toward an Understanding of the Ritual Clown," in *New Perspectives on the Pueblos*, ed. Alfonso Ortiz (Albuquerque: University of New Mexico Press, School of American Research Advanced Seminar Series).

HINTON, LEANNE
1977 "Havasupai Songs: A Linguistic Perspective" (Ph.D. diss., University of California, San Diego).

HOFMANN, CHARLES
1968 *Frances Densmore and American Indian Music*, Contributions from the Museum of the American Indian, Heye Foundation, no. 23 (New York: Museum of the American Indian, Heye Foundation).

HOIJER, HARRY
1938 *Chiricahua and Mescalero Apache Texts*, University of Chicago Publications in Anthropology, Linguistic Series (Chicago: University of Chicago Press).

HUEBENER, G.
1938 "The Green Corn Dance At Santo Domingo," *El Palacio* 45:1-17.

HYMES, DELL
1962 "The Ethnography of Speaking," in *Anthropology and Human Behavior*, ed. Thomas Gladwin and William C. Sturtevant (Washington, D.C.: Anthropological Society of Washington).
1964 "Introduction : Toward Ethnographies of Communication," in *The Ethnography of Communication*, ed. John J. Gumperz and Dell Hymes. *American Anthropologist*, Special Publication, vol. 66, no. 6, pt. 2:1-34.

JEANCON, JEAN A.
1927 "Indian Music of the Southwest," *El Palacio* 23:438-47.

JETT, STEPHEN C., AND VIRGINIA S. HARRIS
n.d. *Navajo Architecture: Style, History, Geography* (Tucson: University of Arizona Press, in press).

JOHNSON, BRODERICK H. (ed.)
1969 *Denetsosie* (Rough Rock, Ariz.: Rough Rock Demonstration School, Navajo Curriculum Center).

JONES, HESTER
1931 "The Fiesta of San Geronimo at Taos," *El Palacio* 31:300-302.

JONES, RICHARD D.
1971 "The Wi'igita of Achi and Quitobac," *Kiva* 36:1-29.

JONES, ROSALIE M.
1968 "The Blackfeet Medicine Lodge Ceremony: Ritual and Dance-Drama" (M.A. Thesis, University of Utah).

KEALIINOHOMOKU, JOANN W.
1965-78 Notes from Hopi fieldwork.
1967 "Hopi and Polynesian Dance: A Study in Cross-Cultural Comparisons," *Ethnomusicology* 11:343-58.
1976 "A Comparative Study of Dance as a Constellation of Motor Behaviors among African and United States Negroes," *CORD Dance Research Annual* 7:17-179.
1978a "Hopi Social Dance Events and How They Function," *Discovery* 27-40.

# REFERENCES

1978b     "Ethnodance," in *The Religious Character of Native American Humanities*, ed. Sam D. Gill (Tempe: Arizona State University, Department of Humanities and Religious Studies).

KEECH, ROY A.
1934a     "The Pecos Ceremony at Jemez August 2, 1932," *El Palacio* 36:129–34.
1934b     "Green Corn Ceremony at the Pueblo of Sia, 1932," *El Palacio* 36:145–49.

KLUCKHOHN, CLYDE, AND DOROTHEA LEIGHTON
1946     *The Navaho* (Cambridge, Mass.: Harvard University Press).
1951     *The Navaho*, 4th printing (Cambridge, Mass.: Harvard University Press).

KLUCKHOHN, CLYDE, AND LELAND C. WYMAN
1940     *An Introduction to Navaho Chant Practice*, Memoirs of the American Anthropological Association, no. 53 (Menasha, Wisc.: American Anthropological Association).

KROEBER, ALFRED L.
1917     *Zuni Kin and Clan*, Anthropological Papers of the American Museum of Natural History, no. 18:39–204 (New York: American Museum of Natural History).

KURATH, GERTRUDE P.
1949     "Dance: Folk and Primitive," in *Dictionary of Folklore, Mythology and Legend*, ed. Maria Leach, 1:276–96 (New York: Funk and Wagnalls).
1950     "Ritual Drama," in *Dictionary of Folklore, Mythology and Legend*, 2:946–49 (New York: Funk and Wagnalls).
1953     "Native Choreographic Areas of North America," *American Anthropologist* 55:60–73.
1957     "The Origin of the Pueblo Indian Matachines," *El Palacio* 64:259–64.
1959     "Cochiti Choreographies and Songs," in *Cochiti: A New Mexico Pueblo, Past and Present*, by Charles H. Lange (Carbondale: Southern Illinois University Press).

KURATH, GERTRUDE P., AND ANTONIO GARCIA
1970     *Music and Dance of the Tewa Pueblos*, Museum of New Mexico Research Records, no. 8 (Santa Fe: Museum of New Mexico Press).

LADD, HORATIO O.
1891     *The Story of New Mexico* (Boston: D. Lothrop Co.).

LAIRD, W. DAVID
1977     *Hopi Bibliography* (Tucson: University of Arizona Press).

LAMPHERE, LOUISE
1977     *To Run After Them: Cultural and Social Bases of Cooperation in a Navajo Community* (Tucson: University of Arizona Press).

LAMPHERE, LOUISE, AND EVON Z. VOGT
1973     "Clyde Kluckhohn as Ethnographer and Student of Navaho Ceremonialism," in *Culture and Life: Essays in Memory of Clyde Kluckhohn*, ed. Walter W. Taylor, John L. Fischer, and Evon Z. Vogt (Carbondale: Southern Illinois University Press).

LANGE, CHARLES H.
1951     "King's Day Ceremonies at a Rio Grande Pueblo, January 6, 1940," *El Palacio* 58:398–406.
1954     "An Animal Dance at Santo Domingo Pueblo, January 26, 1940," *El Palacio* 61:151–55.
1959     *Cochiti: A New Mexico Pueblo, Past and Present* (Carbondale: Southern Illinois University Press).

# References

LANGE, CHARLES H., AND CARROLL L. RILEY (eds.)
1966 *The Southwestern Journals of Adolph F. Bandelier*, vol. 1 (Albuquerque: University of New Mexico Press).

LASKI, VERA
1958 *Seeking Life*, Memoirs of the American Folklore Society, vol. 50 (Philadelphia: American Folklore Society).

LA VIGNA, MARIA
n.d. "Newly Composed Music for a Winter Ceremony: The Turtle Dance Songs of San Juan Pueblo" (Ms. 1977).

LAWRENCE, D. H.
1924 "Dance of the Sprouting Corn," *Theatre Arts Monthly* 8:447–57.

LEIGHTON, ALEXANDER H., AND DOROTHEA C. LEIGHTON
1949 *Gregorio, the Hand-Trembler*, Papers of the Peabody Museum of American Archaeology and Ethnology, vol. 40, no. 1 (Cambridge, Mass.: Harvard University).

LEROY, JAMES A.
1903 "The Indian Festival at Taos," *Outing* 43:282–88.

LÉVI-STRAUSS, CLAUDE
1966 *The Savage Mind* (Chicago: University of Chicago Press).

LI, AN-CHE
1937 "Zuni: Some Observations and Queries," *American Anthropologist* 39:62–76.

LINTON, RALPH
1936 *The Study of Man* (New York: Appleton-Century-Crofts).

LIST, GEORGE
1963 "The Boundaries of Speech and Song," *Ethnomusicology* 7:1–16.

LOMAX, ALAN
1968 *Folk Song Style and Culture*, American Association for the Advancement of Science, no. 88 (Washington, D.C.: American Association for the Advancement of Science).

LUCKERT, KARL W.
1975 *The Navajo Hunter Tradition* (Tucson: University of Arizona Press).
1977 *Navajo Mountain and Rainbow Bridge Religion*, American Tribal Religions 1 (Flagstaff: Museum of Northern Arizona).

LYON, LUKE
1975 "A Calender of Pueblo Fiestas," *New Mexico Magazine* 53:6–17, 39–40.

McALLESTER, DAVID P.
1952 *Navajo Creation Chants*, pamphlet to accompany album of 5 records produced by the Peabody Museum, Harvard University.
1954 *Enemy Way Music*, Papers of the Peabody Museum of American Archaeology and Ethnology, vol. 41, no. 3 (Cambridge, Mass.: Harvard University).
1956 "The Role of Music in Western Apache Culture," in *Selected Papers of the Fifth International Congress of Anthropological and Ethnological Sciences, September 1-9: Men and Cultures*, ed. Anthony F. C. Wallace (Philadelphia: University of Pennsylvannia Press).
1961 *Indian Music in the Southwest* (Colorado Springs, Colo.: Taylor Museum).
1978 "A Different Drum: A Consideration of Music in the Native American Humanities," in *The Religious Character of Native American Humanities*, ed. Sam D. Gill (Tempe: Arizona State University, Department of Humanities and Religious Studies).
n.d. "The First Snake Song," in *Theory and Practice: Essays Presented to Gene Weltfish*, ed. Stanley Diamond (The Hague: Mouton and Co., in press). Ms. 1976. Excerpted in Witherspoon, 1977.

# REFERENCES

McALLESTER, DAVID P., AND DONALD N. BROWN
1962    *Music of the Pueblos, Apache and Navaho*, LP record and booklet (Colorado Springs, Colo.: Taylor Museum).

McCOMBE, LEONARD, EVON Z. VOGT AND CLYDE KLUCKHOHN
1951    *Navaho Means People* (Cambridge, Mass.: Harvard University Press).

MANNHEIM, L. ANDREW
1974    "Photography, Technology of," *Encyclopaedia Britannica* 14:328-46.

MASON, J. ALDEN
1920    "The Papago Harvest Festival," *American Anthropologist* 22:13-25.

MATTHEWS, WASHINGTON
1892    "A Study of Butts and Tips," *American Anthropologist* 5:345-50.
1894    "Songs of Sequence of the Navajos," *Journal of American Folklore* 7:185-94.

MERRIAM, ALAN
1967    *Ethnomusicology of the Flathead Indians*, Viking Fund Publications in Anthropology, no. 44 (New York: Viking Fund).

MERTZ, PIERRE
1974    "Motion Pictures, Technology of," *Encyclopaedia Britannica* 12:540-55.

MILLER, HUGH M.
1970    "Polynesian Dance Films in Color with Sound," *Ethnomusicology* 14:315-20.

MILLS, GEORGE T.
1957    "Art: An Introduction to Qualitative Anthropology," *Journal of Aesthetics and Art Criticism* 16:1-17.
1959    *Navaho Art and Culture* (Colorado Springs, Colo.: Taylor Museum).

MINDELEFF, COSMOS
1898    *Navaho Houses*, Annual Report of the Bureau of American Ethnology no. 17, pt. 2: 469-517 (Washington, D.C.: U.S. Government Printing Office).
1900    "Houses and House Dedication of the Navahos," *Scientific American* 82:233-34.

MINDELEFF, VICTOR
1891    *A Study of Pueblo Architecture: Tusayan and Cibola*, Annual Report of the Bureau of [American] Ethnology no. 8:3-228 (Washington, D.C.: U.S. Government Printing Office).

MOON, SHEILA
1970    *A Magic Dwells* (Middletown, Conn.: Wesleyan University Press).

NAVAJO TIMES
1971    July 29 issue.
1971    September 2 issue.
1972    June 8 issue.
1973    March 22 issue.
1973    November 29 issue.
1975    July 31 issue.
1977    April 21 issue.
1978    March 9 issue.

NETTL, BRUNO
1953    "Observations on Meaningless Peyote Song Texts," *Journal of American Folklore* 66:161-64.
1954    *North American Indian Musical Styles*, Memoirs of the American Folklore Society, no. 45 (Philadelphia: American Folklore Society).
1969    "Musical Areas Reconsidered: A Critique of North American Indian Research," in *Essays in Musicology in Honor of Dragan Plamenac on His 70th*

# References

        *Birthday*, ed. Gustave Reese and Robert Snow (Pittsburg: University of Pittsburgh Press).
NEWCOMB, FRANC J.
1956    "Navajo Symbols in Sand Paintings and Ritual Objects," in *A Study of Navajo Symbolism* by Franc J. Newcomb, Stanley Fishler, and Mary Wheelwright. Papers of the Peabody Museum of Archaeology and Ethnology, vol. 32, no. 3 (Cambridge, Mass.: Harvard University).
1964    *Hosteen Klah: Navajo Medicine Man and Sand Painter* (Norman: University of Oklahoma Press).
NEWCOMB, FRANC J., AND GLADYS A. REICHARD
1937    *Sandpaintings of the Navajo Shooting Chant* (New York: J. J. Augustin).
NEWMAN, STANLEY
1965    *Zuni Grammar*, University of New Mexico Publications in Anthropology, no. 14 (Albuquerque: University of New Mexico Press).
NICHOLAS, DAN
1939    "Mescalero Apache Girl's Puberty Ceremony," *El Palacio* 46:193–204.
NORMAN, ROSAMUND
1960    "A Look at the Papago 'Wikita'," *Masterkey* 34:98–101.
OPLER, MARVIN K.
1939    "The Southern Ute Dog-Dance and its Reported Transmission to Taos," *New Mexico Anthropologist* 3:66–72.
OPLER, MORRIS E.
1942    "Adolescence Rite of the Jicarilla," *El Palacio* 49:25–38.
1946    *Childhood and Youth in Jicarilla Apache Society*, Publications of the Frederick Webb Hodge Anniversary Publication Fund, vol. 5 (Los Angeles, Calif.: Southwest Museum).
1965    *An Apache Life-Way* (New York: Cooper Square Publishers). First published in 1941.
ORTIZ, ALFONSO
1969    *The Tewa World* (Chicago: University of Chicago Press).
1972    "Ritual Drama and Pueblo World View," in *New Perspectives on the Pueblos*, ed. Alfonso Ortiz (Albuquerque: University of New Mexico Press, School of American Research Advanced Seminar Series).
OSTERMANN, FATHER LEOPOLD
1917    "Navajo Houses," *Franciscan Missions of the Southwest* 5:20–30.
PANCOAST, CHALMERS L.
1918    "The Last Dance of the Picuris," *American Museum Journal* 18:308–11.
PANDEY, TRILOKI N.
1978    "Some Reflections on Zuni Religion," in *The Religious Character of Native American Humanities*, ed. Sam D. Gill (Tempe: Arizona State University, Department of Humanities and Religious Studies).
PARSONS, ELSIE CLEWS
1922    *Winter and Summer Dance Series in Zuni*, University of California Publications in American Archaeology and Ethnology, no. 17:169–216 (Berkeley: University of California).
1925 (ed.)    *A Pueblo Indian Journal 1920–1921*, Memoirs of the American Anthropological Association, no. 32 (Menasha, Wisc.: American Anthropological Association).
1932    *Isleta, New Mexico*, Annual Report of the Bureau of American Ethnology no. 47:193–446 (Washington, D.C.: U.S. Government Printing Office).
1933    *Hopi and Zuni Ceremonialism*, Memoirs of the American Anthropological Association, no. 39 (Menasha, Wisc.: American Anthropological Association).

## REFERENCES

1936a   *Hopi Journal of Alexander M. Stephen*, pt. 1 (New York: Columbia University
(ed.)    Press).
1936b   *Taos Pueblo*, General Series in Anthropology, no. 2 (Menasha, Wisc.: George Banta Publishing Co.).
1939a   "Picuris, New Mexico," *American Anthropologist* 41:206–22.
1939b   *Pueblo Indian Religion*, vols. 1 and 2 (Chicago: University of Chicago Press).

REICHARD, GLADYS A.
1934   *Spider Woman: A Story of Navajo Weavers and Chanters* (New York: Macmillan Co.).
1939   *Navajo Medicine Man* (New York: J.J. Augustin).
1944   *Prayer: The Compulsive Word*, Monographs of the American Ethnological Society, no. 7 (Seattle: University of Washington Press).
1950   *Navaho Religion: A Study of Symbolism*, vols. 1 and 2, Bollingen Series 18 (New York: Bollingen Foundation).
1963   *Navaho Religion*, 2d ed., Bollingen Series 18 (New York: Pantheon Books).

RHODES, ROBERT
1977   *Hopi Music and Dance* (Tsaile, Ariz.: Navajo Community College Press).

RHODES, WILLARD
1952   "Acculturation in North American Indian Music," in *Acculturation in the Americas, Proceedings and Selected Papers of the Twenty-ninth International Congress of Americanists*, ed. Sol Tax, 2:127–132 (New York: Cooper Square Publishers).

ROBERTS, DON L.
1964   "A Brief Guide to Rio Grande Pueblo Dances," *Quarterly of the Southwestern Association on Indian Affairs* 1:12–15.
1972   "The Ethnomusicology of the Eastern Pueblos," in *New Perspectives on the Pueblos*, ed. Alfonso Ortiz (Albuquerque: University of New Mexico Press, School of American Research Advanced Seminar Series).

ROBERTS, HELEN H.
1923   "Chakwena Songs of Zuni and Laguna," *Journal of American Folklore* 36:177–84.
1927   "Indian Music from the Southwest," *Natural History* 27:257–65.
1936   *Musical Areas in Aboriginal North America*, Yale University Publications in Anthropology, no. 12 (New Haven, Conn.: Yale University Press).

ROEDIGER, VIRGINIA M.
1941   *Ceremonial Costumes of the Pueblo Indians* (Berkeley and Los Angeles: University of California Press).
1961   *Ceremonial Costumes of the Pueblo Indians*, 2d printing (Berkeley and Los Angeles: University of California Press).

ROESSEL, ROBERT, JR.
1967   *Indian Communities in Action* (Tempe: Arizona State University Bureau of Publications).

ROYCE, ANYA P.
1974   "Choreology Today: A Review of the Field," *CORD Research Annual* 6:47–84.
1977   *The Anthropology of Dance* (Bloomington: Indiana University Press).

RUSSELL, FRANK
1975   *The Pima Indians*, re-edition with introduction, citation sources, and bibliography by Bernard L. Fontana (Tucson: University of Arizona Press). First edition, 1908.

SAPIR, EDWARD
1949   "Why Cultural Anthropology Needs the Psychiatrist," in *Selected Writings of*

# References

*Edward Sapir in Language, Culture, and Personality*, ed. David G. Mandelbaum (Berkeley and Los Angeles: University of California Press).

SAXTON, DEAN, AND LUCILLE SAXTON
1969 *Dictionary: Papago and Pima to English/English to Papago and Pima* (Tucson: University of Arizona Press).
1973 *O'otham Hoho'ok A'agitha: Legends and Lore of the Papago and Pima Indians* (Tucson: University of Arizona Press).

SCHECHNER, RICHARD
1977 *Essays on Performance Theory, 1970-1976* (New York: Drama Book Specialists, Publishers).

SCHWARTZ, DOUGLAS W.
1956 "The Havasupai 600 A.D.-1955 A.D.," *Plateau* 28:77-85.
1959 "Culture Area and Time Depth: The Four Worlds of the Havasupai," *American Anthropologist* 61:1060-70.

SEKAQUAPTEWA, EMORY
n.d. Personal communication to Joann Kealiinohomoku.

SHEETS, MAXINE
1966 *The Phenomenology of Dance* (Madison: University of Wisconsin Press).

SIMMONS, LEO W. (ed.)
1942 *Sun Chief* (New Haven, Conn.: Yale University Press).

SINGER, MILTON
1958 "The Great Tradition in a Metropolitan Center: Madras," *Journal of American Folklore* 71:347-88.
1972 *When a Great Tradition Modernizes* (New York: Praeger Publishers).

SLOANE, ERIC
1962 "The Man Who Invented the Hoop Dance," *New Mexico Magazine* 40:3-5,36.

SMITH, MICHAEL G.
1975 *Corporations and Society: The Social Anthropology of Collective Action* (Chicago: Aldine Publishing Co.).

SMITHSON, CARMA L.
1959 *The Havasupai Woman* (Salt Lake City: University of Utah Press).

SMITHSON, CARMA L., AND ROBERT EULER
1964 *Havasupai Religion and Mythology* (Salt Lake City: University of Utah Press).

SNYDER, ALLEGRA F.
1965 "Three Kinds of Dance Films," *Dance Magazine* 39:34-39.

SORENSON, E. RICHARD
1967 "A Research Film Program in the Study of Changing Man," *Current Anthropology* 8:443-69.

SPENCER, KATHERINE
1957 *Mythology and Values: An Analysis of Navaho Chantway Myths*, Memoirs of the American Folklore Society, vol. 48 (Philadelphia: American Folklore Society).

SPENCER, VIRGINIA C., AND STEPHEN C. JETT
1971 "Navajo Dwellings of Rural Black Creek Valley, Arizona-New Mexico," *Plateau* 43:159-75.

SPIER, LESLIE
1928 *Havasupai Ethnography*, Anthropological Papers of the American Museum of Natural History, vol. 29, no. 3:83-292 (New York: American Museum of Natural History).

# REFERENCES

1929    "Problems Arising from the Classification of the Havasupais," *American Anthropologist* 31:213-22.

SPINDEN, HERBERT J.
1915    "Indian Dances of the Southwest," *American Museum Journal* 15:103-15.

STACEY, REID
1907    "Some Zuni Ceremonies and Melodies," *The Music-Lover's Calendar* 2:54-61.

STEVENSON, MATILDA C.
1904    *The Zuni Indians: Their Mythology, Esoteric Fraternities, and Ceremonies*, Annual Report of the Bureau of American Ethnology no. 23:1-608 (Washington, D.C.: U.S. Government Printing Office).

STEWARD, JULIAN H.
1931    "Notes on Hopi Ceremonies in the Initiatory Form in 1927-28," *American Anthropologist* 33:56-79.

SUNDBERG, JOHAN
1969    "Articulatory Differences Between Spoken and Sung Vowels in Singers," *Speech Transmission Laboratory Quarterly Progress and Status Report* (Stockholm), April 15, pp. 33-46.

SWEET, JILL D.
1976    "Space, Time, and Festival: An Analysis of a San Juan Fiesta" (Ms), pp. 1-14.

1978    "Ritual Play, Role Reversal and Humor: Symbolic Elements of a Tewa Pueblo Navajo Dance," paper presented at the CORD/ADG Conference, Honolulu.

TAYLOR, WALTER W., JOHN L. FISCHER, AND EVON Z. VOGT (eds.)
1973    *Culture and Life: Essays in Memory of Clyde Kluckhohn* (Carbondale: Southern Illinois University Press).

TEDLOCK, BARBARA
1973    "Kachina Dance Songs in Zuni Society: The Role of Esthetics in Social Integration" (M.A. Thesis, Wesleyan University, Middletown, Conn.).

TITIEV, MISCHA
1944    *Old Oraibi: A Study of the Hopi Indians of Third Mesa*, Papers of the Peabody Museum of American Archaeology and Ethnology, vol. 22, no. 1 (Cambridge, Mass.: Harvard University).

1960    "A Fresh Approach to the Problem of Magic and Religion," *Southwestern Journal of Anthropology* 16:292-98.

1972    *The Hopi Indians of Old Oraibi* (Ann Arbor: University of Michigan Press).

TROYER, CARLOS
1904a    *Traditional Songs of the Zuni Indians* (Newton Center, Mass.: Wa-Wan Press).

1904b    *Zuni Lover's Wooing, or Blanket Song* (Philadelphia: Theodore Presser Co.).

1904c    *Invocation to the Sun God* (Philadelphia: Theodore Presser Co.).

1904d    *The Sunrise Call or Echo Song* (Philadelphia: Theodore Presser Co.).

1904e    *Incantation Upon a Sleeping Infant* (Philadelphia: Theodore Presser Co.).

1909a    *Hymn to the Sun* (Philadelphia: Theodore Presser Co.).

1909b    *Sunset Song* (Philadelphia: Theodore Presser Co.)

1909c    *Indian Fire Drill Song* (Philadelphia: Theodore Presser Co.).

1913    *Indian Music Lecture: The Zuni Indians and their Music* (Philadelphia: Theodore Presser Co.).

n.d.a    *Rise Ye, Hunters Brave*, unpublished musical score located in the Yale University Musical Score Archive, New Haven, Conn.

# References

n.d.b    *Now Rest Thee in Peace*, unpublished musical score located in the Yale University Musical Score Archive, New Haven, Conn.

TURNER, VICTOR
1967   *The Forest of Symbols* (Ithaca, N.Y.: Cornell University Press).
1969   *The Ritual Process* (Chicago: Aldine Publishing Co.).

UNDERHILL, RUTH M.
1938a   *A Papago Calendar Record*, University of New Mexico Bulletin no. 322, Anthropological Series, vol. 2, no. 5 (Albuquerque: University of New Mexico Press).
1938b   *Singing for Power: The Song Magic of the Papago Indians of Southern Arizona* (Berkeley: University of California Press).
1939   *Social Organization of the Papago Indians*, Columbia University Contributions to Anthropology, vol. 30 (New York: Columbia University Press).
1946   *Papago Indian Religion* (New York: Columbia University Press).

U.S. BUREAU OF THE CENSUS
1973   *Census of Population, 1970, Vol. 1, Characteristics of the Population, Part 33, New Mexico* (Washington, D.C.: U.S. Government Printing Office).

VAN GENNEP, ARNOLD
1960   *The Rites of Passage* (Chicago: University of Chicago Press). First published in 1908.

VENNARD, WILLIAM
   *Singing: The Mechanism and the Technic*, rev. ed. (New York; Carl Fischer).

VILLASEÑOR, DAVID
1963   *Tapestries in Sand* (Healdsburg, Calif.: Naturegraph Company).

VOEGELIN, C. F., AND R. C. EULER
1957   "Introduction to Hopi Chants," *Journal of American Folklore* 70:115-36.

VON SYDOW, C. W.
1965   "Folktale Studies and Philology: Some Points of View," reprinted in *The Study of Folklore*, ed. Alan Dundes (Englewood Cliffs, N.J.: Prentice-Hall). Originally published in 1948.

VORSE, MARY H.
1930   "Deer Dance in Taos," *The Nation* 131 (August 13):178-79.

WAGNER, ROLAND
1975a   "Pattern and Process in Ritual Syncretism: The Case of Peyotism Among the Navajo," *Journal of Anthropological Research* 31:162-81.
1975b   "Some Pragmatic Aspects of Navaho Peyotism," *Plains Anthropologist* 20:197-205.

WALKER, WILLARD
1966   "Inflectional Class and Taxonomic Structure in Zuni," *International Journal of American Linguistics* 32:217-26.

WALLACE, ANTHONY C.
1966   *Religion: An Anthropological View* (New York: Random House).

WATERS, FRANK
1950   *Masked Gods* (Albuquerque: University of New Mexico Press).

WEAD, CHARLES K.
1900   "The Study of Primitive Music," *American Anthropologist* 2:75-79.

WHITE, LESLIE A.
1932   *The Pueblo of San Felipe*, Memoirs of the American Anthropological Association, no. 38 (Menasha, Wisc.: American Anthropological Association).
1935   *The Pueblo of Santo Domingo, New Mexico*, Memoirs of the American Anthropological Association, no. 43 (Menasha, Wisc.: American Anthropological Association).

# REFERENCES

1942    "Louis H. Morgan's Journal of a Trip to Southwestern Colorado and New
(ed.)    Mexico, June 21 to August 7, 1878," *American Antiquity* 8:1–26.
1962    *The Pueblo of Sia, New Mexico*, Bulletin of the Bureau of American Ethnology no. 184 (Washington, D.C.: U.S. Government Printing Office).

WHITMAN, WILLIAM
1947    *The Pueblo Indians of San Ildefonso*, Columbia University Contributions to Anthropology, no. 34 (New York: Columbia University Press).

WILLIAMS, AUBREY W., JR.
1970    *Navajo Political Process*, Smithsonian Contributions to Anthropology, no. 9 (Washington, D.C.: Smithsonian Institution Press).

WILSON, EDMUND
1956    *Red, Black, Blond, and Olive: Studies in Four Civilizations: Zuni, Haiti, Soviet Russia, Israel* (New York: Oxford University Press).

WITHERSPOON, GARY
1974    "The Central Concepts of Navajo World View: I," *Linguistics* 119:41–59.
1975a    "The Central Concepts of Navajo World View: II," *Linguistics* 161:69–87.
1975b    *Navajo Kinship and Marriage* (Chicago: University of Chicago Press).
1977    *Language and Art in the Navajo Universe* (Ann Arbor: University of Michigan Press).

WYMAN, LELAND C.
1936    "The Female-Shooting Life Chant: A Minor Navaho Ceremony," *American Anthropologist* 38:634–53.
1952    *The Sandpaintings of the Kayenta Navaho*, University of New Mexico Publications in Anthropology 7 (Albuquerque: University of New Mexico Press).
1960    *Navaho Sandpainting: The Huckel Collection* (Colorado Springs, Colo.: Taylor Museum).
1963    *The Red Antway of the Navaho*, Navajo Religion Series, vol. 5 (Santa Fe: Museum of Navajo Ceremonial Art).
1970a    *Sandpaintings of the Navaho Shootingway and the Walcott Collection*, Smithsonian Contributions to Anthropology, no. 13 (Washington, D.C.: Smithsonian Institution Press).
1970b    *Blessingway* (Tucson: University of Arizona Press).
1972a    "A Navajo Medicine Bundle for Shootingway," *Plateau* 44:131–49.
1972b    "Navajo Ceremonial Equipment in the Museum of Northern Arizona," *Plateau* 45:17–30.
1972c    "Ten Sandpaintings from Male Shootingway," *Plateau* 45:55–67.

WYMAN, LELAND C. AND CLYDE KLUCKHOHN
1938    *Navaho Classification of Their Song Ceremonials*, Memoirs of the American Anthropological Association, no. 50 (Menasha, Wisc.: American Anthropological Association).

# Index

Aberle, David F., 162
aesthetics, 33–34. *See also* ritual drama, aesthetics of
Adair, John, 162
Ak Cin, Arizona, 261
Albuquerque Inter-tribal Dancers, 120
Alvarez, Albert, 271n
*American Heritage Dictionary*, 57
Anderson, Robert, 171
Anglo, 167, 174–75, 192–93, 244, 272
Anthropological Film Center, Santa Fe, 101
Athapaskan, 167
antidotes, Hopi 57–58
Apache, 34, 35, 71; Chiricahua 126, 158; Cibique, 126; Jicarilla, 126; Mescalero, 126, 312–13; raids on Papago, 241
Appelman, D. Ralph, 297
arbor. *See also* structures, ritual
audiences, of ritual drama, 322–26; Anglo-American, 322; Havasupai, 292–93, 323–25; Hopi, 323–26; Mescalero Apache, 323–25; Navajo, 322–25; Papago, 323–24; Pueblo, 323; Taos, 322, 325; Zuni, 30–33, 322–23, 325–26
augmentation, principle in Navajo ritual symbolism, 234–35

Baboquivari High School, Sells, Arizona, 248
Bahr, Donald M., 6n, 239, 271n, 277
Bailey, Florence Merriam, 72, 162
balance, 128, 149
Bala-Sinem Choir, Fort Lewis College, Durango, Colorado, 330

Bandelier, Adolph F., 117
Barnes, Nellie, 8
Barthelmess, Christian, 73
Basso, Keith H., 156
Bateson, Gregory, 6n
Bauman, Richard, 155, 172, 174
Beaglehole, Earnest, 39, 58
Beck, Peggy, 6n
Bidney, David, 91n
Black, Robert A., ix
blacks, 51, 110
Blanchard, Kendall A., 164
Blue Eyes, 235n
Breuninger, Evelyn P., 126
Brown, Donald N., ix, 4, 74, 101, 104, 317, 333, 341–42
Brugge, David M., 162, 164, 196n
Buffalo Dance. *See* dances, list of
buildings and structures, Navajo blessing of: Cultural Center at the Chicago Circle Campus, 169; EPI/Vostron plant, 168; Etsitty hogan, 197; Fort Defiance PHS hospital, 196, 198; Fred Harvey Hotel El Navajo, Gallup, 168, 179, 186, 191, 197–98; Gallup Stadium, 186; General Dynamics plant, 168; Kinlichee Chapter House, 168; Museum of Navajo Ceremonial Art, 192; Newberry Library Center, 169; Tribal Council Chamber, 168; Western Navajo fairgrounds, 168
Bunzel, Ruth 9, 11–12, 21–22, 33, 34n
Bureau of Indian Affairs Boarding School, San Xavier, Arizona, 249
burlesques, Tewa female, 320
Buttree, Julia M., 119

361

## INDEX

calendar, ceremonial, 10–13; Pueblo, 108–24
cameras, 95
Canyon Records, 272
Catholic, 104, 109
Catholic, church, 264; mass, 295; missionary, 184; nun, 110; priest, 104, 110
Cavallo-Bosso, J. R., 10
ceremonies, list of: Blessingway, 278; *celkona*: as an intervillage festivity, 262–63; dance movements of, 267–68; definition of term, 258–59; description of, 244–54; in Piman ethnography, 240–48; list of performers, 265; list of recorded ceremonies, 242; music of, 266–67; purpose of, 259–63; sequence of events, 246–47. *See also* dances, list of *and* songs. Corn Grinding, Santa Ana, 123; curing, Navajo: Ghostway, 161; Holyway, 161; Lifeway, 161; curing, Papago, 239; Enemyway, 315; Girls' Coming-of-Age, Papago, 240; Girls' Puberty, discussion of, 126–28, 146–55; Mescalero Apache, 313, 318, 320, 323–24, 330; purpose of, 155; rite of confirmation and intensification, 153–54; Harvest, Papago, 310–11; House Blessing, 317, 321, 325, 327: classification of, 162; focus of, 165–66; historical development and purpose of, 166–67; marking of the hogan, 178–80; myth, 171; personnel of, 176; prayers of, 180–86; private version of, 172–73; public version of, 172–77; research of, 164–65; ritual components of, 161, 170, 191–92; ritual drama in, 170–72; songs of, 188–91; symbolism of, 179–80; Kachina, Santa Ana, 116; Kwirana, San Felipe, 115; Nightway, 316, 323, 328; Purification, Papago, 240; Shalako, 316; Shootingway, 317, 326: features of, 203–4; interpretations of, 230–35; myth of, 201–3; Sun, Papago, 243–44; Wine, Papago, 314; Winter Solstice, Zuni, 316; Yeibichai, 315–16, 323
ceremonies. *See also* dance; dances, list of; feasts, *and* festivals
Chapple, Eliot D., 6n
Chemehuevi, 278
Chesky, Jane, 246, 261–62, 264, 271–73
child rearing, Hopi, 59–67

Children's Shrine, Santa Rosa, 255
Chilkovsky, Nadia, 94
Chinle, Arizona, 236
Christian Church, 3
circularity, 128; Mescalero Apache, 147, 149–50
Clark, Laverne H., 126
Clitso, Keel, 184
Clown Society, Picuris, 72, 313
clowns 29–30, 32–33, 54, 57–58, 64, 72, 76, 137, 139, 308, 327; Eastern Pueblo, 105, 117; Hopi, 46–47, 312–13; Taos, 313; Zuni, 9, 29–33, 325. *See also* Mudheads
Cochití Dam, 121
Coconino Plateau, Arizona, 277
Cohen, Felix, 194
color, symbolism of, 132–33, 144
Columbia University, 235
Comanche, 71
communication, high-context, 152
compensation of ritual drama *personae*, 318–19; baskets, 318; blankets, 318; cash, 318; food, 318–19; jewelry: *see* personal adornment
Conference for Eastern Navajo Educators, 169
Coon, Carleton S. 6n
Corn Dance. *See* dancers, list of
Corn Pollen Queen, 176, 194
costume, ritual, 29–30, 88, 93, 148–51, 153–54, 309, 334; armband, 177; belts, 51, 309, leather, 137; blouse, 268–69; body painting, 157–58; boots, cowboy, 252, 268–69, women's, 80; bow tie, black, 273; chaps, 83–84; concho belt, 177; dress, black manta, 76, 80, buckskin, 157, cloth, 157, girls', 143, war, 245, woman's, 65, 110, 252, 269; G string, 142; garters, 51; hat, cowboy, 252, 269; hats, old style, 177; head band, 142, 177; head covering, 137; headdresses, 112, 137, 149, 158, 309; heel bands, skunk tail, 76; jacket, 269; jeans, blue, 268–69; kilt, 65, 80, 137, 149, 268, 309, Hopi, 76; Levis, 142; mantle, buckskin, 75; moccasins, 43, 76, 128, 309, buckskin, 137, 142, 149, 177; of Mountain Gods, 148–52; Navajo, 177, 230; overblouse, buckskin, 128, 148; purses, 321; repair of, 341; robe, buffalo, 177; sash, 137, 149, 177, 268–69; scarf, 252, 268–69; shawl, 140, 252,

362

# Index

scarf, 252, 268–69; shawl, 140, 252, 269; shirt, 142, 268–69, cotton, 177, velvet, 177; shoes, 177; skirt, 52, 177, 268–69; skirt, buckskin, 128, 130, 148; slacks, 252, 268; suitcoat, 177; T-shirt, 252, 268; trousers, 177, 268; tunic, 268; vest, buckskin 177. *See also* paraphernalia, ritual
Covered Wells, Arizona, 260
creativity, role of, 326–30
Crow-Wing, 39
Crownpoint, 197
curers, 329
Curly, River Junction, 162
Curly, Slim, 162
Curtis, Edward S., 73, 162
Curtis, Natalie, 8, 162
Cushing, Frank Hamilton, 7–8

dance, analysis of Picuris and Taos dances, 74–75, 85–90; discussion of Southwestern Indian, 313–315; music, *chicken scratch*, 272; patterns of movement, 313–15; style, New Mexico, 314. *See also* ceremonies; dances, list of; *and* motion pictures
dancers, clown, 261; Mountain God, 136
dances, list of: Acoma, at Santo Domingo, 116; African and Jazz, 95; *Antegeshare* (Footlifting), 105, San Ildefonso, 115, 117, Santa Ana, 116; Animal, 104, 308–10: Picuris, 85, 314, San Felipe, 114, Taos, 72, 87, 311, 314; Apache, *Gahan*, at Zia, 110; Aztec, at Laguna, 120; Back and Forth, Havasupai, 310, 313, Mescalero, 313, Mojave, 313, Navajo, 315; Basket, 105; Jemez, 122, Picuris, 73, 75, 119, San Felipe, 123, San Ildefonso, 115, 117, San Juan, 105, 115, Santa Ana, 116, Santa Clara, 105, 116, Santo Domingo, 120; Bean, 38, 50, Hopi, 105–6; Belt, San Ildefonso, 115: *see also* Sash; Bird, 310; Borrowed, Eastern Pueblo, 105, 108; Bow and Arrow, 105: Jemez, 113, San Felipe, 121–23, San Ildefonso, 117, San Juan, 111, 116, Santo Domingo, 111, Tesuque, 124; Bow Priesthood, 10, 12; Buffalo, 97: Acoma, 112, Cochití, 110–13, 122, Jemez, 111, 122, Laguna, 114, Picuris, 75, San Felipe, 114, 122, San Juan, 111, 119, Santa Ana, 116, 123, Santa Clara, 96, 111, 118, Santo Domingo, 111, 116, 121, 123, Sandia, 111, Taos, 72, 86–88, 111, Tesuque, 124, Zia, 124, Zuni, 321; Butterfly: Picuris, 114, San Felipe, 111, San Juan, 115, Sandia, 111, 123; *celkona*, 263–70, Gu Aji village, 250–54; Child Coming Out, 11–12; Children's, Taos, 73; Christmas, Cochití, 121, Isleta, 122; Circle, 12, 311, 313, 325: Havasupai, 283–86, 311–13, Hopi, 313, Mescalero Apache, 310, 313, Navajo, 310, 313, 315, Papago, 311, 313–14, Santo Domingo, 116, Zuni, 313; Cloud, San Juan, 115; Comanche: Cochití, 122, Nambé, 121, San Ildefonso, 111–12, San Juan, 108, 119, Santa Clara, 119, Santo Domingo, 116, Zuni, 13; Corn, 97, 104, 107, 109, 119: Cochití, 107, 110, 117–19, Isleta, 107, 120, Jemez, 107, 110, 117–18, Laguna, 107, 120, Picuris, 75, 82–84, 89, 119–20, 314, San Felipe, 107, 118, 123, San Ildefonso, 118, 120, San Juan, 119, 187, Sandia, 107, 118, Santa Ana, 107, 110, 117–19, 123, Santa Clara, 119, Santo Domingo, 107, 110, 118–20, 124, 330, Taos, 72, 107, 111, 119, 314, Tesuque, 121, Zia, 107, 119, 195; Corn Maiden (*Pogonshare*): San Juan, 115, Santa Clara, 116, Tesuque, 124; Corral, 315; Council of the Gods, 12; Crow, Zia, 110–11; Deer, 105: Acoma, 112, Cochití, 122, Picuris, 75–85; 87; 89–92, 119, San Ildefonso, 111, San Juan, 106, 115–16, Santa Clara, 116, Taos, 72–73, 88, 124; Devil, 152; Dog, (*Halowa*), 73; Dragonfly Medicine Society Initiation, 12; Eagle: Acoma, 112; Cochití, 111, 122, Jemez, 110, Laguna, 114, 120, San Felipe, 114, 122, Sandia, 111, Santo Domingo, 117; Easter, 112, 117; Elk: Cochití, 111, Nambé, 121, Picuris, 73, 75; Evergreen, Isleta, 113; Feast Day, 107, 120: Acoma, 120, Isleta, 120, Jemez, 121, Laguna, 120, Nambé, 121, San Ildefonso, 111; Sandia, 118, Santa Clara, 119, Tesuque, 121, Zia, 119; Feather, 315, Picuris, 75; Fire, 315; First Night Shootingway, details of, 211–17; Footlifting (*Antegeshare*), 105, San Ildefonso, 115, 117, Santa

363

# INDEX

dances, list of—*cont*.
Ana, 116; Foreign, 104, Game Animal, 106, 111–12: Cochití, 107, 113, 122, Jemez, 107, 110, 111, 122, Nambé, 121, San Felipe, 107, 112, 114, 121–23, San Ildefonso, 107, 111, Santa Ana, 107, 111, 116, 123, Santa Clara, 96–97, Santo Domingo, 107, 116, Zia, 107, 110, 124; Ghost, 276, 278, 293; Going in the Middle Dance (Parrot), 105: San Felipe, 114–15, Santo Domingo, 117; Good Kachina, 11; Governor's, Acoma, 112; Green Corn, San Felipe, 114, San Juan 117; *Halowa* (Dog), 73; Hand, Taos, 117; Harvest, 10, 12–14, 107: Havasupai, 313, Jemez, 121, San Juan, 120, Taos, 313, Tewa, 313; *Hemis* Kachina, 105, 115; *Hemis Kachinmana*, 105; *hilili*, 11, 13; Hoop, 335; Hopi, Jemez, 110, San Felipe, 114, San Felipe, 114, Santo Domingo, 116, 121, 123; Hopi Buffalo, San Juan, 111, Tesuque, 111; Hopi Kachina, San Felipe, 123; Horse, Santo Domingo, 124; Hunting, 111, San Felipe, 122–23, Santo Domingo, 124; Jemez People, 12; Kachina, 12–13, 308; Eastern Pueblo, 104–05, Hopi, 314, Zuni, 314; Kachina Society, 10; Kiowa, 98, San Felipe, 122; Kiowa Shield, Jemez, 113; Koeyihiyna, 272; Koshare Society, San Felipe, 114; Laguna Corn, Jemez, 118; Laguna Rain God, Cochití, 122; Line, 310, 314, San Felipe, 114; Masked, Hopi, 278; Maskless Kachina, 105, 107, 112: Isleta (Laguna Colony), 113, Jemez, 110, San Felipe, 110, Santa Ana, 110, Zia, 110; Matachina, 108, 314: Jemez, 110, 121, San Felipe, 108, 114, San Felipe, 108, 114, San Ildefonso, 123, San Juan, 108, 123, Sandia, 123, Santa Clara, 111, 116, Santo Domingo, 108, 116, Taos, 72, 87, 124, Yaqui, 314; Medicine Society, 10, Zuni, 311; Mexican, San Felipe, 114, 180, Santo Domingo, 116; Mixed Animal, 11, Hopi, 12, Mountain Sheep, Picuris, 119, San Felipe, 122; Navajo, Cochití, 122, Jemez, 113, San Felipe, 112, 114, 123, Santo Domingo, 117, 123–24; Navajo Skip, San Felipe, 112; Night, 50, 316, Isleta, 113, Sandia, 111, Santo Domingo, 111, Night Kachina, 10, 12–13, 50; Northern Tiwa, 4; Old Child Coming Out, 12; Paiute, Santo Domingo, 116; Parrot, 105, San Felipe, 114–15, Santo Domingo, 117; Pecos Bull. *See* Corn, Jemez *above*; Plains Butterfly, San Felipe, 123; Plains, Zia, 110; *Pogonshare* (Corn Maiden), San Juan, 115, Santa Clara, 116, Tesuque, 124; *Powamua* (Snake), 38, 41–42, 50, 114; Race, Picuris, 73; Rain, 152; Rainbow, Jemez, 110. *See also Pogonshare*; Round, Papago, 250, 261; Run in the Middle, Papago, 243, 272; Saint's Day, Taos, 73; Sandaro, Santo Domingo, 116; Sash, Santa Clara, 111. *See also* Belt; Scalp, 12, 72; Secret, 105; Semi-Secret, 105; Shalako, 10, 12, 14, 35n; Shield, Picuris, 73; Sitting at Stool, 12; Skip-Trot, Navajo, 315; Skipping, Papago, 317, 323, Slender Toad, 12; Snake *(Powamua)*, 38, 41–42, 50, 114; Social, 105, 108, 311, Havasupai, 293, Hopi, 314, Zia, 118; Social, Spanish, 330; Squash Blossom. *See* Pogonshare; Squaw, Navajo, 228; Summer, 10–11, 14, 30; Summer Rain, 11; Sun, Papago, 260, 272; Sundown, Taos, 72, 121; Supai, Santo Domingo, 124; Sweathouse, 325; Traditional Round, Sil Nakia, 261; Transvestite, San Juan, 115; Turtle, 105, Isleta, 113, San Ildefonso, 117, San Juan, 123, Taos, 72–73, 110, 308; Ute Bear, 24; Ute, Santo Domingo, 124; War, Jemez, 110, Picuris, 73, Zia, 124; Winter, 10–11, 14; Women's, San Ildefonso, 115; Women's Medicine Societies', Hopi, 314; Yellow Corn, San Juan, 115

dances, movies of. *See* motion pictures
dances, Plains, 335
dances, Plains style, 336
Deer Dance. *See* dances, list of
Densmore, Frances, 2, 8–9, 112, 116, 119, 244, 272, 277
deities, God 131, 133, in Navajo Ceremonies, Buffalo People, 199, 202; Changing Woman, 165–66; Coyote, 202; Dark Wind, 201–2;

## Index

deities—*cont.*
Enemy Slayer, 205; Holy Boy, 201–02; Holy Girl, 202; Holy People, 165, 167, 170–71, 181, 200, 202; Holy Young Man, 201–03, 205; Jackrabbit, 202; Lightning, 202; Moon, 199, 201–02; Mother Earth, 179, 184; Mountain Woman, 166; Sandhill Crane, 215; Snake Girls, 199; Snake People, 201; Spider Woman, 205; Stars, 202; Sun, 166, 179, 199–202, 205; Talking God, 179, 205; Water, 202, 205; Water Woman, 166; Winds, 199, 202; Wood Woman, 166; Yellow Wind, 201–02;
deities, in Zuni ceremonies, Blue Corn Girls, 16–17; Moon Mother, 23; Yellow Corn Girls, 16–17
directionality, Mescalero Apache, 147–49, 158
Dobyns, Henry, 276
doctrine of signatures, Hopi, 58–59, 61, 66, 68
Dodge, Henry Chee, 167
dogs, Navajo, 322–23
Domínguez, Fray Francisco Atanasio, 72
Doris Duke Foundation, University of Arizona, 271n
Dozier, Edward, 104
drama, presentational, 37
drama, representational, 37
dramatic techniques, Hopi, 51–53
drumming, Plains style, 335
Durán Ramos, 76, 78, 85, 88–90, 92
Driskell, Wanda, x
Dutton, Bertha P., 108

Eagle Dance. *See* dances, list of
East Mountain, Arizona, 158
Eickemeyer, Carl and Lillian, 72
*El Palacio*, Navajo issue, 164
epidemics, among Havasupai, 278
Estergreen, Marion, 72
ethnicity, Mescalero Apache, 146
ethnohistory, Mescalero Apache, 125, 147
Euler, Robert, 276–77

falsetto, 309, Hopi Mother, 51; Southern Athapaskan, 312
farming, Havasupai, 277
Farrer, Claire R., ix, 4, 159, 312–13, 320, 328, 332, 338, 340–41
feasts, Havasupai communal, 294; Papago Saguaro Wine, 239, 250
Feld, Steve, 101

Fergusson, Erna, 39, 72, 112, 119
festivals, Havasupai Harvest, 294; Havasupai Peach, 278; Havasupai Prayer Stick, 260; Papago Harvest, 239, 243
Fewkes, Jesse Walter, 2
fiesta, San Geronimo, Taos, 121
Fillmore, John Comfort, 7, 34n
film, types of, 95, 98
films of dances. *See* motion pictures
First Mesa, 40–41, 45, 47, 49–51, 65, 67n–69
Fishler, Stanley A., 162
Fontana, Bernard, 273
food, in Hopi drama, for ransom, 63; as payment, 63; mentioned, 135, 145, 155, 157; Mescalero Apache, 135, 155
food, list of: apples, 135, 157; beans, mesquite, 157; beans, pinto, 157; berries, 157; candy, 135; chili stew, 135, 157; coffee, 135, 157; fry bread, 135, 157; fruit, canned, 157; Kool-Aid, 157; meat, dried, 157, raw, 157; mescal, 157; nuts, 157; oranges, 135, 157; potato, 135; salad, macaroni, 157; salad, potato, 157; watermelons, 157; yucca flowers, 157
Fort Sumner, 178
Foster, Kenneth, 94
four (number), symbolism of, 128, 147–50, 309
Franciscan Fathers, 162, 235
Franciscans, 244
Fred Harvey Hotel Indian Arts Program, 236
Freud, Sigmund, 60
Frisbie, Charlotte J., ix, 5, 162, 177, 188, 195, 197, 277, 317, 325, 327, 339–40

Gallup, 95
games, Hopi, 51; Papago, 248, 262–63
Garcia, Antonio, 97, 109, 112, 115, 121, 124, 315, 328, 339
Garcia, Carlos, 328
Ge Oidak, Arizona, 261–62
Geertz, Clifford, 342
gestures, Hopi dramatic technique, 52
gifts, exchange of, Papago, 248, 259; in Hopi Ogres drama, 42–43
Gila River Reservation, 241
Gill, Sam D., 162–63, 180–81, 185, 231–32, 236
Gilman, Benjamin Ives, 7

# INDEX

Gilpin, Laura, 196
give-aways, in Mescalero Apache Girls' Puberty Ceremony, 135
Gobernador Knob, 179, 184, 187
Goggin, John, 108
Grant, Blanche C., 72
Grants, 17
Great Basin, 298
Griffith, James, 6n, 272
Grossinger, Richard, 6n
Grunn, Howard, 34n
Gu Aji village, Arizona, 248–50, 260, 262, 264, 273
Gunst, Marie L., 243–45, 260

Hadas, Elizabeth, x
Haefer, J. Richard, ix, 5–6n, 277, 329
Haile, Father Berard, 162, 164, 166, 235–36
Hale, Kenneth, 271n
Halpern, Ida, 277
Halseth, Odd, 171, 197
Hano. *See* Tewa Village
Harper's Ferry, West Virginia, 156
Harris, Virginia S., 165
Harvey, Byron, III, 54
Hatcher, Evelyn P., 163
Havasu Canyon, 277
healing ritual, 64–66
Herzog, George, 2, 9, 16, 18, 22, 34n, 73–74, 276–77
Hewett, Edgar L., 119
Hhb, 192, 197
Hieb, Louis A., 54
Hinton, Leanne, ix, 5–6n, 157, 284, 300, 312, 339–40
hogan. *See* structures, ritual
Hoijer, Harry, 156, 162
homeopathy, Hopi, 57–59
homeostasis, 54
Hopi drama, medicinal value of, 64
Hotevilla, 50, 330
Houston Control, 23
Hualapais, 276
Huckel, John F., 236–37
Huebener, G., 119
Huerfano, 183
Hymes, Dell, 322

impersonation, Hopi female, 44; Hopi male, 44
impersonators, Mountain God, 154
Indian days, Papago, 248
Intensification, rite of, 153–154

Jemez, 35
Jett, Stephen C., 165
Jones, Hester, 72
Jones, Rosalie M., 95

Kachina Village, 11, 31
Kachina, kinds of, cave men, 330; chipmunk, 330; Hopi, 312–13; Mickey Mouse, 330; Santa Claus, 330; Zuni, 311, 313, 325
Kachina Cult, Hopi, 61
Kachina Dance. *See* dances, list of
Kachina parades, 50
Kachina Society, 41
*kahopi* definition of behavior, 65; personages, 64–65
Kealiinohomoku, Halla, 67
Kealiinohomoku, Joann W., ix, 4, 6n, 39, 95, 99, 326, 328, 330, 339–40
Keech, Roy A., 119
Kiowa, 71
Kisly, Paul, x
kivas, 334, Back Wall, 10; Brain, 10; Corn Kernel, 10, 12, 21, 24; Dung, 10; Small Group, 10, 21, 23, 31; Wall, 10
Klah, Hosteen, 162
Kluckhohn, Clyde, 162–64, 231, 235–37
*Koshare*, San Felipe, 114–15
Koyemshi. *See* clowns and Mudheads
Kurath, Gertrude, ix, 2, 4, 6, 101, 109, 112, 115, 121, 314–15, 326, 339

Ladd, Horatio O., 73
Laird, W. David, 6n
Lamphere, Louise, 6n, 162, 164, 237
Lang, Richard W., 157
Lange, Charles H., 110, 111, 116–19
Laski, Vera, 105
laughter, Hopi children, 54
LaVigna, Maria, 123–24
Lawrence, D. H., 118
Leighton, Dorothea C., 162, 166
LeRoy, James A., 72
Lévi-Strauss, 156
Linton, Ralph, 85
List, George, 277
Lomax, Alan, 291–92, 295
Luckert, Karl W., 6n, 164, 196
Lukachukai, Arizona, 199–200, 208, 235
Lyon, Luke, 108

McAllester, David, ix, 5, 6, 10, 162–63, 197, 330–31, 339–40, 342
McLaughlin, Jennifer, x
Mansfield, Portia, 97, 102

# Index

Manuel, Frances, 271n
Maricopas, 272
Martínez, Pat, 76, 78, 84, 88, 90, 92
Matthews, Washington, 2, 162, 235n
medicine, Hopi, 58–59, 66, Hopi prescriptive, 64–65; Western, 58, 293; Zuni, 322
Medicine Men's Association, 167, 193
Merriam, Alan, 277
Mescalero, New Mexico, 156
Mescalerao Apache Mountain Gods, 312, 314
Mesoamerica, 167
Mexican, 110, 114. See also Spanish
Mexico, 272
Miguelito, 235n, 237
Miller, Hugh, 96–97, 101–2
Mills, George T., 163
Mindeleff, Cosmos, 164
Miss Navajo, 176, 194
Mitchell, Frank, 162–63, 320
mnemonic devices, 331, 341
Mojaves, 278
Montezuma church, Gu Aji, Arizona, 264
Morgan, Lewis H., 73
Moslem 121
motion pictures, analysis of, 97; list of Indian dance films, 93; Blackfeet Sun, 95; Nambé Eagle, 102; Nambé Round, 102; Nambé Snake, 102; Navajo Night Chant, 94; Powwow, 98; Puyé Cliffs, Ange'ing, 101, Basket, 101, Blue Corn, 101, Bow and Arrow, 101, Buffalo, 101, Buffalo and Deer, 101, Butterfly, 101, Cloud, 101, Comanche, 101, Dog, 101, Eagle, 101, Fertility Bull, 101, Harvest, 101, Rainbow, 101, Yellow Corn, 101; San Ildefonso, Bow and Arrow, 101, Eagle, 101, Rain, 102, Snowbird, 102; San Juan Buffalo, 102, Comanche, 102, Corn Maiden, 102, Deer, 102, Dog, 102, Matachine, 102, Parrot, 102, Rainbow, 102, Yellow Corn, 102; Santa Clara, Feast Day Corn, 101, Buffalo, 101, Game Animals, 101, Sun Basket, 101–2; Tesuque, Corn, 101, Eagle, 102, prospects of, 98–101; purpose of, 94–95; value of, 93–94
Mountain-around-which-traveling-was-done, 201–2
Mountaintop Way, 323
movies. See motion pictures
Mudheads, 32, 40, 45, 48

music, Havasupai, 277–79; jazz, 105; Maricopa, 277; popular, 105
musical event, goals of, 294
musical style, California, Yuman, 276–78, 310–11; Great Basin, 278, 311; Havasupai, 300n, 311; Hopi, 300n; Pima, 9; Pueblo, 9
myth, Children's Shrine, 272
myths, Navajo, Blessingway, 171; Emergence and Creation, 170; Kinaaldá, 171

Nambé Falls, 120
National Science Foundation Cooperative Fellowship, 196
National Anthropological Film Center, Washington, D.C., 101
Native American Church, 3
Navajo, 5, 34, 35, 40, 44, 51, 278, 309–10
Navajo Community College, 228, 331
Navajo Health Authority, 167
Navajo Mountain 164
Navajo Times, articles on House Blessing, 168–69, 173, 177–78, 183–84, 191, 196–97
Ndé, 154
Ndembu, 153
Negroes, 51, 110
Nettl, Bruno, 2, 277–78, 290
Newcomb, Franc J., 162, 235n
Newman, Stanley, 35
Nicholas, Dan, 126
number, symbolism of. See four

Office of Navajo Economic Opportunity Culture Project, 331
ogres, 310, 327, Hopi, 40–45
Ojo Caliente, 11
Oklahoma, 86
Old Age Home, East Mountain, 130
Olla Maidens, Zuni song composers and performers, 320–21
Opler, M. E., 126
Opler, Marvin K., 73
Oraibi, 49–50
Oraibi, Old, 55
Ortiz, Alfonso, 6n, 52–53, 109, 271
Ostermann, Father Leopold, 162

paintings, meal and pollen, Blue Corn Person, 192; Blue Squash Plant, 192; Changing Woman's House, 191; Pollen Boy, 191. See also sand-paintings
Paiutes, 278
Pancoast, Chalmers Lowell, 73

367

# INDEX

Pandey, Triloki N., 6n
Pan-Indian Movement, 335
Pan-Indianism, 392–30
Papagería, 241, 255, 267
Papago, Club of Phoenix Indian School, 249
Papago Cultural Awareness Office, 248
Papago Culture Day, 249,
paraphernalia, ritual, 261, 263: antlers, 75, 80, 83–85, 111, 113; arrows, 43, 142, 212; arrowheads, 178, 219; bag, pollen, 130, 133; basket, 106, 131, 133, 135, 145, 224, 310, 318, burden, 135, 149, *hoa*, 252–53, 267, Navajo, 177–78, 220; beads, 80, 83, 148; bells, 51, 83, 90, 137, 139, cow, 139, 151, sleigh, 30, 334; bird effigy, 106; birds, painted wooden, 206; blade, hacksaw, 221; blanket, 67, 141, 158, 206, 212, 216, 220–21, 226, Pendleton, 177; blanks (cartridges), 142; boughs, spruce, 178; bow, 43, 52, 113; bowls, Pueblo ceremonial, 177–78; bows and arrows, 51, 55, 76, 82, 89, 142; branches, evergreen, 80, oak, 131; brush, eagle feather, 220; buckskin, white, 144; bugle, 118; bull roarer, 220, 309; bundle, ceremonial; 216, 219, 223; calendar sticks, Papago, 240–41; can, trash, 157; canvas, white, 131; capes, 309; cattle, 157; cedar, 227; cedar bark, 217; chairs, folding, 143; cloth, 142, 222, 224, 318, orange, 212; coals, 207; cornmeal, 33, 43, 174, 178, 212, 309; cotton, 222; crook, shepherd's, 51; darts, 208, 212; deer head, 111; deerskin, 117; dippers, 142, gourd, 212; discs, painted wooden, 206; dish, glass, 212, 215; fan, feather, 252; feathers, 205, 207, 222, eagle, 80, 83, 131, 137, 144–45, 149, 220, 268; parrot, 110, peacock, 110, turkey, 75; figurines, 43; fire, ritual, 217–18; fire drill, 217; firewood, 217; flowers, 310, red paper, 268; food, used in burlesque actions, 245, 262; fur pieces, 309; gramma grass, 131; grass, 149; greasewood, 227; gun, 106, 118; hairs, turkey–beard, 222; herbs, 212, 215, 217, 220; hides, buffalo, 334, cow, 334; hoop, oak 218, 220, 222, 224; horns, (*See* antlers *above*); *iagta*, 252–53, 260–61, 266, 269–70, 272, birds,
250, 269, clouds, 250, 269–70, flower, 270, moon, 270, mountain, 270, pole, 250, 269, rainbows, 261, 269–70, saguaro pole, 270, sun, 270; incense, 207; jewelry, (*See* personal adornment); jewels 205, 222, 230; jinglers, (*See* tinklers, cone); knives, 142; lassos, 52; mask, 29, 49, 55, 68, helmet, 29, Hopi, recovery by FBI, 50, Nataska, 49–50, Santa Claus, 63, mat, cowhide, 141, skin, 132; meat, piece of, 80; medicine bundle, 130, 177; medicine, powdered, 212, 216, 224, mica, 218; money, 135; musical instruments, 258, 276, 313, baton, ceremonial, 312, bull-roarers, 312, drums, 76, 82, 106, 118, 121, 157, 312, two-headed log, 11, fiddle, 121, flutes, 120, 122, guitar, 121, Pueblo, 309, rattles, gourd, 312, hide, 312, hoof, 312, shell, 312, sticks, 312, notched, 115, 267, spruce, 76, whistles, 226, 312, reed, 206, 224; Navajo, 193; neckpiece, beaver fur, 214, 224, otter fur, 214, 226; ochre, red, 144; pail, 220, 250; pail, of emetic water, 218; paper, 268; pelts, 76, 78, 82–83; pickup truck, 226; pigments, colored, 207, 220; piñons, 135; point, beargrass, 217; pokers, wooden effigy, 217–20; pollen, 132, 147, 149, 181, 205, 223–24, 327, corn, 178–79, 184, 309; pot, cast iron, 157; pouch, buckskin pollen, 178–79, pollen, 223–24; shoulder, 177; prayerstick, 21, 208, 315; quiver, 76, 82; rattles, 43, 76, 80, 82–83, 89, 113, deer hoof, 141, 143, gourd, 30, 252–53, 267, 322, turtle shell, 30, 322, wooden, 30, 334; ribbons, 268–69, 310; rifle, 142; root, yucca, 206; rug, 177; sand, colored, 211; sandpaintings, (*See specific entry by name*); sandstone, pieces of, 221; Santiago, 118; santo, 110, 118; saws, 51–52; shaft, lightning-struck oak, 217; shell, 212, 216, 224, perforated, 8; skins, 318, deer, 111, 177, fox, 177, wildcat, 76; snakes, wooden, 206, 212, 220; staff, 51; stew, meat, 209; stick, 89, 137, 139, 142–43, 151, 310, bundle of, 244, lightning, 43, scratching, 130; streamers, red, 137; string, woolen, 211–12; strip, cloth, 213, 217;

368

# Index

paraphernalia—*cont.*
  yucca, 211, 218; stone, mirage (aragonite); 178; stones, precious, 178; tablita, rainbow-shaped, 110; tinklers, cone, 128, 137, 139, 151; tobacco, 131, 142, 149; tube, drinking, 130, jointed reed, 221–23; tules, 131, 143; turquoise, 128; twigs, spruce, 76, 208; wand, ceremonial, 253, dance, 310, feathered, 212, 216, snake, 223; water, sacred, 178; whips, yucca, 32; yucca, 178; yucca-root suds, 143. *See also* costume, ritual; personal adornment, ritual; *and* structures, ritual
Parsons, Elsie Clews, 50, 73–74, 87, 109, 112, 114, 119
payment, for dancing, bean sprouts, 42; blanket, 158; bread, 43; corn kernels, 47; cornmeal, 43; horse, 158; meat, 43; money, 158; shawl, 158; tobacco, 43
Pearl Harbor, 22
Peñasco, 72
Perry-Mansfield Camp, Steamboat Springs, 102
personages, ritual, description of, Hahaiwuhti, 40, 68; Heheya (Silly Boys), 40, 68; Hopi, description of, 39–40, 68; Kiva Chief, 40, 43–44; Mescalero Apache, 126–27, 130–31; Na'amu, Nataska Father, 40, 68; Nataska Uncles, 40, 68; So'owuhti, 40–44, 68; Soyokmana (Natas), 40, 68; Susuyukte, 40, 43–44, 68
personal adornment, ritual, bracelets, 177; clay, black, 245; earrings, 177; in Hopi Ogre Dance, 43–44, 63; jewelry, 128, 140, 151, 318; necklaces, 177; paint, 137, 268–69, face or body, 83, 110, red, 132, white, 143, white clay, 268; painting, Navajo body, 209, 215, 216; rings, 177
Phoenix, Arizona, 246
Phoenix Indian School, 250
Pima (Piman), 9, 240–41, 244, 247, 262, 271n–72, 310
Pinedale-Coolidge-Smith Lake, 236
piñon, 40
Plains, 24, 34, 167, 298
plazas, Back Wall, 30; Big, 30; Rat's Place, 30; Torn Place, 12, 30
Polacca, 47, 334
Powwow, 136, 142, 240, 261, 316–317, 324, 336; Algonquian, 96; Navajo, 169; Pan-Indian style, 136
pragmatism, Hopi, 62–66
Pueblo, 167. *See also* specific pueblos
Pueblo Grande, 197
"pulling" of Hopi children, 43, 45
Puyé Cliffs, 96–97, 120

Quijotoa, 243, 248–49
Quitobac, Sonora, Mexico, 261

races, ceremonial, Hopi, 51; Isleta, 177, Kick-Stick, Cochití, 117; Papago, 243, 246, 260, 262; Taos, 186, 190
Rain Dance. *See* dances, list of
Rainbow Bridge, 164
Ramah-Atarque, 236
reciprocity, principle in Navajo world view, 232
record hops, rock'n'roll, Navajo, 228
Red Moustache, 200, 203, 235
Red Power movement, 336
Reichard, Gladys A., 162–63, 180–81, 231, 234, 235n, 237
Research and Projects Office, Southern Illinois University, Edwardsville, x
Rhodes, Robert, 328
Rhodes, W., 329
Rim of the Emergence Place, 165, 170–71
Rimrock Navajos, 164
ritual drama, aesthetics of, 339: Apache holy men, 340; Eastern Pueblo, 341; Havasupai, 339–40; Hopi dancers, 359; Mescalero Apache, 341; Navajo, 339, House Blessing Ceremony, 340, Shootingway, 342; Pan-Indian, 341; Pueblo, 341; Southern Athapaskans, 340; Southwestern Indian, 339; Tewa, 339; White Mountain Apache, 339; Zuni Medicine Society, 339; change in, 333–36, change in as reflected by: *celkona* songs, 334, Havasupai Harvest Festival, 334, Medicine Songs, 334, Personal Songs, 334, Rain Songs, 334; Hopi Ogres drama game, 334; Mescalero Apache Girls' Puberty Ceremony, 334–35, hand gambling, 334, horse racing, 334, War Dancer costumes, 334; Navajo Girls' Puberty Ceremony, 334, House Blessing Ceremony, 335; Pan-Indianism, 335–36; Papago Girls' Puberty Ceremony, 334, Harvest Festival, 334, Powwows,

ritual drama—*cont*.
335–36, Rodeos, 335; Picuris Clown Society, 335; ritual drama calendars, 334; Taos Hoop Dance, 336, Horse Tail Dance, 336, Shield Dance, 336, Yuman Bird Songs, 336, Line Dance, 336; Zuni Buffalo Dance, 335; children's, 4, 53–57; comparison of three Hopi mesa villages, 47–51; definition of, 3, 37; Eastern Pueblo, 4, 103–8; future directions of, 337–43; Havasupai, 310, 313; Hopi 4, 37–38, 56; Hopi ogre, 4, 312, 326; Kachinas, 311; Mescalero Apache, 309–10; Navajo, 311, 327; operational definition of, 343; Papago, 310–11, 313; Pima, 313; presentation techniques, 311–13; Pueblo, 308; rehearsal of, 315–17; transmission of, 330–33; Buffalo Song, 333; Cochití, 333; Curing Songs, 332; Eastern Pueblos, 333; Havasupais, 332, Peach Festival, 333; Hopi, 332; Hopi Longhair Song, 333; Hopi-Tewa Corn Kachina Song, 333; Kachina Song, 332; Lipan Apache, 332; masked ceremonies, 333; Medicine Society Songs, 332; Mescalero Apaches, 332; Moccasin Game Songs, 333; Mojaves, 333; Navajos, 333; Picuris, 333; Papagos, 332–33; San Juan, 333; Santo Domingo, 333; Turtle Dance Song, 333; Yeibichai, 333; Zunis, 332–33
ritual structures. *See* structures, ritual
Roberts, Don L., 104, 333
Roberts, Helen H., 2, 9, 16, 33, 277
Robertson, Bill, 124
River People, 240, 243, 260
rodeo, 246, 317, 324
Roediger, Virginia M., 112
Roman Catholic. *See* Catholic
Romancito, Mark, 330
Rough Rock Demonstration School, 331
Rough Rock Navajo Mental Health Program, 169
Royce, Anya P., 6n
Russell, Frank, 240–41, 243, 260, 272–73

Salt River People, 241
San Carlos, Apache, 126
San Juan, 99
San Xavier del Bac, 241, 244, 248–49, 255, 264
sandpaintings, 207–9, 211, 213, 220, 230, 234, 236, 326, 331; collections of, Goldwater, Museum of Northern Arizona, 237; Walcott, U.S. National Museum, 237; Wetherill, 236; specific names of, bead chant, 230; buffalo, 207–8; earth and sky, 209; snakes, 207
Sandoval, Albert G., Jr., 200, 235n
Sandoval, Albert G. "Chic", Sr., 197, 209
Santa Clara, photography at, 96
Santa Rosa, Arizona, 255
Santa Rosa School, Arizona, 248
Sapir, Edward, 91n, 162, 277
Schechner, Richard, 154
School of American Research, x, 156–57, 343; Advanced Seminar, 164, 271; Advanced Seminar on Southwestern Indian Ritual Drama, ix, 2–3, 103, 307
Schroeder, Ella, x
Schwartz, Douglas, ix, 156, 276, 278
Second, Bernard, 125, 146, 152, 156, 158
Second Mesa, 47, 49, 57, 68
Sekaquaptewa, Emory, 328
Sells, Arizona, 250
Sheets, Maxine, 91
Shipalovi, 45
Shirley Farr Fellowship, 196
Shungopavi (Chimpovy), 49
Sichomovi, 68
Sil Nakia, Arizona, 248, 255, 261, 273
Simmons, Leo, 39, 55–56, 58
Singer, Milton, 127, 172
singers, role of, 317–319; Havasupai, 318; Mescalero Apache, 317; Mojave, 318; Navajo, 310, 317–318; Papago, 318; Pueblo, 310, 318
singing style, California-Yuman, 298; Havasupai, 311; Hopi, 311; New Mexico, 311; Plains, 335
Sloane, Eric, 72
Smithson, Carma Lee, 276
songs, 276–77; American Indian, 7, 9; borrowing of: Anglo-Americans, 329–30; Havasupai, 329; Havasupai-Chemehuevi, 330; Havasupai-Hopi, 330; Havasupai-Mojave, 330; Havasupai-Navajo, 330; Havasupai-Yuman, 330; Interpueblo, 330; Navajo-Hopi, 330; Papago, 329; Papago-Yaqui, 330; Plains, 329; Pueblo-Havasupai, 330; Pueblo-Navajo, 330; Pueblo-Plains, 330; Taos, 329; Ute, 329; Zuni, 13–14; composition of Kachina, 20–26; fully worded, discussion of, 286–90;

# Index

songs—*cont*.
 name sections, 9–33; performance of, 29–33; rehearsal of, 26–29; structure of, 14–20, Kachina, 14–20; titles and types of: Bird, Mojave, 278; Blanket, 8, 34n; Blessingway, Navajo, 188–89, 192, 196–97: Chief Hogan, 165, 188–89, 196–97; Corn, 188; Corral Dance, 196; Dawn, 188, 204; Foundation of the Songs, 189; Good Luck, 188; Hogan, 164, 166, 188–89; Shootingway Snake, 163; Talking God, 188–89, 196–97; Twelve Verse, 188; Bow Priesthood, 13; Buffalo Dance, 87; Bundle Drum, 19, 25; *celkona*, 254–58, 266–67, 327: Bird, 248, 263; Bluebird series, 241; Morning Star's Visit as a Woman, 266; Name Giving, 243, 248, 259, 262; Chemehuevi salt, 278; clowns, 9; Comanche, 9, 21, 24; Corn Dance, 9; Corn-Grinding, 9, 34n; Coyote Society, 13–14; Crazy Grandchild, 21; Deer Dance, Picuris, 92; Deer Hunting, 13; Deer Village Mountain, 16–17; Downy Feather on a String, 16–17, 21, 29; Entrance, 106; Good Kachina, 9, 16, 21–22; Havasupai, 276–78, 329: Circle Dance, 279–80, 283–87, 290, 293–97, 303, Funeral, 279–80, 295–96, Gambling, 279, Horse, 278, 280, Hunting, 279, Love, 279, 292, Medicine, 278–79, 292–93, 296, 305, Personal, 279, 292, 304–5, 320, previous study of 276–77, Rain, 279, Story, 279, 292, Sweathouse, 278–85, 287, 290–91, 293–97, 301–3, 318; *hilili*, 20, 25, 27–29, 31; Incantation Upon a Sleeping Infant, 34n; Indian Fantasia, 34n; Indian Fire Drill, 34n; Invocation to the Sun God, 34n; Kachina, 9–10, 28, 31, 34, 34n, 117; Kachina Call, 25; Kachina Dance, 14–16, 18, 29; Kachina Society, 13–14, 26, 33, 35; Laguna Chakwena, 9; Limbo Rock, 34; Log Drum, 21, 25; Love, 14; Lover's Wooing, 8, 34n; Maskless Kachina, 9; Medicine, 310; Medicine Society, 13, 24–25, 33–34, 34n; Mescalero Apache, 126, 329; Mescalero Apache Love, 320; Mojave, 328; Navajo, 328; Now Rest Thee in Peace, 34n; Painted Red, 16; Papago, 329; Petting, 84; Pima, 329; Powwow, 14; Rabbit Skin Blanket, 9; Rain Priesthood, 13; Red Beard, 16; Rise Ye, Hunters Brave, 34n; Sacred, 13; Salt Lake Mountain, 16–17, Shina No Yoru, 330; Shootingway, Navajo, 207–9, 228, 230: Buffalo, 204, Cattail, 204, Coyote, 208–9, Dawn, 204, First, 204, 209, Fish and Thunder, 204, Holy People, 204, Holy Young Man, 203, 209, House Raising, 208, Leader Prayer, 221–22, Night, 208–9, Night People 209, Snake, 203–5, 213–16, 230, Snake People, 224, Sun, 302, Thunder, 203, Tobacco, 222–23; Small Eyes, 22, Smoke Youth, 22; Social, 34n; Stephen Foster, 34; Swing Low, Sweet Chariot, 24; Sunset Song, 34n; Taos, 329; They Went to the Moon Mother, 22; Tumanpa, Mojave, 278; Winter, 12; Yuman, 329; Zuni, 315, 328; Zuni Impressions: An Indian Suite, 34n; Zuni Kachina, 327–38; Zuni Lover's Wooing, 34n
Sonora, Mexico, 239
Southern Athapaskan, 309
Southern Ute, 73
Southwest Foundation for Audio-Visual Resources, Santa Fe, 101
space, use of by Hopi in drama, 51
Spanish, 124. *See also* Mexican
Spanish-American, 72
speaking in tongues, 296
Spencer, Katherine, 236
Spencer, Virginia C., 165
Spier, Leslie, 276, 333
Spinden, Herbert J., 73
spirits, Havasupai, 296
Stacey, Reid, 8
Stephen, A. M., 39, 58, 63, 162
Stevenson, Matilda Coxe, 2, 9, 30, 333
Steward, Julian H., 39, 58
structures, ritual altar, 110; arbor, 133, 150, 157, cooking 133, 135, 157, 323; doorslabs, rock, 178; hogan, discussion of, 165–66, forked-stick, 189, mentioned, 167, 208, 226–27, 323; houses, Shalako, 334; lodge, Holy, 130–32, 140–45, 147–50; poles, ritual drama, 310; summer solstice, 11; tents, 133, 157, tipi, 131, 133, 142, 147, 150, 157

371

# INDEX

Sundberg, J., 298
sweatbath, Havasupai, 293, 295
Sweet, Jill D., 6n, 102
symptoms of *communitas*, 46

tape recorder, use of, 332
Taylor Museum, Colorado Springs, 237
Tedlock, Barbara, ix, 3, 156, 315, 323, 326–329, 339–41
Tewa Village, 40, 45, 67, 334
"The Compulsive Word," discussed concerning Navajo ceremonies, 231–34
Theodore Presser Company, 8
Third Mesa, 49, 68
time, Hopi use of in drama, 51–52
Titiev, Mischa, 6n, 39, 50, 56–58, 63
Tiwa, 71–72, 74
Troyer, Carlos, 7–8, 33n
Tsosie, Denet, 200, 203, 213, 232, 234
Tucson, Arizona, 248
Turner, Victor, 6n, 46, 153

Underhill, Ruth M., 241, 244–45, 248, 258, 260, 268, 272–73, 333
University of New Mexico, 102
University of New Mexico Press, x
Ute-Aztecan language, 271

Van Gennep, Arnold, 6n, 153
Van Horn, Ann, x
Vennard, William, 297
vocables, 6, 8, anatomy of 279–90; and aesthetics, 296–99; and communication, 291–96; definition of, 275; Havasupai, 339–40;
Voegelin, Carl, 277
Vogt, Evon Z., 236–37
Vorse, Mary, 72

Walker, Willard, 35
Wallace, Anthony C., 6n
Walpi, 50–51, 68
Walters, A. L., 6n
Ward, Hank, 290
Washington, D. C., 156, 183
Waters, Frank, 72
Wead, Charles, 7
Wetherhead Resident Fellowship, 156
Wheelwright, Mary C., 162
Wheelwright Museum, Santa Fe. *See* Museum of Navajo Ceremonial Art
Whispering Waters, 11
White, Leslie B., 112
White Singer, 236
Whitney M. Young Jr. Memorial Foundation, 156
Williams, Aubrey, W., Jr., 197
Williams, Carroll and Joan, 101
Wilson, Edmund, 35
Wimett, Sarah, x
Window Rock Lodge, 184
Winnie, Ray, 199–201, 203, 209, 222, 235n
witches, Hopi, 55, 60
Witherspoon, Gary, 6n, 162–63, 168, 196, 232
women, role of in ritual drama, 319–21: Acoma, 320; Havasupai, 320; Hopi-Tewa, 320–21; Mescalero Apache, 320; Navajos, 319–21; Papagos, 319; San Felipe, 320; Santo Domingo, 320; Taos-Picuris, 320; Tewa, 320; Zuni, 320–21
Wyman, Leland C., 162–64, 197, 231, 235n, 237

Zuni Mountains, 25
Zuni Salt Lake, 16

/970.4972728>C1/